THE FORD TRI-MOTOR
1926-1992

THE FORD TRI-MOTOR

4-AT-48 is shown in front of the terminal at the Ford Airport in late 1931. The beautiful new Dearborn Inn on the left, one of the first airport hotels in the United States, opened on July 1, 1931. The former Monarch Foods 4-AT, still bearing their emblem on the rudder, was now owned by V.N. Johns and operated as Independence Air Tours in conjunction with the Dearborn Inn. H.H. Timken's 5-AT-89 is at the right with his logo on the side. (Ford Archives)

1926-1992

William T. Larkins

Schiffer Aviation History
West Chester, PA

Acknowledgements

This project began in 1950. My book *The Ford Story*, published in 1957, contains the names of those who assisted at that time. Since then the following individuals have contributed new material, enthusiasm and support:

Richard S. Allen, Jess C. Barrow, J. Roger Bentley, Edward G. Betts, John W. Caler, Robert Casari, Owen Darcey, R.E.G. Davies, Bob Davis, John M. Davis, James H. Farmer, Leslie N. Forden, Harry Gann, Robert E. Garrard, Ronald M. Gerdes, Daniel P. Hagedorn, Dick Hagelthorn, Steven J. Hudek, George Hardie Jr., Marion H. Havelaar, Walter M. Jefferies Jr., Joseph P. Juptner, Ted Keener, Burton Kemp, Art Krieger, Paul Matt, Mitch Mayborn, Jack McNulty, Matthew Miller, K.M. Molson, H.J. Nash, Tim O'Callaghan, Douglas D. Olson, Robert Parmerter, Bob Pauley, Everett J. Payette, Ed Peck, Rudy Profant, Boardman C. Reed, Matt Rodina Jr., Fred W. Roos, Winthrop Sears, Warren D. Shipp, Rudolph A. Stahl, Emil Strasser, Frank Strnad, Lawrence Smalley, Ken Sumney, Chris E. Swain, John Underwood, Adolfo Villasenor, Ray Wagner, Gayle Williams, Kenneth D. Wilson and Harry Yerex.

Four individuals require special mention. Jack Barbery, indefatigable researcher and generous friend, has shared the results of many hours of tedious work in the FAA files in Oklahoma City. Pete Bowers has pleaded, cajoled and continuously contributed material for a revised and updated edition. Dan R. Post, knowledgeable publisher of Ford auto books, for encouragement and support over many years. Lastly, Carl Apollonio has guided the book through difficult times since June 1988 and his perserverence and interest brought about this beautiful volume.

The problems with photo credits increase with age as photographs pass from the person that took them through various collectors who often have bought collections from someone else who did not record the photographer. Wherever possible the name of the person that took the photo is given. If this is not known then the source of the print used in this book is listed. Many of the factory photos are original yellowing prints that were saved by the late Gordon S. Williams. The late Steve Hudek collected and copied a massive number of photos at his own expense, including Ford factory views, and to conserve space the credit line "Hudek" indicates the much longer title that Steve was proud to put on his photos in recent years: "Stephen J. Hudek Aeronautical Archives." To them and all of the others who have contributed my sincere thanks and appreciation.

This book has been based in part on interviews or correspondence with the following individuals who have been personally involved with the Ford Tri-Motor:

W. Ray Allemang, Herbert W. Anderson, Bob Anson, Robert N. Baron, W. Joe Barrows, Ken Blaney, Melvin G. Bowen, Lon Brennan, R.H. Brooks, Arthur Buchner, Paul L. Carpenter, Walter M. Cary, Allan Chaney, Harold Chin, Clare Coe, John A. Collings, Kathryn B. Creedy, Eddie DeLarm, William H. Dowling, Ernest E. Dryer, Lee Flanagin, Eugene O. Frank, Lawrence G. Fritz, Gordon H. Fountain, Dale Glen, Bernie Godlove, E.B. Brownie Gray, John Guglielmetti, Robert E. Hayden, Bob Henry, William H. Hightower, Carles J. Hirst, Glen H. Hoppin, Richard E. Hulse, Perry G. Hutton, Mrs. Leona Inman, Donald M. Ives, Robert R. Johnson, Thunder Johnson, Frank H. Jerdone, George F. Kreitzberg, Otto E. Kirchner, Stanley E. Knauss, Jim Larkin, Norman Layman, Charles Le Master, John Louck, Charles E. Mathews, Gaylord Moxon, Frank D. Oergel Jr., David Ohlwiler, Byron G. O'Hara, W. Kelly Owen, Irv Perch, Paul Poberezny, George H. Prudden, William B. Stout, Laurent Savaard, Frederick D. Smith, Stan Stanton, Penn Stohr Jr., Floyd Tohline, D.W. Tommy Tomlinson, Tom Towle, Harry Volpe, Arthur E. Walker, William G. Walker, Robert Waltermire, Rex Williams, Jerry Wood and Donald Wong.

William T. Larkins

Book Design by Robert Biondi

Photo on Page 1: Details of the nose of an Army Air Corps C-9 (29-224) on July 2, 1929. The Air Corps painted a legend on the side of their planes in the late 1920s giving weights and capacities for the individual airplane as shown in the box on the right. *(Ford Archives)*

Dust jacket photo courtesy of Michael O'Leary.

Library of Congress Catalog Number: 92-60363

Printed in the United States of America.
ISBN: 0-88740-416-2

We are interested in hearing from authors with book ideas on related topics.

Published by Schiffer Publishing Ltd.
1469 Morstein Rd.
West Chester, PA 19380
Please write for a free catalog.
This book may be purchased from the publisher.
Please include $2.95 postage.
Try your bookstore first.

Contents

Introduction

The Ford Tri-Motor, together with the complimentary engineering and thought that surrounded its development during the formative years of American air transport, remains to this day a fine example of good engineering, planning and production.

The production and refinement of this aircraft, and the accompanying research and development of ground and air aids to airline management carried on by the Ford Motor Company, was unquestionably one of the most important factors in the historical development of air transportation in this country. The design of an aircraft is not always the deciding factor in its success. Quite often, as with the Ford Tri-Motor, a series of supporting circumstances and the accident of time and place produce a legendary airplane.

It was the application of a modified assembly line

production by the world's largest automobile manufacturer to a continuously refined design, backed by extensive advertising and publicity concerned with safety at a time when such dependability and safety was crucial, that put Ford ahead of all of its competitors. The value of the corporate name "Ford Motor Company" cannot be underestimated and the result is best indicated by a study of the contemporary transports.

William B. Stout and his Liberty-powered 2-AT brought about Henry and Edsel Ford's interest in aviation in 1924. Both a small factory and a flying field were built by Ford and leased to Stout for further research and development. Out of this start came the first tri-motor as well as a company air freight line. In 1925 Ford bought out the Stout Metal Plane Company and thus began active participation and encouragement of aircraft design and production which was to last through 1932.

Below: The end of the 1930 Ford Air Tour with the factory and Greenfield Village in the background. The Tri-Motors are 5-AT-60 (#5) flown by Harry Russell, and 7-AT-1 flown by Myron Zeller. (Ford Archives)

Much more than just an airplane had been created. Due to the vision and support of Edsel Ford, William Mayo and Bill Stout, many other important items were developed. Ford built a model airport and aircraft factory, paved a runway for the first time, built a model passenger terminal and airport hotel, developed radio communications and an airway radio beacon system. One of the most unusual things developed was a unique Ford training school for pilots. As part of their continuing program of developing safe flying the Ford Motor Company publicly stated in January 1929, "Purchasers of planes are welcome to send their own men to our school for this special training, if they meet the requirements. But we must ask them to consider our decision of their fitness final. So important do we regard this provision, that we reserve the right to decline to deliver a Ford plane unless the pilot who will fly it meets with the approval of the officials of our training school."

In addition, during 1927 an intensive campaign was carried out by the Ford Motor Company to educate the public in the safety, dependability and pleasure of flying in the new all-metal tri-motor transports. An editorial of the period sums this up by saying, "His advertising has done more to popularize flying among the reading public than all the stunts that have ever been stunted, at the risk of neck and limb . . ." These advertisements, which appeared in the magazines *Saturday Evening Post*, *Literary Digest*, *National Geographic*, *American Boy*, *Town and Country*, *World's Work*, *Review of Reviews*, *Spur*, *Vanity Fair* and *Sportsman*, through a combined circulation of 6,158,912 reached an estimated fifteen to twenty million people in the United States, Canada and overseas. Seventeen of these advertisements make up the book *Lift Up Your Eyes* and provide a valuable historical record to this period of aviation development.

A large number of people in the United States have had their first airplane ride in a Ford Tri-Motor, usually as a result of barnstorming rides in the countryside as regular airline travel was limited to the few who could afford it in the post depression era.

By the end of 1927 fourteen tri-motors had been built. 1928 and 1929 were the big production years for this

The first Flivver and 4-AT-1 on exhibit at a show on December 8, 1926. Note the long forward landing gear strut that was soon changed to a more conventional structure. (Ford Archives)

plane, with a total of 149 being turned out during this period – the Prohibition-bound "Roaring Twenties" era of Ruth Chatterton, Greta Garbo, Rudy Valee etc., as well as the start of the shattering stock market crash.

A wave of distress selling, starting on October 24, 1929, and climaxing on the 28th, resulted in a 14 billion dollar loss on the New York Stock Exchange and plunged the United States into a depression that lasted through 1935. In March 1930 the new Ford Roadster was selling for $435, the Tudor Sedan for $500, and the top price Town Sedan for $670. The heavier Dodge 6 was priced at $835, and in January 1931 a new one-ton General Motors truck could be purchased for $675. At the same time, a year and a half after the stock market crash, fur coats, rugs and other non essentials etc., were being advertised as "drastically reduced."

It was in this financial atmosphere that the 5-AT was being manufactured and sold. Even with the price reductions announced in May 1930 it became increasingly difficult to find a market for $50,000 airplanes. The airlines were becoming saturated and only a new design with radical improvements could justify such expenditures. The new twin-engine, low-wing Boeing 247, with a retractable landing gear and higher speed was the next star on the transport horizon. This plane, and the subsequent TWA developed DC-1, brought improved performance. With the introduction of the DC-3 and its economy of operation the Ford passed out of the airline business in the United States.

The all-metal construction, stressed so much by the Ford advertising campaign of the late 1920s, proved its worth in later years. The life span of the average airplane in the 1920s was relatively short and so it is not surprising to find the Ford Company timidly stating in their 1929 advertising that "no Ford plane has yet worn out in service", and, "Consequently we now feel buyers of Ford planes run little if any danger that the planes will become obsolete before they have completed their period of usefulness – a period which we now know to be not less than four years." Later, in 1932, they admitted that when the 5-AT-B's were built that their estimated life was 2,500 flying hours. But TWA had already put 3,000 hours on each plane and was sending them back to the factory to have wing mail bins installed in the belief that they were good for another 2,000 hours. Stout's dream of the value of metal construction was only beginning to pay off and even he never dared to predict that some Ford Tri-Motors would still be flying 65 years after being built and that one would accumulate 23,000 hours of flying time.

Probably to the surprise of its engineers and builders this rugged airplane entered a whole new field of endeavor – that of the heavy duty freight carrier – which was to last far longer than the period for which it had been originally designed and built.

The man who gave the Ford its second life was Lowell Yerex, pioneer founder of the Central American airline TACA (Transportes Aereos Centro Americanos) with headquarters at Tegucigalpa, Honduras. Together with its subsidiaries TACA-Guatemala, TACA-Costa Rica and TACA-Nicaragua the airline flew at least 27 different 5-AT's. Some started flying freight and passengers as early as 1934, with others being added through the 1930s. From 1942 through 1947 sixteen were operated under Nicaraguan registry. Most, if not all, of these had large cargo doors cut into the side and some had sliding or removable hatches installed in the top of the fuselage to enable the loading of heavy machinery. In addition to the flying of freight at least one plane was modified with a 600-gallon fuselage tank to carry diesel oil and flew 2,400 gallons per day to the La Luz Mine in Nicaragua.

Thc Ford Tri-Motor was manufactured in seven basic models, plus various minor modifications. A single-engine freight carrier, a large 40-passenger tri-motor, and two small single-place Flivvers were also built. The Ford Tri-Motor was used by all of the major airlines in the United States at one time or another, as well as by the Army, Navy and Marines.

The Ford has been looped, rolled and flown upside down. Many an unbeliever was converted by Harold Johnson and his spectacular flying at the National Air Races in Cleveland. If a snap roll at 800 feet didn't do it, then surely they were convinced by three low-level loops ending in a one-wheel landing!

The Ford has been flown on wheels, floats and skis. It has been used to carry neon signs for night sky advertising, as well as searchlights and public address systems; it has been used as a tanker for aerial refuelling; it has served as a steady platform for parachutists – both military and Forest Service fire fighters. Since World War II it has been used as an agricultural aircraft for spraying crops, grass and forests. Two have been converted to air tankers ("borate bombers") and used on forest fires. But its greatest fame has come from two distinct operations. One, for which it was designed, has been as a sturdy and reliable passenger transport. The second, for which is was not designed, has been as a remarkable heavy duty freight carrier. Its career in this regard far surpasses any other prewar American transport except the DC-3.

When the research was first started on the Ford Tri-Motor in 1950, culminating in the publication of the book *The Ford Story* in 1957, the basic premise was that a history of each individual airplane would provide the most complete history of the overall subject. This policy has been continued so that the basic foundation of this book is as much information as possible on the individual life history of each airplane. It is probably impossible to obtain a photo of every individual Ford built but this has been a continuing effort. This book is the end result of 41 years of collecting information on the Ford and as such is unique among American aviation publications.

Unfortunately, even this amount of time has not answered many questions and has, in fact, created new

The completely new Ford 4-AT-1 at the factory in June 1926. The resemblance to the 2-AT is apparent, but the refinement over the Stout 3-AT led to a successful airplane. (Hudek)

ones. It is as if "the more you learn the less you know." It would be fascinating, for example, to find the 8-AT in Colombia today. But that would just open up a whole new range of questions such as, "Where has it been since 1938?... Did it fly for the Sanabria Mines?... Who flew it?... Where was it during World War II?... Did it crash? ... Is it still intact enough to rebuild and fly" etc. In other words, what has it been doing for 53 years!

Indeed the largest area of unknowns still revolves around Central and South America. An interesting phenomenon of the past twenty years has been the uncovering of a number of photographs, original and in publication, that prove the existence of a Ford with a visible foreign registration that cannot be documented as to individual identity. These are noted in the appropriate places in this book and remain a notable frustration. They may never be identified as government records now bordering on being 60 years old, in these countries torn by political upheaval, are less and less likely to be saved. Pilots log books are an excellent source of documented information but seldom if ever identify the airplane by anything other than its registration or military serial number. Thus a photo and a logbook may verify XH-TAL as a Ford Tri-Motor but which one and where it fits into the complete history may never be known.

Regardless of this, if this book is read carefully and the index, appendix, tables and photo captions are consulted, the result will be the most complete information available on a very famous aircraft.

The basic history of each airplane is in Chapters 7 and 8 and the planes are referred to throughout this book by their factory serial number so that the reader can refer to these chapters for the background on the specific aircraft being discussed.

There are some myths that have been perpetrated over the last twenty years, much of it caused by one author blindly copying from another, so that the following should be pointed out:

1. Bill Stout Designed the Ford Tri-Motor. This flat statement has been repeated endlessly but is simply not true. The far more complex story is described in Chapter 1 but the evidence has been there for many years in Bill Stout's autobiography "So Away I Went." In it he lists all of his designs but very carefully avoids saying that he designed the Ford Tri-Motor. He writes that he worked on the Tri-Motor and he also states that he believed his greatest contribution to aviation was his successful effort to interest Henry Ford in aviation and aircraft production.

2. There Has Never Been A Structural Failure In The Ford Tri-Motor. Although the Tri-Motor had a remarkable record in this regard there were instances as a reading of Chapter 10 will indicate. No aircraft is immune to damage

if enough stress, strain and continual use are applied. Certainly the major damage to so many Fords on the ground from wind storms should be ample evidence of this potential.

3. The Ford Tri-Motor Was Named The "Tin Goose." The first publication of this name in connection with the Tri-Motor seems to be in the June 1929 issue of *Western Flying* when D.W. Tommy Tomlinson refers to flying "the Big Tin Goose." Then in February 1939 John Collings wrote his nostalgic piece "Farewell, Tin Goose." Writer Ralph Hancock claimed in 1970 to have invented the term but did not use it in his 1940 article on TACA. A review of the bibliography will show clearly its continued popular use since the 1950s.

A continuous search for 35 years failed to turn up anything other than Larry Fritz's clear recollection that it was used around the Ford plant when he was there in 1927. Finally, in 1988, tenacious researcher and aviation enthusiast Everette Payette found one answer in the Monroe, Michigan, newspaper. A so far unnamed Associated Press writer did two stories in December 1925. The plane was, of course, the single engine Liberty powered 2-AT and not the Tri-Motor which had not yet been built. The first story on December 30th is headlined, "One of Henry's Tin Geese Is Storm Victim" and further mentions in the story about, ". . . the Miss St. Petersburg, one of Henry Ford's 'tin geese' members of the fleet of four . . ." The second story on December 31st is headlined, "3 Tin Geese In Wreck, Nashville." The question still remains as to the origin of the term "Tin Goose", but it obviously was not coined for the Tri-Motor.

4. They All Went To South America. This is heard in hangar flying stories by pilots more than seen in published material, but is a theme that has continued over the years. It seems to be primarily the result of geographical ignorance; simply not knowing the difference between Central America and South America.

5. Lindbergh Sat In That Seat. There has been a rash of newspaper stories in Florida and the Southeast in the past two years that have been a misunderstanding at the very least. Al Chaney has been barnstorming with 4-AT-38 (N-7584), and the stories about Lindbergh and Henry Ford have grown. This is summed up by the story in a Columbia, South Carolina, newspaper which stated in October 1988 that Chaney said, "Charles Lindbergh was the first pilot of this airplane . . . and where you're sitting in the co-pilots seat once sat Henry Ford. As a matter of fact, Edsel Ford was sitting somewhere in the back on the same flight."

The facts are, as described further in Chapter 7, that Charles Lindbergh, Henry Ford and Edsel Ford flew together only once and that was on August 11, 1927. NC-7584 was not built until thirteen months later in September 1928.

Chapter 1
Development Of An Idea

The Ford Tri-Motor, like all production airplanes and other such pieces of complex machinery, came about as a result of many influences, many people and much experience in actual use.

The plane, as we know it today, combined the ideas, talent and far-sighted genius of Bill Stout, his associate engineers, and the vast resources and influence of the Ford Motor Company under the able direction of William B. Mayo. A simple comparison of the original 3-AT and the final 5-AT-D shows better than any description how this plane evolved through constant change and improvement to a final product that hardly resembles the original in any way other than the fact that it was a three-engine, all-metal monoplane.

In addition, the true historical value of the Ford Tri-Motor involves far more than just the design of an airplane. The impact of the Ford Motor Company entering the struggling aviation industry, the extensive safety advertising campaign carried on by the Ford Motor Company and the developments in airport design and factory production techniques pioneered by Ford all had an equal influence on air transportation and flying in the United States from 1926 to 1933.

The Ford Tri-Motor brought all-metal construction to an infant industry still building with wood, wire and fabric, the materials of World War I. To a public accustomed to open-cockpit flying, in an era of wing walkers and dare-devil stuntmen, the Ford Tri-Motor brought a new dependability and safety. For the first time in the United States air transportation became a national reality, climaxed by transcontinental airlines pioneered and developed with Ford Tri-Motors. The impact of the Ford Motor Company on aviation is one of the lesser known milestones in our history. The value of the corporate name "Ford Motor Company" cannot be under-estimated and the results are best indicated by a study of the contemporary transports that never reached production status – much less are still flying after 65 years. Bill Stout has stated that he believed his greatest contribution to aviation was his successful effort to interest Henry Ford in aviation and aircraft production.

To pinpoint the specific beginning of any design is often a purely academic question. Certainly the first physical tri-motor in this design series was the 3-AT, but

A rare photo of the 3-AT with the original Stout factory behind it on December 10, 1925. This building, the 3-AT a 2-AT and 13 Wright Whirlwind engines were destroyed in a fire on January 17, 1926. (Larkins Collection)

Ford

this has to be viewed in relation to the 2-AT single engine all-metal transport that fathered it and which was the main influence on Henry Ford entering aviation. But, from the standpoint of Bill Stout the designer, the 2-AT was itself the result of his earlier experience in designing and building the small three-place, all-metal 1-AS "Air Sedan."

Since no better basis of qualification exists than the system of model designations we will assume that this story begins with the little Stout 1-AS "Air Sedan" which first flew at Selfridge Field, Michigan, on February 17, 1923. It was originally powered with an OX-5 engine of 90 hp which proved to be underpowered. This was replaced by a 150 hp Hisso engine and the plane flew many times before being retired.

Satisfied with the design, and the practicability of all-metal construction coupled with the cantilever wing, Stout sought a way to improve the plane for the air transport business that he foresaw to come. Since the OX-5 was too light for the job, and the Hissos were not readily available, he turned to the war-surplus 400 hp Liberty in-line engine. To use this meant the complete redesign of the plane, and with the approval of his company's directors, Stout and his engineers stretched the 1-AS into a larger plane built around the huge Liberty engine. Much of the work on this design was done by George H. Prudden, Chief Engineer of the Stout Metal Plane Company at the time. At the time of his death in 1964 he was working for Lockheed and in their company obituary they make the statement that, "Prudden was the first to design and build an all-metal airplane in the U.S."

The new eight-passenger plane was named the "Air Pullman" (after the dependable and sturdy railroad car) and was flight tested by Walter Lees at Selfridge Field in 1924. At the time that the plant was moved from Detroit to Dearborn in late 1924 the plane was designated 2-AT and re-named "Air Transport."

The 2-AT was a rugged, advanced design for the period and proved its value many times over while in operation on the Ford freight line. In regard to this it is pertinent to quote from a 1952 letter from Bill Stout to the author concerning the development of this plane and the later tri-motor: "I am as interested as you are in getting this all straightened out as I think it will show some rather remarkable safety records for this plane in spite of the fact that it was designed out of a C.A.A. [sic] handbook of about twelve pages, was in a considerable amount imaginary and was structurally designed by a man just out of the University of Minnesota graduating as a specialist on reinforced concrete structures. Much credit should be given to George Prudden, now at Lockheed, for having established many of the fundamentals of internal design now used on all planes."

Opposite:
William B. Stout; genius, inventor, promoter and guiding influence behind the development of the Ford Tri-Motor and Stout Air Lines. (Bill Balogh)

It was at this time that Edsel Ford became interested in Stout's activities, and after exchanging ideas with him he was prompted to invest in the future development of aviation by building an airport and providing a building, on lease, for the further development of the Stout 2-AT. Harold H. Emmons, Bill Stout and Edsel Ford selected the site for the new airport, and after six months work clearing trees and leveling the ground had constructed a building and two runways, one 3,700 feet long and the other 3,400 feet long. This was formally announced in the company house organ "Ford News" for July 15, 1924 as follows: "For the purpose of encouraging aircraft development the Ford interests will erect a modern factory building devoted to research in aviation. The buildings will be used by the Stout Metal Plane Company and the Aircraft Development Corporation." The field was completed in November 1924 and officially dedicated as Ford Airport on January 15, 1925. The Aircraft Development Corporation announced on January 8, 1926 that it was going to build the largest metal-clad airship in the world, two and a half times the size of the Shenandoah, at the Ford Airport.

With the passage of the Kelly Air Mail Act in February 1925 Henry Ford became interested in this additional aspect of aviation. He approached Stout with the idea of starting an experimental air freight line between Dearborn and Chicago. With typical Ford abruptness and decision the airline was founded and put into operation in one week, devoted solely to the business of one company, on April 13, 1925. The first flight was made with the first Stout 2-AT named "Maiden Dearborn I." The second plane, "Maiden Dearborn II", was placed into service on April 27th creating daily service to Chicago. On June 26th a third plane was added with service to Cleveland.

Aviation writer John Neville graphically described the emotional climate surrounding this flight, a thing so commonplace today that we often do not appreciate the progress that has been made in such a short time: "Before a few officials of the Ford and Stout companies and several newspapermen, Eddie Hamilton, who had been employed by Ford as chief pilot, took the plane off on its initial flight to Chicago. So high was the interest in the new experiment, and so marked was the doubt that everything would go smoothly, that for nearly a week thereafter Bill Stout and his associates – plus the inevitable newspapermen – gathered at the field every afternoon to watch the big plane return from its 'hazardous' trip to Chicago."

During July 1925 Henry Ford made the initial advances to Stout for the Ford Motor Company to purchase his company. The transaction was quietly made at the end of the fiscal year, and officially announced on August 8, 1925 in the "Ford News"; "Ford Motor Company became a manufacturer of airplanes July 31st by purchasing all

The little Stout 1-AS Air Sedan that shows the general layout and design of the later Tri-Motor. (Hudek)

The next progression in the design with an enlarged fuselage, wing and more powerful Liberty engine called the 2-AT Air Transport. With no national registration of aircraft in 1925 this plane was identified only as "Maiden Dearborn IV." (G.S. Williams)

stock and assets of the Stout Metal Airplane Company. The building of Stout all-metal planes will henceforth be carried on by the Stout Metal Airplane division of the Ford Motor Company. Operations will be continued in the factory built at Ford Airport, Dearborn, where four planes have already been built and others are under construction. Mr. Stout, who developed the present model, after 15 years of experimentation, and was a pioneer in building an all-metal monoplane of the thick-wing type, remains in charge of plane manufacture, while his personnel of expert engineers and mechanics also has been retained.

The Stout plant and manufacturing equipment has been purchased by the Ford Company for the purpose of accelerating airplane development by backing the design with the diversified resources and experience of the Ford organization. The scope of experimental operations will be widened, while manufacture of the present type, which has proved highly successful in Ford air freight service, will be continued on a larger scale. The Stout plant was closed down Friday, July 31st for inventory, and opened Monday, August 3, 1925, under new management.

The association of the Stout Metal Airplane Company with the Ford organization began less than a year ago, when on completion of the airplane factory built at the Ford Airport, October 14, 1924, Henry Ford and Edsel Ford contributed its facilities to the development of the Stout plane, of which only one of the present kind then existed.

The Stout plane was selected as being the most highly developed type in America, and because it appealed to Mr. Ford as the most logical, dependable, and safe."

There were either ten or eleven 2-AT's built in 1924

and 1925, but because this was two years before any government licensing of airplanes or pilots was required incomplete records exist for detailed information. The summary of records found to date are as follows:

Serial No.	Registration	Remarks
2-AT-1	none	Built 1924, "Maiden Dearborn I"
2-AT-2	none	Built 1925, "Maiden Dearborn II"
2-AT-3	none	Built 1925, "Maiden Dearborn III"
2-AT-4	NC-2431	Built 8-25, "Maiden Dearborn IV", crashed 2-4-28 while landing in fog at Wayne, Michigan.
2-AT-5	NC-2432	Built 10-25, "Maiden Dearborn V", had flown 1,331 hours as of 9-27. Lost in crash at Cleveland 4-28.
2-AT-6	NC-1494	Built 11-25. Had flown 1,155 hours by 9-27. Grounded 8-11-28, junked.
2-AT-7	NC-2243	Built 1925. Florida Airways 1926, Stout Air Services 1927.
2-AT-8	TN-3944	Built 12-25, to Florida Airways. Repossessed 12-27, to Stout Air Services. Temporary Number to fly from Tampa to Dearborn.
2-AT-9	unknown	No information. Possibly the plane tested with the new P&W Wasp.
2-AT-10	ID-1493	Built 11-25. By Sept 1927 had flown 609 hours. Identified lic.
2-AT-11	TN-2244	Built 1925. To John Wanamaker & Company, NYC, for a month, back to Stout Air Services. To Betz Air Lines, Hammond, IN 2-20-28.

All 2-AT's were grounded by the Department of Commerce on August 11, 1928 due to structural weakness in the wings. As it was economically unfeasible to modify the planes to meet the new standards they were all retired from service.

The first six 2-AT's flew daily for the company freight line in 1925. In 1926 over one thousand flights were made without an injury when the Ford Motor Company formally contracted for Air Mail Routes No.6 (Detroit-Cleveland), and No.7 (Detroit-Chicago), and flew two and three times a day with a payload of 1,000 to 1,500 pounds per trip.

The great contribution to commercial aviation made by the Ford Company in pioneering the company air line, and the air mail service, was well stated by C.M. Keys, President of the Curtiss Aeroplane & Motor Company in an address he made in Philadelphia in March 1926: "Mr. Ford was the first in the air, operating a line of all-metal

One 2-AT was modified with the 14th P&W Wasp engine. The VIP's are William B. Mayo (Chief Engineer, Ford Motor Company), Frederich B. Rentschler (President of Pratt & Whitney Aircraft Company), George J. Mead (Vice President of P&W), and Colonel Edward A. Deeds (Chairman of the Board of Directors of P&W). (P&W)

ships from Detroit to Chicago and later from Detroit to Cleveland, for the transportation of mail. His operating experience is very freely offered to all other operators. His whole operation has been public spirited and generous and was in fact the starting point of organized commercial aviation in this country."

This sentiment is further enforced by the statement of an anonymous commentator in a Detroit newspaper at the time that Ford took over the Stout Company who said, "Ford's entrance into aviation means progress in three departments: commercial flying, passenger flying, and national defense . . . If Stout never did anything else for aviation but interest the Fords he did a great service for our civilization."

With the advent of the light-weight, Wright air-cooled radial engine the whole picture changed and it was then possible to build a multi-engine plane without using the heavy and cumbersome Liberty engines. Thus Stout proceeded, together with George Prudden, Otto C. Koppen and John G. Lee, to modify a stock Liberty-powered 2-AT into the first tri-motor. As can be seen by the photographs this involved removing the Liberty from the nose and replacing it with a Wright Whirlwind low on a Sikorsky-type "bow", and installing two more radial engines in the leading edge of the wing. The center section was widened and an open cockpit placed above the wing.

This first tri-motor, the 3-AT, made at least three flights but performed poorly due to the center section stalling out whenever the engines were throttled back by test pilot "Shorty Schroeder", thus making it almost impossible to land power-off. Before this could be corrected the plane was destroyed, along with an early Stout "Air Pullman" used by the Post Office Department, and 13 Wright Whirlwind engines, in a $500,000 fire. This disastrous fire destroyed the Stout Metal Plane factory at Ford Airport on Sunday, January 17, 1926.

A little-known item is that Captain George Wilkins, commanding the forthcoming Detroit Arctic Expedition, made a statement to the newspapers on the 19th that the new three engine all-metal plane was being built for the expedition. William Mayo, chief engineer of the Ford Motor Company and president of the Detroit Aviation Society that was financing the expedition, said that "work on the plane that was burned had been rushed day and night for three months to have it ready for shipment this week." The 3-AT was to have been shipped to Seattle as a reserve to two Fokker planes according to Wilkins.

Shortly after the factory fire plans were made by the company to build a new and larger facility and continue with the tri-motor development. Henry Ford, however, was annoyed at the failure of the 3-AT design and so replaced Stout by Harold Hicks as chief engineer. A new design emerged under the direction of Hicks and Tom Towle, the open-cockpit 4-AT with the engines below the wings.

The evidence appears to indicate that the first Ford Tri-Motor was designed and build by a group of engineers under the direction of Harold Hicks. However, in fairness to Tom Towle, M.E. Yale 1920, who is the only person who has ever publicly sought to prove that they designed the Ford Tri-Motor, the following is his statement:

> "Mr. Stout made a preliminary free hand arrangement sketch of a methods of converting this single-engine Liberty "Air Pullman" into a three engine ship using Wright J4 air-cooled engines. The conversion was made and critically flown, and was burned up in the Stout Metal Airplane Company fire shortly thereafter; when Ford bought out Stout, I was requested to take all drawings to the Ford Laboratories the Saturday afternoon before the Sunday night fire; and a many times larger airplane factory, on the same site, was under way almost before the ashes were cold. Mr. William B. Mayo, Chief Engineer of the Ford Motor Company, then asked the writer to design a three engine passenger airplane in the Ford Laboratories. This became the Ford Tri-Motor. The writer personally made the original three-view layout drawing of the proposed ship, unassisted. It was designed by the only one there, at the time, who could formally, stress analyze an entire airplane structure for the various conditions of flight and landing; as well as, mathematically calculate the proposed airplane's performance. The writer still has in his possession a blueprint copy of the layout design, signed and dated by himself at the time. Detail drawings were made up with the help of Ford auto body draftsmen."

Tom Towle also listed himself as "Chief Engineer of the Aircraft Division of Ford Motor Company, 1926-1928." Further statements by Towle, in addition to some different remembrances by John G. Lee who was there at the same time, are contained in two fascinating articles in the Fall 1970 issue of the *Journal of the American Aviation Historical Society*.

Later, under the direction of William Mayo and Harold Hicks, an enlarged staff including A. Buchner, E. Dart, Harry Karcher, Otto Koppen, Ross, Wright and Parker Van Zandt developed and refined the 5-AT airline transport.

The significant part that William Mayo played in the development of the Tri-Motor is described in the following editorial from *Aero Digest* of May 1931:

> "The patron saint of American aviation in certain of its phases, is "Bill" Mayo. It was through him, then an important official in the Ford Motor Company, that Henry Ford became interested in and finally purchased the Stout Metal Airplane Company, putting his vast resources behind the development of practical airplanes to do practical work.
>
> "It was under William Mayo's inspiration, also, that the first exclusively passenger airline in America was started, and he inaugurated the world's first wholly freight-carrying airline.

The Stout designed and developed tri-motor, model 3-AT, that was a 2-AT with three air cooled engines in place of the liquid cooled Liberty. It proved to have poor performance during the few flights that were made with it by Major Shorty Schroeder. (Ford Archives)

Ever since, these wonderful facilities have operated ceaselessly, with an astonishing record for safety and efficiency. The freight planes have borne, to date, more than ten million pounds of Ford material, of one kind or another, in inter-service between Detroit, Chicago, Cleveland and Buffalo, to say nothing of much longer flights on occasions.

"At the time that the first exclusively passenger airline was started under William Mayo's guidance, a group of notables gathered in Detroit and were stirred by his enthusiasm to create in the office of the Ford Airplane Company a new organization for the carriage of Air Mail. It was christened National Air Transport Company, and was one of the first commercial organizations to take over an Air Mail contract.

"Nor did this wonderful man, Mayo, confine his efforts to his own City of Detroit. The organization of the Western Air Transport at Los Angeles, also was fostered and assisted by this far-sighted man. He was represented at the original meeting and invested his personal funds in the young enterprise.

"William Mayo's work, moreover, has been singularly without thought of his own profit. He has given the welfare of the industry the greater portion of his genius. The experimental work now being carried on under his direction will not be exclusively or even principally for the benefit of those enterprises with which he is personally associated, but for the welfare of that industry which serves human flight, in which unquestionably, he is one of the outstanding geniuses.

"After the Ford purchase of the Stout Metal Airplane Company the development of the tri-motor ships and other experimental work has been entirely under William Mayo's business supervision and today the Ford Tri-Motor transport planes occupy a position recognized by every operator in the world.

"When he passes on to his reward Henry Ford will leave behind him many evidences of genius. None will be more striking than the record of the fact that he gave William Mayo his great opportunity.

"For a few years, indeed, nearly every successful airline in the country had Mayo's name upon its board; all work to this day under his close advise and counsel. If American Air Transport has a father that father is named Mayo – William B."

Some mention should be made of the resemblance between the Ford Tri-Motor and the Fokker tri-motor transports. Their external features were, in fact, so closely alike that the average layman could identify the Ford only because of its "washboard" metal construction. The assertions that the Ford was a copy of the Fokker are not true, however, although the Ford design derives ideas from both the Fokker and Junkers airplanes.

Anthony Fokker's statement on this subject is interesting and deserves a place in this history as it represents the thoughts of several people at the time: "In 1925 I brought over the first three-motored plane, a ship which created a sensation in the industry, and gave Ford something more to imitate. Many people have thought I opposed Henry Ford's copying of this tri-motored airliner. Actually his imitating that machine in all-metal construction has been a great help to me."

Another published claim, in the same vein, is that of Thomas Hamilton, founder of the Hamilton Metalplane Company of Milwaukee, Wisconsin. Eugene Wilson states, of Hamilton, that "He had, however, established his own Metalplane Company and built a high wing metal monoplane that, he claimed, antedated the Ford", and "This plane, according to Tom, had been the prototype from which the Ford Tri-Motor had evolved." This claim should be judged by comparing Stout's early developments with the realization that the Hamilton Metalplane Company was founded in 1927.

The 4-AT-1 was designed and built in a remarkably short time, being test flown in just over four months. A new design was laid down, as can be seen by a comparison

William B. Mayo, the most important person in the development and refinement of the Ford Tri-Motor. (Hudek)

of the photos of the 3-AT and 4-AT, and the entire airplane was hand-built. This is quite an achievement for a three-engine, all-metal aircraft of some seventy-foot span. The new design was an eight passenger transport with an open cockpit and tail skid, three wright J-4 engines, and a marked resemblance to the 2-AT, particularly in the fuselage, windows and tail group.

The 4-AT-1 was test flown by Major R.W. "Shorty" Schroeder on the morning of Friday, June 11, 1926. The plane was airborne in seven seconds and flew for 55 minutes before Henry Ford, Edsel Ford, a few executives of the Ford Motor Company and the company pilots.

In the afternoon it flew again for 45 minutes before a large crowd of company officials and representatives of National Air Transport, Colonials Airways, Western Air Express and Florida Airways.

It is hard for us today to look at this primitive transport and understand the following enthusiastic description of it given at the time: "The cabin of the plane is larger than that of the other Ford planes and is fitted with comfortable swivel reclining chairs for eight passengers, a separate room for freight and baggage, toilet facilities, and equipped for the utmost of safety and comfort in operation." It must be viewed from the standpoint of what else was flying as a "transport" in the summer of 1926.

The one Ford pilot who had been in Chicago in the morning was there for the afternoon flight. The Ford pilots, as remembered by Larry Fritz in 1969, were Dean Burford (302), John Collings (267), Larry Fritz (327), Pat Gallup (216), Eddie Hamilton (366), Perry Hutton (547), Ross Kirkpatrick (?), Leroy Manning (307) and Major Shorty Schroeder (6988). Their pilots license numbers have been added from Government records to further identify these real pioneers in aviation.

The Ford Motor Company built a model factory and flying field at Dearborn and pioneered many of the developments that we take for granted today such as concrete runways, radio and navigational aids, an airport hotel and administration building, and a dirigible mooring mast. The mast was first used by the Army dirigible RS-1 on September 18, 1926 and later by the USS Shenandoah.

The 108-room hotel named "Dearborn Inn" was leased to a private operator. This magnificent structure shows in the background of a number of photos taken at the factory and is still in operation today.

Some idea of the type of design and construction of the factory can be gained from the following company announcement made in October 1929: "All of the present buildings at the site of the Ford aviation activities will be retained and additions will be made so as to permit on a larger scale the efficient production and movement of parts toward assembly. All airplane manufacturing operations will be concentrated in the single factory at Dearborn. Provisions will be made for the production there of parts now being made in the Rouge plant of the Ford Motor Company, while facilities for the finishing and trimming of the cabin interiors of the big air transports will be so enlarged that twelve planes may be handled on the trim line at the same time. Architecturally, the plant additions will be of the style dictated by the airplane. They will conform in general appearance to the hangars and to the Ford experimental laboratories in the immediate vicinity of the airplane factory, being long and low so as to constitute no interference for incoming or departing planes at the airport and no barrier to the wide visibility required for flying. The big increase in floor space will make possible the production of one tri-engine, all-metal air transport a day. Throughout the early part of the year (1929), the production schedule has been three planes a week, but a short time ago the rate was stepped up by an additional plane weekly.

Building plans call for the erection behind the present factory of a unit duplicating the present one in size and immediately connected with it as to double the floor space of the plant. In addition, on the north end the building will be extended to within about 90 feet of Airport Drive, giving still more floor space. On the north end of the

Aerial view of the Ford aircraft factory and field on July 29, 1929. The brand new 5-AT-62 (NC-403H) for Pan American Airways is third from the left in the lineup of Tri-Motors. (Ford Archives)

present plant a mezzanine floor will be built to extend southward a distance of six bays. When completed the factory will extend 640 feet along Oakwood Boulevard and 253 feet along Airport Drive. Its exterior will be of the same materials as were used in the present structure. Bedford limestone and fire-clay brick, with steel sash and doors and cement tiled roof. The exceptional lighting arrangement and the ventilation system of the present factory will be carried out faithfully in the new buildings. At present the factory is 500 feet in length. The new building will be 140 feet longer. An entrance to the northwest corner, convenient to the intersection of Airport Drive and Oakwood Boulevard will admit to the general offices, the accounting, employment and stock departments, the office of the superintendent and others. The mezzanine floor will be devoted to the drafting room, employees' rooms, and other uses." The buildings are still there and the airport field has been used for a number of

Exterior of the new passenger terminal built by Ford as a model for other airports to follow in the development of airline use. It is shown on February 3, 1928. (Ford Archives)

Interior of the Passenger Terminal on the same date. (Ford Archives)

years as an automobile test track.

One word in this company statement is worth commenting upon. This is the term "tri-engine." This is the technically correct term for piston engines, as "motors" are electric and "engines" are combustion powered as in "diesel engine." It is interesting to note that at least one photo exists showing 4-AT-5 with the name "TRI-FORD" on the fin. There must have been considerable discussion over adopting a popular name because Charles Lindbergh himself, writing in the May 1928 National Geographic Magazine, uses the terms "TRIPLE-MOTORED PLANES" and "triple-motored ships." The other deciding factor was the already established term "tri-motor" being used by Anthony Fokker. It is the author's judgement that those in charge decided upon the name "Tri-Motor", with a dash between the two words, in order to establish a Trademark for the Ford airplane to distinguish it from all other planes with three engines.

1928 and 1929 were the main years for production of the Ford Tri-Motor and the factory employed approximately 500 skilled workers plus management, engineering and flight test personnel. Sales were at an all-time high in 1929 when the October stock market crash changed the entire future of the factory. An attempt was made to set up a European sales center in 1930 when Ford opened a facility with hangars and shops in England. Named "Ford Airfield", it was the former Comper Aircraft Company factory at Hooton Park, Cheshire. Five aircraft were assembled but the anticipated sales did not develop.

Two misconceptions about the Ford have existed for some time. The first is the notion that the lower hp 4-AT's were built first and then the Wasp powered 5-AT's were designed and production changed to them. A study of the following table "Ford Tri-Motor Production By Date" will clearly show that this was not the case and that, in fact, the two models were build simultaneously in 1928 and 1929. The second is that the serial number indicates the order of production. Most recent writing about the Ford has made this mistake, such as 5-AT-74 (N-414H) being "the 74th Ford built" etc., whereas it was actually the 155th Tri-Motor built. As can be seen each model started with number one so the serial number is not an indication of when the plane was built.

Ford Tri-Motor Production

(Listing by Date)

6-11-26	4-AT-A	4-AT-1	Open cockpit
11-2-26	4-AT-A	4-AT-2	
1-28-27	4-AT-A	4-AT-3	
1-29-27	4-AT-A	4-AT-4	First military; Navy XJR-1
3-28-27	4-AT-A	4-AT-5	
5-12-27	4-AT-A	4-AT-6	First company a/c; Stand Oil
7-22-27	4-AT-A	4-AT-07	
8-1-27	4-AT-A	4-AT-8	
8-22-27	4-AT-A	4-AT-9	
9-10-27	4-AT-A	4-AT-10	First on floats, 1st export
10-11-27	4-AT-A	4-AT-11	
10-26-27	4-AT-A	4-AT-12	
11-17-27	4-AT-A	4-AT-13	Second military; Army C-3
12-14-27	4-AT-A	4-AT-14	
3-20-28	4-AT-B	4-AT-15	Byrd's South Pole a/c
3-30-28	4-AT-B	4-AT-16	
4-12-28	4-AT-B	4-AT-17	
5-1-28	4-AT-B	4-AT-18	
4-28-28	4-AT-B	4-AT-19	
5-10-28	4-AT-B	4-AT-20	
5-18-28	4-AT-B	4-AT-21	
6-1-28	4-AT-B	4-AT-22	
6-16-28	4-AT-B	4-AT-23	
6-16-28	4-AT-D	4-AT-24	
7-2-28	4-AT-B	4-AT-25	
7-14-28	4-AT-B	4-AT-26	
7-21-28	5-AT-A	5-AT-1	First 5-AT
7-24-28	4-AT-B	4-AT-27	
7-31-28	4-AT-B	4-AT-28	
8-3-28	4-AT-B	4-AT-29	

8-10-28	4-AT-B	4-AT-30	
8-15-28	4-AT-B	4-AT-31	
8-22-28	4-AT-B	4-AT-32	
8-28-28	4-AT-B	4-AT-33	
8-30-28	5-AT-A	5-AT-2	
8-31-28	4-AT-B	4-AT-34	
9-5-28	4-AT-B	4-AT-35	
9-7-28	4-AT-B	4-AT-36	
9-10-28	4-AT-B	4-AT-37	Modified to 4-AT-D
9-13-28	4-AT-B	4-AT-38	
9-17-28	4-AT-B	4-AT-39	To 9-AT-1 in 1930
9-22-28	4-AT-B	4-AT-40	
9-22-28	4-AT-B	4-AT-41	
9-26-28	4-AT-B	4-AT-42	
9-29-28	5-AT-A	5-AT-3	
10-1-28	4-AT-B	4-AT-43	
10-3-28	4-AT-B	4-AT-44	
10-8-28	4-AT-B	4-AT-45	
10-12-28	4-AT-C	4-AT-47	One only 4-AT-C
10-17-28	4-AT-B	4-AT-48	
10-24-28	5-AT-B	5-AT-4	First 5-AT-B; Lindbergh
10-26-28	4-AT-B	4-AT-49	
10-30-28	4-AT-B	4-AT-50	
11-2-28	4-AT-B	4-AT-51	
11-8-28	5-AT-B	5-AT-5	
11-9-28	4-AT-B	4-AT-52	
11-13-28	4-AT-B	4-AT-53	
11-22-28	5-AT-B	5-AT-6	
11-27-28	5-AT-B	5-AT-7	
12-1-28	5-AT-B	5-AT-8	
12-4-28	5-AT-B	5-AT-9	
12-6-28	5-AT-B	5-AT-10	
12-10-28	5-AT-B	5-AT-11	
12-12-28	5-AT-B	5-AT-12	
12-14-28	5-AT-B	5-AT-13	
12-19-28	5-AT-B	5-AT-14	
12-21-28	5-AT-B	5-AT-15	
12-27-28	5-AT-B	5-AT-16	
12-29-28	5-AT-B	5-AT-17	
1-8-29	5-AT-B	5-AT-18	
1-10-29	5-AT-B	5-AT-19	
1-11-29	4-AT-B	4-AT-54	
1-15-29	4-AT-E	4-AT-55	First 4-AT-E
1-17-29	4-AT-E	4-AT-56	
1-18-29	5-AT-B	5-AT-20	
1-23-29	5-AT-B	5-AT-21	
1-25-29	5-AT-B	5-AT-22	
1-26-29	4-AT-E	4-AT-57	
1-29-29	4-AT-E	4-AT-58	
1-31-29	5-AT-B	5-AT-23	
2-7-29	5-AT-B	5-AT-24	
2-11-29	5-AT-B	5-AT-25	
2-12-29	4-AT-E	4-AT-59	
2-18-29	4-AT-E	4-AT-60	
2-19-29	5-AT-B	5-AT-26	
2-21-29	5-AT-B	5-AT-27	
2-22-29	4-AT-E	4-AT-61	
2-26-29	5-AT-B	5-AT-28	
2-28-29	5-AT-B	5-AT-29	
3-5-29	5-AT-B	5-AT-30	
3-8-29	5-AT-B	5-AT-31	
3-14-29	5-AT-B	5-AT-32	

The factory on April 19, 1929, with new planes coming down the assembly line. 5-AT-34 in the foreground is on exhibit today at the Flying Lady Restaurant and Museum at Morgan Hill, California. (Ford Archives)

3-20-29	5-AT-B	5-AT-33	
3-22-29	5-AT-B	5-AT-34	
3-26-29	5-AT-B	5-AT-37	
3-28-29	5-AT-B	5-AT-36	
4-3-29	5-AT-B	5-AT-35	
4-5-29	5-AT-B	5-AT-38	Army
4-6-29	5-AT-B	5-AT-39	
4-9-29	5-AT-B	5-AT-40	
4-11-29	5-AT-B	5-AT-41	
4-16-29	4-AT-E	4-AT-63	
4-17-29	4-AT-E	4-AT-64	
4-19-29	5-AT-B	5-AT-42	
4-23-29	5-AT-B	5-AT-43	
4-25-29	5-AT-B	5-AT-44	
4-26-29	5-AT-B	5-AT-45	
5-1-29	4-AT-E	4-AT-65	
5-14-29	6-AT-AS	6-AT-1	
5-18-29	5-AT-C	5-AT-46	First 5-AT-C
5-23-29	5-AT-C	5-AT-47	
5-29-29	4-AT-E	4-AT-80	Army C-9, 29-220
5-31-29	6-AT-A	6-AT-2	Modified to 7-AT-1
6-3-29	4-AT-E	4-AT-81	Army C-9
6-4-29	5-AT-C	5-AT-50	Demonstrator for England
6-5-29	5-AT-C	5-AT-48	
6-7-29	4-AT-E	4-AT-82	Army C-9
6-8-29	5-AT-C	5-AT-49	
6-11-29	6-AT-A	6-AT-3	To 5-AT-94
6-13-29	5-AT-C	5-AT-51	

Above: One of the company planes used on the Ford Freight Lines to carry automobile parts between plants in March 1927. (Ford Archives)

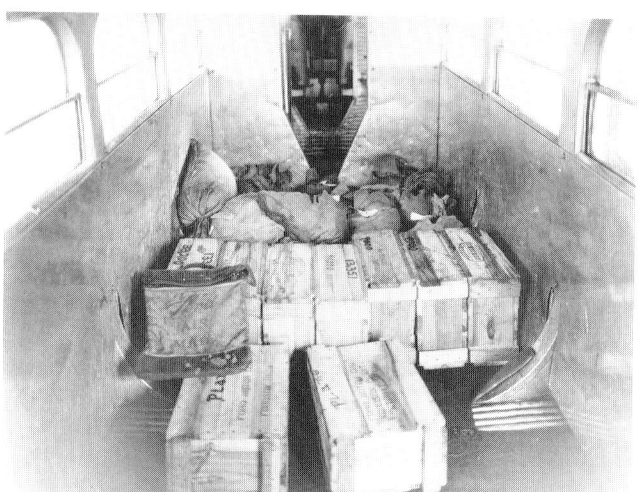

Left: An interior view showing the car parts in wooden boxes on the floor of the 4-AT. (Hudek)

6-14-29	4-AT-E	4-AT-83	Army C-9
6-17-29	5-AT-C	5-AT-52	
6-18-29	4-AT-E	4-AT-84	Army C-9
6-20-29	4-AT-E	4-AT-85	Army C-9
6-21-29	5-AT-C	5-AT-53	
6-21-29	4-AT-E	4-AT-86	Army C-9
6-24-29	5-AT-C	5-AT-54	
6-25-29	5-AT-C	5-AT-55	
6-26-29	5-AT-C	5-AT-56	
6-27-29	5-AT-C	5-AT-57	
6-29-29	5-AT-C	5-AT-58	
7-1-29	4-AT-E	4-AT-46	
7-5-29	5-AT-C	5-AT-59	
7-5-29	5-AT-C	5-AT-60	
7-6-29	4-AT-E	4-AT-62	
7-10-29	4-AT-E	4-AT-66	To 11-AT-1 in March 1930
7-12-29	5-AT-C	5-AT-61	
7-15-29	5-AT-C	5-AT-62	
7-16-29	5-AT-C	5-AT-63	
7-18-29	5-AT-C	5-AT-64	
7-19-29	5-AT-C	5-AT-65	
7-26-29	5-AT-C	5-AT-66	
7-27-29	5-AT-C	5-AT-67	
7-30-29	8-AT	8-AT-1	Single-engine 5-AT
8-2-29	4-AT-E	4-AT-67	
8-3-29	5-AT-C	5-AT-68	
8-7-29	5-AT-C	5-AT-69	
8-10-29	5-AT-C	5-AT-70	
8-14-29	4-AT-E	4-AT-68	
8-17-29	5-AT-C	5-AT-71	
8-21-29	4-AT-E	4-AT-69	
8-23-29	5-AT-C	5-AT-75	
8-26-29	5-AT-C	5-AT-72	
8-28-29	4-AT-E	4-AT-70	
8-30-29	5-AT-C	5-AT-73	
9-4-29	5-AT-C	5-AT-74	Company demonstrator
9-5-29	5-AT-C	5-AT-76	
9-13-29	5-AT-C	5-AT-78	
10-8-29	5-AT-C	5-AT-77	
10-29	5-AT-C	5-AT-79	X-419H
11-5-29	5-AT-C	5-AT-80	Tests with engines in wing
12-18-29	5-AT-C	5-AT-81	
12-27-29	5-AT-C	5-AT-82	
1-20-30	5-AT-C	5-AT-88	
2-10-30	5-AT-C	5-AT-89	
3-28-30	5-AT-C	5-AT-90	
4-2-30	5-AT-C	5-AT-83	
6-25-30	5-AT-C	5-AT-94	Converted from 6-AT-3
10-31-30	5-AT-C	5-AT-84	
11-10-30	5-AT-C	5-AT-85	
11-20-30	5-AT-C	5-AT-86	
11-21-30	5-AT-C	5-AT-87	
12-19-30	5-AT-C	5-AT-96	
12-27-30	5-AT-D	5-AT-91	First 5-AT-D; Army C-4A
1-30-31	5-AT-D	5-AT-92	Army
2-5-31	5-AT-D	5-AT-93	Army
2-12-31	5-AT-D	5-AT-95	Army
2-24-31	5-AT-D	5-AT-97	
3-25-31	5-AT-D	5-AT-98	
4-2-31	5-AT-D	5-AT-99	
4-7-31	5-AT-D	5-AT-100	To 13-A in 1931
4-7-31	5-AT-D	XB-906-1	Bomber
4-15-31	5-AT-D	5-AT-106	
4-17-31	5-AT-D	5-AT-102	
5-1-31	5-AT-D	5-AT-101	
5-31	5-AT-D	5-AT-103	
5-8-31	5-AT-D	5-AT-104	
5-27-31	5-AT-D	5-AT-108	
6-9-31	5-AT-D	5-AT-110	
7-31	5-AT-D	5-AT-107	
7-31	5-AT-D	5-AT-111	
7-24-31	5-AT-C	5-AT-79A	Formerly 6-AT-2
7-27-31	4-AT-F	4-AT-71	One only 4-AT-F
12-31	5-AT-D	5-AT-105	Delivered 12-23-31 to USMC
12-31	5-AT-D	5-AT-109	Delivered 2-17-32 to USN
3-32	5-AT-D	5-AT-112	
3-17-32	5-AT-D	5-AT-114	
3-31-32	5-AT-D	5-AT-113	
4-25-33	5-AT-D	5-AT-115	
6-7-33	5-AT-D	5-AT-116	Last Ford built, to PAA

An interesting photo of the 4-AT-1 blasting itself out of the mud on November 27, 1926. Note the two pilots in the open cockpit and streamlined prop spinners not seen on the later production Ford Tri-Motors. (Ford Archives)

The 4-AT-1 on February 4, 1927 showing the change to an enclosed pilots cockpit that remained standard from then on. (Ford Archives)

Summary of production:

Year	Number
1926	2
1927	12
1928	54
1929	95
1930	11
1931	19
1932	4
1933	2
Total	199

The Ford Motor Company ceased manufacturing Tri-Motors in September 1932. The decision was probably reached as a result of a combination of various issues; the tightened market and economy of the depression era, the overall loss incurred in the production of the airplanes, the diminishing necessity for a three-engine aircraft, the need for a faster and more economical design for airline use, and the personal diminishing interest on the part of Henry Ford caused by the deaths of three test pilots in crashes.

The final closing of the Tri-Motor Sales Department is described in the following news story from the New York Times for September 18, 1932: "News that Ford was interested in unloading its present stock of Tri-Motors developed several weeks ago when airline operators were asked to bid on a fleet of eight aircraft which were at the Ford field. No line cared, however, to tie up the capital needed for the deal and no offers were received. Since then the company has disposed of two to the Navy and expects to sell the remaining six at extremely low prices." Evidently the last two airplanes, 5-AT-115 and 5-AT-116, were not even completed in 1932 for the CAA records show them to be manufactured in April and June 1933. It appears that Ford decided to delay any further work on them until a customer had been obtained. Aircraft production ended and the factory doors closed for the last time on June 8, 1933.

Prices

The original price for the 4-AT model was $42,000 delivered at the factory. In May 1930, when price reductions went into effect for all Ford airplanes, the price dropped to $40,000. Only four years later the sale price had dropped to $5,000. Chalon Carson advertised his 4-AT-E, with a total time of 1600 hours, for sale for $9,000, but at the same time Jerry Wood was asking only $5,000 for his 4-AT-E with a total time of 800 hours (*Aero Digest*, August 1934).

The 4-AT-1 rounding a pylon at the 1926 Philadelphia Air Races. (U.S. Air Service via Bowers)

Two years later the price for a used 4-AT varied between $3,750 (4-AT-62) to $5,000 (4-AT-48). In 1938 Jerry Wood was down to $3,950 (*Aero Digest*, May 1938), and 4-AT-48 was offered for $3,750 (*Aero Digest*, August 1938). It was not until after World War II that the price of a used 4-AT rose again.

The 5-AT always sold for more than the 4-AT because of its larger engines and better carrying capacity. The original price was $55,000, reduced to $50,000 in May 1930. The 7-AT with its odd engine combination dropped from $51,000 to $47,000.

Prices for used 5-AT's started to show up in the mid-1930s with one being Litzenberger's 5-AT-C (NC-420H) advertised for $4,600 (*Aero Digest*, September 1937). The Babb Company was a major clearinghouse for Ford's being sold abroad and in January to June 1937 their advertisements listed a 5-AT-D for $6,500 and a 5-AT-C for $6,000. The upward trend seemed to start with the Aero Brokerage Service Company of Los Angeles who listed a 5-AT-C for $13,500 (*Aero Digest*, March 1939). In the next year TACA Honduras advertised ten Wasp Fords for sale at $15,000+ each (*Aero Digest*, July 1940).

Jerry Wilson advertised his 5-AT-39 for $27,000 in September 1956 and the venerable 5-AT-74 was advertised for $47,600 in Aviation week for May 27, 1957. In November 1957 Jack Adams A/C Sales offered a Ford "painted yellow with green and white trim" for $26,300. By January 1966 the price for 5-AT-11 had risen to $45,000 in a Trade-A-Plane ad. Within a short time the price for this same plane had risen to $78,000 (*Trade-A-Plane*, October 1968).

Inflation and rarity finally took over and Island Airlines offered their 4-AT-38 for sale for $950,000 (*Trade-A-Plane*, February 1982). 4-AT-55 had been put up for auction the same month, asking $500,000, but was not sold when the highest bid was only $320,000. Irv Perch was the first to break the seven digit figure with his ad in the *Wall Street Journal* (September 6, 1978) offering 5-AT-34 for sale for $1,250,000. He has kept to this price over the years, turned down one million dollars at the 1990 Santa Monica Auction and brought the plane back to Morgan Hill. The pristine 5-AT-8, totally rebuilt by Harrahs Automobile and Boat Shop, was sold at the auction following Bill Harrah's death for $1,500,000. The October 1991 Museum of Flying Auction at Santa Monica, California, saw the sale of 4-AT-38 for $650,000.

Chapter 2
Construction and Model Designations

Construction

The construction of the Ford Tri-Motor was a novel and unique idea in the United States in 1926, but it was not the first all-metal plane to be built in this country. It was, however, the first such aircraft of such large size, and with three engines. It was also backed by the biggest name in American production.

There is no question about the Germans being first with this concept, Junkers having built the all-metal, tri-motored, low-wing G-23 monoplane with a 95-foot span carrying a crew of two and ten passengers. This plane was flown from Russia to Switzerland in late 1924.

The following technical description of the Ford Tri-Motors, based on official company statements regarding its construction describes in general terms the basic materials and construction details applicable to all models. The Ford Tri-Motor was an all-metal cantilever high wing cabin monoplane. It was constructed from heat treated aluminum alloy channels riveted together and covered with corrugated "Alclad" alloy, an aluminum coated duralumin sheet. Duraluminum is an exceptionally strong metal, light in weight, and having the strength of steel.

The all-metal feature of the Ford Tri-Motor has many well understood advantages over other materials. Both from the standpoint of low upkeep expense and long life, metal offers economy and security in its freedom from rotting, warping and splitting, tearing – in its resistance to wear and vibration – in its definitely determined strength, and in its unvarying good appearance. This is taken for granted today but in 1926 it was an era of wood, wire and fabric. Steel tube construction became standard for fuselages about this time but that was still fabric covered.

The one drawback of metal, corrosion, is eliminated or delayed by the use of "Alclad" alloy on all exposed wing, fuselage and control surfaces. Pure aluminum is highly resistant to corrosion and "Alclad" alloy combines the corrosion-resisting quality of pure aluminum with the strength of duraluminum. A sheet of "Alclad" alloy is something like a sandwich. The two surfaces are corroding-resistant 99.7% pure aluminum. Between these two surfaces is the strength-providing duraluminum. "Alclad" alloy can be rolled into a sheet as thin as paper and still

The 5-AT production line on May 28, 1929. From left to right are 5-AT-54, 5-AT-53 and 5-AT-52. (Ford Archives)

6456-5-28-29

have the same proportionate sheath of pure aluminum on its surface. The aluminum is an integral part of the sheet.

Another astonishing peculiarity is that it resists corrosion at its edges, or where the rivet holes expose the duralumin core. Such edges have been exposed to as much as eighteen months attack by salt water without the slightest deterioration.

All of the exposed parts of the Ford Tri-Motor that are made of duralumin were coated with a moisture-proof, protective lacquer. As these parts are never subjected to wear, friction or abrasion, the coating was a positive preventive of corrosion.

Metal is a determinate material, that is its characteristics may be pre-determined with accuracy. All-metal construction offers additional strength and fire resisting qualities not available in other materials, safety factors that were as important as the three engines in selling the Ford to the operators of the day.

Fuselage

The fuselage, rectangular in shape with a rounded deck, was constructed entirely of duralumin with "Alclad" alloy covering. The structure was formed into sections from duralumin sheets. The sections were assembled together by means of gussets and duralumin rivets. This made a structure similar to that of a steel building or bridge.

Wing

The Ford wing was an internally braced structure of monoplane design built on the principle of a cantilever bridge. It was composed of three units: the root or center section above the fuselage, and two wing sections. The root section is a high lift airfoil section of constant thickness. The wings are tapered in both plan and front elevation, changing gradually from the root section to a high speed thin section at the extreme tips.

The wing structure consists of three main spars. To distribute the loads among the spars they are interconnected at regular intervals by means of rib trussing. Five auxiliary spars located transversely and intermediately between the main spars carry the loads to the rib trusses and thence to the main spars. The entire wing was covered with corrugated "Alclad" alloy riveted to the spars. All rivets in the wing could be easily inspected as no blind rivets were used. The sections were riveted together by means of gusset plates into a rigid structure of homogeneous material proportionately designed to permit uniform deflection.

An excellent detailed view of a 4-AT on skis on March 10, 1930. (Ford Archives)

Ken Fryling, Ford Project engineer for Kal-Aero, rolling corrugated alclad skin for a 4-AT restoration. (E.J. Payette)

Wicker seats and the sparse interior of 4-AT-2 show the start of the Ford Tri-Motor series. (From the Collections of Henry Ford Museum and Greenfield Village)

Wing skin being formed on the frame. (Ford Archives)

4-AT-55 on the production line on December 20, 1928. The clean, well lighted aircraft factory was a model for the aviation industry to follow. (Ford Archives)

The wing center section is permanently attached to the fuselage and carries the outboard engines. To this center section two outer wing panels are attached by six bolts each. These are of a standard size, identical for the 4-AT and 5-AT, and thus the extra area is obtained solely by increasing the span of the center section. This ingenious device saved the expense of manufacturing two different sets of wings for the two models. The 5-AT added roughly four feet to the span and 3,400 pounds to the gross weight.

A passenger shakes hands through the open window of a 4-AT, a vivid contrast with the multi-paned windows in the pressurized cabins of today's airliners. (Hudek)

Cabin Interior and Equipment

The interior of the cabin in the standard planes was covered with Ford Aero Board made of two thin sheets of aluminum with a balsam wood core. This provided an excellent surface for the interior decorations and in addition adds to the soundproofing and cleanliness of the cabin.

Passenger chairs in the early models, of both the 4-AT and 5-AT versions, were of wicker construction. Several different sizes and styles were built as well as a later combination metal frame and wicker back. The final version was an aluminum seat covered with leather in color to harmonize with the interior of the cabin.

Large cabin windows provided the passengers with an excellent view of the ground while in flight. They were made of non-shattering glass and equipped with individual pull shades. Electric cabin lights were provided over the windows in later models, particularly the 5-AT-C and 5-AT-D.

The toilet compartment is located at the rear of the cabin. Space for luggage is provided in the wing compartments of the center section on both sides of the fuselage and doors in the cabin ceiling provide access to these storage areas. Later modifications requested by TWA led to additional retractable wing bins in the outer wing sections.

Special equipment provided for the Club models included berths, over-stuffed chairs, divan, radio, typewriter desk. ice boxes, cupboards, stewards galley and carpets.

Early wicker seats in one of the first 4-AT's. (Hudek)

Pilots Compartment

The pilots compartment in the front of the plane is separated from the passenger cabin by a bulkhead on both sides of the fuselage, with a door on later models. Window shapes in the pilots compartment differed with various models but all had a sliding panel on the left and right hand side.

Later model wicker seats in a 1928 4-AT. (From the Collections of Henry Ford Museum and Greenfield Village)

The first 5-AT's also had wicker seats although they were of an advanced design as can be seen in this photo of the interior of a TAT airliner. (TWA)

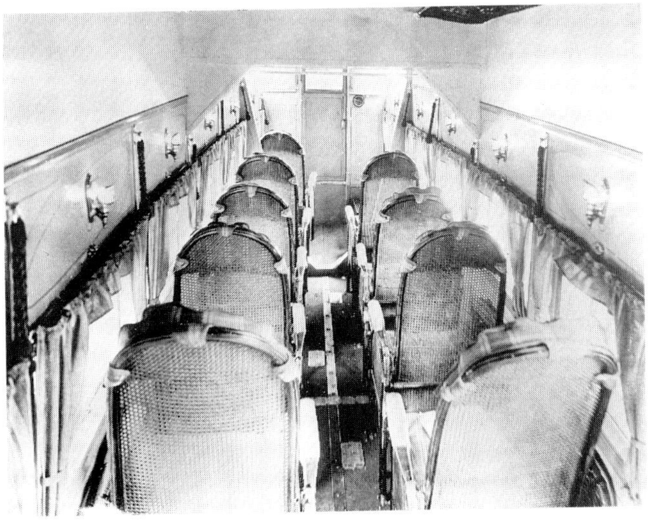

A rear view of these same wicker seats in the 5-AT. (TWA)

The standard aluminum and leather seats used on the majority of airlines. This view shows a Northwest 5-AT. (G.S. Williams)

The final model of the metal-leather seat in 5-AT-106, a 5-AT-D used by Pacific Air Transport in 1931. (Ford Archives)

The same seats were installed in the first Army C-4A (5-AT-91) as this January 1931 photo shows. (Ford Archives)

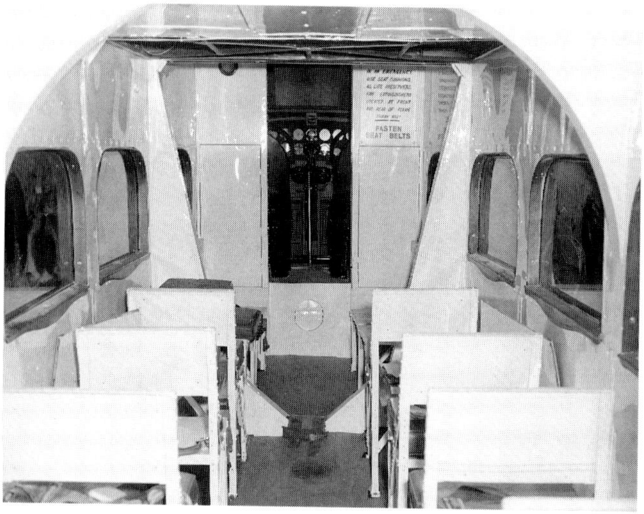

By comparison the sparse interior of Island Airlines 4-AT-42 shows their functional appearance as re-built by Kal-Aero in 1980. (E.J. Payette)

Interior of 5-AT-11 after overhaul by Pacific Airmotive at Lockheed Air Terminal in 1961. The paratrooper style benches folded up to allow cargo to be carried at the same time. (Bude Donato)

Dual controls were installed so that the plane could be flown by either pilot and many Ford airline pilots have described how it was necessary for both pilots to handle the controls at the same time in rough weather to keep the plane flying on course.

On all models except the 5-AT-D the instruments for the wing engines were mounted on a strut above the engine. An exception was 5-AT-89, a 5-AT-C Club Model, and possibly on all six of the "C" Club models.

The cockpit of C-4A, 31-401, on January 9, 1931. (Ford Archives)

Still another variation in cockpit detail with 5-AT-106 on April 17, 1931. (George Hardie)

A typical late 4-AT instrument panel and cockpit arrangement. This view shows 4-AT-84 (Air Corps C-9, 29-224) at the factory on September 26, 1928. It is interesting to note that the throttle handles are smaller than the engine switches on the Ford Tri-Motor. (G.S. Williams)

An unidentified instrument panel on June 10, 1929. This is probably a 5-AT-C. (Ford Archives)

TWA's modification of the instrument panel as a result of the use and improvement in radio communication. This photo shows 5-AT-34, NC-9651. (TWA)

An unidentified 5-AT instrument panel with the interesting addition of three starter switches to the left of center. (Hudek)

Landing Gear

The landing gear is of the wide tread split axle type, with the wheels located just under the wing engines so that maximum control can be had on the ground and in cross-wind landings. It consists of a specially designed axle with rear brace tube and shock absorber strut. Landing shocks are taken up by shock absorbers of a type developed after years of experimentation. Recoil mechanism was incorporated to take all rebound so that the plane makes contact with the ground softly and with no bounds, even in a severe landing.

Axle fittings are made integral with the ends of axle tubes by the flash weld method developed by the Ford Motor Company. Maximum tube strength is obtained in the weld by this process. Since the axle tubes are of steel special care must be taken to prevent rust and corrosion on the inside, so before the axle tubes were assembled to the plane they were drilled at each end, then boiled in oil for a period of twenty minutes. When the boiling operation was completed the tubes were drained and the holes plugged. The entire tube was then coated on the outside with cadmium plate, a rust resistant.

Brakes

The landing wheels on the Ford plane were fitted with hydraulically operated brakes so that both wheels could be locked when "running in" the engines or warming them up; one or both wheels could be released for steering on the ground. Without a crew to assist, the plane could turn around in its own length on the ground, even in strong cross winds, assuring positive control. The linings operated in a "V" type brake drum on the wheel rim. The braking torque is carried from the wheel rim directly to the brake reaction plate. This construction prevented any stressing of the wheel spokes.

The brake control lever (popularly called a Johnson Bar) was mounted between the pilots seats, easily accessible from either side. Upon pulling the control lever directly aft the brakes were equally applied to both wheels. On pulling diagonally aft and to the right the right wheel only is affected and similarly by pulling diagonally aft to the left the left wheel only is affected.

The brake lever looks like the gear shift lever in a Ford Model A automobile. This method of braking in a Ford is always startling to the modern pilot who is used to toe or heel brakes and is one of the things that old timers feel makes Ford pilots "men of distinction." However, because it is difficult to use if flying solo most of the Fords from the 1960s on have replaced it with modern foot brakes, often from the Vultee BT-13.

The tail wheel structure of 5-AT-39 in 1963. When American Airlines rebuilt it they added a stainless steel nameplate to the end of the fuselage, something that most observers have missed. (W.T. Larkins)

Tail Wheel

All of the early 4-AT models were built with a tail skid, normal for 1926 and early 1927, but these soon gave way to tail wheels with the advent of airline use. The tail wheel, developed by Otto Koppen and other Ford aeronautical engineers. is sprung on rubber shock absorbers in the same manner as the landing gear. It has a 165 degree radius of action. A steering fork was provided by the company to hook over the tail wheel axle so that the plane could be backed up by hand and easily moved about the field or in the hangar. Wheels are mounted on roller bearings which facilitates handling by a small crew.

Control Surfaces

All Ford Tri-Motors were fitted with dual side-by-side control. This was arranged with an aisle between the two seats. which are up forward just to the rear of the front engine, but out in front of the leading edge of the wing so that vision is clear.

The engine controls were located between the pilots on a decorative polished metal column. The three engines were handled by three separate control levers, so nested together that they could be worked as one or individually.

Wheel control was used, with stirrups for the rudder control. Control surfaces were built of duralumin, carefully proportioned to size and shape and are mounted on ball bearings.

The ailerons are of the Airfoil Counterbalance type. Their controls are of the cable and horn design, the cables being carried inside the wings along the front spar to the fuselage and thence to the control wheels. Each aileron is controlled independently from the cockpit section. Numerous inspection windows are provided near the points where the cables traveled over the pulleys.

The general size and shape of the tail surfaces and the ailerons afford excellent control throughout the entire range of action. Elevator and rudder are high, providing unusually generous ground clearance. The stabilizer is rectangular in shape, built upon two main spars which are connected with diagonal trussing. The stabilizer is easily adjusted in flight by means of a control handle placed above the pilots head in the cockpit. The elevators are attached to the stabilizer with self-aligning ball bearing hinges. The controls for the rudder and elevators are of the cable and horn type. The cables run through fair leads on the outside of the fuselage where they are in position for immediate and maximum inspection at all times.

The external rudder and elevator controls on 4-AT-55 in October 1951. (W.T. Larkins)

Detail of the horizontal stabilizer and control wires on the same plane. (W.T. Larkins)

Power Plant and Mounts

In general the 4-AT was powered with Wright "Whirlwind" engines and the 5-AT with Pratt & Whitney "wasp" engines. Experimental modifications and other models are described in the text.

Each engine is enclosed in a separate nacelle. The nacelles also contain the oil tanks, oil lines, starters and carburetors. The engine mounts are made of Chrome Molybdenum tubing. The intersection of the tubes in the mount is reinforced by gusset plates. The entire mount is boiled in oil inside and out, the oil entering the interior of the tubes through small holes at the end of each tube. After draining the holes are plugged with self-threading screws. To prevent the steel tube members from rusting or corroding the exterior of the mount is coated with Kepolac.

The propellers are all-metal. The blades are machined from duralumin forging and assembled in a forged steel hub.

All of the oil tanks are of welded wheel aluminum equipped with baffles to insure maximum strength and to control the oil flow through the tanks. Government specification rubber hose and fittings, together with durable hose clamps, is used throughout the oil system.

Hand inertia starters are furnished as special equipment. Electric starters and generators are also used, furnished at extra cost on specified airplanes.

Instruments are provided for each engine which show the oil temperature, oil pressure and R.P.M. On the outboard engines the instruments are easily visible to the pilot day or night since they are electrically illuminated.

They are mounted on a panel located on the inner strut, above the outboard engine nacelle, on the fuselage side of both engine nacelles. The disadvantage of this system is that the right hand engine instruments are difficult to read from the left seat if flying solo but it should be remembered that at the time of the design of the Ford that it was intended by the company that it be flown by a crew of two at all times. This sometimes meant that a steward, or mechanic, sat in the right hand seat, but someone was available to read the instruments for the pilot.

Engine mount detail on 4-AT-1 on April 5, 1927. (Ford Archives)

A Maddux Air Lines Mate (mechanic/co-pilot) greasing an engine on a new 4-AT. (EAA Library)

Fuel System

Full gravity feed for the center engine is provided. Planes equipped with a Wasp center engine (i.e. the 4-AT-C, 5-AT-A, 5-AT-B, 5-AT-C, 5-AT-D, 7-AT-A, 9-AT-A and XB-906) are provided with an auxiliary fuel pump.

Three fuel tanks, two large and one smaller for reserve, are located in the center section of the wings, the most protected position in the plane. They are readily filled through the top of the wing. Tanks are easily inspected and removable through panels located in the cabin ceiling. They are made of aluminum with standard welded joints.

Equipment

Standard equipment for all Ford Tri-Motors was: Altimeter, Gasoline Gauges, Booster Magneto, Magnetic Compass, Air Speed Indicator, Oil Pressure Gauges, Turn and Bank Indicator, Clock, Tachometers, Engine Primers, Inertia Starters, Instrument Lights, Cabin and Navigation Lights, and necessary handling equipment.

Interiors and Equipment

Some information on interior colors and added equipment is contained in a Ford sales list for April 1932. It also gives an insight into flying time as of March 1, 1932, as well as special prices for Demonstrator aircraft:

4-AT-18, Total Time(TT) 1,984 hours. Cardboard trim. $10,000.
4-AT-28, TT 1,718 hours. Cardboard trim. $10,000.

4-AT-34, TT 1,732 hours. Bakelite trim, exterior painted with zinc chromate and 2 coats of aluminum lacquer. $12,500.

4-AT-3, TT 3,722 hours. This is powered with 3 Wright J6 300 hp engines, and has high speed equipment consisting of the lowered engine mounts and air foil rings. We will install 11 Ford reclining passenger chairs and freshen the interior trim throughout. It has new 44" Bendix wheels, landing lights, and

Good engine detail on the 9-AT-1 with the P&W Wasp Junior. At the factory on April 3, 1930. (Ed Peck)

Hamilton Standard Propeller Service mechanics working on a new prop on TAT's "City of Washington." (John Underwood)

Almost all of the Ford Tri-Motors had the wing engine instruments mounted outside on a strut as shown in this 3-22-29 photo. (Ed Peck)

brackets for parachute flares. Many new parts have been installed on this plane for test purposes so that much of the structure has been replaced with brand new parts. Weight empty 7,022 lbs., licensed at 10,130 lbs. Useful load 3,108 lbs. Bonded for radio. High speed 138 mph. Economical cruising speed 113 mph. $17,500. 4-AT-67, TT 1,507 hours. Has new type sloping windshield. We will provide 11 new Ford reclining passenger chairs and interior trim. The extras include landing lights, brackets for parachute flares and Lux fire extinguisher. Bonded for radio. The high speed is 132 mph, and the economical cruising speed 107 mph. $24,300.

4-AT-64, TT 129 hours. Is practically an unused 4 AT plane, powered with 3 Wright J6 300 hp engines. Has high speed equipment consisting of lowered engine mounts and airfoil rings. It has been flown only two or three trips away from Dearborn. Two extras include landing lights, brackets for parachute flares and Lux fire extinguisher, also an air speed indicator and an altimeter installed in the main passenger compartment. The 11 Ford reclining chairs and the cabin boy stool at the door are upholstered in green leather. The aero board interior trim is cream, lined in green. The high speed is 138 mph, and the economical cruising speed 113 mph. $39,000.

9-AT-1, TT 1,761 hours. This is a 4-AT plane, powered with 3 Wasp Jr. engines of 300 hp. Has high speed equipment consisting of lowered engine mounts and airfoil rings. The plane itself is about two years old. It is equipped with 10 Ford reclining passenger chairs upholstered in rich dark red leather. The walls above the windows are tapestried in figured velour matching the chair colors. Among the extras on this plane are landing lights, brackets for parachute flares, Lux fire extinguisher, and the exterior has been given a priming coat of zinc chromate and two finishing coats of aluminized lacquer. High speed 138 mph, economical cruising speed 113 mph. $28,000.

13A-1 (5-D-100), TT 59 hours. This is powered with one Wright Cyclone 600 hp engine in the nose and two Wright J6 300 hp engines outboard. Except for the use of the Wright engines instead of Wasps, this plane is similar in all respects to the Model D tri-motor which is our current production model. The high speed is 145 mph, and the economical cruising speed is 117 mph. There are a number of expensive extras installed on this plane including electric starters, a large size storage battery, a 25-ampere generator, landing lights, brackets for parachute flares and Lux fire extinguisher. The interior has the new paneled transfer finish and the interior trim includes 13 new Ford armchairs. This plane won the Ford Reliability Tour for 1931. $48,000.

5-AT-74, TT 249 hours. As a Seaplane: equipped with two all-metal floats giving a capacity of 13 passengers plus crew; powered with 3 Wasp 425 hp engines. The extras include electric starters, a large size battery, generator, anchor and quick release, brackets for parachute flares, Lux fire extinguisher, internal and external priming coat of zinc chromate and two external finishing coats of aluminum lacquer. As a seaplane the high speed is 135 mph, economical cruise 108 mph. $45,000. 5-AT-74, TT 249 hours. As a land plane the high speed is 150 mph, and the economical cruising speed is 120 mph. Same extras as listed for the seaplane except wheels and struts in place of the pontoons. $35,500.

An inspection form signed by Robert M. Baron for a brand new 5-AT-D contains a wealth of detailed information. This notarized "Airplane Weight Affidavit" of 4-25-33 for 5-AT-115 lists the following: Exterior paint – none except window trim in Aluminum lacquer. Interior paint – Robin Egg Blue, Deep Crimson, Black Borders, Aluminum Lacquer toilet, Grace Green cockpit, Red Leather seat trim, Aluminum Company chairs, 11 side lights with Amber colored deflectors. Interior of wings, center section and fuselage sprayed with zinc chromate and aluminum lacquer; rear panels of "zero" bulkhead extend to the ceiling – sloping windshield; small wheel fenders; auxiliary running lights; 2-place cockpit heater; standard cabin heater for winter; center section and outboard instrument panels indirectly lighted; no hand booster; booster coil in each nacelle. 5-AT-115 was built with one 126 gallon fuel tank each in the right and left wing panels and one 103 gallon tank in the center section. The three engines each had an 11 gallon oil tank. Two baggage compartments of 400 pounds each were in the center section, plus two wing mail compartments of 400 pounds each. Information in the FAA files for 5-AT-116, the last Ford Tri-Motor built, shows a few minor changes. The interior was Berry Red on the lower section and Robin Egg Blue above the windows. The Church toilet seat was Dark Pearl. 5-AT-116 was equipped with Warner wheels and brakes, and Goodrich Silvertown low pressure tires. By comparison 5-AT-115 had Bendix wheels and brakes.

An earlier 5-AT-D, 5-AT-113, had a simpler interior of zinc chromate and aluminum lacquer with a trim of Walnut Transfer and Aero Board decalcomania. The most interesting note is the one describing the exterior paint as "White Gold" over zinc chromate. These three planes were in the last group to be sold and the differences can probably be explained by the fact that they had originally been intended for different customers for which the sale did not go through.

There was an interesting modification of 5-AT-4 for TAT that approached being a Club Model. This plane had built-in berths, a refrigerator for food, a metal desk and letter file, a typewriter and stenographers table and six upholstered chairs. The cabin panelling consisted of layers of sheet aluminum with balsa wood in between, 1/4 inch thick, of a walnut color with appropriate designs symbolic of aviation. This flying office was for the use of Col. Charles Lindbergh and Major Thomas Lanphier for the survey work necessary to lay out the 1929 air-rail route across the country. After this work had been completed the plane was rebuilt back to airline standards and put into service by TAT.

Exterior Colors

As is obvious from all of the photographs in this book the majority of Ford Tri-Motors had little or no color. The dark blue trim applied by American Airways was typical of the additions made by the owners after the planes left the factory.

The Royal Typewriter, Texaco and Monarch Food airplanes are the generally known exceptions because photos of them have been published over the years. The little-known Fords of the Curtiss-Wright Flying Service are the most colorful of all, but because there have been no photographs of them they have not gotten any recognition.

As a publicity program for their widespread activities around the United States, the Curtiss-Wright Flying Service painted four of their 4-AT's with a solid colored fuselage. One was Red, one was Blue, one was Green, and one was Orange. The only other known photo of an example of this, complete with the large company name in white on the side, is shown in the upper left hand corner of the photo on page 594 of *The National Geographic* Magazine for May, 1933.

Performance Characteristics

Oddly enough, there are no figures given for take off and landing distances for the Ford Tri-Motor in either the company pilots manual, "Book of Instruction, Ford All-Metal Monoplane", or in any Ford advertisements.

Over the years there have been a lot of "hangar flying" stories about Fords doing impossible things, and because of this there is a general misunderstanding today about the normal operating performance of the plane. While it is true that an empty plane, with a good headwind, and a deliberate attempt to make a short take off, gives credence to these stories it does not represent anything other than special circumstances. For example Paul Poberezny has been able to take off in the EAA Ford, in a 15 mph wind, in 150 feet. This is the proverbial "three plane lengths" that is often written about. But, this is with an empty 4-AT that has been modified to use 450 hp Wasps and that in no way represents the standard 4-AT with 220 hp wrights and a full load.

In the interesting flight evaluation by NASA pilot Fitzhugh Fulton Jr., he also describes short field performance with the Island Airlines 4-AT-42 and states, "The normal lift off distance with a 10-15 knot wind was around 300 feet at light gross weight and was probably 800-900 feet when fully loaded." He also states that landing distances were generally 500 to 600 feet, but that, "the airplane could be stopped in under 300 feet of ground roll with a slight head wind by using a 3 point touchdown and moderate braking."

Both former Johnson Flying Service pilot Jim Larkin, and Bernie Godlove, concur that a normal, safe operating performance for a loaded Ford would be about the same as that of the DHC-6 Twin Otter. The statistics for the Twin Otter are a take off run of 620 feet (1,040 feet over a 50-foot obstacle), and a landing run of 700 feet (990 feet over a 50-foot obstacle). Larkin remembers using all 1,400 feet of the Mackey Bar strip, and that the McCall runway was 2,500 feet long. The Moose Creek strip was 1,700 feet long and surrounded by mountains and trees.

Some further comparisons are shown by the Pan American flights to the Parcoy Mine in Peru. Here, in the real world of Ford performance pushed to the limit, a strip was built 65 feet wide by 3,300 feet long at the mine at altitude of six thousand feet. The other end of the operation was in a dry lake bed at ten thousand feet and its strip was 65 feet wide by 2,950 feet.

The most critical performance hazard with the Fords has always been an engine out on takeoff, as is discussed further in Chapter 10.

It is interesting to note the difference between the pilots manual for the Ford Tri-Motor and the company advertising. It was clear to the Ford engineers that this was a severe problem, particularly with the left engine, but there is no hint of it in company sales literature. The pilots manual states, for example, "An outboard engine failing when starting on the take off is apt to dangerously swerve the ship and, due to the low air speed, the rudder will not be powerful enough to correct it." In addition it warns, "It is extremely bad practice to open the throttles for a take off while the ship is rolling rapidly from a previous landing. Should an outboard engine fail under these circumstances, the ship would swerve sharply and be very difficult to control." A graphic example of the problem is the embarrassing accident to NC-9646 at Clovis, New Mexico, during the opening of the air-rail service.

This extremely rare photo of 4-AT-23 is taken from a portion of a hangar photograph found by B.C. Reed in 1992. The fuselage is probably red with white lettering that reads, "World's Oldest Flying Organization, Curtiss-Wright, Los Angeles, California. Grand Central Air Terminal, Glendale, California." (Boardman C. Reed)

The Model 4-AT-A on November 2, 1926. Preliminary sales for future Tri-Motors were already under way with National Air Transport. (Ford Archives)

Model Designations

MODEL 4-AT-A

Memo 2-9 issued in 1928; revised 9-25-28.
Serial numbers 4-AT-1 to 4-AT-14.
Army C-3, Navy XJR-1
3 Wright Junior J-4 of 220 h.p.

The first 14 planes are easily distinguishable, in photos taken at the time they were built, by the exhausts from the two wing engines. These rose vertically from the rear of the engines to pass through the leading edge of the wing and out the top. The exhaust pipes were raised about four inches above the top surface of the wing. Since the hot exhaust pipes passed through the wings near the gasoline tanks it was felt that there was a possibility of explosion and fire if gasoline fumes came in contact with the pipes, as had happened with disastrous consequences on some Junkers airplanes with a similar arrangement, so from early 1928 on this system was abandoned and all Fords from then on used short top or side exhaust stacks for the wing engines. The early 4-AT-A's were so modified so later photos of these planes do not show this design.

The windshield and cabin roof area around the pilot's compartment sloped backwards at a sharp angle. Nearly all of the 4-AT-A's were built with tail skids but these were subject to later change. There were changes in the cabin windows from the original half-moon shape to the next clerestory "streetcar" pattern with the rounded corners on the top panes. There were also changes and improvements in the size and shape of the rudder.

A production 4-AT-A (4-AT-9) showing the engine exhaust stacks going up through the wing. This was discontinued shortly afterward when problems arose with hot exhaust igniting fuel vapor. At the factory on September 8, 1927. (G.S. Williams)

MODEL 4-AT-B

ATC 87 (superseding Memo 2-10) of 11-19-28, revised 2-4-30. Serial numbers 4-AT-15 to 4-AT-23, 4-AT-25 to 4-AT-36, 4-AT-38 to 4-AT-39, 4-AT-41 to 4-AT-46, and 4-AT-48 to 4-AT-53. 3 wright J-5 of 220 h.p.

All 4-AT-B's have the familiar three-piece cabin windows consisting of a single piece on top with round corners, and a two-piece panel on the bottom in which one panel could be slid open for fresh air.

The slope of the windshield is no longer a valid recognition feature as a straight, vertical windshield appears on about half of these planes. It is possible that all of those were modified at a later date.

A check of photographs of planes in this group shows only one, 4-AT-35, with any kind of engine speed ring or cowling. An attempt was made to correlate the type and number of nose engine nacelle vents (which vary from the left to right side) and although this showed that the majority had 32 vents it is felt that this is inconclusive evidence as a recognition feature. The Ford Motor Company "Parts Price List" shows that showed the group of planes 4-AT-1 to 4-AT-22 inclusive have the same type of exhaust manifold assembly, so therefore there may be a change between 4-AT-22 and 4-AT-23.

The Model 4-AT-D (4-AT-24) while owned by Reed and Clemm in the 1930s. (G.S. Williams)

MODEL 4-AT-C

Memo 2-11 issued 10-27-28.
Serial number 4-AT-47 only.
1 P&W Wasp of 450 h.p. in the nose, and 2 wright J-5 of 220 h.p. under the wings.

The first Model 4-AT-E (4-AT-54) at the factory on February 27, 1929. The nationality letter "N", for the United States, was not required on aircraft that did not fly outside of the U.S. in the early formative years of the Department of Commerce, Bureau of Aeronautics. (Ford Archives)

MODEL 4-AT-D

Memo 2-322 for 4-AT-24 issued 1-23-31.
Serial numbers 4-AT-24, 4-AT-37 and 4-AT-40.
All three 4-AT-D's had the 5-AT-A wing root with 4-AT-B wing panels and fuselage. 4-AT-24 had three Wright J-4's of 200 h.p., 4-AT-40 had three Wright J-6's of 300 h.p., and 4-AT-37 had one Wright J-6 of 300 h.p. in the nose and two Wright J-5's of 220 h.p. in the wings.

The one and only Model 4-AT-F (4-AT-71) at the factory on July 28, 1931 when it was only one day old. (George Hardie/EAA)

MODEL 4-AT-E

ATC 132 issued 3-30-29 with later revisions.
Serial numbers 4-AT-54 to 4-AT-70, and 4-AT-80 to 4-AT-86.
Army C-9, Navy JR-2
Three Wright J6-9 of 300 h.p.

The distinct similarity between the Ford 4-AT and the Fokker F-10 is shown in this photo. The Standard Air Lines F-10 is in the center with a Ford on each side. The Maddux Ford is 4-AT-33, NC-7119. (UC Bancroft Library)

A rare photo showing 4-AT-10 on floats. Date and location are unknown. (Hudek)

With one exception (4-AT-67) all of these planes had the vertical windshield as a recognition feature. Starting with 4-AT-59 the fuselage cabin windows were the smaller 5-AT rectangular type with four square corners, a marked change from all earlier 4-AT models.

The engine nose vents vary considerably, some having 32, some 4 plus one large vent, two with three vents, and four with six vents. There seems to be no way to visually distinguish c/n 4-AT-54 through 4-AT-58 as 4-AT-E's other than the fact that they were equipped with the 300 h.p. J6-9's which clearly show the exhaust collector plate and pipes in front of the cylinders. (The exhaust collection pipes for the Wright J-5 are behind the cylinders).

MODEL 4-AT-F
ATC 441 issued 8-10-31.
Serial number 4-AT-71 only.
3 Wright R-975 (J6-9) of 300 h.p.
Only one 4-AT-F was built and it was the most refined of the series with a slightly increased gross load, NACA cowlings on the wing engines, new one-piece windows, and three vents plus one large scoop on the nose engine nacelle.

MODEL 5-AT-A
Memo 2-32 (2-7-29)
Memo 2-282 (10-10-30) for 5-AT-1 only.

The Model 5-AT-A sold to Pratt & Whitney Aircraft Company. This photo shows 5-AT-1 in its original form with the sloping windshield and rounded windows of the 4-AT-B. Probably taken upon delivery in August 1928. (Pratt & Whitney)

The same 5-AT-1 completely rebuilt to 5-AT-C configuration in 1931. The plane was for the personal transportation of Col. Deeds, Chairman of the Board, and he often kept it on a private strip next to his estate in Fairfield, Ohio. (P&W)

Serial numbers 5-AT-1 to 5-AT-3.
3 P&W Wasp of 420 h.p.
These first 5-AT's had the appearance of being 4-AT's with P&W Wasp engines as they had the sharply rearward sloping windshield, the round-top cabin windows. 5-AT-1, as first built, had two less cabin windows.

Col. Deeds had his 5-AT-1 rebuilt to 5-AT-B standard in 1930 and this included raising the wing six inches (thus dropping the engines six inches with respect to the wing), moving the wing engines forward four inches, wheels and struts streamlined, ring cowls added to the wings engines, and P&W type high nose cowl and sunken collector rings on the wing engines. The ring cowl on the center engine restricted visibility and did not effect any increase in speed, so was removed. The improvements increased the speed from 135 mph to 155 mph. The speed of 155.2 mph was determined by the Army Air Corps during a demonstration at Dayton with the engines turning 2100 rpm. See the photos of 5-AT-1 before and after "modification", a term that does not adequately describe a total rebuilding.

MODEL 5-AT-B

ATC 156 issued 6-4-29 with revisions, and Memo 2-12 of 2-16-29. Serial Numbers 5-AT-4 to 5-AT-45
Army C-4

MODEL 5-AT-C

ATC 165 (6-14-29) and 296 (2-12-30), Memo 2-240 (7-26-30), 2-242 (7-28-30), 2-518 (11-4-35).
Serial Numbers 5-AT-46 to 5-AT-90, 5-AT-94, 5-AT-96.
Navy JR-3, RR-4.
There were no easily discernable differences between the 5-AT-B and 5-AT-C and since both models underwent various modifications after they were built it is almost impossible to identify the correct model in a photograph without being able to read the registration number. The C had two more passenger seats and the fuselage was five inches longer.

Many of the B's and C's were modified by the factory to the "High Speed" configuration in 1930 and 1931. This included lowering the wing engines six inches, "Speed

The Model 5-AT-B (5-AT-14) at the factory on February 5, 1929. The standardized refinements now associated with the Ford Tri-Motor are apparent in this photo. (Hudek)

The Model 5-AT-C (5-AT-81) at the factory on 8-21-30. (Ford Archives)

The same plane being tested on twin floats on 5-9-30. Many tests were run by the Ford Motor Company while the planes were still in their ownership.

Rings" (thin cowls around the wing engines), "Wheel Streamlines" (pants) and other minor changes. This was done, for example, to 5-AT-15 (a B) in January 1931 and to 5-AT-49 (a C) in December 1930. Other changes included the backward sloping windshield to a vertical one, an example being 5-AT-16 (a B) changed in January 1932. American Airlines did their own modification to add six inches to the chord of the stabilizer on their 5-AT-B's. Wing mail bins were installed and removed at various times by the airlines. And, of course, roof cargo hatches and such changes were done by operators such as South American Gulf Oil, Pan American-Grace and TACA long after the planes had left the factory.

The airlines were constantly working on improvements to the Ford in airline service. An example of this was the design and installation or rubber engine mounts on 5-AT-51 in October 1932, three years and four months after the plane was built. The flight test was made on October 12, 1932, and the favorable results showed that it eliminated the rumble in the cabin caused by the center engine, as well as dampening out the vibrations so noticeable in the cockpit. The flight test summary states that, "The instruments did not vibrate and the rudder pedals and control wheel also were free from vibration", and that

The same finish on 5-AT-97. The circular pattern is "spotted" before corrugation by being burnished with a machine brush, cork, rotors, emery and oil. This special treatment was even applied to an entire airplane including the propellers for display at a trade show. 5-AT-88 is a model 5-AT-C, 5-AT-97 is a model 5-AT-D. Note the differences in the engine nacelle and exhaust. Photo taken at the factory on March 6, 1931. (Ford Archives)

The beautiful "Birds-Eye Finish" applied to 5-AT-88, the Club Model that went to Prince Bibesco of the Federation Aeronautic International (FAI) and became CV-FAI. The nose engine exhaust is funneled through an air chamber to provide heat through floor ducts. Note the different, polished exhaust on the wing engine. (Ford Archives)

The Model 5-AT-D at the factory 5-13-31. 5-AT-101 was registered NS-1 (U.S., State Use, Number One). It was fitted as a Club Model and sometimes referred to as Model 5-D. In 1931 Clarence M. Young, Chief of the Aeronautics Branch, traveled 30,000 miles by air in NS-1. The plane was used in 1933 experiments with blind landings. James L. Kinney, D of C test pilot, flew it at Newark, NJ, where equipment had been installed for the tests. Over 200 landings were made on instruments with radio direction. (G.S. Williams)

The Model 5-AT-E with the wing engines moved up and faired into the leading edge of the wing. This was 5-AT-80 and it was rebuilt back to normal 5-AT-C standard after the tests were completed. It is shown in front of Greenfield Village on 5-28-30. (Hudek)

"it was possible to converse in the cabin in a tone of voice only slightly above normal." The test was conducted by senior pilots Paul Richter and Larry Fritz.

MODEL 5-AT-D

ATC 409 (3-30-31) and Memo 2-504 (5-28-35). Serial Numbers 5-AT-91 to 5-AT-93, 5-AT-95, 5-AT-97 to 5-AT-116. Army C-4A, Navy RR-5.

The 5-AT-D was known as the "very high wing Ford" and "the big Ford" because of the readily apparent difference in height. The D was eight inches higher than the C, an easily discernable fact when the distance between the top of the cabin windows and the bottom of the wing is compared between the C and D models.

The second main recognition feature of the D is the square cabin door on the right side. All other Ford models had the door with rounded top and bottom. The third distinguishing item was the removal of the windows behind the pilots producing a distinctive square-cut ap-

A later August 6, 1930, closeup photo showing the installation and fairing behind the engine. (Ford Archives)

pearance not seen on any other models except the 4-AT-F.

The greater height allowed more head room in the cabin, and together with larger doors in the ceiling of the cabin allowed freer inspection of the wing center section and fuel lines and removal of the fuel tanks. Cabin windows were of one-piece safety glass with a new form of air intake at the leading edge of each window. A new type of rearward slanting windshield was developed on the later D's which was good for night flying because it eliminated the glare from airway beacons that had been passed. All parts of the metal structure were treated with zinc chromate and sprayed with aluminized lacquer when assembled.

An interesting sidelight is the following story. During the original preparation of this history in the 1950s it was impossible to find any good material on the 5-AT-D. By comparing photographs of the C and the D, and measuring the number of corrugations in the fuselage skin between the top of the windows and the forward underside of the wing, the 5-AT-D was found to have seven more than the 5-AT-C. From the Parts Price List it was known that the height of the glass in the cabin windows was 13 and 11/16th inches. Again studying the photos, with a 7x jewelers loupe, it was shown that this figure equalled 12 corrugations. Dividing one by the other equalled 1.14 inches per corrugation. This figure times seven equals 7.98 inches. Two years later when the official figures for the 5-AT-D were finally uncovered it was found that the difference in height between the C and D was eight inches. A more recent measuring of an actual plane shows these figures to be accurate but slightly different. The actual corrugations are 10 to the foot, or 1.2 inches per corrugation, equalling 8.4 inches.

The first 5-AT-D built was 5-AT-91 for the U. S. Army. Reference to the table "Ford Production by Date" shows how production went into the D model and did not follow the factory serial numbers consecutively.

MODEL 5-AT-E
No ATC.
Serial number 5-AT-80
The single 5-AT-E was an experimental modification of a 5-AT-C with the outboard engines mounted in the wings. For the purposes of these tests the Pratt & Whitney Wasps were replaced by Wright Whirlwind J-5's. Tests were run in the summer of 1930 with the wing engines moved up, a few inches at a time, until they were completely faired into the wing.

The plane was flown by test pilot Leroy Manning on flights between Dearborn and Chicago and showed the expected increase in speed. The landing speed, however, also went up. The engines in the wings acted as a spoiler at high angles of attack and the lift fell off badly. Since landing speed, and distance, was still a prime factor in airline operations at that time the Ford engineers reverted back to the original design.

Unfortunately so much of the skilled engineering work that was done at Ford has gone unpublished that most people do not realize what a refinement the final 5-AT-D was in the evolution of the Ford Tri-Motor.

Deluxe Club Models

The 5-AT-C and 5-AT-D were also available in what the company described in their advertising as a "deluxe club plane, a winged yacht, beautiful as a jewel, comfortable as your club, equipped for high-speed flying without sacrificing any of the luxurious accommodations which distinguish it."

The usual configuration for a Club model was nine passengers and a crew of two (pilot and mechanic). They contained a kitchenette on the left side of the fuselage which can be identified by two circular windows, folding berths, radio cabinet, writing desk and bookcase, seven overstuffed chairs, a two-place divan, card tables and serving trays, refrigerator, thermos cases, lavatory with toilet, running water, towel racks, and closets for luggage, guns, fishing tackle or golf clubs.

The walls and ceiling were sound-proof and the entire interior beautifully trimmed and decorated in choice fabrics. The cabin had individual ventilation at each window, dome and wall lights and a heat register in the floor. The kitchenette and lavatory were provided with tile walls.

The interior of 5-AT-68 (G-ABFF) illustrates one example. This plane was equipped with six reclining chairs upholstered in steel gray silk moire, piped with silver gray leather, and a six foot divan upholstered in red leather with an overcast of green.

The sidewall trim was heavy silk of a coral rust shade done in a modern design. A similar fabric, of shades of peach, blended with the gray that was used for the ceiling trim and the floor carpet of walnut shade. The lights were diamond shaped, fitted with opal glass, and mounted above the seats for reading. All interior metal fittings were plated with chromium.

Trays fitted to the arm rests of the seats for writing, reading or serving lunch. A large table could be mounted on the arms of two pairs of seats that face each other.

Each Club model was furnished with a set of silverware by Lux.

Another Club Plane interior was that of 5-AT-89 (NC-429H) sold to H.H. Timken and the Timken Roller Bearing Company. It was displayed at a 1930 Ford Transportation Exhibit in Chicago. Seating eight passengers it had its cabin walls and ceiling padded with two inches of sound-proofing material. The cabin was trimmed

Interior of a 5-AT-C Club Model for six passengers utilizing two rearward facing seats. At the factory 2-11-30. (G.S. Williams)

The luxurious interior of the 5-AT-C Club Plane for Prince Bibesco (5-AT-88) contrasts with the earlier interior of 4-AT-2 as shown on page 31. (Ford Archives)

in cloth, the head lining finished in a light tan cord material, the side walls above the windows in walnut brown and below the windows in a handsome fawn. The floor was covered with a maroon and taupe modernistic rug.

Six reclining over-stuffed chairs were installed in addition to a two-place davenport, the cushions of which were built up with coil springs to add to their comfort. The seats and davenport were upholstered in brown striped material, as well as two pillows. Four of the seats were grouped so that a card table could be attached to the arms by means of sockets, which could also hold individual serving trays.

In the ceiling, just above the davenport, a folding standard size berth was furnished with a special light weight mattress, sheets, blankets and pillows, all of which would fold into the berth when it was not in use as in a railway pullman car.

The forward part of the cabin held a combination writing desk, radio cabinet and book case in black walnut. The radio set, which could receive from stations 150 miles away, was concealed in a compartment in the rear of the fuselage but the operating dials were built into the desk. The loud speaker was built into the ceiling in the center of the cabin. Windows were of the single-pane style and did not open. This was done to minimize noise and make possible better control of ventilation because a special ventilator was built into the wall in front of each window. Heat was supplied by small registers in the aisle. Lighting was by specially designed dome lights and diamond shaped side lights on the walls directly above the seats.

A kitchenette was built opposite the entrance door and partitioned off from the rest of the cabin. A combination aluminum sink, drain-board and hot plate with shelf and closet space above and below made it possible to serve a club lunch. Felt-lined racks held cups, saucers, plates and glasses. Water was supplied by an overhead tank. The hot plate was heated by Pyrofax, a concentrated gas contained in a small tank in the cabinet. It had a small dome light, ventilator and electric fan, as well as an additional round window for light.

A lavatory was built to the rear of the kitchenette with a toilet, wash bowl with running water, towel rack, soap dispenser and mirror. In addition, in a small space to the side, partitioned off by a curtain, was a storage area for clothes, golf bags or a gun rack.

The entire fuselage and wings of this plane had the "Bird's Eye" burnished finish, as well as the engine nacelles, wheel pants etc., giving the impression of "having been burnished with thousands of small over-lapping circular patterns such as are frequently found on the inside of watch cases." In addition to this all steel parts were chrome plated resulting in a spectacular appearance.

Another unusual feature of this Club Plane was the fact that the tachometer, oil pressure gauge and oil temperature gauge for the wing engines was moved from the outer engine nacelle strut to the cockpit instrument panel.

Additional improvements on this model included a new fire extinguisher system and newly developed landing lights that gave a bright spot ahead and at the same time a soft light to the left and right in the immediate foreground.

The Club models sold in the $68,000 price range and the following nine are known to have been built:

5-AT-60	G-ABHO	Ford demonstrator in England, sold to Lord Lovelace.
5-AT-68	NC-409H	Company demonstrator, to G-ABFF.
5-AT-75	NC-415H	Demonstrator, sold to Firestone Tire and Rubber Company in October 1929.
5-AT-88	CV-FAI	Prince Bibesco, F.A.I., Romania.
5-AT-89	NC-429H	H.H. Timken, Timken Roller Bearing Co.
5-AT-90	NC-430H	Continental Oil Company, Okla homa.
5-AT-99	NC-432H	5-D Demonstrator, to Marshall Chang Hseuh-Liang, China, in March 1932.
5-AT-101	NS-1	Dept. of Commerce, Bureau of Air Bureau of Air Commerce, Washington, DC.
5-AT-107	NC-440H	European demonstrator, to G-ACAE, sold to the Honorable A.E. Guiness, Dublin, Ireland in 1932.
5-AT-112	NC-438H	Ten passenger Club, sold to SCADTA in Colombia in September 1934.

MODEL 6-AT, 6-AT-S

ATC 173 (7-26-29), Memo 2-97 (7-23-29, revised 7-23-30). Serial Numbers 6-AT-1 to 6-AT-3.

The 5-AT-C model powered with three Wright J-6 engines. This design combined the more economical 4-AT engines with the larger wing and cabin interior of the 5-AT-C. Three planes were built as follows:

6-AT-1; G-CYWZ, CF-BEP; 6-AT-S, 6-AT-A

FF 5-14-29. Delivered to the Royal Canadian Air Force for experiments in forest dusting. Destroyed 3-2-39 when hit by a Hawker "Hurricane" taking off at Vancouver. Remains sold and moved to Whitehorse where it was eventually buried.

6-AT-2; ID-8485, NC-8485, China; 6-AT-A, to 7-AT, to 5-AT-C FF 5-31-29. In August 1929 while still at the factory it was rebuilt into model 7-AT by replacing the Wright J-6 in the nose with a 450 hp P& Wasp. In a letter dated 8-28-29 the Ford Company notified the Department of Commerce that the factory serial number was being changed to 7-AT-1. In February 1931 two Wasps were installed in the wing positions and other changes were made to reconvert the plane back to 5-AT-C standard (ATC-165) and the serial number was changed to 5-AT-79A. It was sold to American Airlines, Chicago, on 8-20-31. Sold 3-26-36 to the Aviation Manufacturing Corporation, Chicago, IL, who in turn sold it on 4-4-36 to the Central Aviation School, Hangchow, China. American Airlines overhauled the engines and ferried it to the West Coast for crating and shipment to China by boat.

6-AT-3; NC-8486, China -; 6-AT-A, 5-AT-C Special. FF 6-11-29. Sold 7-19-29 to Colonial Western Airways, New York City. 2-20-30 Colonial Air Transport, New York, NY. Leased to Universal Aviation Corporation from May to June 1930. Returned to the factory in June and converted back to model 5-AT-C. The outboard P&W Wasp engines were installed six inches lower than standard under Group 2-240 approval. It was test flown for the second time on 6-25-30 and re-designated 5-AT-C serial number 5-AT-94. 12-16-32 American Airways, St. Louis, MO. It was overhauled at their base, the cockpit changed and strengthened, and the factory serial was now listed as "5-AT-C Special No.3." 5-12-34 American Airlines, Chicago, IL. 4-1-36 Aviation Manufacturing Corporation, Chicago, IL. 4-26-36 Central Aviation School, Hangchow, China. American installed overhauled Wasp engines and ferried the plane to the West Coast for crating and shipment to China by boat.

MODEL 7-AT

7-AT-1; NC-8485; 7-AT; to 5-AT-C

ATC-246 (9-30-29)

Serial Number 7-AT-1

The 6-AT-2 was modified by putting a 420 hp P&W Wasp in the nose and retaining the Wright J-6 wing engines. It was the winner of the 1929 and 1930 Ford Air Tours in this configuration. The plane was rebuilt at the factory in 1931 and reverted back to its original 5-AT standard with three 420 hp Wasps.. It was test flown as 5-AT-79A on July 24, 1931 and delivered to American Airways on November 7, 1931 as a 5-AT-C.

MODEL 8-AT-A

8-AT-1; NX-8499, NC-8499; 8-AT-A

Memo 2-485 (8-16-34)

The 8-AT-A was the most radical departure from the normal standard for the Ford Company as it, being a single engine airplane, stood in direct contradiction to all the years of Ford advertising regarding the necessity of three engines for safety. A standard 5-AT-C fuselage and wing were modified to operate as a single engine cargo plane.

The Model 6-AT on floats for the Royal Canadian Air Force. The Wright engines are clearly shown, as are the two permanently attached ladders for seaplane operations. (Larkins Collection)

The Model 7-AT during the 1929 Ford Air Tour. The 7-AT-1 was flown by Myron E. Zeller and placed third in the race which was won by points accumulated under a formula allowing for the differences in the size and power of the planes. The Tour was accompanied by four Ford Tri-Motors: George Chapline, flying Wright Aeronautical's NX-7864; Rodney Lamont, flying Standard Oil of Indiana's NC-9676; Lester Bryant, flying Firestone Tire's NC-9614; and Ralph Wickford flying the Curtiss Flying Service's NC-7865. (Hudek)

The 7-AT in the September 1930 "Sixth Annual National Air Tour for the Edsel B. Ford Reliability Trophy and the Great Lakes Light Plane Trophy." It carried Tour No. 6 on the rudder and was flown by Harry Russell. Both photos show the P&W Wasp in the nose and the two Wright J-6's in the wing positions. (Ford Archives)

The Model 8-AT single engine freighter on July 31, 1929 with a P&W Hornet geared engine. (Hudek)

The 8-AT with a Bliss Jupiter engine, three-bladed prop and modified cowl, on 9-23-29. (P&W)

The final version with a 700 hp Wright Cyclone. By the time it was sold to Pacific Alaska Airways in 1934 it had been modernized and an additional row of cabin windows was added. (Ford Archives)

The aircraft was flown with six different engines.The original engine was a Pratt and Whitney Hornet A, geared 2:1, when it was first flown on 7-3029. A P&W Hornet B, geared 3:2 was also tried. The next engine installed was a Bliss "Jupiter" model 9000 of 535 hp (British Bristol Jupiter radial engine built in the United States under license). On 1-30-31 a 575 hp Wright Cyclone was installed. On 47-31 this was changed to a Hispano Suiza model 12NB in-line engine of 650 hp. At some subsequent time the plane was remodeled, cabin doors installed, equipped with a larger 700 hp Wright Cyclone GR-1820F-1 engine, and sold in that configuration to Pacific Alaska Airways, Fairbanks, Alaska on 5-31-34. At this time it was licensed to carry 11 passengers and 2 crew (12,000 lbs.), or as a cargo plane with 2 crew (12,500 lbs.). Sold 8-3-37 to Charles H. Babb, Glendale, CA, for $1,750. Sold 10-21-37 to James M. Markley Jr., Coral Gables, FL. Sold 3-26-38 to The Sanabria Mines Ltd., Guapi, Colombia.

There was a Ford advertisement stating that Tri-Motors could be returned to the factory to be re-built into single engine freighters. There is no evidence that this ever happened. In addition Chris Swain, longtime Tri-Motor enthusiast, claims that Harry Karcher told him years ago that serial numbers 4-AT-71, 73, 75, 77 and 79 were built on the line as 8-AT's with a double left-hand door. This had been done on the basis of letters of intent from prospective customers for which the orders were eventually cancelled. Karcher said that the planes were then re-built back to 4-AT configuration with 4-AT-71 becoming the 4-AT-F. He also said that 4-AT-72, 74, 76 and 78 were to be regular 4-AT's that were cancelled. This probably explains how the Army Air Corps got serial numbers 80-86.

MODEL 9-AT-A

ATC 307 (4-2-30)

9-AT-1; NX-7585, NC-7585; NC-423H; 9-AT-A The 9-AT-A was a 4-AT-B with three Pratt and Whitney "Wasp Junior" engines of 300hp. Engine serial number 1 was installed in the nose, No.3 on the left and No. 4 on the right. Experimental license X-7585 was issued 9-15-30 to

The 9-AT was 4-AT-39 modified and as a result there has been confusion over the years because different records have reported it as both 9-AT-1 and 4-AT-39. (Hudek)

The beautiful Model 9-AT with P&W Wasp Junior engines. 9-AT-1, shown here at the factory on March 10, 1930, was the only one built. Note the extensive Ford advertising under the wing and on the side of the fuselage. (Ford Archives)

The most impressive sales presentation ever launched for the Ford Tri-Motor was at the August 1931 Detroit Air Show. 5-AT-D, NC-432H (5-AT-99) is on the left on a carpeted floor with flowers and chairs; in the middle next to a wing section with some of the skin removed to show the inside structure, a kneeling giant is holding up the beautiful 13-A; and on the right is the 8-AT. (Ford Archives)

Another view of the display from the side showing the 8-AT with the French Hispano-Suiza engine and its four-bladed propeller. The photo was taken on April 13, 1931. (Ford Archives)

test this configuration with the outboard nacelles lowered 7-1/2 inches. The registration was changed to NC-423H, the model designation from 4-AT-B to 9-AT-A, and the serial number from 4-AT-39 to 9-AT-1. Sold 1-26-34 to Harold A. White, Tegucigalpa, Honduras. Export Certificate E-935 was issued in February 1934.

MODEL 10-A

A four-engine design of 26,500 lbs. gross weight that was not built. As can be seen in the photo of the wind tunnel model it had two engines on a pylon, one tractor and one pusher, plus two engines in the wings. The four Pratt & Whitney Hornets developed a total of 2,300 hp. The design was modified into the model 12-A, and eventually into the 14-A.

MODEL 11-AT

11-AT-1; X-8404, NC-8404; 11-AT to 4-AT-B

4-AT-66, a 4-AT-E, was modified in March 1930 to be powered by three 225 hp Packard-Diesel engines. It was flown 4-2-30 and tentatively classified as model 4-AT-G. When a decision was made to publicly advertise the model for sale, as was done, it was assigned the model number 11-AT, and the new factory serial number 11-AT-1. No record has been found of any ATC or Memo Number having been assigned to the Diesel Ford. The engines were advertised as having more safety, due to less

Wind tunnel model of the four-engine 10-A that was not built. The tractor-pusher arrangement was used on various aircraft of the late 1920s so it was not unique to Ford. The design was modified to the Model 12-A, which was not built, and eventually into the Model 14-A. (Ed Peck)

An interesting model of a proposed twin-engine flying boat in October 1928. Note the wing, rear fuselage and tail that are typical of the Tri-Motor. (Bob Pauley)

The first of two "Flivver" planes designed by Otto Koppen in a program headed by test pilot Harry Brooks. This plane, assigned Identified No. 268, first flew in July 1926. It had a span of 22 feet, length 16 feet, wing area of 97 square feet and was powered by a 3-cylinder, 36-hp Anzani engine. It was flown by Charles Lindbergh before Henry Ford and many spectators on August 11, 1927 and that may have been the final incentive that got him to fly in an airplane for the first time that day. The plane is currently on exhibit in the Henry Ford Museum at Greenfield Village. (Ford Archives)

The second Flivver was registered as a Model 2-F when the Department of Commerce assigned it Identified No. 3218 on October 24, 1927. It had a span of 25 feet, length 16 feet 9 inches and a wing area of 92 square feet. It was powered by an experimental Ford AC engine of 41 hp designed by Harold Hicks. The first Flivver had a straight wing, but this one had a slight dihedral and four supporting struts. Both planes were painted blue and silver with a large white "Ford" on the side. Harry Brooks was lost at sea in this plane off Melbourne, Florida, on February 25, 1928, after making a record-breaking flight from Detroit to Titusville. The damaged plane washed ashore and both Harold Hicks, and Al Esper, in their 1951 oral interviews state that it was brought back to Dearborn and re-assembled. Henry Ford had envisioned a vast program of aerial Model T's but cancelled the entire project after this fatal accident. (Ford Archives)

fire hazard from diesel fuel, more economical to operate, and having no radio interference. The pilots comments about the vibration and fumes were not mentioned. A full page ad appears on page 18 of *Western Flying* for September 1930. In July 1934 Ford modified it back to a 4-AT-B standard with Wright J-5 engines of 220 hp.

MODEL 12-A

A modified 10-A design, changing from four-engines to three with one Hispano Suiza of 1,000 hp and two P&W Hornets of 575hp each. Not built, developed into the 14-A.

The Model 11-A powered by three Packard Diesel engines. The photo shows it at the Ford factory on April 2, 1930. Although it was advertised as a viable option for Ford operators the fumes and vibration, common to all diesel powered aircraft, were such that none were ever sold. This plane started life as a 4-AT-E (4-AT-66) and was at first called a model 4-AT-G. That designation was changed to 11-A and the serial number changed to 11-AT-1. After its failure to sell it was modified back to model 4-AT-E and reverted back to its serial number 4-AT-66. (Hudek)

The Model 13-A with a Wright Cyclone in the nose and two Wright J6 Whirlwinds in the wings. It was flown by Harry Russell to first place in the July 1931 Ford Air Tour. The photo was taken on July 28, 1931, three days after the Tour and the plane still carries its number 5 on the side. (G.S. Williams)

The Model 14-A on March 3, 1932. The plane was designed to carry 40 passengers and the three French Hispano-Suiza engines made it a true Ford Tri-Motor. The top engine was 1,100 hp and the two wing engines were 715 hp each. Bill Stout writes in his autobiography that it was cut up with torches and scrapped. There are conflicting reports on whether or not it flew. (Ford Archives)

The large metal emblem on the fuselage to the rear of the cabin door was similar to a locomotive Builders Plate. This was not the aircraft nameplate which was usually placed on the right side of the instrument panel. (E.J. Payette)

MODEL 13-A

13-A-1; NX-433H, NC-433H; 5-AT-D to 13-A to 5-AT-D ATC 431 (6-22-31)

5-AT-D, 5-AT-100, was modified in March 1931 to become the model 13-A by the installation of a Wright Cyclone R-1820-E of 575 hp in the nose, and two wright R-975's of 300 hp each in the wings. Tests were run with a three-blade prop on the nose engine. When first licensed as NC 7-15-32 the seating capacity was limited to six passengers and a crew of two. In August 1932 the plane was remodeled back to model 5-AT-D, with three P&W Wasp engines of 420 hp each. In addition, as the plane was being sold to Pangara, the wing fuel tanks were increased to 499 gallons total, and the designation changed back to 5-AT-D under ATC 409.

MODEL 14-A

14-A-1; NX-9660; 14-A

The huge 40-passenger tri-motor, built about February 1932, was the final development in the long line of Ford transports. A further modification of the design studies for the 10-A and 12-A that was built and taxi tested. It mounted two 715 hp Hispano Suiza engines in the wings and one Hispano Suiza. of 1,000 hp above the center section. The plane had a span of 110 feet, a length of 80' 10", and a height of 23' 7." It was fitted with a smoking room in addition to the main cabin, two lavatories and a stewards galley.

The plane never did fly, and the non-steerable tail wheel broke through the fuselage during taxi tests. Bill Stout comments in his book *So Away I Went* that "Work did go on, however, with the big plane until its final fiasco. It was exhibited in one show as a marvelous structure, which it was, and then cut up with torches for the scrap heap. It didn't fly, but they learned a lot from it." On June 23, 1933, Ford wrote to the Department of Commerce that the plane was being dismantled and asked that the license be cancelled.

Chapter 3
Airlines

From the very beginning the Ford Tri-Motor exerted a very strong influence on American air transportation and the development of what we know today as the major United States airlines. See Appendix 10, Part 1, for a list of 115 airlines that have used the Ford Tri-Motor worldwide.

In July 1927, when Maddux Air Lines took delivery of their first 4-AT-A, commercial air travel was for the most part uncomfortable and daring. One of the first and most important jobs that had to be done was that of mass education to the new era of safe, dependable and comfortable air travel for the general public. The Ford Motor Company pioneered this type of program with their full page advertisements in all types of magazines, including such non-aviation journals as the National Geographic. This tremendous, widespread advertising campaign which is said to have been substituted for previously planned announcements of the forthcoming V-8 automobile, is one of the most important contributions that Ford made to aviation.

Some of the feeling for this early attempt to dignify air travel is conveyed in the following statement from the 1928 Maddux Air Lines time-table: "Standard equipment for the daily passenger service of Maddux Air Lines is the Ford all-metal 12-passenger, parlor monoplane, powered with three Wright Whirlwind motors, a single one of which carried Colonel Charles A. Lindbergh's 'Spirit of St. Louis' across the Atlantic. Genuine comfort as well as the luxury of speed is the keynote of the huge craft, with its easy chairs, wide windows and ample foot-room suggesting complete relaxation and rest. No dust, dirt or smoke is associated with a transport of this type. raising it above all other transportation mediums for cleanliness. A rest room is conveniently located. Rack space for hats, coats and other light encumbrances is provided, besides the regular luggage storage."

Old flying stories are usually embellished somewhat but the following one from an American Airlines press release makes an interesting contrast with the previous statement about the rest room being conveniently located:

"On some of the Fords there was a lavatory between the cabin and the mail compartment. A retired Captain recently

This typical crowd surrounds Stout Air Lines 4-AT-28 at the Ford Airport. Note props turning near the people, a common hazard in the 1920s. (Larkins Collection)

Grover A. Whalan and Amelia Earhart christening the nose of TAT's "City of New York" in the Pennsylvania Railroad Station as part of the ceremonies opening the TAT air-rail service in July 1929. (Larkins Collection)

Lawrence G. Fritz in the uniform of Commodore of Maddux Air Lines. He and famed Navy pilot Tommy Tomlinson built the fledgling airline into one of the major parts of Transcontinental & Western Air. He later set up Southern Air Fast Express (SAFEWAY) in Texas, became a Major General in the AAF in World War II, and retired as a Vice President of American Airlines. (Larkins Collection)

recounted an embarrassing experience of one of his co-pilots. 'We were flying between Memphis and Cleveland. Before one stop the co-pilot had gone back to sort the mail. While there a passenger went to the lavatory. Meanwhile, I was letting down and the co-pilot tried to get back up front. He pushed on the door. But the passenger slammed it shut. The co-pilot waited. Finally, he pushed on the door and said, I've got to get to the cockpit. I'm one of the pilots.' Asked the startled passenger: 'What have you got, a pilot on each end?'"

Another story regarding the co-pilots duties with the mail was told by a pilot in 1963: "After the co-pilot served the box lunches he would go to the rear of the airplane and sort the mail in order to have the right sack ready to unload quickly at the next landing. I flew as co-pilot once and had to go back there. You leaned over the mail bin, riding backward in the tail, bouncing around with a flashlight in your hand trying to read the names on the mail sacks. I turned around to get out of the bin and was so sick I could hardly see – it's the only time I've ever been sick in more than 30 years of flying. You had to get the right sack off at the right place, too. If you goofed, you had to work for two weeks without pay."

The Ford Tri-Motor became the basis of the first major airline service in the country when Transcontinental Air Transport was formed to provide, in conjunction with two railroads, the first air-rail route across the United States. After months of preparation, which included laying out the route and building ground facilities, the service was started in July 1929. The following in-depth study of this is an attempt to identify for the first time who was involved with the first flights.

The following is the result of research over the past twenty years to attempt to define exactly who flew what and where on this famous inaugural T.A.T. Air-Rail route. There were seven different aircraft involved in nine starts and eight flights.

Passengers going West left New York City at 6:05 P.M. in the evening and rode the train all night to Port Columbus, Ohio, where they transferred to the Ford Tri-

Arrival of the first Maddux Ford at Rogers Airport, Los Angeles, on July 27, 1927. This was 4-AT-7 with temporary registration 3114 (this shows on the wing in some photos), later becoming NC-1102. It was flown by Larry Fritz and the impressive passenger list included William B. Mayo, Eddie Hamilton, J. Parker Van Zandt, Jack Wiles, Lamar Nelson, W.J. Fleming and Harry Macpherson representing Jack Maddux. Some idea of the change in attitudes over the years is shown by the Los Angeles Times description of the plane as "The giant plane circled the landing field several times before attempting to make a landing and police, aided by attaches of the airport, strove in vain to keep the crowd back until the monster came to a standstill." This "monster" is the same as the "little" Ford flying for Island Airlines for so many years. (L.G. Fritz)

William Mayo on the left, and Jack Maddux on the right, pose with vintage cars in front of 4-AT-7. Maddux was the Lincoln car dealer in Los Angeles and offered to start an airline with the Tri-Motors if their performance was such that they could be flown from the factory, over the mountains, to Los Angeles. (L.G. Fritz)

Rare markings on a Ford shortly after the merger of Transcontinental Air Transport, Maddux Air Lines and Western Air Express. The S's were a public relations man's idea of showing speed in flight. (Larkins Collection)

Motor and flew during the day to Indianapolis, St. Louis, Kansas City, Wichita, and Waynoka, Oklahoma. From there they again took the train during the night to Clovis, New Mexico. In the morning they boarded another Ford Tri-Motor for the flight to Albuquerque, Winslow, Kingman, and Los Angeles. The East-bound trip was the reverse. On the inaugural trip two Fords flew each leg as follows:

1. WESTBOUND, Port Columbus to Waynoka (7-8-29)
NC-9648 CITY OF COLUMBUS 5-AT-C c/n 5-AT-57
Pilots: Dean W. Burford and H.J. Zimmerman Courier: D.W. Dudley
Passengers:
Miss Amelia Earhart, Assistant to the General Manager, T.A.T. Col. Paul Henderson, Vice President, T.A.T. Paul Henderson, Jr., Son of Colonel Henderson Miss Betty Brainerd, Associated Newspapers, NYC U. Grant Border, U.S. Border & Sons, NYC Col. Edgar S. Gorrell, President, Stutz Motor Co., Indianapolis Albert A. Garthwaite, Vice President, Lee Tire Co. Conshohocken, Penn., S.W. Higgins, Dennison Manufacturing Co., Boston, Mass. Daniel M. Sheaffer, Chief of Passenger Transportation, Pennsylvania Railroad J.W. Brennan, Central Traffic Manager, T.A.T.

Maddux Air Lines had an active publicity department and was quick to photograph movie stars with their airplanes. This photo shows Dolores Del Rio and Arthur Edmund Carew. (John Caler)

2. WESTBOUND, Port Columbus to Waynoka (7-8-29)
NC-9645 CITY OF WICHITA 5-AT-B c/n 5-AT-8
Pilots: Harry W. McGee and George C. Price
Passengers:
William Chaplin, Associated Press, NYC Mrs. John T. Litch, Boston, Mass. Miss M. A. Salomon, Chamber of Commerce, Brooklyn, New York Mrs. G.P. Putnam, New York City Mrs. F.C. Kenney, Indianapolis, Ind. E.E. Greiner, Springfield, Ohio William James Bryant, Nation's Business, Washington, D.C., Carl Larsen, Fox Movietone News Charles Tice, Fox Movietone News

3. WESTBOUND, Clovis to Los Angeles (7-9-29)
NC-9649 CITY OF SAN FRANCISCO 5-AT-Bc/n 5-AT-20
Pilots: Stephen R. Shore and Wesley Phillipi
Passengers: James Bryant, William Chaplain, E.E. Greiner, Col. Paul Henderson, Paul Henderson Jr., Fritz Hinkle, Carl Larson, Mrs. John T. Litch, Miss M.A. Salamon, Charles Tice, ?

Note: All TAT references state that there were 10 passengers on each aircraft, and other statements refer to a waiting list to fly the route, so there should be 10 names for each flight. There was a crew of 3 on each flight; two Pilots and a Courier.

4. WESTBOUND, Clovis to Los Angeles (7-9-29)
NC-9644 CITY OF WASHINGTON 5-AT-B c/n 5-AT-7
Pilots: Charles A. Lindbergh and Edward A. Bellande
Passengers: (From a hand written manifest signed by the pilots above plus the following passengers) A. Garthwaite, Conshohocken, Pa. D.M. Sheaffer, Phila, Pa., Mrs. G.P. Putnam, Rye, N.Y. S.W. Higgins, Boston, Mass., Amelia Earhart, New York, N.Y., Anne Lindbergh, U. Grant Border, New York, Chauncey T. Lamb, Hinsdale, Ill, E.S. Gorrell, Indianapolis, Ind., Betty Brainerd, New York City, "With Colonel Charles Lindbergh at the controls, the CITY OF WASHINGTON swooped gracefully down to a three-point landing at 5:42 pm, 24 minutes after the City of San Francisco piloted by R.W.Shore had unloaded her passengers. Lindberg was due in first but on account of strong tail winds, of which pilot Shore took more advantage, the City of San Francisco beat him to the finish . . . though it was in no sense a race . . . With Lindbergh's ship emptied of its human cargo, the City of Washington became the center of a distinguished group . . . as Gloria Swanson . . . broke a bottle of grape juice over the planes nose formally christening the craft."

5. WESTBOUND, Clovis to Los Angeles (7-9-29)
NC-9646 CITY OF LOS ANGELES 5-AT-Bc/n 5-AT-9
Pilots: J.B. Stowe and ?
Passengers: See No.3.

Lineup of two Maddux 5-AT's and two 4-AT's. 5-AT-17 is in the foreground. Maddux Air Lines operated 16 Ford Tri-Motors between August 1927 and April 1931 when the planes on hand at that time were transferred to Transcontinental & Western Air. (Peter M. Bowers)

Another publicity shot with United Parcel Service and 5-AT-10. The boxes are labeled "United Parcel System Air Express Division" and are marked for Portland, Seattle and San Francisco. Maddux flew from Los Angeles to San Francisco where the cargo could be transferred to Pacific Air Transport. (Peter M. Bowers)

A 700-pound calf about to be flown in a Stout 4-AT on November 26, 1927. Note the exhaust stains on the top of the wing from the early exhaust pipes that went up through the wing and out the top. (Bob Pauley)

"The second plane prepared to follow but in taxying across the field preparatory to the getaway a gust of wind lifted one wing and a combination of other unfavorable circumstances threw the ship into a slow ground loop across plowed land. One wing of the ship brushed against the windows of the hangar office, breaking several panes of glass as the ship came safely to a stop. Thereupon the City of San Francisco was wheeled out and substituted for the slightly damaged plane." (*New York Times*, 7-10-29). Senate Document 319 states "Plane ground looped into hangar on take off. Cause: Pilot claimed outboard engine stopped. Cause charged to material and personnel."

6. EASTBOUND, Los Angeles to Clovis (7-8-29)
NC-9646 CITY OF LOS ANGELES 5-AT-B c/n 5-AT-9
Pilots: Charles A. Lindbergh and Edward A. Bellande
Passengers: A.L. Rocklein, Los Angeles Examiner (also given as A.M. Rochlen), Terril Delapp, Los Angeles Times, Jack Scanlon, Los Angeles, M.D. Schatzman, Los Angeles, Thomas B. Eastland, San Francisco, Director T.A.T R.W. Millar, Banker, Los Angeles Mrs. Charles A. Lindberg, Major C.C. Moseley, Vice President, T.A.T. Dr. W.J. Furie, Long Beach, Calif. (Purie?) Eugene Coughlin

Note: One minor problem remains. Although the Columbus Citizen reports that, "Mrs. Lindbergh will fly as a passenger as far as Winslow, Ariz., where she will alight and await her husband's return as pilot of the City of Washington", the Los Angeles Times states, "Col. Lindbergh, however, left the ship at winslow, Arizona, and will depart from there this morning bound for Los Angeles at the helm of the City of Washington . . ." If Lindbergh got off at Winslow, stayed overnight with his wife and then returned from there the next day, then who took his place as pilot on the two flights between Winslow and Clovis?

7. EASTBOUND, Los Angeles to Clovis (7-8-29)
NC-9651 CITY OF PHILADELPHIA 5-AT-Bc/n 5-AT-34
Pilots: Stephen R. Shore and Wesley Phillipi
Passengers: Albert Hitchin, Insurance Broker, Los Angeles, R.K. Rochester, Vice President Pennsylvania Railroad, Mrs. R.K. Rochester, Miss Velva Darling, Los Angeles John B. Austin, President, Chamber of Commerce, Los Angeles, Turner Wills, Los Angeles, Mrs. R.K. Rochester, A.C. Hart, Dr. R.B. Von Kleinsmid

8. EASTBOUND, Waynoka to Port Columbus (7-9-29)
NC-9647 CITY OF INDIANAPOLIS 5-AT-Bc/n 5-AT-21
Pilots: Harry W. McGee and George C. Price
Passengers: R.K. Rochester, Philadelphia Mrs. R.K. Rochester, Philadelphia, Harry Brundage, St. Louis, Charles Walker, New York, Velva Darling, New York, J.B. Austin, Los Angeles, E.F. Padberg, St. Louis, H.E. Trader, St. Louis, E.F. Eddy, St. Louis

9. EASTBOUND. Waynoka to Port Columbus (7-9-29)
NC-9648 CITY OF COLUMBUS 5-AT-C c/n 5-AT-57
Pilots: Dean W. Burford and Jack Zimmerman (?)

Charles Lindbergh's famous "City of Columbus" (5-AT-4) which served as his flying office while laying out the new route for the start of the air-rail service in 1929. He had a desk for himself and a stenographer in place of the usual passenger seats. (P&W)

A huge crowd turned out at Glendale to watch Charles Lindbergh and Eddie Belande pilot the first TAT plane to head Eastbound on the new air-rail service on July 8, 1929. The plane is 5-AT-9, NC-9646, the "City of Los Angeles." (Hudek)

Airplane christening was a common practice in the late 1920s. This was the opening of "Queen City Airlines" at Watson Airport, Cincinnati, Ohio on August 28, 1928. (Paul Matt)

Proof of the change of the name on 5-AT-4 (NC-9606) from "City of Columbus" to "City of New York" so that it could be placed in Penn Station for the christening ceremonies by Amelia Earhart. (Hudek)

5-AT-51 (NC-8413) was a visitor to Port Columbus during the exciting opening ceremonies on July 8, 1929. It was less than a month old and was probably being used as a press plane while on its way to be delivered to Maddux Air Lines in Los Angeles. (TWA via Ed Betts)

A rare night shot of 5-AT-37 with the interesting name "City of Saint Louis" spelled out rather than St. Louis. (Ed Peck)

INFORMATION

Passengers: Tien Lai Huang ("The Chinese Lindbergh") Albert Hitchin Turner Willis

10. PENNSYLVANIA STATION, New York City (7-7-29)
NC-9606 CITY OF NEW YORK 5-AT-Bc/n 5-AT-4
This non-flying Ford was christened by Amelia Earhart (with a bottle of Canada Dry Pale Ginger Ale), before a thousand people in the Pennsylvania Railroad Station at the start of the first West bound trip. She watched The Airway Limited train being christened by Dorothy Stone, and then boarded the train for Columbus.

11. PORT COLUMBUS, Ohio
NC-9607 THE KANSAS CITY 5-AT-Bc/n 5-AT-5
A TWA photo (T2383 by Cresswell, K.C. MO) shows this Ford being christened by a woman and two men on a platform. This may have been done prior to the start on July 8th. Evidently the name was chosen because of the otherwise awkward sounding "City of Kansas City."

Over the years there has been a great deal of confusion over this first air-rail flight and a striking example is shown by a 1984 book on U.S. Airlines that makes the incredible statement that the airplane was loaded on the train and carried all night! This book states: ". . . The carrier used the Tri-motor on the New York to Los Angeles run, with it being loaded on a train for an overnight run to Columbus. Frome here, it flew the next day to Waynoka, Oklahoma, where it was placed aboard

The "City of Columbus" (5-AT-4) was the only 5-AT to have a window behind the passenger door. This was probably installed as part of Lindbergh's office layout and was a non-standard modification not seen on the airline version. (Larkins Collection)

5-AT-4 in the Pennsylvania Railroad Station in New York City as part of the opening ceremonies for TAT. (Ford Archives)

a Santa Fe train for an overnight trip to Clovis, New Mexico. The next day it completed its trip to Los Angeles."

Perhaps the following official schedule makes it clear when the passengers were on the train and when they were on the airplane.

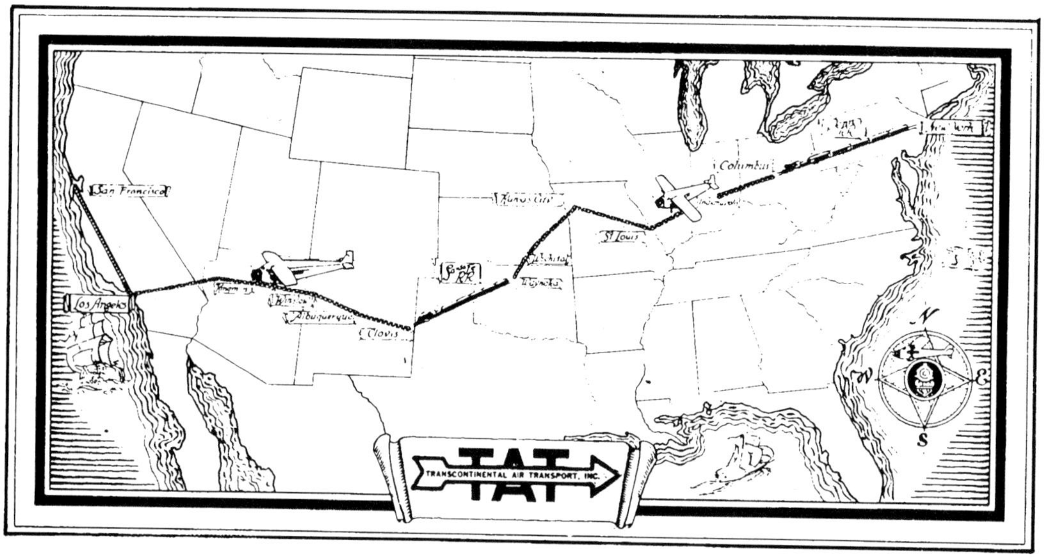

SCHEDULES

(Subject to change without notice)

WESTBOUND Read Down			EASTBOUND Read Up	
		PENNSYLVANIA RAILROAD		
"THE AIRWAY LIMITED"				
6.05 PM	**ET**	Lv. New York City	Ar. 9.50 AM	ET
7.55 AM	ET	Ar. Port Columbus, Ohio	Lv. **7.46 PM**	**ET**
			"THE AMERICAN"	
		TRANSCONTINENTAL AIR TRANSPORT, INC.		
8.15 AM	ET	Lv. Port Columbus	Ar. **7.13 PM**	**ET**
9.13 AM	CT	Ar. Indianapolis	Lv. **4.37 PM**	**CT**
9.28 AM	CT	Lv. Indianapolis	Ar. **4.22 PM**	**CT**
12.03 PM	**CT**	Ar. St. Louis	Lv. **2.15 PM**	**CT**
12.18 PM	**CT**	Lv. St. Louis	Ar. **2.00 PM**	**CT**
2.47 PM	**CT**	Ar. Kansas City	Lv. 11.58 AM	CT
3.02 PM	**CT**	Lv. Kansas City	Ar. 11.43 AM	CT
4.56 PM	**CT**	Ar. Wichita	Lv. 10.10 AM	CT
5.11 PM	**CT**	Lv. Wichita	Ar. 9.55 AM	CT
6.24 PM	**CT**	Ar. Airport, Waynoka, Okla.	Lv. 8.55 AM	CT
		SANTA FE RAILWAY		
"THE MISSIONARY"				
11.00 PM	**CT**	Lv. Waynoka, Okla.	Ar. 8:10 AM	CT
8.25 AM	CT	Ar. Clovis, N. M.	Lv. **11.35 PM**	**CT**
			"THE SCOUT"	
		TRANSCONTINENTAL AIR TRANSPORT, INC.		
8.10 AM	MT	Lv. Portair, Clovis, N. M.	Ar. **6.54 PM**	**MT**
10.17 AM	MT	Ar. Albuquerque, N. M.	Lv. **5.10 PM**	**MT**
10.32 AM	MT	Lv. Albuquerque, N. M.	Ar. **4.40 PM**	**MT**
1.12 PM	**MT**	Ar. Winslow, Arizona	Lv. **2.29 PM**	**MT**
1.27 PM	**MT**	Lv. Winslow, Arizona	Ar. **2.14 PM**	**MT**
2.31 PM	**PT**	Ar. Kingman, Arizona	Lv. 11.33 AM	PT
2.46 PM	**PT**	Lv. Kingman Arizona	Ar. 11.18 AM	PT
5.52 PM	**PT**	Ar. Los Angeles, Calif.	Lv. 8.45 AM	PT

Combinations of TAT plane and train service are possible from many other points with equally valuable time savings. Inquire at any travel or ticket office.

A special Pullman car, on the train operated by the Pennsylvania Railroad, was designated "The Airway Limited" and was specially equipped with compartments and drawing rooms. There were 11 Ford Tri-Motors assigned to the route, and all pilots were selected personally by Col. Lindbergh.

In preparation a "dress rehearsal" period in which the Tri-Motors were flown some 50,000 miles, carrying 261 passengers, was undertaken before inauguration of regular service on the announced "Day We Are Properly Ready."

If you had been in the right place at the right time during those preceding months you could have had a free ride such as that described in the following story in the *Clovis Journal*: "Dr. Moore, now (1962) a Clovis dentist but then a teenaged boy just out of high school remembers the flight well and says it was a comfortable one. Dad and I were at the airport, Dr. Moore recalls, looking around and the agent asked us if we wanted to go to Los Angeles. This was before service started and T.A.T. was giving people goodwill rides to get them acquainted with the service. we said no but told him we would like to go to Albuquerque so we rode over there, caught the afternoon plane back, and arrived in Clovis after dark. They didn't have lighted runways then but just flooded the whole airport with light from hundreds of floodlamps. The trip was calm and enjoyable and they didn't even give us parachutes, desiring to instill in us a feeling of how safe we were. On the way back we were flying quite low and would lean out the window and throw newspapers at cowboys on the plains."

The first official East-to-West trip arrived at Los Angeles at 5:18 pm on July 9th. Only two passengers went all the way from Los Angeles to New York City. Ticket No.1 was held by Albert S. Hichen, a Los Angeles insurance broker. No mention is made of the name of the

Celebrities posed with the "City of Los Angeles" prior to its departure from Glendale on July 7, 1929. Left to right are: Douglas Fairbanks, Major C.C. Moseley, unidentified, Anne Morrow Lindbergh, Mary Pickford (who christened the plane), Colonel Charles Lindbergh, Dudley Steele and John Bowers. (TWA)

Bobbie Trout meeting Elinor Smith upon arrival at Los Angeles on the TAT air-rail service prior to the start of their endurance flight attempt. (Hudek)

Franklin Young and Lynn Berkenkamp in TAT uniforms in 1931. (Ken Blaney)

second person in the Los Angeles newspapers. The first West-to-East trip arrived at New York City at 10:35 am on July 10th.

Col. Lindbergh, accompanied by his wife, flew a Maddux Air Lines Ford Tri-Motor from Los Angeles to San Francisco on July 10th, inaugurating that company's increased service to the area. The Los Angeles Times states "San Francisco" but the landing was made at Alameda Airport which was the northern terminal for Maddux Air Lines. Likewise the "Los Angeles" airport was actually Grand Central Air Terminal at Burbank.

An interesting sidelight is that Henry and Edsel Ford arrived for the ceremonies at Port Columbus on July 8th by train although a company Tri-Motor also flew there for the same occasion. They were there among the participants in a breakfast given in the T.A.T. hangar following the departure of the two Ford Tri-Motors. It was hosted by T.B. Clement, General Traffic Manager of T.A.T., and included William B. Mayo (who had flown in) and Harvey Firestone. The Fords returned to Dearborn by Ford auto, dropping off Harvey Firestone at Akron on the way.

There is some contradiction over the identity of the "City of Columbus" that departed there on July 8th. The Ohio State Journal (7-6-29, pg.1) states that the City of Columbus is the "newest TAT vehicle made, resembling in every way and replacing the original City of Columbus fleet flagship now in the TAT hangars in New York."

A May 1931 TWA document from the FAA files in Oklahoma City identifies the City of Columbus as NC-9648 (5-AT-57). This plane, a new 5-AT-C, first flew on June 27th and was delivered to T.A.T. on July 3, 1929. This same document lists the "City of New York" as NC-9606 (5-AT-4). Does this mean that the original "City of Columbus (NC-9606) was the plane christened in the railroad station and NC-9648 was the plane in Items 1 and 8?

Ford Motor Company photo No. 6916 shows NC-9606 in the Pennsylvania Railroad Station and has a date of 11-6-29 on the negative - but that may be the date it was copied and added to the Ford Company files. It was not taken at the same time as the photo of Amelia Earhart christening the "City of New York." Proof of this theory has finally been located in the publication "The Making of An Airline - TWA, A Pictorial History" (*ALPA*, NY, 1981). There on page 13 is a photo of NC-9648 as the "City of Columbus" at the start of the flight from Port Columbus.

Coast to Coast by Plane and Train in 48 Hours July 7-9, 1929

The long months of preparation to build the first major transcontinental air-rail system, on the route laid out by Charles Lindbergh in his executive Ford Tri-Motor, came to fruition in July 1929. The official description, in the language of the times, reads as follows:

"Step aboard the perfectly equipped "Airway Limited" of the Pennsylvania railroad. It leaves New York at 6:05 P.M., and an excellent dinner is being served as you go aboard.

"An hour in the club or observation car, a restful night in berth, compartment, or drawing room, and you arise from breakfast as the "Airway" approaches Port Columbus.

The great plane stands at the passenger station, its propellers whirring idly. Pilots and Courier are in attendance. Enter the

TAT's "City of Wichita" that flew the University of New Mexico football team from Albuquerque to Los Angeles on October 11, 1929. They played Occidental College in Los Angeles and flew back home in time for classes on Monday. From right to left are H.W. Beck, Western Traffic Manager of TAT; Tom Popejoy, manager of the New Mexico team; and George Ellsworth, manager of the Occidental team. The photo was taken upon arrival at L.A. (TWA)

TWA modified some of its 5-AT's to use a jump seat for the Steward next to the cabin door. This one is on 5-AT-51, TWA No.601. (TWA)

Dignitaries on hand for the first flight of the all-air 36-hour transcontinental flight by Transcontinental & Western Air. Left to right are: Postmaster General Walter F. Brown, Harris M. Hanshue (President of TWA), Roy Black, Colonel Lindbergh, Jerome T. Congleton (Mayor of Newark, NJ), Charles Gillen (Commissioner of Public Parks in Newark) and Amelia Earhart. The flight left from Newark Airport on October 25, 1930. (Larkins Collection)

G.E. Ruckstell, President of Grand Canyon Airline, and Edith McManus, Hostess, in front of the clean GCA 5-AT. See chapter 7 for the story on her aerial wedding. (Irving Kravitz)

5-AT-54 of Pan American Grace Airways at the "airport terminal" at Pacasmayo, Peru. The plane was named "Santa Rosa." (PAA)

cabin with nine fellow passengers, relax in the comfortable chairs with their reclining backs and prepare to enjoy your flight.

"The earth floats lazily by below you - low level fields wooded lands, ribbons of paved roads - bodies of water - small towns - America from a new viewpoint. You pause for fifteen minutes at Indianapolis, St. Louis, Kansas City and Wichita, the day's flight ending at Airport, Waynoka, at 6:24 o'clock.

"In mid-morning a cup of bouillon is served aloft. A Fred Harvey luncheon is served aloft between St. Louis and Kansas City and in mi-afternoon hot or iced tea is served aboard the plane.

"A set-out Pullman awaits at Waynoka, ready for immediate occupancy and is attached to the "Missionary" of the Santa Fe railroad later in the evening.

"Another comfortable night in a Pullman, breakfast at the Harvey House in Clovis, New Mexico, a trip in the Aero car to Portair, Clovis, where the second day's plane trip begins.

"West of Clovis the landscape rises toward the mountains, and wide desert spaces separate the ranges. Visibility increases and mountains as far away as 100 miles are easily seen.

America, seen from the air, is a country of magnificent expanses.

"Luncheon and the mid-morning and mid-afternoon refreshments are again served aloft by Fred Harvey.

"Brief stops are made, as on the previous day, at Albuquerque, New Mexico; Winslow, Arizona; Kingman, Arizona, and, late in the afternoon, Los Angeles, California. The Hero car takes you to downtown Los Angeles in ample time for dinner and the evening's business or social engagements.

"You have crossed the continent in 48 hours.

"You have traveled with the utmost comfort, luxury and speed - but above all you have gained a deeper understanding of the vast and beautiful country that lies between East and West coasts.

"Passengers bound for San Francisco may leave by train the same evening or remain in Los Angeles over-night to leave by air early next morning.

"TAT service, while transcontinental in its scope, is an extension of existing transportation facilities throughout the United States. The service will be found a convenience in connection with other transport schedules in the East, the Middle West and the great Southwest. It is, in a word, the highest achievement of American Transportation."

Perhaps this glowing description by the carrier is not the full story as many pilots and passengers have written of the noise, sickness and fatigue involved in long trips on the Ford Tri-Motor. One passenger, Ellen Williamson, who flew the air-rail route all the way from New York to Los Angeles wrote, "It took me a week to recover. Besides being quite deaf from the roar of the motors, and dizzy from the constant rolling and yawing, as well as a little queasy from the more gentle motion of the trains at night, I ended up just plain tired from all the hectic rushing from one moving object to another. It saved thirty-six hours, and I was glad that I'd done it once, but never again."

The grand scheme for air-rail travel lasted just over one year. On October 2, 1930 Transcontinental and Western Air Inc. (TWA) was formed by the combination of Transcontinental Air Transport, Maddux Air Lines, Pittsburgh Aviation Industries and Western Air Express as a result of the Post Office granting a joint air mail bid.

Within a few weeks, on October 25th, this new airline opened the first all-air crossing of the United States. The new service was advertised as 36 hours, 12 less than the previous air-rail route. The price was $200 one-way and included an overnight stay. The first East to West flight left Newark, NJ, at 8:10 am on the 25th and arrived at Alhambra Airport, Los Angeles, at 8:00 pm on the 26th.

This Ford was flown by H.G. "Andy" Andrews, with co-pilot Joseph Russell, and the passenger list was full of dignitaries; Walter F. Brown (Postmaster General), W.I. Glover (Assistant Postmaster General), E.B. Wadsworth (Superintendent of Airmail), Harris Hanshue (President

Pioneer pilot Art Burns with TWA No. 606 (5-AT-57). Burns flew passengers on an airline to Catalina Island in 1919. (TWA)

5-AT-61 of Pan American Grace Airways, named "San Pablo." Note the use of US MAIL under the wing and the Army Air Corps style tail stripes. (R.E.G. Davies)

Pan American Airways 5-AT-30. (PAA)

Pacific Alaska Airways 8-AT on skis. (Hudek)

The 8-AT again in a rare photo of it being moved across a river in Alaska on a raft. The plane is on wheels, not floats. (Hudek)

Charles Lindbergh arrives in Mexico on the opening flight of Cia Mexicana from Brownsville, Texas, to Mexico City in 1929. 5-AT-12 carries interesting mixed markings of both the U.S. registration NC-9661 and the Mexican registration M-SCAN. It later became X-ABCB when the Mexican Government changed their system of civil registrations. (Adolfo Villasenor)

of TWA), C.M. Young (Assistant Secretary of Commerce for Air), Amelia Earhart, Louise Thaden, and J.C. Cowdin. The first West-to-East flights were by two red Fokker Tri-motors of the former Western Air Express. They left Los Angeles at 5:19 am on the 25th and arrived at Newark at 7:38 pm on the 26th. This was preceded by two minutes by a mail plane, carrying 268 pounds of mail, flown by Lamar Nelson and Orman Gove that may have been a Ford.

The other early airline that was a major user of the Ford was Pan American Airways and it's subsidiaries Pan American Grace Airlines and Cia Mexicana de Aviacion. Charles Lindbergh was again a prominent figure in the early operations and he personally flew PAA Fords on route selection and first flight opening ceremonies. The center of Pan American's Ford operations was Brownsville, Texas, and from there Ford service went to Mexico, Guatemala, San Salvador, Nicaragua, Panama, Colombia, Ecuador, Peru, Bolivia, Chile, Argentina, Uruguay, Paraguay and Brazil. The basic passenger and air mail service to these countries between 1929 and 1933 was provided by the Ford Tri-Motor. It's replacement on PAA service was the Douglas DC-2.

A small, little-known, subsidiary of Pan American was Panama Airways established in December 1936 to fly tourists across the Panama Canal. Using Ford Tri-Motors flying between Balboa and Cristobal, a distance of 35 miles, the $14.00 trip only took 29 minutes. The service was coordinated with cruise directors so that up to 36 round trips were possible in one day. Although they also operated DC-2's the passengers preferred the Ford for it's better view of the Panama Canal. It was also possible to pass through the canal by ship and take the round trip flight for an additional aerial view before rejoining the cruise. In 1937 there were 43 cruise ships carrying 16,000 passengers in and out of Cristobal and 3,000 of those flew on the Panama Airways sightseeing flights.

The life span of the average wood and fabric airliner of the 1920s was relatively short so it is not surprising to read Ford Company ads timidly stating in 1929 that "no Ford plane has yet worn out in service", and "consequently we now feel buyers of Ford planes run little if any danger that the planes will become obsolete before they have completed their period of usefulness a period which we now know to be not less than four years." Later, in 1932, they admitted that when the 5-AT-B's were built that their estimated life was 2,500 flying hours. But TWA had already put 3,000 hours on each plane and was sending them back to the factory to have wing mail bins installed in the belief that they were good for another 2,000 hours.

Finally, in late 1934, TWA did replace their fleet with DC-2's and this prompted an article titled "TWA Ford Tri-Motors Retired" which began: "Like faithful old fire-horses, unshod and retired to a life of ease amid green

5-AT-11 (X-ABCC) at the terminal in Brownsville. Note use of PAA emblem with their subsidiary Cia Mexicana. (Harry Gann)

In contrast this is the frugal, but functional, gate used by Cia Mexicana at Tijuana, Mexico. (Larkins Collection)

TACA Guatemala's 5-AT-26 in front of one of their many hangars. This is one of the passenger versions used by TACA throughout Central America. (Jim Harvey)

Pan American Airways System

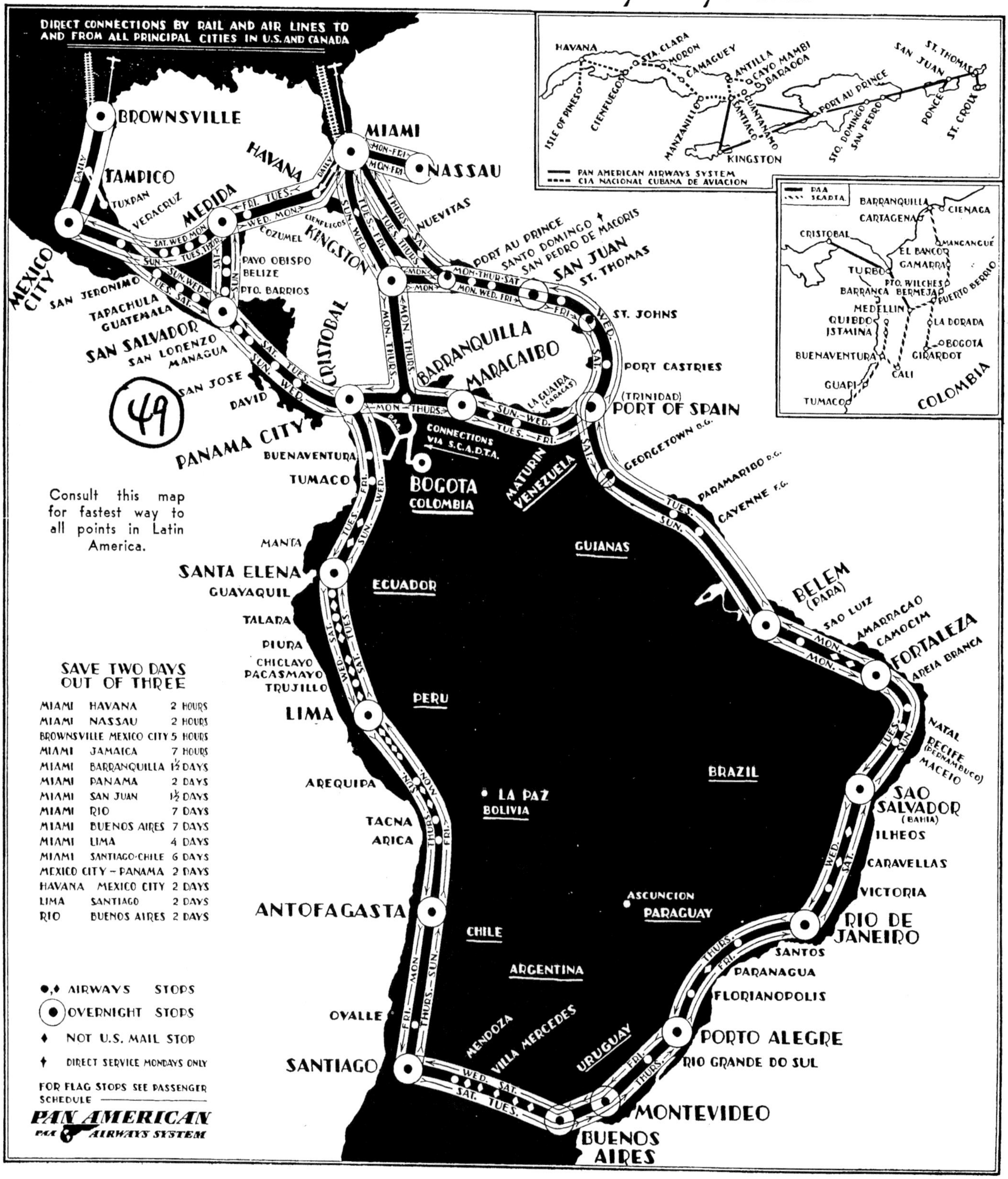

A typical passenger gate of the late 1920s. The American Airways 5-AT carried the "Colonial Division" name under the logo. (AA)

pastures, a fleet of veteran tri-motored airplanes is facing retirement after almost a decade of active service on the mid-transcontinental airway between New York and Los Angeles."

Later, in 1939, John Collings, pioneer Ford test pilot and airline executive, wrote an article "Farewell, Tin Goose" in which he said, "I know the end is in sight for the old girl" and "She was and is a thoroughbred, but her days are almost up."

But the rugged Tin Goose fooled them all. Far from retiring to green pastures she entered the hardest working period of her life. Stout's dream of the value of metal construction was only beginning to pay off and even he never dared to predict that Fords would still be flying in 1992 and that one had 22,900 hours to it's credit.

The man who gave the Ford its second life was Lowell Yerex, pioneer founder of the Central American airline TACA (Transportes Aereos Centro-Americanos) with headquarters at Tegucigalpa, Honduras. Together with its subsidiaries TACA-Guatemala, TACA-Costa Rica and TACA-Nicaragua the airline flew at least 27 Wasp-powered Ford Tri-Motors. Some started flying freight and passengers as early as 1934, with others being added through the 1930s. From 1942 through 1947 sixteen Fords were operated under Nicaraguan registry. Most, if not all, of these had large cargo doors cut into the side and sliding or removable hatches installed in the top of the fuselage to enable the loading of heavy machinery. In addition to the flying of freight at least one plane was modified with a 600-gallon fuselage tank to carry diesel oil and it flew 2,400 gallons per day to the La Luz Mine. At least six TACA Fords were lost in crashes during this period of rugged and hazardous flying. For more detailed information see Chapters 6, 9 and 10.

While hardly an airline, for sixteen years after World War II, 5-AT-11 (XA-HIL) flew steadily between Mazatlan and the San Luis Mine at Tayoltita, Mexico. This plane single-handedly built a world wide reputation for dependability and service that has not been equalled by any other Ford. During this time she flew 5,376 hours and carried more than 65,000 passengers, 436 tons of mail, 4,790 tons of express and 2,165 tons of freight.

Operating under the general management of Bert Brown, and known as TATSA, this little airline provided the only transportation in and out of the mine during eight months of the year. Captain Jesus Delgadillo, of TATSA, flew this Ford for a total of 4,477 hours without an incident - a remarkable record of mountain flying from a single 1,200 foot runway buried at the base of a box canyon with 4,000 foot walls.

And, of course, there is the airline that has gotten the most publicity in the last thirty years and that is Island Air Service/ Island Airlines at Put-in-Bay, Ohio. It seems as if there isn't a magazine or newspaper that hasn't at some time run an article on this operation and the older the Fords got the more wonderment crept into the reporters stories.

It is no wonder that Island got so much coverage when they operated such a unique service of daily flights between small islands in Lake Erie with an average flight time of ten minutes between takeoff and landing. Add to this two 1928 airplanes, and a pilot (Harold Hauck) with 11,000 pilot hours in a Ford Tri-Motor, together with a claim of flying 35,000 passengers a year and one has the makings of grand adventure.

The airline did not start with any such background. Milton Hersberger started a small operation in 1930 with a New Standard D-25 and named it Erie Isle Airways. By

5-AT-11 (XA-HIL) landing at the San Luis Mining Company strip at Tayoltita, Mexico. Part of the small community lies below the approach to the single runway. (Adolfo Villasenor)

5-AT-69 on the TWA commute service in New York City. (Henry Arnold)

Another view of 5-AT-69 showing the thick wing chord and the technique of taxying seaplanes with two engines. (Larkins Collection)

1936 it had grown and with his partner R.N. Anderson they bought their first Ford (4-AT-38) in November. The company's legal title at that time was Air Tours Inc., of Put-in-Bay, Ohio. During the life of the Island operation of the Ford they owned seven planes as follows (by date of purchase): 4-AT-38, 4-AT-5, 4-AT-42, 4-AT-53, 5-AT-40, 5-AT-27 and 5-AT-11. In 1953 the company name had been changed to Travelair Taxi Inc., of Sandusky, Ohio. For further information see Chapters 8, 9, 10 and the Bibliography.

Milton Hersberger may well have gotten the idea for his Island Air Service Ford operation from a visit to New York City in 1931. The Curtiss-Wright Corporation established a similar service in September 1931 with two Fords (4-AT-49 and 4-AT-51) and the inauguration of the Metropolitan Air Ferry Service.

This interesting 55-mile route carried rail passengers and tourists between North Beach Airport, Newark Airport and Floyd Bennett Field. The fare was $2.00 between airports and $5.00 for the round trip. The triangular route was flown every hour on the hour from North Beach and became so popular that night flights were added that extended the schedule to 9:00 pm, returning at 10:00 pm. The route was at 2,000 feet altitude over Manhattan and the hope was that tourists would take the flight just as they would try the subway.

In the first month of operation the Air Ferry carried 2,259 passengers and the Fords flew 18,405 miles. 4-AT-49 had the large words AIR FERRY painted on the side of the fuselage. The entire operation had been set up and supervised by Major William B. Robertson and probably would have been successful if it had not been for the Depression. Unfortunately, it did not last a year and the two Fords were sold in 1932.

Island Air Service 4-AT-42 at Peninsular Airport, Ohio, in February 1952. (Clay Jansson)

Rare photo of a Ford with the Universal Air Lines division of the Robertson Aircraft Corporation. This plane is 4-AT-29. (Hudek)

5-AT-33 of Colonial Air Transport. (John Stiles)

Another short-lived attempt at New York City commuter flying with a Ford was undertaken by TWA in 1935. This exotic service involved 5-AT-69 on floats, flying from a downtown "Skyport" at the foot of Wall Street and another at the end of Thirty First Street, to Floyd Bennett Field. The purpose was to transport passengers and mail from downtown Manhattan to Floyd Bennett to connect with the new DC-2 flights to the west coast.

TWA pilot Bill Piper, just out of the Navy with seaplane experience, was put in charge of getting the operation started with NC-410H, TWA No. 620. In July and August he prepared the plane and tested it along with Harlan Hull, Pat Gallup and Jack Zimmerman. On August 29th it was approved for operation on floats by the Department of Commerce and some goodwill flights were made for the Mayor and members of the TWA Board of Directors.

The service was planned primarily on the delivery of mail to Floyd Bennett which was expected to become the designated air mail field in place of Newark, New Jersey. However, the Mayor of Newark and influential people such as the President of the Pennsylvania Railroad blocked this appointment. The official mail field was kept at Newark and the passenger load did not justify the seaplane operation so it was shut down in a few months and the plane sold to SCADTA in Colombia in February, 1936.

One of the interesting stories involved in this flying took place during the preliminary testing. As Bill Piper tells it,". . . Harlan Hull, the system Chief Pilot, (and a former Marine pilot) came out to see me and asked if the ship was ready to fly. May answer was a quick 'Let's give it a try!' The next morning we were airborne for one of the most thrilling flights ever . . . underneath the 59th Street and George Washington bridges, and a tour of the New York skyline, the Statue of Liberty, Long Beach and Eastern Long Island . . . all from an altitude of 50 feet."

Piper may have thought that this was the first time that a Ford had flown under a bridge, but it had been done in 1929 with a load of passengers. Maddux Airlines, operating between Los Angeles and Oakland, sometimes found the fog too thick in the Oakland hills to make a direct flight. On one or more occasion, the 4-AT flew under the Carquinez bridge on the Sacramento River, in

Northwest Airlines 5-AT-48 in flight. (Paul Matt)

Helen Richey and pilots for Central Airlines in December 1934. From left to right in front of 5-AT-67: Duke Slimon, Mac McDonough, Slim Carmichael, Bill Day, Al Carl, Merle Moltrop, Trow Sebree, Helen Richey, Jack Fife, Al Brooks, and Jim Gott. Central Airlines leased 5-AT-28, 5-AT-43 and 5-AT-57 from American Airlines. (Ken Sumney)

5-AT-69 of the New England and Western Air Transportation Company in 1930. This airline was the only one to paint a large HANDS OFF on the rudder of their Fords. (Ken Molson)

5-AT-58 of Northern Air Transport at Seattle. The Ford flew between Nome and Fairbanks, Alaska. (G.S. Williams)

5-AT-58 on skis in the Alaskan winter. (Peter M. Bowers)

Eastern Air Transport 4-AT-63 photographed at Atlanta, Georgia. (Eastern Air Lines)

The rarely seen airway beacon emblem of American Airways on the side of 5-AT-14 at Boston on April 8, 1931. (Donald Ives)

5-AT-67 with the markings of the Colonial Division of American Airways. Note the name on the hangar. (George Hardie Jr.)

5-AT-39 with the Colonial Division of AA. Compare this photo with the one in Chapter 12 to see the differences between the same plane in 1932 and 1992. (Larkins Collection)

NC 9683
Ford
TRI-MOTOR
6
S.A.F.E.Way
AIR LINES
S.A.F.E.
AIR LINES

order to circle around and come back down San Francisco Bay to Alameda Airport. Jack Collier relates the story about how he and Maurice Murphy "had gone under it one day in thick going" to Tommy Tomlinson (*Western Flying*, June 1929).

An interesting footnote to the airline history involves the first woman airline pilot in the United States. Helen Richey, a young pilot with experience in an endurance flight and winner of the 1934 Women's Air Derby, applied for a job with Central Airlines who was at the time flying Fords leased from American.

She made her first official flight as a co-pilot with Horace Stark in Ford 5-AT-67 from Washington, DC, to Detroit, Michigan, on December 31, 1934. There is a photo of her in the New York Times for January 1, 1935, standing in the door of the Ford shaking hands with Assistant Postmaster General William Howes prior to the takeoff.

In less than a week the Department of Commerce Bureau of Aeronautics (now the FAA) suggested to the airline that it took the strength of two men to pilot a Ford in bad weather so Helen resigned rather than be a "fair weather pilot." This raised a mild feminist furor at the time and was summed up by Amelia Earhart who said a year later, "The pilots union refused to take her in, not because of lack of ability but because she was a female. The result of this action was that the Department of Commerce refused to let her fly passengers in bad weather, so the poor girl could not do her part at all and had to resign." Dept. of Commerce officials responded by saying, "It was not an order, not an attachment to her transport license, it was just an informal suggestion made to the airline." At the same time Ruth Nichols and Ruth Haviland both agreed that transports took hard, physical work to fly. Nichols suggested that research was needed to design a separate rudder motor.

In December 1935, undoubtedly under pressure from the press and others, the Bureau of Aeronautics hired Helen Richey to join two other women pilots (Louise Thaden and Helen McCloskey) in a program to assist municipalities in marking rooftops to aid airmen in flight.

Southwest Air Fast Express 5-AT's lined up in the early days of their operation under the direction of Larry Fritz. (George Copeland)

SAFEWAY employees demonstrating the strength of 5-AT-29's wing in October 1930. (George Copeland)

AA Captains J.D. "Ted" Lewis and Paul L. Carpenter on the inauguration of the first two-way radio service on American Airways. Note the radio mast on the rear of the fuselage. (Paul L. Carpenter)

Merrill H. Grix testing an experimental compressed air starter for the Ford Tri-Motor. The pressure on the gauge reads 28 pounds. This 1931 proposal was not adopted. (Ford Archives)

TWA's 5-AT-41 and American Airways 5-AT-44 together in the early 1930s. Note the radio masts added to the top of the rear fuselage by both airlines. (Ed Peck)

This photo is interesting because it shows National Air Transport markings on 5-AT-5 that was delivered to Transcontinental Air Transport (TAT) 14 days after it was built. Was this a mistake at the factory, or was it a handy airplane that was available for painting for publicity photos for NAT? (Hudek)

Rare NAT markings on a 5-AT-D (5-AT-103). Most photos of the NAT/United D's show Pacific Air Transport or United Air Lines markings. (United Air Lines)

A late photo of a United Air Lines 5-AT-D in flight. The PAT Fords all had names assigned, this one for 5-AT-106 was PUGET. (Boeing Airplane Company)

Spokane, Washington, city officials flew to Seattle to inspect Boeing Field on September 14, 1930. Standing in front of Mamer Air Transport's 4-AT-55 are left to right: A.D. Butler, Nick Mamer, Thaddeus Lane, A.J. Fabian, Mayor Frank Edwards, Dr. Ralph Hendricks, LeRoy Lambert and A.W. Burch. (Larkins Collection)

The 5-AT-D's had double-unit wing bins as shown in this photo of a new Pacific Air Transport plane. The wing bins were opened and closed with the use of a long hand crank as shown in the photo. (Boeing Airplane Company)

TWA developed a single-unit wing bin for mail and baggage in 1932. This photo of 5-AT-34 was taken on April 13, 1932. This was so successful that Ford adopted the idea for the 5-AT-D and they were factory built. (G.S. Williams)

Stewardess Edna Eishen with Mrs. Eleanor Roosevelt in front of a United Air Lines 5-AT-C. This was possibly taken on the Chicago to Kansas City route, and it is rare to see the name United Air Lines on a C model. (Larkins Collection)

A publicity photo for Pacific Air Transport (PAT) "on PAT's fifth birthday" of September 13, 1932. It shows excellent detail of the square door of the 5-AT-D model. (Peter M. Bowers)

TWA's answer was to convert a Ford Tri-Motor and call it General Air Freight. This was used on the Chicago to New York City line in October 1936. The TWA hostesses posed for the photo are Elnora Knotts and Alberta Tyne. (TWA via Ed Betts)

A photo of early small package air freight being loaded on an American Airways 5-AT. (American Airlines)

Chapter 4
Corporate and Private Use

The potential use of the airplane in sales promotion and executive transportation was understood and developed early in the production of the Ford Tri-Motor.

The first plane to be delivered for this purpose was 4-AT-6 for the Standard Oil Company of Indiana. It was delivered on May 21, 1927 - the day that Lindbergh landed in Paris. It was named "Stanolind I" and was the first airplane to be owned by a non-aviation commercial organization in the United States.

The plane was used frequently to carry members of the Board of Directors and other executives on trips requiring fast travel. When not being used for that purpose it toured midwest cities taking public officials and businessmen on goodwill flights to promote aviation. These were particularly aimed at those persons who had never flown before and this was a policy carried out by many of the other business owners. A second Tri-Motor "Stanolind II", 5-AT-42, was purchased in May 1929. It was badly damaged a month later in a Kansas hurricane while on the ground for the night. After being sent back to the factory and rebuilt it was re-named "Stanolind III" and returned to service in July 1929.

During the time that the two planes were operated by Standard Oil of Indiana they carried without charge some 25,000 passengers over a total of more than 200,000 miles in approximately 2,200 flying hours.

The second Ford sold to a business was the Royal Typewriter Company "Air Truck." This specially modified 4-AT-A (4-AT-8) sold for $46,000 and had a freight interior built to carry 210 portable typewriters in racks, plus a desk for a shipping clerk in the rear of the cabin. A hatch was cut into the floor at the rear so that typewriters could be dropped by parachute, three at a time, to Royal distributors. This technique was developed to eliminate the necessity of landing at these points on a cross-country flight – or so the public relations department said!

The plane was delivered to Hadley Field, New Jersey, on August 4th, 1927, and from there went to Curtiss Field, New York, and then to the Royal Typewriter plant at Hartford, Connecticut. The initial business trip, with John A. Collings as pilot, was from the plant at Hartford to Baltimore, Maryland. Later that month they flew from

4-AT-48 was sold to the president of Reed, Murdoch and Company by the Arthur Hatch, manager of the Lincoln sales department, while they were both travelling on a train. When it came time for delivery Mr. Stevens, president of Reed Murdoch, insisted on coming to the plant and turning the check over to Hatch personally. From left to right in this November 28, 1928 photo are William B. Mayo, Edsel Ford, Mr. Stevens and Arthur Hatch. (Ford Archives)

INDEPENDENCE
Ford
7863

The Teenie Weenies inside the Monarch Food Company flying salesroom. Special racks held the sample canned goods on the sides of the cabin and on the center overhead structure. (Ford Archives)

Hartford to Havana, Cuba, and return.

The parachuting of the typewriters had been tested in Detroit and worked well. It was demonstrated to the press at Curtiss Field on August 5th with one lot dumped from a 700-foot altitude, and another at 250 feet above the ground. There is a photo of the typewriters descending by parachute in the New York Times, 8-5-27, page 15. This demonstration led to a semi-humorous editorial concerning the "future" possibilities of such delivery, including the hazards of parachuting pianos, particularly if the chutes did not open.

By November 1927, 45 flying days after delivery, the plane had flown 14,350 miles to 114 cities in 27 states, and had made parachute deliveries to 62 additional points. The plane was, however, sold shortly afterwards and the delivery program discontinued.

Another modified Ford was 4-AT-48 purchased by the Reid, Murdoch Company of Chicago. The interior of the cabin was made into a flying salesroom with racks to hold two hundred different items of food products from their Monarch Foods line. The plane was named "Independence" for the Independent Grocers of their midwestern territory. Two children dressed as the "Teenie Weenies", a General and a Policeman, accompanied the plane on some public relations tours.

This Ford probably had the most lettering on it of any ever built. From the rear one could see the large words MONARCH on the top of the left center section, TEA on the top of the left elevator, COFFEE on the top of the right center section and COCOA on the top of the right elevator. The large name INDEPENDENCE was in billboard fashion on both sides of the fuselage with the Monarch Lion trade mark on both sides of the nose and rudder.

In addition, under the cabin windows, in letters about four inches high, were the words Monarch Teenie Weenies, Sweet Pickles, Peanut Butter, Wheat Hearts, Pop Corn, Toffies, Sardines, Peas, Asparagus, Lima Beans and Corn.

The Ford made a tour of several states and was visited by ten to fifteen thousand people, including students from the high schools in Uniontown, Pennsylvania, which closed so their pupils could inspect the airplane. A former Ford employee, who wishes to remain unnamed because of guilt, fondly remembers looking forward to the plane coming to the plant for service as those on the night shift could help themselves to the jars of Toffies.

The Nekoosa-Edwards Paper Company of Wisconsin was another of the pioneer industrial owners of the Ford Tri-Motor. They purchased 4-AT-43, a 4-AT-B, in October 1928 and flew it for three years on company business, primarily carrying customers from the midwest area to and from the mills and offices at Port Edwards. In June 1931 it was sold to Major Leslie G. Mulzer, who had previously been the pilot of the plane for the company.

The Continental Oil Company, of Ponca City, Oklahoma, flew their Curtiss Robin and their Ford 5-AT-C Club Model (5-AT-90) on an extensive 11,985 mile sales trip through 30 states and two Canadian provinces in the summer of 1931. The purpose was to visit the principal points of the company's twelve marketing divisions. An average of 160 miles a day was maintained and the division managers and their assistant accompanied the party in each division. The conveniences afforded, the mobility, value of sales consummated and extent of publicity and good will obtained made the tour a great success.

Not all of the business flying was in the East for the Standard Oil Company of California bought a brand new 4-AT-B (4-AT-19) in May 1928. It was flown to San Francisco where it was christened "Standard of California" by Elizabeth May Hanna, daughter of one of the Board of Directors.

In addition to the usual promotional trips many educational flights were undertaken such as those given for the Secondary School Principals Convention in Oakland, California, in March 1929. The Ford carried 800 passengers on flights over the city, consisting of delegates to the convention, visiting educators, members of the local board of education etc. In most instances those that flew had never been in an airplane before.

See Appendix 10, Part II, for a full list of all the Fords used for business purposes.

4-AT-6 was purchased new by the Standard Oil Company of Indiana. The large Ford emblem was on the nose on the early 4-AT's and was moved to behind the cabin door on later models. The plane was one day old when this photo was taken on May 13, 1927. (Ford Archives)

Standard Oil of Indiana's second Tri-Motor was 5-AT-42 and it was named "Stanolind II" when this photo was taken on May 7, 1929. (Ken Wilson)

A specially modified "Air Truck" was built for the Royal Typewriter Company. 4-AT-8 had a trap door built into the floor to enable the crew to drop typewriters by parachute to dealers in small towns where the plane could not land. At the Ford plant on July 29, 1927. (Hudek)

The plane was named "Independence" to honor the independent grocers that purchased their line of canned foods, some of which are readable on the side of the fuselage. A platform with stairs was placed outside the fuselage so that customers and friends could view the inside of the cabin and cockpit. The Teenie Weenie characters were a General and a Policeman and are believed to have been based on popular comic strip characters of the period. The lettering around the Monarch Foods emblem reads "Leadership for 75 Years." (Ford Archives)

Barnstorming - Old and New

The Ford has been involved in various forms of barnstorming from 1928 to 1991, some of the most low budget hand-to-mouth existence and some bordering on luxury. Those before the depression were first class, those during the 1930s extremely frugal and basic, those after World War II much better.

The first operation was more a matter of taking people for a ride in a new airplane in conjunction with their car dealer than a true barnstorming, ticket-selling sales pitch. Leo Rocca, a partner in the Washington, DC, agency for Ford and Lincoln cars organized Universal Flyers in 1928 and bought a new 4-AT (4-AT-37) in September 1928. Ray Loomis, a former Ford freight line pilot, was hired along with Charles Wolber, a Wright engine mechanic at Ford Airport, as mechanic. The advertising literature stressed the experience of the crew and the safe operation including the fact that Wolber, "spends four hours each day checking and inspecting the big plane before he gives it an OK so that it may fly."

They carried 4,122 passengers in the first month of a detailed plan to send the plane across the United States in a year and a half tour to be sponsored by the Ford and Lincoln dealers in every state. Beautiful, numbered tickets were printed for the "Aerial Tour" and were available from the auto dealers showrooms for $5.00. Loomis bought the Ford in June 1931 and continued to operate it on his own until 1934. An ex Air Corps and air mail pilot, his brochure carried the interesting statement, "He holds the world's record for carrying more passengers than any other pilot."

The next plane used was 4-AT-55 (NC-9612) and it was indirectly involved in barnstorming. Nick Mamer bought the plane new at the factory for his air service for $50,000. He and Art Walker picked it up and flew it away on Sunday, April 1, 1929. (They heard about that later from the Ford factory where such things were not supposed to happen on a Sunday). By the time they got back to Spokane, Washington, in the first week of May they had

4-AT-43 flown by Leslie G. Mulzer for the Nekoosa-Edwards Paper Company. Note the use of the company logo NEPCO under the right wing in the same manner as Ford had done with their name for advertising purposes. (Nekoosa-Edwards)

Standard Oil Company of California was the third oil company to buy a new Ford as is shown in this view of 4-AT-19 taken on May 7, 1928. (G.S. Williams)

Continental Oil Company's beautiful 5-AT-90 at Ponca City, Oklahoma. Professional pilots who took pride in their planes would make sure that all three propellers were in the same position when the plane was on public view. (Hudek)

sold enough rides at $5.00 each for once around the field to pay for the plane. Although this was a true barnstorming operation the main difference was that the customers got to ride in a brand new airplane.

The more common, and better known, depression era barnstorming with used airplanes came between 1931 and 1940. Jerry Wood was the largest of them all, incorporating as "Air Tours" long before Milton Hersberger used that name, and he had a number of planes and pilots. In addition to his Ford 4-AT-56, he operated two Boeing 80-A tri-motors. Pilots who flew for him, many of whom later became senior airline pilots, were John M. Barchard, Harold J. Cary, W.M. "Red" Cary, Stephen Darius, J.M. "Mac" Gilmour, A.J. Hartman, J.E. "Red" Matthews, Woods C. "Penny" Rogers, Earl Thomas, Loren D. Webb and Robert E. Windett.

There was lots of competition, and some of those that flew Fords as barnstormers during the 1930s were Keith Cantine, Ben Gregory, Capt. O.M. Goodsell, Slim Hightower, Charlie Hunter, Art Inman, Fred Kane, "Pop" Keightly, Capt. Ray Loomis, Hunter Moody, Major Leslie Mulzer, Joe Musleh, Dale Smith and Mel Swanson. In 1930-1931 Howard F. Maish barnstormed a 4-AT over 175,000 miles in the U.S., Canada and Mexico.

Jerry Wood described part of the scene: "Ray Loomis owned several Fords from 1928 to 1938 under the name of Universal Flyers. He was a rough, tough, price-cutting competitor. He cleaned a town like a vacuum cleaner. He never gave nor asked any favors, yet with all, he was a nice guy, a fine pilot, and perhaps the most consistent and aggressive of all the Ford barnstormers during that period." Ben Gregory was carrying passengers at 50 cents each in 1933. He would keep the people waiting in a "bull pen", 14 at a time, and two ground assistants would load them in and out. He flew up to 1,000 feet, one turn over town, and back to the field in a glide to save money. He polished his system to the point that he could get the people on and off in 90 seconds.

Firestone Tire and Rubber Company bought 4-AT-57 to promote business in 1929. (Larkins Collection)

4-AT-57 was delivered to Akron, Ohio, on May 29, 1929. From left to right are Harvey S. Firestone Jr., William B. Stout and Harvey S. Firestone. (Larkins Collection)

Some ladies in typical 1929 dress ready for a flight in the Firestone 4-AT-E. (Henry W. Arnold)

The company replaced their 4-AT with the two-month old Ford demonstrator 5-AT-75 in October 1929. This photo was taken in August 1930 when the plane was visiting the factory. (Ken Wilson)

Some women were involved in barnstorming, such as Art Inman's wife Leona, and some of the flavor of that type of flying is told by Mrs. Leona Inman Pemberton:

"I don't think I would be considered a Ford Tri-Motor pilot, as most of my flying time was cross-country in the Co-pilots seat, and hostess on charter flights etc. Being Mrs Inman made me part owner of the Ford as well as several other planes, consequently I was "grounded" most of the time, selling tickets to keep the planes loaded with passengers, operate the public address system, keep cars and people out of the propellers, food and water to the pilots and crew, tie-down staples, ropes and sledge hammer ready in case a "line squall" type thunder storm, which we had plenty of back in the middle west.

"'Complaints' that was a big one. The Sheriff often paid us a visit, we were making too much noise over the hospital or flying too low over town, truth of the matter was we were "revving" up the engines on purpose to attract attention for more business. Nearby farmers came dashing out all shook up, we were frightening the chickens, cows and horses, not being used to planes as we did most of our barnstorming on fields such as cow pastures, wheat stubble and even alfalfa fields. I also did some advance work billing towns etc."

The rock bottom experience was that of Reg Pattinson and Wayne Parmerter. They bought NC-9612 for $3,000 in Burbank, California, in October 1936. At that point they had half a tank of gas and $30 in cash. So they started out to barnstorm their way home. Their experience was typical of the depression and they didn't get home in Witt, Illinois, until May 1937. For those interested in the stop by stop details Robert Winston wrote a fascinating article in the September 1939 issue of The Sportsman Pilot. One different angle took place at an unnamed town in Texas where they sold "advertising space" on the side of the Ford at $5.00 per sign. This was the same airplane that Mamer and Walker had barnstormed when new.

World War II put a stop to barnstorming and it didn't start again with a Ford until John Louck bought 5-AT-74 (N-414H) in October 1959. Louck, a former crop duster and AAF pilot, had 11 fields in 9 states but gave up all of this to realize his lifetime ambition of barnstorming a Ford Tri-Motor. In 1988 he carried 17,000 passengers, including 2,800 in five days at Rockford, Illinois. He operated in the Chicago and Mid West area until 1965 when he sold his Ford to American Airlines.

This short summary doesn't do justice to Louck and the great contribution that he made to the preservation of N-414H. If it was not for John Louck, that plane would probably not be in existence today as the senior, most experienced Ford still flying. Some of the heartache and effort that John and his wife Katherine put into this can be appreciated from the following excerpts from a 1989 letter:

"Upon my arrival in Florida I found the remains of a Ford and that was about all. As I was stuck with the deal, and not wanting to back out, my two men and I started to work on the Ford to get it 'ferryable.' There was Florida sand, wasp nests, green frogs, snakes etc., all over the Ford. After two weeks of work from daylight to dark and driving over 1,000 miles for small parts here and there we got it ready to test hop. It was about an hour before dark we took her up and I had never flown a Ford before. I overshot the field 3 times and it was nearly dark before I got her down. We left the next morning for Monmouth, Ill. We made 132 miles the first day. The rest were not so good. We left Florida in the first week of October (1959) and arrived at Monmouth December 16th. 68 days to make 1,700 miles in an airplane. The mishaps, breakdowns, troubles, heartbreaks would fill a book. But one thing for sure I knew every bolt, nut or any

5-AT-1 after being rebuilt to 5-AT-C standards. (P&W)

part of a Ford Tri-Motor. I have never cussed, discussed, threatened and petted any airplane so much in my whole flying career. But one thing did happen, I became so attached to the Ford that I got mad at anybody that said anything against it. And they said plenty. Most of my flying friends thought I had gone off my rocker and my family looked at me like I was a stranger. One thing they didn't realize was it was not the Fords fault for all the trouble but the previous owners who had treated it with no care at all.

"The second week of January 1960 after arriving home we were changing an engine when the hoist slipped catching me under the engine. It tore the muscle out of my shoulder and put me in the hospital for three months. After getting back on my feet in April I started to barnstorm and the next thing the FAA comes along and grounds my Ford because they say the engines are obsolete. So I started to do battle with them. My wife, friends etc., thought that this was the end of the Ford escapade but they didn't understand. I had only begun to fight. After a long drawn out battle with the FAA and $15,000 expenses I finally got the Ford relicensed, but I was about broke as a tornado had struck my town and wiped out my airport except for two buildings. I had parts of airplanes as far away as three miles.

"Luckily my Ford was at another airport or I would have lost her for sure. Well everybody thought I would sure sell the Ford now as I was broke, in debt, and winter was coming but I didn't. I just went deeper in debt and decided to give her another try next season." All of this paid off and Louck flew some 100,000 passengers in N-414H while he owned it.

Another corporate aircraft was 5-AT-89 flown by the Timken Bearing Company. (P&W)

Phillips Petroleum Company named their 5-AT-78 "Woolaroc II", keeping the original name for their famous Travel Air. This photo was taken on October 1, 1930 at the factory. (Hudek)

The next Ford was 5-AT-34 purchased by Gaylord Moxon in 1964 and flown until it was sold to Irv Perch in October 1969. Moxon ran a first class business with his wife and two assistants in red vests selling tickets, plastic model kits of the Ford and copies of the British Profile on the Tri-Motor. His peak appearance was probably at the world famous Nut Tree Restaurant, Gift Shop and aviation book store near Vacaville, California, where customers could ride a miniature train from the restaurant to the tree-lined airport. Moxon also attended all of the air shows in California and around the West.

The reborn N-414H took up the barnstorming circuit again in 1972 when Charles LeMaster bought her from American Airlines.

Christening the plane "The Kansas Clipper" LeMaster operated around the Mid West and at the EAA annual convention at Oshkosh. He flew the plane for five years before selling it to Grand Canyon Airlines.

The last, and perhaps best known of the modern barnstormers, is Allan Chaney of Newark, Ohio. After buying the rebuilt 4-AT-38 from Island Airlines he flew the plane for six years up and down the East Coast, the South and the Mid-West selling rides at $20 each for adults ($30 to sit in the co-pilots seat), and $10 for children. His red, white and blue Ford became a familiar scene in Florida over the years as he spent winters barnstorming up and down the state so it is fitting that it should now be a resident of the Weeks Air Museum in Miami.

It is unlikely that we will see any more barnstorming with Ford Tri-Motors because of the steep rise in insurance premiums, the crowded traffic-controlled airspace, and the risk of loosing an airplane in an accident that is now becoming worth a million dollars.

Above: The pilot of 5-AT-77 demonstrating the open cockpit window as well as the new voice microphone for air to ground radio transmission. (Western Electric Company)

Left: The Bell Telephone Laboratories 5-AT-77 was used for extensive experiments to develop air to ground radio communication. Note the radio mast on the rear fuselage. (P&W)

A factory photo of 4-AT-31 as it actually appeared just before delivery to Maddux Air Lines in August 1928. (Hudek)

The same photo retouched with the name of a prospective buyer "Broadmoor Hotel, Colorado Springs." The name is painted on the photo, not the airplane. This was done several times with the name "Ford" on early company photos. Ford correspondence files list the following names of prospective customers for the Ford Tri-Motor: Broadmoor Hotel, B & H Air Service, Erwin Wasey Company, L.A. Air Service, New York Air Terminals, D. Barr Peat, Roosevelt Flying Corp., and Southern Air Transport Flying Service. (Hudek)

Edwin Link, on the left, in front of the Link Aeronautical Corporation 4-AT-58 that he occasionally flew. Note the dangerous but common practice of the 1930s to be photographed in front of moving propellers. (Larkins Collection)

Another variation on the neon sign carrier was 4-AT-42 used by Mike Murphy of Findlay, Ohio, in 1940 and 1941. This photo shows it when it was advertising Marathon Gasoline and Oil. NC-7684 flew from 1941 to 1972 for Island Airlines. (Logan Coombs)

The Quehl Sign Company used 4-AT-27 in 1929 for nightime advertising with a neon sign. The under side of the wing and center of the fuselage was painted matte black to improve the appearance of such ads as GIVE US BEER. The plane flew from Lunken Airport in Cincinnati, Ohio. (Paul Matt)

A Maddux Ford was used by MGM as an aerial cutting room during the filming of Ramon Navarro's "Gold Braid." George Hill the director, on the right, and Blanche Sewell, film cutter, are supervising the loading of the equipment. Motion picture film was edited on the numerous flights between San Diego and Hollywood. (John W. Caler)

Cast and crew of the RKO movie "The Man Who Found Himself" on the set with 4-AT-24. (James Farmer)

Right: 4-AT-24 and the camera crew at Union Air Terminal, Burbank, in 1937. (Walt Jefferies)

Larry Fritz flew this Maddux Ford to Truckee, California, for scenes for the movie "The Red Dance", a film about Russia before and after the revloution directed by Raoul Walsh and starring Dolores Del Rio. The filming was done in January 1928 with 4-AT-7. (L.G. Fritz)

4-AT-27 later in its operation. The windshield has been changed and the name FORD added under the wing. This is a typical scene at a small dirt field airport where thousands of people got their first plane ride in a Ford Tri-Motor. (Hudek)

Universal Flyers 4-AT-37, a 4-AT-D, at Washington, D.C., on December 12, 1928. "Fly Under the Auspices of Your Ford Dealer" is painted on the side, and the front states "This Ship Uses Gulf-No-Nox Motor Fuel and Gulf Pride Lubricants." It was at the start of the barnstorming operation and the total passengers carried was only 2,223. (Larkins Collection)

4-AT-55 after arriving in Spokane and being named "West Wind." (John C. Mitchell)

Mrs. Leona Inman with 4-AT-23. (Leona Inman)

The ultimate in a high class operation by Moxon in 1967 at the Nut Tree in California. Grace and Gaylord Moxon are in the center. In addition to tickets they sold plastic model kits of the Ford and copies of the British Profile. Left to right: Robert Marcum, Grace Moxon, Gaylord Moxon, Robert Setterberg. (W.T. Larkins)

Above: A typical scene from the barnstorming days of the 1930s. This is 4-AT-67 operated by Westchester Airways. (Charles Thompson)

Below: 4-AT-23 in flight with the name "Inman Brothers Flying Circus" on the side. (Art Krieger)

Al Chaney flying 4-AT-38 by the Statue of Liberty in New York Harbor on July 4, 1986. (Al Chaney)

Arthur Bussy stands in front of 4-AT-58 at Floyd Bennett Field in May 1932. He advertised for four paying passengers to fly with him to Harbor Grace and across the Atlantic to London. The plane is United Air Services' "Miss Albany." (Larkins Collection)

The professional sign at the Nut Tree Restaurant gave advance notice to the public weeks before the arrival of the Ford Tri-Motor, a sharp contrast with the sudden arrival of a Ford in a dirt field in the early 1930s. (W.T. Larkins)

Al Chaney at the controls of 4-AT-38 checking the runway prior to takeoff with another load of passengers. (Al Chaney)

4-AT-35 flying formation with the Goodyear Blimp NC-7A. (Larkins Collection)

Chapter 5
U.S. Military

U.S. Army

Thirteen Fords were built for the U.S. Army Air Corps, plus the single XB-906 Bomber that was a company proposal and not on a military contract. The first plane, a C-3, was delivered to Wright Field on February 8, 1928.

The production consisted of: 1 C-3 (AC 28-348), 7 C-3A's (29-220 to 29-226) re-designated as C-9 upon delivery; 1 C-4 (29-219) and 4 C-4A's (31-401 to 31-404).

As may be seen in the following individual aircraft histories, Air Corps history cards did not designate the squadrons that individual planes were assigned to, but rather the Base or Field. Because of this it is difficult to document squadron service for the Army Fords but photos and accident reports do identify use by the 3rd Attack Group, 1st Pursuit Group, 17th Pursuit Group, 38th Pursuit Squadron, 94th Pursuit Squadron, 53rd School Squadron, 57th Service Squadron, 58th Service Squadron, 60th Service Squadron and 71st Service Squadron.

Individual Histories, U.S. Army Air Corps

28-348 C-3 4-AT-13 FF 11-17-27

Received at Wright Field 2-8-28 as model XC-3, designation changed to C-3 in November 1928. 5-16-29 Mitchell Field. 6-4-29 Wright Field. 8-24-29 Chanute Field. 4-23-30 Fairfield Air Depot. 6-9-30 Chanute Field. 7-23-31 Fairfield Air Depot. 8-4-31 Chanute Field. 1-12-32 Wright Field. Surveyed at Wright 7-9-32. TT 1,273 hours.

29-219 C-4 5-AT-38 FF 4-5-29

Received at Bolling Field 6-9-29. Went on a two months long cross country flight of 70 flying hours with Capt. Harry A. Dingu as pilot. 12-5-29 Fairfield Air Depot. 1-21-30 Bolling Field. (Damaged 7-22-30 at March Field when hit by soldiers in a truck). 4-18-31 Ford Motor Company. 5-27-31 Kelly Field. 7-3-31 March Field. Converted to C-4A on 7-17-31 and used for research and development 7-5-32 to 3-3-33 at which time it reverted to regular flying with the 70th Service Squadron. 4-1-34 to the Western Zone to fly the Air Mail. 5-15-34 March Field. Surveyed at March 4-29-35 and then used for tests of the effects of fragmentation bombs on metal aircraft. TT 2,329 hours.

The end of 29-219. With the engines removed it was tested at March Field in 1935 for the results of fragmentation bombs on all-metal aircraft. (B.C. Reed)

MBING ON

29-220 C-9 4-AT-80 FF 5-29-29
Received at Wright Field 6-14-29. 2-24-30 France Field, Canal Zone (Panama). 2-33 Albrook Field. 4-35 Depot at France Field. Surveyed at France 8-2-35. TT 1,763 hours.

29-221 C-9 4-AT-81 FF 6-3-29
Received at Bolling Field 7-5-29. Accident 3-3-30 at Mitchel Field. 3-26-31 Middletown Air Depot. 4-28-31 Fort Crockett. 10-21-31 San Antonio Air Depot. 12-21-31 Fort Crockett. 6-14-33 San Antonio Air Depot. 11-28-33 Scott Field. 3-13-34 Eastern Zone to fly the Air Mail. 5-12-34 Scott Field, 15th Observation Squadron. 2-11-36 Wright Field. Surveyed at Wright 5-25-36. TT 2,695 hours.

29-222 C-9 4-AT-82 FF 6-7-29
Received at Selfridge Field 6-26-29. Accident 2-2-30 at Alba, Michigan. 2-27-30 Ford Motor Company for repairs. 3-21-30 Selfridge Field. 9-14-31 Fairfield Air Depot. 5-27-32 Selfridge Field. 5-16-33 Chanute Field. 6-13-33 Selfridge Field. Surveyed at Selfridge 8-6-34. TT 1,588 hours.

29-223 C-9 4-AT-83 FF 6-14-29
Received at Mitchel Field 6-29-29. Accident 1-23-30 at Dayton, Ohio. 1-30-30 Fairfield Air Depot for repairs. 3-12-30 Selfridge Field. 1-29-31 Fairfield Air Depot. 2-8-31 Wright Field. Redesignated XC-9 from 5-1-31 to 11-30-31. 11-30-31 Fairfield Air Depot. 1-8-32 Wright Field. Redesignated XC-9 from 2-1-32 to 8-6-32. 8-6-32 Fairfield Air Depot. 11-26-32 Wright Field. Surveyed 2-13-36. TT 1,322 hours.

29-224 C-9 4-AT-84 FF 6-18-29
Received at Fort Crockett 6-29-29. 8-16-29 Wright Field. 12-17-29 Fairfield Air Depot. 1-4-30 Selfridge Field. 6-13-30 Fairfield Air Depot. 8-15-30 Wright Field. 2-1-31 Kelly Field. 10-27-31 Fort Crockett. Accident 12-2-31 at Fort Crockett when Lt. Foster taxied into a gas truck. 3-3-32 San Antonio Air Depot. 2-34 Central Zone to fly the Air Mail, probably operating out of Barksdale Field. Surveyed at San Antonio Air Depot 11-1-34. TT 1,794 hours.

29-225 C-9 4-AT-85 FF 6-20-29
Received at Brooks Field 6-29-29. Accident at Brooks 7-15-29. 7-931 San Antonio Air Depot. 9-9-31 Brooks Field. 10-12-31 Randolph Field. Damaged in forced landing 1-29-32 at Bissel, Arkansas. 1-5-33 Barksdale Field. 8-15-33 San Antonio Air Depot. 2-12-34 Maxwell Field. 2-16-34 Barksdale Field. 3-30-34 Central Zone to fly the Air Mail. 6-5-34 Barksdale Field. Surveyed at Barksdale 5-1-36. TT 2,924 hours.

The first Army Air Corps Ford Tri-Motor, AC 28-348, with the Wright Field number P506 on the rudder. (Air Force Museum)

The same plane in later service with a parachute jumper leaving the plane which has had its door removed. (Peter M. Bowers)

29-226 C-9 4-AT-86 FF 6-21-29
Received at Fort Crockett 6-29-29. In April 1930 was serving with the 60th Service Squadron as an ambulance plane. 7-9-30 San Antonio Air Depot. 7-25-30 Fort Crockett. 8-1-30 Selfridge Field. 10-28-30 Fairfield Air Depot. 1-11-31 Fort Crockett. 8-16-32 San Antonio Air Depot. 2-14-33 Chanute Field. 5-16-33 Selfridge Field. 6-14-33 Chanute Field. 2-23-34 Central Zone to fly the Air Mail. 5-9-34 Chanute Field. 8-15-34 Fort Crockett. 2-19-35 Barksdale Field, 3rd Attack Group. Surveyed at Barksdale 9-3-35. TT 2,528 hours. Destroyed in a test on 1-25-36 to determine the effect of machine gun fire on metal aircraft.

31-401 C-4A 5-AT-91 FF 12-27-30
Received at Wright Field 1-9-31. Redesignated XC-4A from 1-31-31 to 3-2-31. 4-3-33 Fairfield Air Depot. 9-1-33 Wright Field. 3-1-34 Eastern Zone to fly the Air Mail. Accident 3-24-34 at Toledo, Ohio. 5-24-34 Wright Field. Accident 1-10-35 when it ground-looped into two Boeing P-12's. 9-5-36 San Antonio Air Depot. 3-1-37 Barksdale Field. 2-10-38 San Antonio Air Depot. Surveyed at San Antonio 5-26-38. TT 2,703 hours.

31-402 C-4A 5-AT-92 FF 1-30-31
Received at Bolling Field 2-5-31. 12-15-31 Wright Field. Redesignated XC-4A from 1-9-32 to 1-19-32. 1-19-32 Bolling Field. 9-14-32 Middletown Air Depot. 10-22-32 Bolling Field. Accident 4-24-33 at Bolling Field. 2-26-34 Eastern Zone for flying the Air Mail. 5-21-34 Bolling Field. 5-8-36 Wright Field. 6-11-36 Fairfield Air Depot. 12-5-36 Wright Field. Surveyed at Wright 7-9-38. TT 2,136 hours.

31-403 C-4A 5-AT-93 FF 2-5-31
Received at Selfridge Field 2-11-31. 2-17-31 Middletown Air Depot. 1-7-32 Selfridge Field. Accident 5-27-33 at Port Columbus, Ohio. 6-5-33 Fairfield Air Depot for repairs. 11-3-33 Selfridge Field. 3-22-34 Eastern Zone to fly the Air Mail. 5-22-34 Selfridge Field. Crashed 6-11-34 at Camp Skeel, Michigan. Surveyed at Selfridge 8-20-34. TT 1,355 hours.

31-404 C-4A 5-AT-95 FF 2-12-31
Received at Langley Field 2-19-31. 11-4-34 Fairfield Air Depot. 12-10-31 Langley Field. 7-7-32 Middletown Air Depot. 8-28-32 Langley Field. 4-18-33 Bolling Field. 1-16-34 Langley Field. 3-6-34 Eastern Zone to fly the Air Mail. 5-21-34 Langley Field. 10-15-34 Middletown Air Depot. 12-31-34 Langley Field. 2-10-37 Middletown Air Depot. 5-1-37 Langley Field. 6-29-37 Mitchel Field. 2-27-38 Chanute Field. Surveyed at Chanute 9-30-38. TT 3,503 hours.

Radio operator adjusts the shortwave radio in 29-226 (4-AT-86) U.S. Army Air Corps.

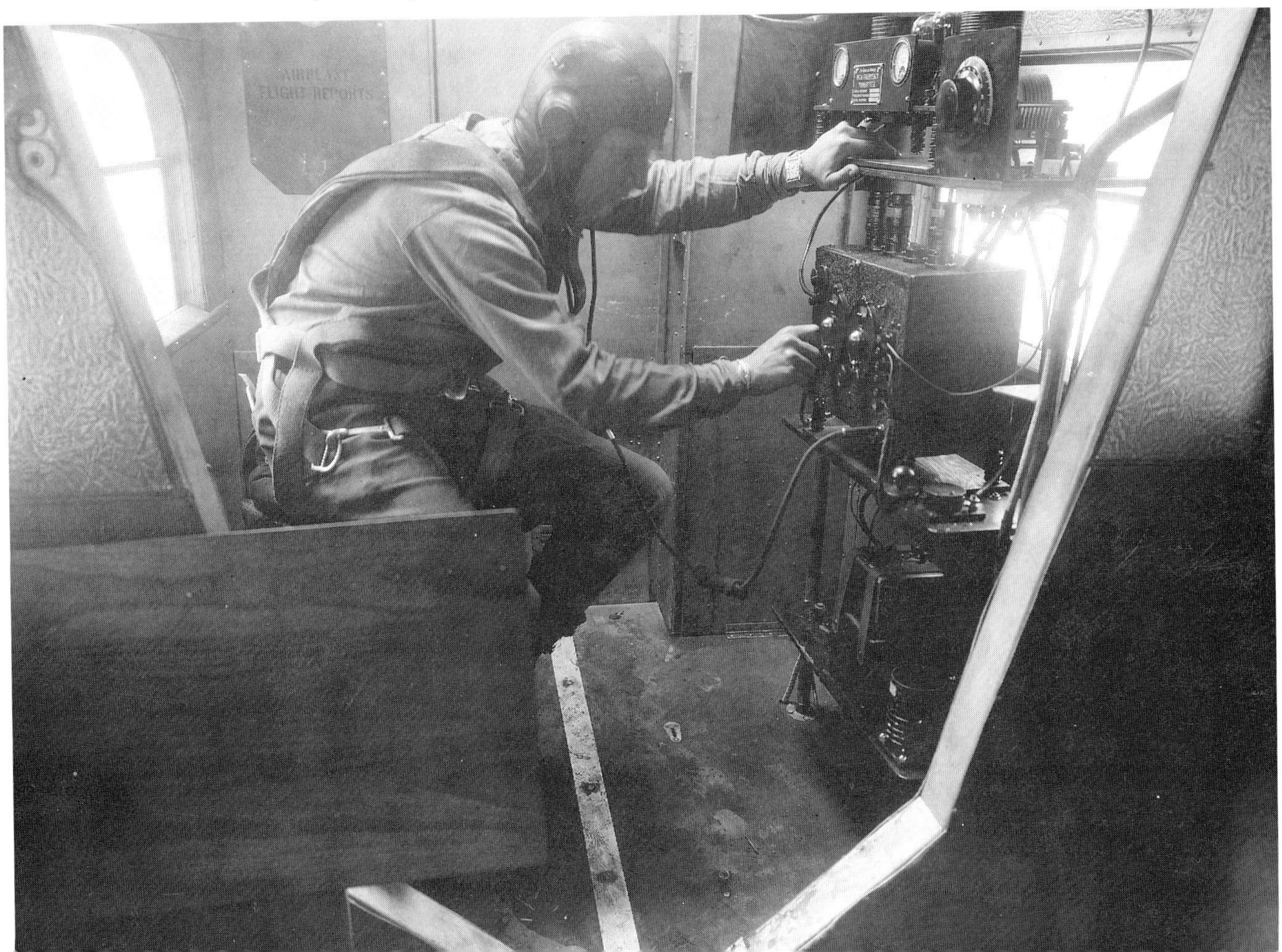

Army Endurance Tests With 5-AT-21

A civil registered Ford Tri-Motor was used by the Army Air Corps in 1929 for flight endurance tests. 5-AT-21, manufactured 1-23-29, was modified and given Identification Mark 9662 on 2-16-29 with additional reserve fuel tanks in the outer wing panels.

After being tested by the Air Corps it was returned to the factory and rebuilt back to 5-AT-B standards and sold to Transcontinental Air Transport with one of their block of reserved registration numbers (NC-9647) being assigned about 4-1-29.

An interesting sidelight to this story is the fact that the Ford Motor Company took it upon themselves to re-assign the number 9662 to 5-AT-29 without prior approval from the Department of Commerce. As a result they were reprimanded by the DofC Bureau of Air Commerce for not getting approval to re-use the registration mark.

A C-9 at Boeing Field, Seattle, Washington. This is probably 29-226 and it carries the insignia of the 20th Pursuit Group on the side of the fuselage. (G.S. Williams)

A C-9 of the 60th Service Squadron. (G.S. Williams)

A C-9 assigned to the 19th Observation Squadron at Scott Field, Illinois. (George Hardie Jr.)

Two Air Corps Fords Destroyed After Being Surveyed

The first, Ford C-9, A.C. 29-226, came to a dramatic ending on January 25, 1936 at Barksdale Field. The transport, which had been serving with the 3rd Attack Group, had been surveyed in September 1935 so the Materiel Division gave permission for its destruction by machine gun fire.

Each fuel tank was filled with 60 gallons of gasoline and the engines were then started by Staff Sgt Young, who

Left: C-9, 29-226, at Mather Field, Sacramento, CA, in April 1930. It was there for Air Corps field maneuvers and carries the red cross of a hospital plane. The crew consisted of two pilots, a flight surgeon and a medical attendant. The seats were removed from the cabin to make room for litters for four to six patients. (U.S. Air Force)

Below: Three C-9's from the First Pursuit Group at Selfridge Field, Michigan. (John Underwood Collection)

The interesting instrument panel of a C-9. The vertical instruments may have been used on all of the C-9's. Note the aircraft nameplate on the right between the spokes of the wheel. There was another version that was rectangular with square corners. (Ford Archives)

The ambulance interior of C-9, 29-226. Plans for the national Civilian Conservation Corps (CCC) included the availability of the C-9 ambulance plane for emergencies. (G.S. Williams)

By comparison, the ambulance interior of C-4A, 31-401. The larger cabin of the 5-AT-D contrasts with the 4-AT-E (C-9). This photo was taken on January 9, 1931. (Ford Archives)

had been the plane's first crew chief, and set to run at 1,000 rpm while three firing missions took place. When approximately 100 rounds from each gun had been fired on the third mission fire was seen to break out in the front of the left engine, spreading rapidly until the plane was a mass of twisted and molten metal.

The results of the firing, which had been observed from dugouts made for the occasion, led to the following conclusions: 1.) That an area seventy yards wide is a proper target for a three-ship element and that the length of the area depends upon the speed of the airplane and capabilities of the gun. 2.) That sweeping fire over an area is effective against material within the area. 3.) That machine gun fire is an effective agent against airplanes on the ground and will immobilize an outfit until all airplanes can be carefully inspected for damage to the interior structure.

The second, C-4, A.C. 29-219, was destroyed at March Field to test the results of fragmentation bombs. These 25-pound bombs were placed inside the fuselage to determine the effect on the metal structure. The engines had been removed and there was no fire involved as with the C-9. Photographs show extensive damage to the sides and top of the fuselage.

Air Corps Ambulance

C-9, Air Corps Number 29-226, was equipped to carry four to six patients plus a flight surgeon and medical attendant in addition to two pilots. It was equipped with a radio, medical instruments, drugs and dressings for emergency purposes, as well as drinking water, sterilized water, antiseptic solutions and splints.

U.S. Army Corps of Engineers

The Army did not want the Public Roads Administration operating in the Canzal Zone during World War II so the Corps of Engineers took over and as part of this set up their own air transportation service.

Eddie DeLarm was loaned by Pan American Airways and he purchased two Fords (NC-5577 and NC-7583) and a converted tri-motor Bach T-11-P (NC-34998), built a hangar and proceeded to fly seven days a week from November 1942 to December 1943 when the operation moved to Costa Rica.

A beautiful photograph of C-9, 29-222, on skis with the insignia of the First Pursuit Group. (Ford Archives)

The new C-4A, 31-401, at Wright Field for evaluation tests and the routine record photography. All Air Corps types, and some civilian visitors, were photographed in seven views with large cameras which produced a high quality 8"x10" negative. (U.S. Air Force)

A C-4A photographed on May 23, 1938. It carries the insignia of the Air Corps Technical School at Rantoul, Illinois so this is probably 31-404. (William F. Yeager)

C-4A, 31-402, in the snow at Newark, New Jersey. The insignia on the side is for the Bolling Field Detachment at Washington, DC. The square to the left of the insignia is the rank placard holder. When a General was aboard his star, or stars, would be displayed in the same fashion as Navy Command planes. (G.S. Williams)

A C-4A from Wright Field, probably 31-401, in a spectacular photo with nine Thomas-Morse 0-17's in flight overhead. (Hudek)

Wright Field's C-4A taking off from Boeing Field at Seattle. (G.S. Williams)

The single Air Corps 5-AT-B that was an oddity. It was delivered as a C-4, 29-219 (5-AT-38), but was re-designated C-4A in July 1931 even though it was not a 5-AT-D model. The paint scheme gives it the look of an American Airways Ford. (G.S. Williams)

The same plane on March 22, 1932 looking a lot more like a standard Air Corps utility transport. (B.C. Reed)

4-AT-37, the 4-AT-D flown for the Army Corps of Engineers in Panama in 1943. (Eddie DeLarm)

He flew 1,280 hours in thirteen months and completed every flight except one on time. That one flight delay was due to an engine swallowing a valve and he had to dump the load of mule feed in order to get back.

DeLarm prided himself on his punctuality and carried it to extremes to impress Colonel Ketchum, the Commanding Officer. As Eddie said, "I'd leave him out in the field at some junction with orders to pick him up at say 4:30 pm. I'd arrive 5 or 10 minutes ahead of time, hide behind a mountain and right on the second I'd pop around and hit the runway right on the button. He never knew how I had outfoxed him, and I'd carry things still further when one of his shavetails would show up one minute late. I'd take off right on the button - that was 6 am - and I didn't give a damn who got left. When the Colonel came I'd flag the chocks out and pour on the coal - not that I wanted to be an old meanie, just wanted to make the Colonel happy."

The XB-906 Bomber

One of the lesser known bomber proposals of the early 1930s was the Ford XB-906, a private venture involving a highly modified 5-AT-D airframe. Because it was only in existence for about five and a half months, and because of the usual Ford secrecy, little has been published on this interesting design.

Flight tested April 9, 1931 at the factory by Leroy Manning, it was a contemporary of the Keystone B-4A and B-6A biplane bombers with open cockpits. The all-metal Douglas Y1B-7 and the Boeing Y1B-9 had not yet been flown by the Army Air Corps.

Official performance tests were made at Wright Field, Dayton, Ohio, on June 27, 1931. The plane was flown by R.C. Moffat and Lt. H.J. Crocker, with ballast making up the weight of the other three crew members normally carried. The actual bomb load installed was 1,784 pounds with the remaining bomb load weight being compensated for by an overload of 36 gallons of gasoline.

Official performance figures from this test, with the throttles opened to stop below 7,000 feet in level flight was as follows:

Altitude	Speed
Sea Level	144.6 mph
5,000 ft	141.5 mph
7,000 ft	140.0 mph
10,000 ft	156 mph
15,000 ft	149.0 mph
18,400 ft	139.5 mph
20,000 ft	118.0 mph

The XB-906 Bomber at Wright Field for evaluation tests and photography in May 1931. It was flown to Wright Field by Leroy Manning on May 12, 1931, and returned by him to the factory on June 1st. While there it was test flown by a group of Air Corps pilots. (U.S. Air Force)

The X9652 on the fin is the civil registration of the plane. It was a Ford company sponsored project submitted as a proposal to the Air Corps. Leroy Manning was killed in the crash of this plane at Dearborn on September 19, 1931 while doing a dive test. (U.S. Air Force)

The average speed was 143.6 mph at 2020 rpm at 1,600 feet. A comparison of performance between the 5-AT-D and XB-906 is as follows:

	5-AT-D	**XB-906**
Empty weight	7,840 lbs.	8,345 lbs.
Gross weight	13,500 lbs.	14,137 lbs.
Maximum speed	150 mph	156 mph
Cruising speed	122 mph	135 mph
Landing speed	64 mph	66 mph
Service ceiling	14,200 ft	18,400 ft
Absolute ceiling	16,100 ft	20,000 ft
Crew + passengers	16	5
Bomb load	2,000 lbs.	
Total horsepower	1260/1350 hp	1500 hp

(Engines were P&W SR-1340E of 500 hp each)

Descriptions accompanying photographs in the company proposal are interesting, particularly in light of the critical comments made by the flight review board. They start out by saying, "The three supercharged Wasp engines in the Ford heavy bomber give it more power than is available for any twin-engine bomber powered with American engines. This high power results in speed and high ceiling. Also, for sea coast defense and long distance attacks any two of the three engines will fly the plane without necessity of jettisoning bombs or fuel. Thus, even if one of the engines is not functioning properly the tri-motor could probably complete its mission or at least save itself and personnel."

In discussing the armament a caption states, "Forward top gun has range of fire of whole upper hemisphere with considerable range in bottom hemisphere. The gun is well above the pilot. The pilot's position is enclosed to give maximum weather and temperature protection. This protection is particularly valuable at the high altitudes obtainable with the Ford Bomber. The transparent hatch above the pilot can be removed instantaneously."

The greatest disparity lies with the description of the pilot's visibility. Ford states, "The narrowed fuselage gives the pilot excellent vision on both sides. He can follow the target no matter which side it is on and later watch the bombs through the grilled floor. He is so far above the center engine it does not obstruct his vision. Rudder brakes facilitate taxying. The auxiliary dual flight control may be installed in any one of three available positions that is preferred by the Air Service." The Bombardment Board reported to the Chief of the Air Corps that, "this airplane is basically at fault in that the high wing, three engine monoplane type so restricts the vision as to prevent its use as a bombardment airplane for formation flying as a predominant requirement." In the original wooden mockup of the XB-906 the pilots cockpit was open and vision to the rear was considered to be adequate. But in enclosing the cockpit in standard Ford

Interior view of the XB-906 looking forward to the lower nose gun, bombardiers position and pilots cockpit overhead. The interior photos were taken at the factory in April 1931. (U.S. Air Force)

Tri-Motor fashion the pilot lost his ability to keep track of other aircraft in formation above and behind.

In addition the Air Corps tests found the plane to be difficult to fly with one wing engine out because of the high rudder forces required. Another deficiency was considered to be the high elevator forces required at low speeds and lack of control when the stabilizer was not rolled back. Another problem was oil on the bombardiers window which was directly below the nose engine. The final report was written as the result of the experiences of six Air Corps pilots flying the XB-906 while it was at Wright Field.

The plane was returned to the factory and lost during further testing. On September 19, 1931, it crashed at Dearborn killing the pilot and mechanic. William B. Mayo told the New York Times that, "so far as he could learn, the fliers, who had been aloft in the plane about an hour, put it into a power dive when at altitude of more than 5,000 feet, and that something apparently went wrong with one of the motors, which seemed to explode." Leroy Manning, the pilot, was Chief Test Pilot for Ford, as well as being a former Army pilot with the 94th Pursuit Squadron at Selfridge Field, so there could not have been a more experienced pilot at the controls.

Army Air Corps Fields Assigned Ford Tri-Motors

Albrook Field	Canal Zone
Barksdale Field	Shreveport, Louisiana
Bolling Field	Washington, DC
Brooks Field	San Antonio, Texas
Chanute Field	Rantoul, Illinois
Fairfield Air Depot	Fairfield, Ohio
Fort Crockett	Galveston, Texas
France Field	Canal Zone
Kelly Field	San Antonio, Texas
Langley Field	Hampton, Virginia
March Field	Riverside, California
Maxwell Field	Montgomery, Alabama
Middletown Air Depot	Middletown, Pennsylvania
Mitchel Field	Long Island, New York
Randolph Field	San Antonio, Texas
San Antonio Air Depot	San Antonio, Texas
Scott Field	Belleville, Illinois
Selfridge Field	Mt. Clemens, Michigan
Wright Field	Dayton, Ohio

The pilots cockpit in the XB-906 Bomber. It was designed and built to be flown by one pilot only, a distinct departure from all previous Ford designs. This change placed the throttles on the left instead of in the center. (U.S. Air Force)

A view showing the two top gunners positions. Note the different arrangement of cabin windows from the standard. (U.S. Air Force)

The top gunners position behind the pilot. (U.S. Air Force)

The first military Ford was 4-AT-4 shown here at the Anacostia Naval Air Station, Washington, DC. Note the elephant-ear ailerons and lack of military markings. (Larkins Collection)

U.S. Navy and U.S. Marine Corps

Nine Fords were sold to the U.S. Navy as follows: 1 XJR-1 (A7526), 2 JR-2's (A8273/A8274), 3 JR-3's (A8457, A8598/A8599), 1 RR-4 (A8840), and 2 RR-5's (A9205/A9206). Five of these (8273, 8274, 8598, 8840 and 9205 went to the U.S. Marine Corps).

The "J" for Utility model designation of the Ford transports, as well as other Navy airplanes, was changed to "R" for Transport in 1931. Both of these designations were the equivalent of the Army's "Service Squadron." Thus the JR-2's became RR-2's and the JR-3's became RR-3's except for A8598 which had been stricken before this change took place.

The Navy was the first service to buy a Ford, taking delivery ten months before the Army received theirs. The XJR-1 was only the fourth Tri-Motor built and this shows the Navy's interest in all-metal aircraft at an early date. The plane was demonstrated to the Navy before purchase and photos show it going through several modifications and updates during the three short years that it was in service. The accompanying photos show exterior changes in the propellers, nose engine, windshield, ailerons and vertical tail surfaces.

The Navy used the XJR-1 during a Navy Day program in October 1927 when nine Navy parachutists jumped from the plane over Washington, D.C. The men taking part in this first of a kind demonstration were: A.F. Starr, T. Dworzymsky, G.F. Hayes, J. Fisher, W. Cooper, T. Nickle, W.F. Scott Jr., T. Clark and R.F. Ryder.

As the Air Corps had done, the Navy also was involved with a civilian plane but this was more of a sales proposal by Ford than an engineering test. 5-AT-74 (NC-414H) was fitted with two 30 foot long Aircraft Products

Model A-27000 floats at the Philadelphia Navy Yard in February 1930. Flight tests showed a top speed of 127 mph, a cruising speed of 103 mph and a stalling speed of 65 mph. Takeoff from the water was in 17 seconds. It was demonstrated as a 20 passenger troop transport or a hospital air ambulance.

A further proposal was made on paper for it to be built as a torpedo bomber which would indicate that plans were under discussion at this time for the XB-906 which flew a year later. The proposal called for the Ford to carry two Mark IV torpedoes weighing 1,800 pounds each. Or, as a bomber with wheels, it would carry a useful load of 6,000 pounds; equivalent to a cargo of pilot, radio operator, bombardier, gunner, three machine guns, two 1,100 pound bombs, 800 pounds of smaller demolition bombs, and sufficient fuel for five to six hours of flight. It is interesting to note the first mention of a single pilot for the Ford Tri-Motor, an idea that was finally realized in the XB-906.

Later in 1930 it was flown to NAS Anacostia for demonstration flights before Navy officials there. Nothing further developed with the Navy bomber concept and all of the Navy Ford Tri-Motors served as transports.

A photo taken a short time later with a large NAVY under the wing. (Everett J. Payette)

The same plane after having its windshield and ailerons changed. It was now designated XJR-1. (U.S. Navy)

Individual Histories, U.S. Navy and Marine Corps

A-7526 XJR-1 4-AT-4 FF 1-29-27
Delivered 3-9-27 to NAS Anacostia. 4-25-27 Naval Aircraft Factory, Philadelphia, for repairs. 5-27 Anacostia. 11-18-27 empennage crushed and right wing broken due to tornado. 8-21-29 to Naval Aircraft Factory for repairs. Stricken at the NAF 4-30-30. TT 971 hours.

A-8273 JR-2 4-AT-59 FF 2-12-29
Delivered 6-21-29 to NAS Anacostia, then to Quantico. 3-29-31 USMC San Diego. 4-28-31 USMC Nicaragua. 8-1-32 to NAF for repairs after crash in Cuba 7-2-32. 12-9-32 West Coast Expeditionary Force VJ-7M. Stricken 1-31-35 at San Diego. TT 1,788 hours.

A-8274 JR-2 4-AT-60 FF 2-18-29
Delivered 6-12-29 to NAS Anacostia. 10-30-30 Wright Aeronautical Corp., Paterson, NJ. 11-10-30 Anacostia. 7-21-31 NAF for painting. 8-5-31 Commander Aircraft Scouting Force (?) Flag Unit, 9-22-31 NAF. 1-25-32 Quantico. 7-6-32 Nicaragua. 1-12-33 Quantico. Stricken 7-31-34. TT 578 hours.

A-8457 JR-3 5-AT-72 FF 8-26-29
Delivered 10-3-19 to NAS Anacostia (used by David Ingalls, Assistant Secretary of the Navy for Air). 1-28-31 San Diego. 9-2932 NAF for overhaul. 2-23-33 San Diego. Stricken 12-31-34 at San Diego. TT 1,594 hours.

A-8598 JR-3 5-AT-82 FF 12-27-29
Released from factory 4-30-30, to USMC. To Nicaragua 5-12-30. Crashed at Ocotal, Nicaragua, 8-4-30. Stricken 9-30-30. TT 119 hours.

A-8599 JR-3 5-AT-83 FF 4-2-30
Delivered 5-21-30 to Quantico. 8-23-30 Nicaragua. 7-18-32 NAF. 1 10-18-32 Nicaragua. 1-12-33 Quantico. Crashed at Virginia Beach near Norfolk 3-22-33. Stricken 5-3-33. TT 272 hours.

A-8840 RR-4 5-AT-84 FF 10-3-1-30
Delivered 11-9-30 to NAS Anacostia. 1-20-31 NAF. 1-28-31 Anacostia. 3-6-33 NAF. 10-10-33 Anacostia.5-1-34 Quantico. 5-23-34 Pensacola. 12-12-34 Aircraft Two San Diego. 9-25-35 NAF for overhaul. 1-16-36 Quantico (nosed up on takeoff 2-1-36). 10-16-36 VJ-6M Quantico. Stricken 5-29-37 at Quantico. TT 148 hours.

A-9205 RR-5 5-AT-109 FF 12-15-31
Delivered 12-23-31 to NAS Anacostia. 12-31-31 to Marine Corps in Nicaragua. 1-12-33 Quantico. 9-17-34 Naval Aircraft Factory for overhaul. 11-15-34 Quantico. 1-18-35 Naval Aircraft Factory. 2-835 Quantico. 10-2-35 NAS Pensacola. Stricken 8-31-37 at Pensacola. TT 1,836 hours.

A-9206 RR-5 5-AT-105 FF 9-25-31?
Delivered 2-17-32 to NAS Anacostia. 12-10-34 Pensacola. Worn out in service, stricken at Pensacola 7-11-40. TT 2,784 hours.

Naval Air Stations Assigned Ford Tri-Motors

Anacostia	Washington, DC
Naval Aircraft Factory	Philadelphia, Pennsylvania
Pensacola	Pensacola, Florida
Quantico	MCAS Quantico, Virginia
San Diego	San Diego, California

Further modification to the XJR-1 with a three-bladed prop on the nose and a 4-AT-B windshield. (Peter M. Bowers)

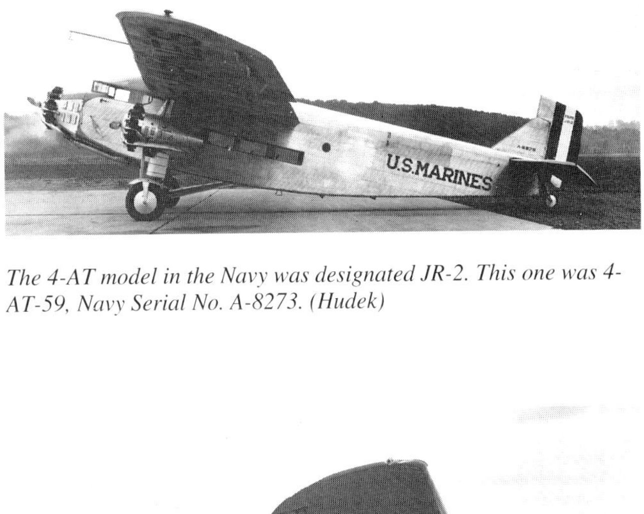

The 4-AT model in the Navy was designated JR-2. This one was 4-AT-59, Navy Serial No. A-8273. (Hudek)

5-AT-105 photographed on December 10, 1937 while assigned to NAS Anacostia. (William Yeager)

5-AT-109 with Marine Corps Air Station Quantico #2 on the rudder. (Larkins Collection)

New 5-AT-82 at the factory April 29, 1930. At this time the Navy-Marine Corps 5-AT-C was designated JR-3. (Ford Archives)

The RR-4 (5AT-84) assigned to NAS Pensacola. Note the wind driven generator on top of the rear fuselage. (R.O. Moore)

The same plane, 5-AT-84, while in service with the U.S. Marine Corps in 1936. (John C. Mitchell)

Chapter 6
Export and Foreign Activities

The use of the Ford Tri-Motor has been world-wide, with perhaps the operations in South America being the best known because of their dramatic appeal. Certainly the pioneering efforts by Pan American to cross the Andes Mountains attracted the attention of newspapers and magazines, as well as early newsreel motion pictures, to make a lasting impression.

All Pan American-Grace Fords flew in Central and South America at one time or another, and most of them probably joined the Fokker Tri-motors in the route encircling South America, which means that they flew over Mexico, Guatemala, Honduras, Nicaragua, Costa Rica, Panama, Colombia, Ecuador, Peru, Chile, Argentina, Uruguay, Brazil, French-Dutch British Guinea and Venezuela.

It has taken over forty years to determine the national registrations in this chapter as documented information is not only scarce but often incomplete and inaccurate. As a result, as will be commented on in various areas, a large number of identifications remain unknown. One of the largest groups is Honduras and it is hoped that some day old TACA records may be found to solve this problem as it is unlikely that any government records have survived years of political upheaval.

Argentina (R)
Three Fords were operated in Argentina by NYRBA under the name New York Safety Airways. NC-1780, an early 4-AT-A, was loaded for shipment from New York in June 1929. Photos taken in Argentina show it with both NC-1780 and R-131 on it at the same time and the name "Rio de la Plata." Two additional NYRBA planes have been identified after many years by records of their engine serial numbers. A fourth plane was registered by Panagra and it is possible that a fifth Argentine registration was also issued to them.

May 1930: 4-AT-68 being loaded on a barge for reloading on to a ship bound for Spain. (Ford Archives)

LUNCHROOM
CB406

The planes were:

Registration	Serial No.	U.S. Reg.	Airline
R-130	5-AT-55	NC-8417	NYRBA "Mendoza"
R-131	4-AT-11	NC-1780	NYRBA "Rio de la Plata"
R-148	5-AT-63	NC-404H	NYRBA
R-176	5-AT-61	NC-402H	Panagra

Pan American-Grace Airways flew Fords on a weekly schedule (with U.S. Registration) from Santiago, Chile, to Buenos Aires, Argentina. The first plane to open this service, named "Santiago", left Buenos Aires on September 4, 1929. It was a ten and a half hour flight via Rosario, Cordoba and Mendoza and the lunch served aboard was reported to have been the first time that this had been done in South America.

Just one month later pilot Raymond Williams, and Panagra Vice President John C. MacGregor, flew the reverse route with the first mail for the United States from Buenos Aires. A lengthy description of the flight by MacGregor (*New York Times* 10-14-29, pg. 16) included the comments, "We left Mendoza at 4 PM, this being the best flying hour over the Cordillera, and we arrived at Santiago at 5:20. Our average altitude over the Uspallata Pass twenty miles south of Mt. Aconcagua . . . was 18,000 feet. Because of the heaters we did not need overcoats . . . the Ford acted magnificently and reached the necessary altitude in forty minutes, with the motors turning at 1,650 revolutions."

5-AT-60 being airlifted out of the Lake Myola lakebed in New Guinea by a Royal Australian Air Force Chinook, of the 12th Squadron, in October 1979. The drogue chute is to stabilize the free swinging fuselage. The Ford, RAAF A45-1, crashed during World War II while evacuating wounded soldiers. (Bruce D. Hoy)

Australia (VH)
Four Fords were registered in Australia, all having come from England. These were, in their order of arrival in Australia:

VH-UTB (5-AT-68) Australian Certificate of Registration No. 501 issued 12-10-34 to Guinea Airways Ltd., Lae, New Guinea. It was operated by them until 10-23-41 when it was written off in an accident at Wau. (Although most of the famous air-freight operations at the Bulolo Gold Mines were carried out with Junkers G-23 and Ju 52 aircraft, VH-UTB did fly parts of a dredge in from Wau just before the outbreak of World War II.

VH-USX (4-AT-68) Australian Certificate of Registration No. 525 issued 5-24-35 to Holden Air Transport Services Ltd., Salamaua, New Guinea. On 6-24-35 the plane had a forced landing due to a collapsed piston, and on 2-20-36 again made a forced landing due to a cylinder barrel splitting. On 5-14-37 the plane was sold to Guinea Airways Ltd., and moved to Lae. It was eventually lost to enemy action in January, 1942.

VH-UBI (5-AT-60) Australian Certificate of Registration No. 554 issued 10-26-35 to Guinea Airways Ltd. The aircraft was involved in an accident 7-21-38 and out of action until 6-4-40. It was then flown until 2-6-42 when it was impressed into military duty and delivered to the Royal Australian Air Force Unit at Townsville, Queensland, and assigned RAAF Serial No. A-45-1. It is believed to have been converted into an ambulance plane and crashed in 1942.

VH-UDY (4-AT-61) Australian Certificate of Registration No. 519 issued 1-8-36 to Holdens Air Transport Services Ltd. Transferred to Guinea Airways on 7-15-37 and operated by them until 2-6-42 when it was also impressed into the RAAF, given the serial A-45-2, and delivered to the RAAF Unit at Townsville.
Recovered in October, 1979, and awaiting reconstruction at the National Museum in Papua, New Guinea. See Chapter 12.

Bolivia (CB)
U.S. Registered Fords of Pan American-Grace operated in Bolivia in 1937 transporting one million pounds of mining machinery over the Andes mountains from La Paz to the Aramayo Mine in the Tipuani Valley. A rough "airport" was constructed at the mine and the machinery was hauled in by loading the Fords through special hatches cut in the top of the fuselage near the door. These

5-AT-55, with both U.S. registration of NC-8417, and Argentine registration R-130, upon its arrival in Buenos Aires in 1930. NYRBA pilot Eddie DeLarm flew the plane, named "Mendoza", from the U.S. to Argentina. (Eddie DeLarm)

The same plane later in the markings of the government airline L.A.N. (Harry Yerex)

were replaced in 1939 and 1940 by three Fords sold to Compania Aramayo de Mines. CB-CAM is the only known registration.

In September 1932 a new 5-AT-D was sold to the airline Lloyd Aero Boliviano. Because of the war between Ecuador and Paraguay it was immediately impressed into military service so may not have ever had a civil registration. Unfortunately it crashed within a month.

The four known aircraft are:

Registration	Model	Serial Number	US Registration
5-AT-D	5-AT-113	NC-9654 (1932)	CB-CAM
5-AT-B	5-AT-17	NC-9639 (1939)	CB-?
5-AT-C	5-AT-77	NC-417H (1940)	CB-?
5-AT-C	5-AT-80	NC-420H (1940)	

Canada (G-CXXX, CF)
Four Fords were registered in Canada as follows:

Registration	Model	Serial No.	Former Registration
G-CARC	4-AT-A	4-AT-10	NC-1077
G-CATX	4-AT-B	4-AT-26	NC-5810
G-CYWZ	6-AT	6-AT-1	None
CF-AZB	4-AT-A	4-AT-3	NC-3041
CF-BEP	6-AT	6-AT-1	G-CYWZ

6-AT-1 was built as a seaplane and was licensed by the Department of Commerce under Memo 2-80. It was first flown on May 14, 1929, purchased by the Royal Canadian Air Force for $92,650 and delivered in June as G-CYWZ.

At that time Canadian government airplanes, including military aircraft, carried a civil registration in the early Canadian series G (Great Britain) - C (Canada). Only the last two letters were painted on the RCAF planes, however, and thus the Ford was known as "Old WZ."

It was initially used by the Civil Government Air Operations Division for experiments in forest dusting, and for this purpose operated from rivers and lakes on large twin Brewster floats. For further information on this period of its life see Chapter 7.

In 1931 WZ carried service personnel for the RCAF Armstrong-Whitworth "Siskin" fighters on the Trans Canada Air Pagent. In 1932 the plane was reconditioned by the RCAF as it was rapidly becoming obsolete.

In 1935 it was reconditioned at St. Hubert airport for radio test work. It was flown from there on August 7th to the RCAF Station at Ottawa (Rockcliffe) and was then allocated on loan to the Controller of Civil Aviation for five months to carry out radio and night flying tests between Ottawa and St. Hubert. During this time the RCAF provided the crew to fly the plane, and much of the experimental work was for the purpose of testing various types of radio compasses. Early in December WZ was transferred again to St. Hubert where there were adequate hangar facilities for the winter months. The plane apparently made its last flight for the RCAF on January 9, 1936 when it made a final radio test flight. It was then put into storage for the winter.

In May 1936 instructions were given to dismantle the aircraft and it remained in a hangar at St. Hubert for the remainder of the year. Although its logbook showed only 494 flying hours since it had been purchased it was in need of extensive repair and overhaul. In view of the fact that the type was no longer in production, and that the RCAF had no need for such an aircraft, it was decided in January 1937 to offer it for sale.

On January 16, 1937, tenders were called for (G.S.2256), the aircraft being listed as dismantled with engines removed, in storage at St. Hubert and in need of complete overhaul. The successful bidder was G.W.G.

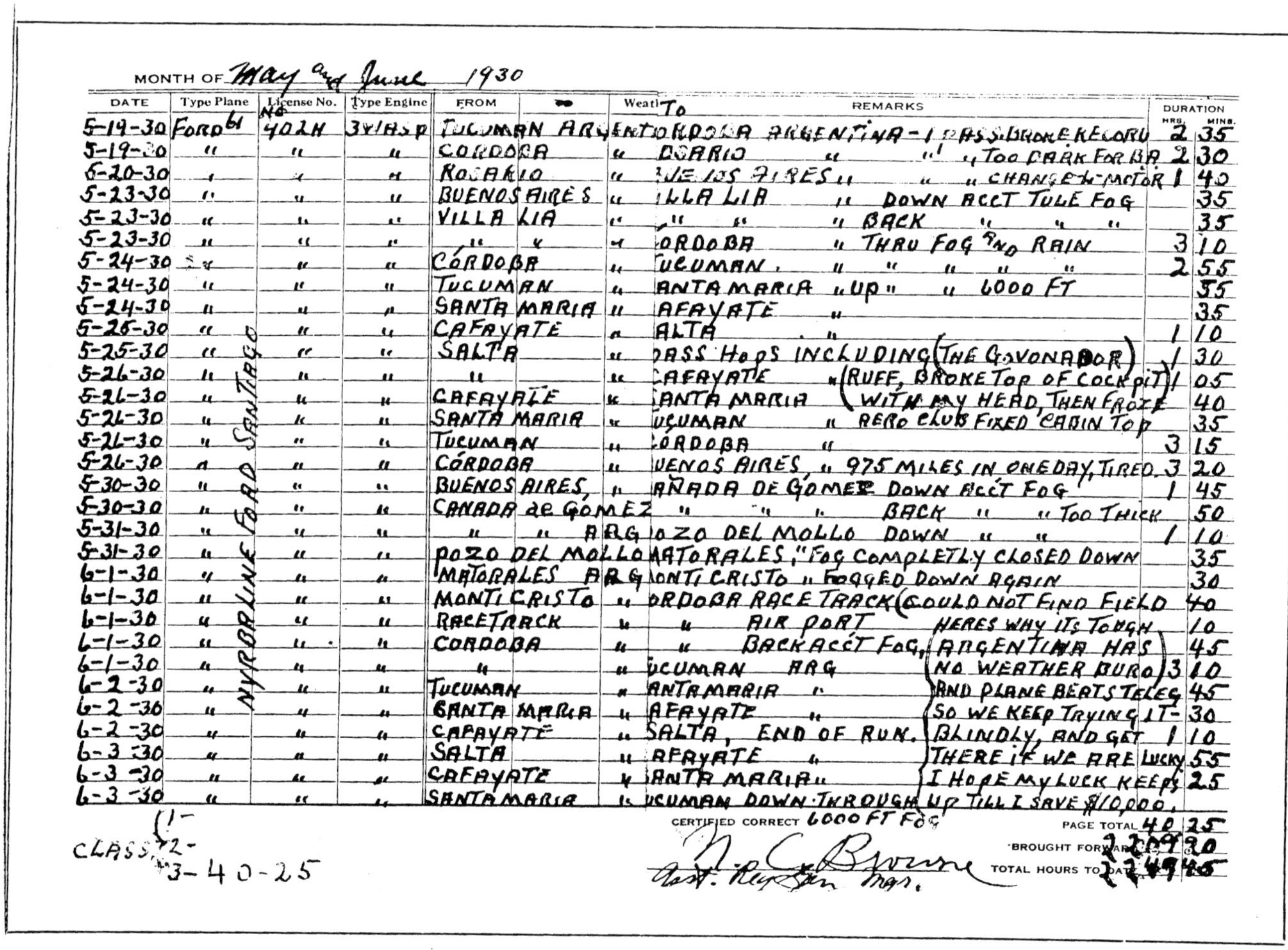

MONTH OF May and June 1930

DATE	Type Plane	License No.	Type Engine	FROM	Weather	TO / REMARKS	HRS.	MINS.
5-19-30	Ford 61	NC 402H	3 Wasp	TUCUMAN ARGENTINA		CORDOBA ARGENTINA - 1 PASS. BROKE RECORD	2	35
5-19-30	"	"	"	CORDOBA	"	ROSARIO " " " TOO DARK FOR BA	2	30
5-20-30	"	"	"	ROSARIO	"	BUENOS AIRES " " " CHANGE 1 MOTOR	1	40
5-23-30	"	"	"	BUENOS AIRES	"	VILLA LIA " DOWN ACCT TULE FOG		35
5-23-30	"	"	"	VILLA LIA	"	" " " BACK " " "		35
5-23-30	"	"	"	" "	"	CORDOBA " THRU FOG AND RAIN	3	10
5-24-30	"	"	"	CÓRDOBA	"	TUCUMAN " " " " "	2	55
5-24-30	"	"	"	TUCUMAN	"	SANTA MARIA " UP " " 6000 FT		55
5-24-30	"	"	"	SANTA MARIA	"	CAFAYATE "		35
5-25-30	"	"	"	CAFAYATE	"	SALTA "	1	10
5-25-30	"	"	"	SALTA	"	PASS HOPS INCLUDING (THE GOVONADOR)	1	30
5-26-30	"	"	"	"	"	CAFAYATE " (RUFF, BROKE TOP OF COCKPIT	1	05
5-26-30	"	"	"	CAFAYATE	"	SANTA MARIA WITH MY HEAD, THEN FROZE)		40
5-26-30	"	"	"	SANTA MARIA	"	TUCUMAN " AERO CLUB FIXED CABIN TOP		35
5-26-30	"	"	"	TUCUMAN	"	CORDOBA "	3	15
5-26-30	"	"	"	CÓRDOBA	"	BUENOS AIRES " 975 MILES IN ONE DAY, TIRED.	3	20
5-30-30	"	"	"	BUENOS AIRES,	"	CAÑADA DE GOMEZ DOWN ACCT FOG	1	45
5-30-30	"	"	"	CANADA DE GOMEZ	"	" " " BACK " " TOO THICK		50
5-31-30	"	"	"	" " ARG		POZO DEL MOLLO DOWN " "	1	10
5-31-30	"	"	"	POZO DEL MOLLO		MATORALES, "FOG COMPLETLY CLOSED DOWN		35
6-1-30	"	"	"	MATORALES ARG		MONTI CRISTO " FOGGED DOWN AGAIN		30
6-1-30	"	"	"	MONTI CRISTO	"	CORDOBA RACE TRACK (COULD NOT FIND FIELD		40
6-1-30	"	"	"	RACETRACK	"	" AIR PORT HERES WHY ITS TOUGH		10
6-1-30	"	"	"	CORDOBA	"	" BACK ACCT FOG, ARGENTINA HAS		45
6-1-30	"	"	"	"	"	TUCUMAN ARG NO WEATHER BURO	3	10
6-2-30	"	"	"	TUCUMAN	"	SANTA MARIA " AND PLANE BEATS TELEG		45
6-2-30	"	"	"	SANTA MARIA	"	CAFAYATE " SO WE KEEP TRYING IT-		30
6-2-30	"	"	"	CAFAYATE	"	SALTA, END OF RUN. BLINDLY, AND GET	1	10
6-3-30	"	"	"	SALTA	"	CAFAYATE " THERE IF WE ARE LUCKY		55
6-3-30	"	"	"	CAFAYATE	"	SANTA MARIA " I HOPE MY LUCK KEEPS		25
6-3-30	"	"	"	SANTA MARIA	"	TUCUMAN DOWN THROUGH 6000 FT FOG UP TILL I SAVE $10,000.		

NYRBALINE FORD SANTIAGO

CLASS 1- 2- 3- 40-25

CERTIFIED CORRECT [illegible signature] Asst. Reg. Gen. Mgr.

PAGE TOTAL 40 25

BROUGHT FORWARD 2209 20

TOTAL HOURS TO DATE 2249 45

A page from Eddie DeLarm's log book while flying 5-AT-55 for NYRBA in May and June 1930. His fascinating personal remarks, such as "Ruff, broke top of cockpit with my head", and "Heres why its tough Argentina has no weather buro and plane beats teleg so we keep trying it blindly, and get there if we are lucky. I hope my luck keeps up till I save $10,000." (Eddie DeLarm)

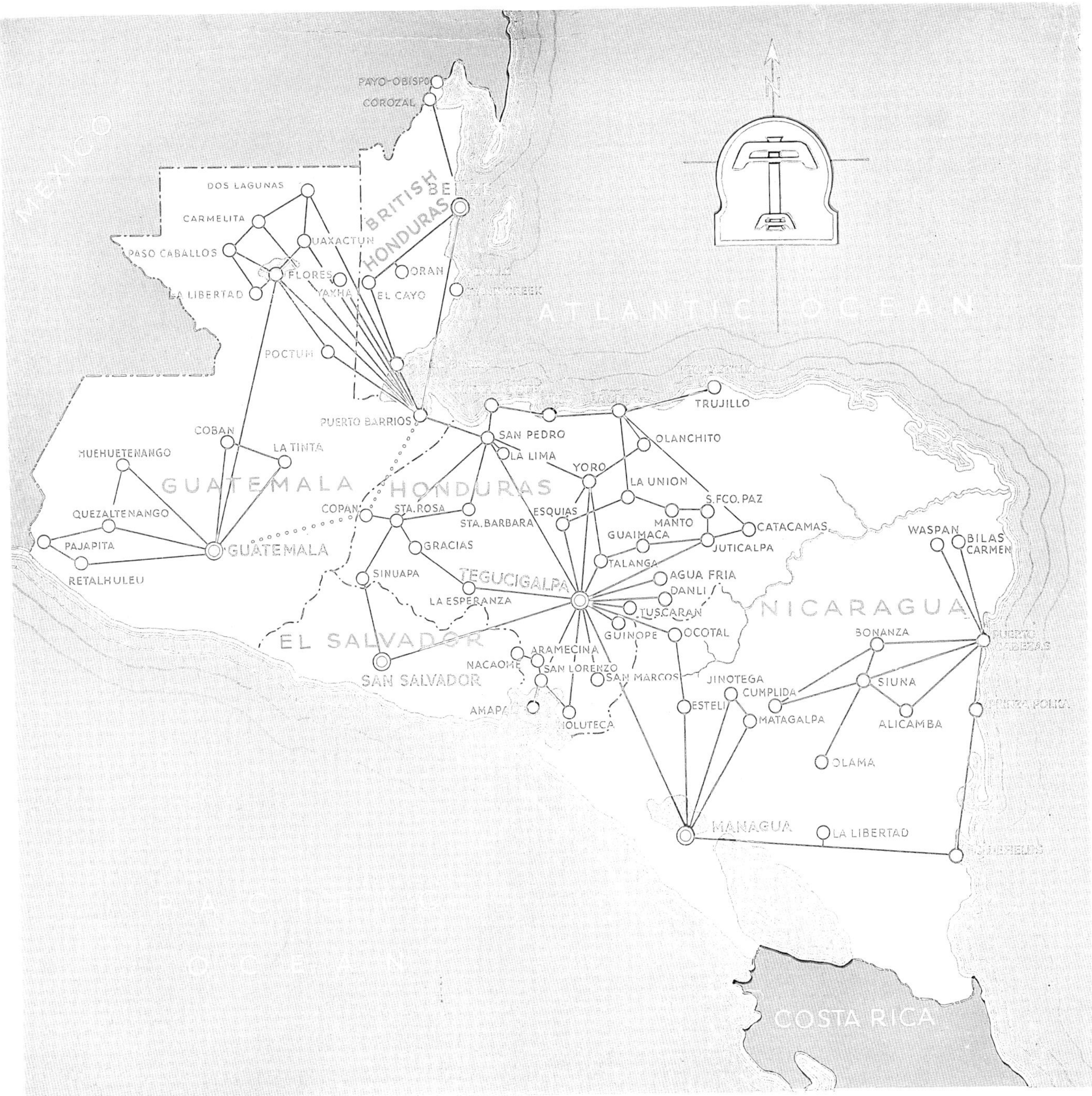

The network of air lines operated by Transportes Aereos Centro Americanos in Central America. In addition to the regular aerodromes shown on the map TACA maintains many auxiliary landing fields throughout British Honduras, Guatemala, Honduras, El Salvador and Nicaragua for special flights when sufficient loads are available.

TACA map courtesy of the Intava World, October, 1939

McConachie of Edmonton, Alberta, who offered $3,500 for WZ and it was sold to him on February 27th by authority of Salvage Minute No. 9543.

It was later assembled and put into flying condition at St. Hubert, at a cost of $8,500, and was operated by McConachie Air Transport under the new civil registration CF-BEP. It was used to carry passengers, mail and freight between Vancouver and Whitehorse. For further information on it's spectacular accident when hit by an RCAF Hawker Hurricane, see Chapter 10.

WZ was one of the few Ford Tri-Motors to operate on wheels, floats and skis and was probably the first tri-motored duster operated on floats in the world.

Chile ("F")

A great deal of confusion has existed over the Fords that went to Chile. There were four Export Certificates issued, and a letter from the Director of Aeronautics in Santiago in 1953 confirmed this and stated that they had been given the identity markings of F-1 through F-4, with the F meaning "Ford", since airline aircraft in Chile in 1930 did not carry civil markings.

Now, however, it seems conclusive from material in the FAA files that only three planes went to Chile. The list is as follows:

Date	Export Cert. No.	Serial No.	U.S. Reg
1-2-30	E-251	5-AT-66	NC-407H
1-2-30	E-252	5-AT-76	NC-416H
11-19-30	E-355	5-AT-85	NC-425H
3-11-31	E-381	5-AT-75	NC-415H

The Export Certificate for 5-AT-75 was requested by the Chilean Government who would not buy the aircraft until it had been issued. After it was issued the decision was changed and they did not buy the plane, and Firestone Tire & Rubber Company sold it instead to American Airways on 10-23-31.

In addition to this there has been the mysterious "ambulance plane." This was mentioned in two places but there is now some doubt that it ever existed. The company house organ "Ford News" for December 15, 1930, described, "the first completely equipped ambulance plane turned out by the Ford factory. Fittings include an emergency operating table to enable surgeons to perform operations while in flight, a complete sterilizing unit, an equipment of instruments and two litters for the transportation of wounded or ill passengers." The second mention was in "Foreign Air News" for 2-27-31, produced by the Civil Aeronautics Board, which states, "A tri-motor ambulance plane has been purchased by the National Air Lines of Chile. It will be used on regular passenger service and is convertible to an ambulance when necessary." One possible answer to this puzzle is that negotiations were going on between Ford and the Chilean government over a proposal to re-build the Firestone Ford as an ambulance plane and that the cost became so expensive that the order was cancelled.

4-AT-61 operating in Australia in 1936 with its British registration G-ABEF before becoming VH-UDY. (N.H. Cranstoun)

5-AT-60 with Guinea Airways Ltd., prior to its being impressed into service with the Royal Australian Air Force in World War II. (M.E. Jones)

4-AT-26 of British Columbia Airways that crashed August 25, 1928. (Peter M. Bowers)

The 6-AT-1, RCAF's "WZ", on skis. (RCAF)

6-AT-1 after service with the RCAF. (Peter M. Bowers)

China

Seven Fords went to China but there has never been any evidence of the use of an international civil registration on any of them. The CNAC planes used names on the nose and small numbers on the tail, as for example "KUNMING #23."

The aircraft, in the order of their shipment to China, are as follows:

Date	Serial No.	U.S. Reg.	Delivered To
7-31*	5-AT-65	NC-406H	Marshall Chang Hseuh-Liang
2-5-32	5-AT-99	NC-432H	Marshall Chang Hseuh-Liang
2-3-35	5-AT-115	NC-9658	C.N.A.C. (#23?)
8-1-35	5-AT-116	NC-9659	C.N.A.C. (#26?)
10-23-35	5-AT-101	NC-15551	C.N.A.C. (#27?)
4-36	5-AT-79A	NC-8485	China Aviation School
4-36	5-AT-94	NC-8486	China Aviation School

*Date of sale. The plane was already in China on a sales tour. The original Export Certificate was issued 1-29-30.

Colombia (F, C, HK)

Colombia operated more Ford Tri-Motors than any other South American country. The total number appears to be

20, plus the single-engine 8-AT.

The list, in the order of their Export Certificate and shipment to Colombia is as follows:

Date	Model	Serial Number	U.S. Reg.	Col. Reg
1934	5-AT-A	5-AT-1	NC-6926	C-210?
1934	5-AT-D	5-AT-111	NC-434H	
1934	5-AT-D	5-AT-112	NC-438H	C-31
1935	5-AT-D	5-AT-106	NC-439H	
1935	5-AT-B	5-AT-6	NC-9643	F-31
1935	5-AT-B	5-AT-16	NC-9638	F-32
1935	5-AT-D	5-AT-104	NC-437H	C-202
1935	5-AT-DS	5-AT-114	NC-9657	
1935	5-AT-D	5-AT-108	NC-9653	C-203
1936	5-AT-C	5-AT-69	NC-401H	(Floats)
1936	5-AT-C	5-AT-67	NC-408H	(Army)

A Chinese Army 5-AT-D, #1801, at Chungking in 1938. (John Underwood)

An Interesting fake photo purporting to show a Chinese 5-AT in flight with the nose engine gone. If it could have been flown at all it would have been so unbalanced that it would be impossible to fly with the elevators in the neutral position. (Peter M. Bowers)

One of the 5-AT's of the China Aviation School at Hangchow. (G.S. Williams)

SACO airliner 5-AT-16 at Roosevelt Field, New York, prior to its delivery to Colombia. (G.S. Williams)

5-AT-89 at North Beach Airport, New York, prior to leaving for Colombia. Note the Shell Oil name painted out on the fuselage and the late airline radio mast. (Larkins Collection)

5-AT-61 with all of its windows removed and converted into a freighter with the Colombian registration C206. (Larkins Collection)

SCADTA's 5-AT-106 in front of one of its hangars in Colombia. The former United Air Lines insignia on the side of the fuselage has been rubbed off but portions still show. (R.E.G. Davies)

1936	5-AT-B	5-AT-44	NC-9687	(Army)
1936	5-AT-C	5-AT-47	NC-9690	(Army)
1936	5-AT-C	5-AT-89	NC-429H	(Army)
1937	8-AT-A	8-AT-1	NC-8499	
1938	5-AT-C	5-AT-86	NC-426	HC-207, HK-1501E
1938	5-AT-C	5-AT-49	NC-8411	
1938	5-AT-C	5-AT-54	NC-8416	C-204
1938	5-AT-C	5-AT-61	NC-402	HC-206
1939	5-AT-C	5-AT-22	NC-9672	C-205
1939	5-AT-C	5-AT-80	NC-420H	C-208

AVIANCA (Aerovias Nacionales de Colombia S.A.) stated in a letter that they operated C-202 (5-AT-D), C-203 (5-AT-D), C-210 (5-AT-A?), and C-270 (5-AT-C). Flying magazine, May 1944, pg. 54, and September 1944 pg. 48, has photos of C-210 and it is named "Santander."

In May 1935 the German controlled Colombian airline SCADTA (Sociedad Colombo-Alemana de Transportes Aereos, taken over by AVIANCA in World War II) bought 5-AT-D NC-9657 from United Air Lines. It was flown to North Beach Airport, New York, for modifications including the installation of an additional door on the left side of the fuselage (the only Ford known to have a door on both sides of the fuselage), and the mounting of 30' 7" long Edo 43-14060 twin floats. Special instruments were added and the plane, now a 5-AT-DS, was licensed as a ten passenger transport with a crew of two or three. The third crew member was a hostess for which a special jump seat was installed. With a gross weight of 14,000 pounds it would cruise at 122 mph at sea level. This Ford, and possibly one other, were purchased for operation out of Barranquilla on the winding Magalena River.

In addition to the civil operation there were four Fords in the Colombian Army. One of these was flown to Bolling Field, Washington, DC, by Colonel Benjamin Mendez, in May 1936. Col. Mendez, a U.S. Army Air Corps trained pilot, brought the ship in for the purpose of meeting the Minister of Colombia, Senor Don Miguel Lopez, and Senora de Lopez, and flying them back to their home in Bogota for the summer.

The four Colombian Army aircraft were in the order of the issuance of their Export Certificates:

5-AT-67	NC-408	HE-1810	issued 1-29-36
5-AT-44	NC-9687	E-1816	issued 2-13-36
5-AT-47	NC-9690	E-1860	issued 3-31-36
5-AT-89	NC-429H	E-1903	issued 4-01-36

C207, another 5-AT freighter. Identity uncertain, probably the plane mistakenly identified as C270 in correspondence from the Colombian government in 1953. Photo taken at Dallas, Texas, in 1941. (Charles Schuler)

Colombian Army 5-AT on floats at the Edo factory in New York. It is probably 5-AT-44. (Larkins Collection)

The first three were purchased from American Airlines and the fourth from Shell Oil Company. All four were overhauled in the AA shops at Chicago. 5-AT-67 was fitted with float reinforcements although floats were not installed. The four planes were ferried to New York. Roger Q. Williams was one of the pilots that checked out the Colombian Army pilots who then flew them from New York to Colombia. They were assigned Fuerza Aerea Colombiana serial numbers 641-644 but no documents have surfaced so far to identify them. FAC 643 crashed in April 1941 while on floats. Photos of the planes at New York show both #2 and #3 on twin floats. FAC 641 remained, in unserviceable condition, until 1944.

Costa Rica (TI)

The identity of the following Fords in Costa Rica has been pieced together over the years from various sources but there has never been any official records from the government to confirm all of the identities. TACA and TAN were both Ford operators, with the TACA Fords moving about between several Central American countries and changing registrations each time.

Fords identified as registered in Costa Rica are:

Registration	Model	Serial Number	U.S. Registration
TI-15	5-AT-B	5-AT-43	NC-9682
TI-33	5-AT-C	5-AT-70	NC-411H
TI-40	5-AT-		

Lineup of three SCADTA Fords at the Techo Airport at Bogota, Colombia. (R.E.G. Davies)

TI-41	5-AT-C	5-AT-78	NC-418H
TI-42	5-AT-C	5-AT-71	NC-412H
TI-43	9-AT	9-AT-1	NC-423H (4-AT-39)
TI-44	5-AT-B	5-AT-31	NC-9673
TI-46	5-AT-C	5-AT-90	NC-430H
TI-51	5-AT-B	5-AT-19	NC-9641
TI-61	4-AT-E	4-AT-23	NC-5577
TI-64	4-AT	4-AT-37?	NC-7583?

Cuba (NM, IM)
Cuba operated at least nine Fords but there may have been more as Cuban records have been impossible to obtain. The most accurate source of information has been the CAA files and the Export Certificates but this would not include any aircraft imported into Cuba from other countries such as Colombia. There are references to a Ford in the Cuban Navy but no further details.

Date	Model	Serial No.	U.S. Reg.	Cuban Reg.	Notes
1929	5-AT-B	5-AT-11	NC-9637	NM-22 [1]	
1931	4-AT-E	4-AT-63	NC-8401		Cubana
1931	4-AT-E	4-AT-69	NC-8407		Cubana
1931	4-AT-E	4-AT-70	NC-8408		Cubana
1936	5-AT-B	5-AT-27	NC-9670	NM-25	Cubana
1938	5-AT-B	5-AT-40	NC-9684	NM-24	Cubana
1943	4-AT-B	4-AT-51	NC-9608	IM-4	
1943	4-AT-E	4-AT-67	NC-8405	IM-3	
1944	4-AT-B	4-AT-31	NC-7117	IM-5	

Note 1: Operated by Pan American from approximately February through April 1929 when the plane then was sold to Cia Mexicana.

Czechoslovakia (OK)
The European demonstrator (5-AT-50) was sold to the state owned airline at Prague and registered OK-FOR about January, 1930. It was destroyed in a crash near Friederichdorf about seven months later. See Chapters 7, 9 and 10.

Ecuador (HC)
No Fords were registered in Ecuador in the pre-war years, but they were flown there by Panagra. Two were reported as being shipped to Guayaquil in August 1929 for service with PAA-Grace. The planes were flown from Detroit to Newark, NJ, and crated there in boxes 48' long and 7' wide. These were placed aboard the Grace Line ship "Santa Cecelia" and described by the New York Times as, "the largest shipment of multi-motored aircraft and parts ever to be transported out of the New York harbor on a single steamer." Colonel Bayardo Tobar from Ecuador flew one of these Fords as co-pilot and wrote that it had a very short life and was scrapped. Perhaps he was referring to NC-8418 that crashed in Chile in April 1931.

In the immediate post-war period of 1946 to 1948 the Shell Company of Ecuador purchased six Fords as follows:

Registration	Model	Shell No.	Remarks
HC-SBC	4-AT-B	2, 4	4-AT-24, accident 4-5-46
HC-SBD	4-AT-B	1, 3	4-AT-29, accident 11-13-46
HC-SBI	5-AT	9	Accident 9-10-46
HC-SBJ	5-AT	10	1948
HC-SBK	5-AT-11		5-AT-67; accident 7-16-47
HC-SBQ	4-AT-B	14	1948

HC-SBI, HC-SBJ and HC-SBK came from Venezuela in May 1946 so they are probably 5-AT-22, 54 and 67 from AVENSA. A photo of HC-SBQ shows it to be a 4-AT-B with three P&W Wasp engines. Overhaul for the planes was done by TACA. The difficult flying from narrow, rough strips at mining camps took its toll and all had crashed or were withdrawn from use by mid-1948.

Guatemala (LG, TG)
Ten 5-AT's were registered in Guatemala, presumably most of them by TACA Guatemala. They were:

Registration	Model	Serial No.	Former NC Number
LG-AAC	5-AT-C	5-AT-52	NC-8414
LG-AAD	5-AT-C	5-AT-73	NC-413H
LG-AAE	5-AT-B	5-AT-28	NC-9671
LG-AAF	5-AT-B	5-AT-36	NC-9681
LG-AAG	5-AT-B	5-AT-26	NC-9669
LG-AAH	5-AT-B	5-AT-14	NC-9663
LG-AAI	5-AT-B	5-AT-18	NC-9640
LG-AAJ	5-AT-B	5-AT-7	NC-9644
LG-AAL	5-AT-B	5-AT-16	NC-9638
LG-AFA	5-AT-C	5-AT-74	NC-414H

LG-AFA was sold by Pan American Airways to Aerovias de Guatemala in May, 1941, for use as a chicle cargo carrier. This airline was later re-named AVIATECA (Empressa Guatemalteca de Aviacion). In March 1950 Robert Waltermire of Choteau, Montana, bought it and brought it back to the United States.

Honduras (XH)
At least 16 Fords were registered in Honduras, and possibly more, but no records have been found to document them. The following list has been compiled from photographs, pilot's letters and other sources. Most of these were operated by TACA Honduras but their identities have been impossible to determine.

Registration	Model	Serial Number	U.S. Registration
XH-TAB	5-AT-C	5-AT-71?	NC-412H
XH-TAH	5-AT-C	5-AT-75	NC-415H

SCADTA Ford 5-AT-C named "Leticia" at Bogota. (R.E.G. Davies)

SCADTA No. 62, a 5-AT-D. (R.E.G. Davies)

XH-TAI	5-AT		
XH-TAJ	5-AT		
XH-TAK	5-AT-B	5-AT-39	NC-9683
XH-TAL	5-AT-C		
XH-TAN	5-AT		
XH-TAO	5-AT-D	5-AT-103	NC-436H
XH-TAR	5-AT		
XH-TAS???			
XH-TAT	5-AT		
XH-TAW	5-AT-B	5-AT-15	NC-9668
XH-TAX	5-AT-B	5-AT-28	NC-9671
XH-TAY	5-AT		
XH-TAZ	5-AT		
XH-?	4-AT-E	4-AT-64	NC-8402
XH-?	9-AT	9-AT-1	NC-423H

An excellent photo showing XH-TAL modified as a "Flying Tanker" appears on page 21 of Western Flying for August 1940. This most interesting modification consisted of adding special cross bracing and a heavy duty floor, plus a 600 gallon fuselage tank, for the purpose of flying diesel oil to the mines. This operation was developed so successfully that the plane could be loaded in eight minutes and unloaded in six. TACA Honduras hauled 2,400 gallons a day in four trips between Alamicambra and Siuna for the La Luz Mine Company. The modification was done by TACA in their own shops at Toncontin and included a ladder on the right side of the nose to enable the pilot to enter the plane from the top.

Two other photos showing TACA modified airplanes appear in *Popular Aviation*, August 1939, pg. 54 (XH-TAZ being loaded through different cargo doors), and *Air News*, May 1943, pg. 15 (XH-TAR).

5-AT-64 operated in Honduras for two years under its U.S. registration of NC-405H while carrying freight to the Agua Fria Mine. The Cia Minera Agua Fria was in the mountains 75 miles from the Pacific Coast and 50 miles from Tegucigalpa. A landing strip was started in the summer of 1934 and the first plane landed on it in September. The loading base was at San Lorenzo, on the Bay of Fonseco, and the Ford had to fly from there at sea level, over 6,000 foot mountains, and back down to 3,500 feet altitude at the mine. A hatch 4 feet by six feet was cut in the top of the fuselage over the door for loading

SCADTA's 5-AT-114 registered C60 and named "Barranquilla" with the airline logo on the side. This is the 5-AT-DS that was modified with a left hand door. (R.E.G. Davies)

5-AT-114 at North Beach Airport in New York. The additional left hand door is just to the rear of the engine. This was constructed and the floats added before it left the U.S. (Larkins Collection)

machinery by a hoist. Between September 1934 and June 1935, all of the equipment for a 50-ton flotation and cyanide mill, a 450 hp diesel hydro-electric plant, two 320-foot compressors, a 150 hp diesel generator set, machine shop equipment, metal fume and penstock pipe and other machinery was flown into the mine. In addition all of the food, clothing and needs of the mine personnel was flown in. It was planned to fly the ore out on return trips once the mine was operating.

Two 4-AT types were exported to Honduras but their registrations and operating histories are unknown. Harold A. White in Tegucigalpa bought 4-AT-64 in November 1933 and 9-AT-1 in February 1934.

Group in front of 5-AT-78 (TI-41) just after its delivery to Costa Rica on October 1, 1939. Left to right are the Aerovias Nacionales maintenance supervisor, Frank Jerdone, Hernando Macaya and Eddie DeLarm. Note the non-standard balloon tire. Roman Macaya bought the plane from the Phillips Petroleum Company for $5,000 and DeLarm flew it from California to Costa Rica. (Eddie DeLarm)

Mexico (M, X, XA, XB)
One 4-AT and 12 5-AT's were registered in Mexico. However, because some went to Mexico, returned to the U.S., and later went back to Mexico there are 23 Mexican Registrations.

The initial Mexican civil registration system, using the letter M, allotted the registrations M-SCAL, M-SCAM and M-SCAN to Cia Mexicana, and M-SCAO to North American Lloyd, Apartado 40, Mexico City. No further details or identities are known.

The later registrations are as follows:

Registration	Model	Serial Number	U.S. Reg
X-ABCA	5-AT-B	5-AT-22	NC-9672
X-ABCB	5-AT-B	5-AT-12	NC-9661
X-ABCC	5-AT-B	5-AT-11	NC-9637
X-ABCD	5-AT-B	5-AT-27	NC-9670
X-ABCE	5-AT-B	5-AT-31	NC-9673
X-ABCF	5-AT-B	5-AT-40	NC-9684
X-ABCO	5-AT-B	5-AT-12	NC-9661
X-ABCU	5-AT-B	5-AT-27	NC-9670
X-ABCV	5-AT-B	5-AT-31	NC-9673
X-ABCW	5-AT-B	5-AT-45	NC-9688
XA-BCX	5-AT-C	5-AT-74	NC-414H
XA-BKS	5-AT-C	5-AT-74	NC-414H
XA-DOL	4-AT-A/E	4-AT-5	NC-1879
XA-FOH	5-AT-B	5-AT-31	NC-9673
XA-FON	5-AT-D	5-AT-103	NC-436H
XA-FUB	5-AT-B	5-AT-8	NC-9645
XA-FUE	5-AT-B	5-AT-39	NC-9683
XA-FUO	5-AT-C	5-AT-64	NC-405H
XA-FUP	5-AT-B	5-AT-18	NC-9640
XA-GIJ	5-AT-C	5-AT-75	NC-415H
XA-HIL	5-AT-B	5-AT-11	NC-9637
XB-KUI	5-AT-B	5-AT-11	NC-9637
XB-NET	5-AT-B	5-AT-8	NC-9645
XB-WAR	5-AT-B	5-AT-39	NC-9683
XB-YIT	5-AT-B	5-AT-39	NC-9683

The registration system changed a third time in the 1930s, allocating XA for commercial, XB for private, and XC for government use. Thus photos will show some Fords with X- and XA- registrations at different times, such as X-ABCW and XA-BCW.

Ford pilots Roman Macaya (President, Aerovias Nacionales), Enrique Malek and Carl Overly in front of the Aerovias Curtiss Kingbird in Costa Rica in 1939. (Eddie DeLarm)

Airlines operating Fords in Mexico were CMA, Cia Mexicana de Aviacion S.A.; LAGOSA, Lineas Aereos Guerrero-Oaxaca S.A.; NAMSA, Negociacion Aerea-Mexicana S.A.; SACSA, Servicios Aereos de Chiapas S.A.; TAJSA, Transportes Aereos de Jalisco S.A.; TAMSA, Transportes Aereos Mexicanos S.A.; and TATSA, Transportes Aereos-Terrestres S.A.

Netherlands (PH)
One Ford (5-AT-42) was sold to Holland and registered PH-AKE on September 4, 1935 for Netherlands Indonesian Airways (KNILM). It was further sold on August 26, 1936, to N.V. Bataafse Petroleum Maatschappij.

Nicaragua (AN)
16 Ford 5-AT's were registered to TACA Nicaragua between 1942 and 2947, and one 4-AT was registered to

5-AT-27 upon delivery to Havana by the Pan American pilot in the center of the group. The others, left to right, are Arturo Perez and Guillermo Delgado (Cia Cubana mechanics), Capt. Manuel Qvevedo (VP of Cubana), Fernando Lopez Porta (Cubana public relations chief), and Armando Menocal (Traffic Manager for PAA at Havana). (Cubana)

Rare photo of a 5-AT with the Aerovias Nacionales emblem on the side. The registration is TI-40. (Gary Kuhn)

5-AT-11, Cuban registration NM-22, landing in Cuba. (Bill Cook)

This 4-AT of Compania Dominicana de Aviacion (CDA) carries the Cuban registration NM4 which would indicate that it was 4-AT-51. (Larkins Collection)

The European demonstrator 5-AT-50 after it was sold to the Czechoslovakian government airline and registered OK-FOR. See Chapter 7. (Tor Johnsson)

HC-SBI landing at Ayuy, Ecuador, on July 15, 1946. (H.C. Kavelaars)

4-AT-29 being operated by the Shell Company of Ecuador at the Arajuno airstrip in 1945. (R.I. Baker)

Tropical Air Transport in 1946.

These were as follows:

Registration	Model	Serial Number	NC Number
AN-AAC	5-AT-C	5-AT-90	NC-430H
AN-AAD	5-AT-C	5-AT-89	NC-429H
AN-AAE	5-AT-B	5-AT-31	NC-9673
AN-AAG	5-AT-B	5-AT-43	NC-9682
AN-AAJ	5-AT-B	5-AT-11	NC-9637
AN-AAK	5-AT-D	5-AT-103	NC-436H
AN-AAL	5-AT-B	5-AT-18	NC-9640
AN-AAM	5-AT-C	5-AT-73	NC-413H
AN-AAN	5-AT-C	5-AT-64	NC-405H
AN-AAO	5-AT-C	5-AT-52	NC-8414
AN-AAP	5-AT-B	5-AT-39	NC-9683
AN-AAQ	5-AT-B	5-AT-4	NC-9606
AN-AAR	5-AT-B	5-AT-13	NC-9667
AN-AAS	5-AT-B	5-AT-8	NC-9645
AN-AAT	5-AT-B	5-AT-7	NC-9644
AN-ABO	5-AT-C	5-AT-75	NC-415H
AN-ACM	4-AT	4-AT-?	

Peru (OA, OB)

Four Pan American Fords were given Peruvian registrations but this may have been done primarily for public relations purposes as only one (5-AT-61) was actually sold and that was to Aerovias Peruanas S.A., a Panagra affiliate.

Pan American Fords flew cargo to the mines from 1934 to 1936 and photos show three types of markings: P27, in a circle, which was simply the Pangra Fleet Number; NC-9639, the U.S. registration; and OA-AAA, a new Peruvian registration. The examples given were all

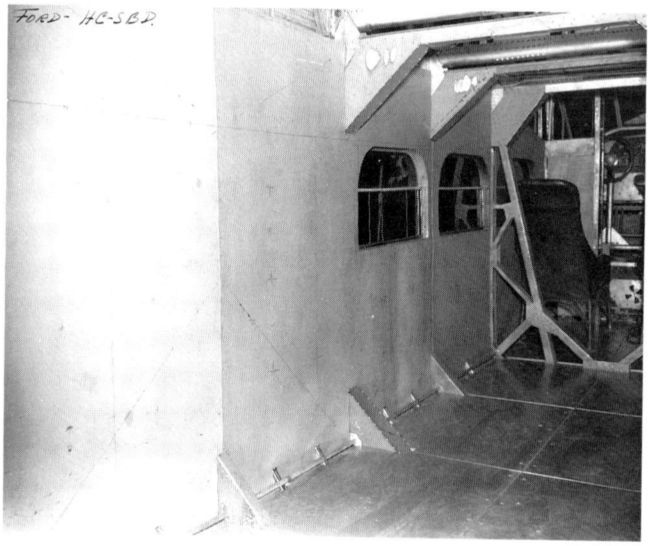

The interior of 4-AT-29 (HC-SBD) in 1945. (Dan Hagedorn)

HC-SBJ at the Shell Mera field on June 2, 1947. The steel beams are for a hangar that was being built. (H.C. Kavelaars)

Another Ford, 5-AT-64, that operated under U.S. registration in a foreign country. NC-405H was owned by Cia Minera Agua Fria (Cold Water Mine), a Los Angeles company, and flew in Honduras for two years. (John C. Mitchell)

5-AT-22 being moved by an early Cia Mexicana "airport tug." (Harry Gann)

Lineup of three Fords in Mexico. Left to right are 5-AT-12, 5-AT-40 and 5-AT-11. Pan American and Cia Mexicana Fords were often seen together. (Pan American)

5-AT-11 and 5-AT-40 of Cia Mexicana with their nose hangars for engine maintenance. (Ford Archives)

5-AT-90 of the Compania Nacional Aviacion (CNA) that operated in Guatemala in 1935 under the U.S. registration NC-430H. Note the bent nose prop. (John Underwood)

5-AT-74 in the Cia Mexicana shops with the registration XA-BCX. The fittings for the seaplane ladder, while flying as the Ford demonstrator NC-414H, still show to the rear of the door. (Adolfo Villasenor)

used on the same airplane.

The four registrations assigned were:

Registration	Model	Serial Number	U.S.Registration
OA-AAA	5-AT-B	5-AT-17	NC-9639
OA-AAB	5-AT-C	5-AT-61	NC-402H
OA-AAC	5-AT-C	5-AT-54	NC-8416
OA-AAD	5-AT-C	5-AT-59	NC-400H

An excellent one-half page photo of OA-AAA in flight over the mountains appears on page 539 of the November 1935 Engineering and Mining Journal. The other half of the same page is a photo of two Fords taken at Huanacopampa airstrip, both carrying the same striped wing and tail surfaces. These wide bands, probably red, were painted three each on the top and bottom of the outer one-third of the wings, and three each on the full surface of each horizontal tailplane. These stripes were very similar to the "Invasion Stripes" used at Normandy in World War II and were used for the same purposes of visibility and recognition.

The largest operation in Peru took place between August and October 1934 when Pan American-Grace

The rare "smooth-skin" 5-AT-8 at Mexico City in 1951. While modern alclad was easy to apply the flat skin lost much of the strength provided by the corrugations. (Jose Villela Jr.)

5-AT-11 in for overhaul at Lockheed Air Terminal, Burbank, CA, in 1949. (B.C. Reed)

5-AT-103 at Lockheed Air Terminal in 1948. Note the large modified cargo door installed during its use by TACA. The plane was being operated by Transportes Aereos de Jalisco (TAJ) and was named "Estrella Fugaz." (B.C. Reed)

modified a Ford and transported 735 tons of mining machinery from Cuzco to the Huanacopampa Mine in the Andes mountains. The Ford was equipped with two 550 hp Wasp engines in the wings, and a 450 hp Wasp SC-1 in the nose. In tests fully loaded it was able to maintain its altitude at 16,000 feet. A large hatch, approximately 9-3/4 feet long and 4-1/2 feet wide, was cut in the top of the fuselage to load the machinery. The interior was fitted with a small trolley set on rails and connected to a hand winch in order to place the cargo in proper relation to the center of gravity of the plane. Arrangements were made for unloading at the minehead, and an electric power line was installed so that night loading and maintenance of the planes could be carried out.

The planes took off from Cuzco at an altitude of 10,900 feet with an average load of 2,345 pounds. They flew across the Andean Divide at 15,000 feet, and landed at the mine which was 12,675 feet above sea level. The flights averaged thirty minutes between stations, with five trips a day. To move the same material by land would have required 7,300 mules with an average time for a round trip of four to five weeks, as contrasted with one hour by plane.

The complete machinery and parts for a 1,500 hp hydro electric generator was flown in, and later a 750 hp addition to that power plant. The heaviest single piece carried was 4,362 pounds. During the first return trips, with an empty plane, 200 pounds of ballast was required in the rear of the fuselage to keep the tail down. This was later eliminated by landing with full power on the center engine. In addition to the 735 tons of machinery flown in, the planes also carried 203 employees and other passengers in a total of 421 trips.

A second job, again using NC-9639/0A-AAA, was carried out between June and August 1936 when Aerovias Peruanas moved 387 tons of machinery to the Sindicato Minero Parcoy Mine. Trucks brought the machinery 125 miles from the Port of Salaverry to an old lake bed near Huamachuco. A 65 x 2,950 foot runway was built out of the gravel and served as a takeoff area. From there the planes flew 252 round trips to another makeshift strip in

A rare photo of 5-AT-39 at Guaymas on March 3, 1954 on its way back to the United States. The Mexican government required a registration to ferry the plane out of the country and XB-WAR was assigned for that purpose. (Calvin Southard)

5-AT-42 being lifted off a barge at Waalhaven airport near Rotterdam, Holland, in May 1935. (H.C. Kavelaars)

5-AT-31 of TACA Nicaragua with its double wing bins open. This was a regular passenger airliner in contrast with the many TACA cargo planes. (Robert L. Taylor)

the basin of a dry river. This landing field was surrounded on three sides by mountain walls and so was accessible from one direction only. A strip 65 feet wide and 3,300 feet long was laid out on the gravel bed, with an additional 985 foot emergency section that curved with the river. An 8-1/2 mile road was built from there to the mine and the machinery was transported up this road on trucks that had been flown in piece by piece and reassembled.

The landing field near the mine was actually lower than the takeoff station so loads were usually arranged as close to 3,080 as possible to 3,000 pounds per trip so that the Fords could get off the 10,000 foot altitude field, fly over the 14,000 foot mountains, and land at the 6,000 foot mine field. Despite all of the difficulties the contract was completed 32 days ahead of schedule without a mishap.

C. Carleton Semple wrote that Elmer Faucett also flew a great deal of air freight to the Parcoy Mine. He is reported to have used two Curtiss "Condor" biplanes, carrying four tons each, as well as one Ford Tri-Motor. The Ford made six to seven round trips a day from Huamachuco. This Ford remains unidentified.

4-AT-21 (NC-5492) was sold to the Government of Peru on June 22, 1933. It has been reported as flying for the Peruvian Air Force in 1940.

Romania (CV)

One Ford was registered in Romania, the beautiful but short-lived CV-FAI. It was named for Count George de la Vaulx, a former president of the Federation Aeronautique Internationale (who was killed in the crash of a Canadian Colonial Fairchild 71 in New Jersey in April 1930), and was washed out in a bizarre accident within a month of the time that it was christened.

Some interesting background to this Ford is given in the following comments from the April 1, 1931 issue of The Aeroplane magazine: "The first of the party to arrive at Heston on that Friday afternoon (March 27, 1931) was Mr. G.W. Higgs, Manager of the Ford Motor Company's Aviation Department in Europe, and Mrs. Higgs. The machine had been assembled at Hooton, and Mr. Higgs eyed the sky with some disquiet as the hour drew near.

In due course the invariably impressive sound and appearance of the Ford, with its three Pratt and Whitney Wasps, set doubts at rest although the crowds of spectators were yet to undergo one of those highly uncomfortable moments which add spice to aerodrome life.

The machine was being flown by Major Aviator Traian Burduloiu, of the Romanian Air Force, and he had some difficulty in matching the flat glide of the Ford with the total absence of wind. His first approach overshot to the extent that he had to put on his engines and go round again. His second was slightly shorter, and provided the thrill of the month. Only after making a three-point landing did the pilot realize that his run, in spite of brakes, seemed likely to carry him through the fence. He put on his three Wasps and took off again in a steep bank to avoid certain trees beyond. Fortunately the Wasps took hold, and the Ford showed itself an excellent flying machine by going through with the maneuver in a condition much more nearly stalled than was good for the onlookers. Mr. H.C. Johnson, test pilot for the Ford Motor Company in Europe, admitted afterwards that there was an uncomfortable session in the machine, but seemed less affected than the spectators. If the pilot does this sort of thing often the machine is likely to come to as tragic an end as did the nobleman after whom it was named." (It did indeed, see Chapter 10).

The Ford was replaced by a tri-motored Junkers Ju 52/3m, also registered CV-FAI. (Photo in *Aero Digest*, May 1932, pg. 96).

Spain (EC)

Two Fords went to Spain, although five registrations exist. These were 4-AT-68 and 4-AT-71. The first of

Four TACA Fords lined up at Puerto Cabezas, Nicaragua, about 1943. (David Ohlwiler)

Rare photo showing mixed registrations. These Fords were 5-AT's XH-TAW, XH-TAX and XH-TAJ. They were moved from TACA Honduras to TACA Nicaragua and the national letters were simply changed from XH to AN making them AN-TAW, AN-TAX and AN-TAJ. (Harry Yerex)

Ed Brice, the TACA Maintenance Supervisor, and Eddie DeLarm in front of a TACA Ford. AN-TAW is in the background on the right. (Eddie DeLarm)

5-AT-18 modified by TACA to carry diesel oil at Alamacamba, Nicaragua, in 1942. The cabin was filled with the oil tanks so a permanent ladder was attached to enable the pilot to enter through the escape hatch over the cockpit. (David Ohlwiler)

these, NC-8406, went to Spain in 1930 and became EC-KKA.

The second, the one and only 4-AT-F (NC-9656), also went to CLASSA (Concesionaires de Lineas Aereas Subvencionades S.A.) and was delivered in October 1931. An outstanding night photo of this plane, as EC-WIO, appears on page 802 of The Aeroplane for September 30,, 1931. In 1932 the ownership changed from CLASSA to LAPE and the registration changed to EC-RRA. The plane later carried the Spanish Air Force Serial 42-8 during the Civil War and later the civil registration EC-BAB.

A side issue brought about by the shipment of the first Ford to CLASSA was its subsequent embargo because of a lawsuit instituted by the Junkers Company of Germany.

Junkers issued an official statement to the press which read in part: "Yesterday the competent law court at Sevilla confiscated a tri-engine Ford monoplane which was destined for the Spanish airways company Classa . . . Junkers having sued the Ford Company in Spain for the contravention of its patents relative to 'wings with a corrugated skin' and to 'directly loaded wings.' As long as Ford made no attempt to export this type of airplane the Junkers Company decided not to take any legal steps with respect to the infringements. This resolution had to be pushed aside, however, as soon as it became clear that Ford intended to force the export of his machines to Europe. The general public first became aware of such intentions through the numerous propaganda flights which, in the summer months, were also extended to Germany. The .Junkers works, therefore, took the first opportunity of an authentic sale of a machine to Spain to proceed against Ford.

"Before detailed commentaries on this can be made, one will, of course, have to await further developments. Owing to some German papers having commented on this occurrence before the legal measures were carried through, some untrue assertions have been published, as, for instance, that Ford had for a long time tried in vain to

Pan American pilot J.R. Nielander found this 5-AT-B in the Nicaraguan mountains and arranged to retrieve it to help in the rebuilding of EAA's 4-AT-E. In 1975 the fuselage was moved to a river, floated on a barge to an ore boat and shipped to Texas. From there it was trucked to Wisconsin. Identification is uncertain but it is probably AN-AAR, 5-AT-13. (Lee Fray)

Interior of the 5-AT from Nicaragua. It had been hoped to use parts to rebuild 4-AT-69, however there were too many differences between the models and the condition was poor as can be seen in this photo of the fuselage interior. (Lee Fray)

Pan American Grace's P27 named "San Fernando." (Hudek)

5-AT-54 loading at Cuzco, Peru, in 1934. (Pan American)

The former 13-A, now 5-AT-100, at the Pan American Grace terminal at Trujillo, Peru on regular passenger service. (R.E.G. Davies)

procure Junkers' licenses and that foreign purchasers of Ford planes had annulled their orders upon hearing of the Junkers-Ford differences. In regard to these statements it must be said that Ford has not applied for Junkers' licenses and that direct proofs for the reasons underlying the said cancellation of orders by foreign companies are not at hand."

The Ford Motor Company counter-sued in the Prague Trade Court, but lost on both counts (corrugated sheet iron body, and construction of a monoplane where freight is carried by means of the frame of the wings instead of the fuselage) in a decision handed down in November 1930. (Further information is covered in the *New York Times* for 1-15-30, pg. 3; 1-22-30 pg. 5; 4-26-30 pg. 3; 4-27-30 pg. 18; 9-12-30 pg. 17; 10-23-30 pg. 8; and 11-28-30 pg. 9).

United Kingdom (G)

Five Fords were registered in Great Britain, with a total of six registrations. G-ABEF had the initials "EF" for Edsel Ford, so when G-ABFF was received it was promptly changed to G-ABHF so that the last two letters would stand for "Henry Ford." The registrations were as follows:

Registration	Model	Serial Number	Next Registration
G-ABEF	4-AT-E	4-AT-61	to VH-UDY
G-ABFF	5-AT-C	5-AT-68	to G-ABHF
G-ABHF	5-AT-C	5-AT-68	to VH-UTB
G-ABHO	5-AT-C	5-AT-60	to VH-UBI
G-ACAE	5-AT-D	5-AT-107	to RAF X5000
G-ACAK	4-AT-E	4-AT-68	to VH-USX

The Ford Motor Company set up an assembly and maintenance base called Ford Aerodrome near Arundel in Sussex. Mr. A.F. Burke was in charge of engineering work and some modifications were necessary for the issuance of a British airworthiness certificate such as the provision for an additional emergency exit, the installation of fully fireproof engine bulkheads, and the mechanical interconnection of the throttle and mixture controls.

In 1930 G-ABHO was flown to Tanganyika, British East Africa, with Lord Lovelace for an elephant hunt on his estates. A photo taken at Cairo of "Lord Lovelace's magnificent air yacht", named "Tanganyika Star" is on page 1155 of The Aeroplane for June 17, 1931.

In August 1934 Capt. Newman and L.S. Whicher flew G-ABHF to Sweden for the first visit of a British Ford to that country. In the same month G-ABHF was flown from Heston to Jersey, Channel Islands, and landed

The beautiful 5-AT-88 Club Model for Prince Bibesco and the Federation Aeronautique Internationale. The Romanian civil registration uses the FAI initials to honor the organization. (John Underwood)

on the beach as no airport existed at that time. G-ACAE, the 5-AT-D, was for some time the largest privately owned aircraft on the British Civil Register. It was impressed into service with the Royal Air Force in World War II.

Venezuela (YV)

Venezuela is another of those countries with no official historical records of aircraft registration. The only known direct sale from the United States is 5-AT-9 (NC-9646) which was sold by the Gulf Oil Company to their subsidiary Mene Grande Oil Company at Maracaibo on October 30, 1937. The Venezuelan registration has been reported as YV-MGO (Mene Grande Oil) but this is not shown in the FAA records. The Texas Petroleum Company flew their 5-AT-4 in Venezuela under it's U.S. Registration of NC-9606.

Three additional Fords, 5-AT-22, 5-AT-54 and 5-AT-61 have been reported as being sold to AVENSA. One photo exists showing YV-AVB which may be one of these three.

4-AT-71 in Spain in the 1930s. (L.S. dePazos)

5-AT-68 on a typical British grass field. (John Underwood)

4-AT-68 in England, 1933. (Larkins Collection)

5-AT-60 while in the service of the British Air Navigation Company. The name "Voyager" is just below the copilots window. (Larkins Collection)

Rare photo of 5-AT-107 in World War II camouflage. The Royal Air Force serial number was X5000. (Peter M. Bowers)

One of the 5-AT's used by AVENSA for cargo work. Another is in the background to the left. The identity of YV-AVB is uncertain and the date and location are unknown. (Larkins Collection)

Interior of the Ford assembly hangar near Arundel, England. From left to right: 5-AT-107, still carrying NC-440H on the wing; 5-AT-60, and 5-AT-68. (Larkins Collection)

5-AT-68 after its registration had been changed to G-ABHF for "Henry Ford." It is shown during a visit to the Schiphol Aerodrome in Amsterdam, Holland, in September 1931. (H.C. Kavelaars)

Chapter 7
Special Events and Operations

Henry Ford's Flight in a Tri-Motor

The fact that Henry Ford once flew in one of his Tri-Motors is well documented, even if the names of the other passengers are uncertain.

When Charles Lindbergh visited Henry Ford with his "Spirit of St. Louis" in August 1927 he invited Henry to fly with him. Ford had steadfastly refused to fly in an airplane and his sudden reversal was a surprise to everyone present. After some quick adjustments to the Ryan to provide an extra seat Lindbergh and Henry Ford took off and flew for 15 minutes. Edsel Ford was next with another 15 minute flight.

Both Fords were pleased and impressed with their flights and in a second quick decision Henry Ford invited Lindbergh to fly in one of his planes. After 4-AT-5 (Temporary No.3022) was brought out Henry decided to make up a party and fly with Lindbergh. The second flight lasted 40 minutes according to Russell Wilks who claims, "I had the honor of being the only newspaperman given permission to make the trip."

It is at this point that different reports of this flight do not agree. Wilks claims to have been the only reporter while the New York Times states that two newspapermen were aboard and does not mention Wilks at all. A third source, the 1944 Ford News Bureau history "Ford And Aviation", likewise does not mention Wilks.

The three sources agree on the following people being aboard this remarkable flight: Harry Brooks (pilot), Col. Charles Lindbergh (co-pilot), Henry Ford, Edsel Ford and Major Thomas Lanphier. Russell Wilks adds himself and gives no further names. The *New York Times* adds William B. Stout, William Mayo, Mrs. Ray Dahlinger, B.E. Martin and Charles E. Sorenson. The Ford News Bureau does not have Bill Stout but adds James Piersol.

Thus Henry Ford flew twice on August 11th, 1927, at Ford Airport in Dearborn. His third and last flight, virtually unknown, was in a Douglas DC-3 on July 12, 1936.

Dr. Rock and party in front of the China National Aviation Corporation (CNAC) 5-AT-115 that flew him to Wuadukwuadu from Yunnan in 1936. From left to right: Bob Black (co-pilot), Dr. Rock (with binoculars), Consul General Harding, Mrs. Byron O'Hara, Bryon O'Hara (pilot), a French banker and a Canadian missionary doctor. (Byron G. O'Hara)

4-AT-5, the 5th Tri-Motor built, and the one in which Henry Ford flew with Charles Lindbergh on August 11, 1927. This is also the only known example of the use of the words "Tri-Ford" as seen on the fin. The #23 is for the 1927 Ford Air Tour when it was flown by Dean Burford and Harry Brooks. (Hudek)

4-AT-10 in Mexico City, December 1927. Bill Stout and Charles Lindbergh's mother flew from Detroit to Mexico City and back in this plane so that she could visit with her son and the Morrow family who were in Mexico City for Christmas. The pilots were Harry Brooks and Harry Russell. While there they took President Obregon of Mexico for a ride in the Ford. On their return they ran into a snow storm near Chicago and had to land in the Robey Race Track. (Adolfo Villasenor)

The Bremen Rescue Flight

In April 1928 the German Junkers W.33L "Bremen" was forced down on Greenly Island, Newfoundland, after a flight from Ireland. A massive rescue operation was launched to save the three pilots and this included 4-AT-10 which had been chartered by the North American Newspaper Alliance.

With Bernt Balchen as the pilot the Ford brought supplies and parts to repair the damaged Junkers so that it could continue its flight to New York. In addition to gasoline and a propeller the Ford brought a new axle and wheels plus wine, beer, food and cigars. Junkers mechanic Ernst Koeppe and Mr. Murphy, representing the New York World and the press, were also aboard. The Ford landed and took off on skis with no difficulty. This Tri-Motor is still in existence and is slowly being restored by Gene Frank in Idaho.

The Ford/Fokker "Christopher Columbus"

One of the most humorous incidents in the long history of Ford airline use took place on November 21, 1928 when Mrs. Calvin Coolidge christened the Pan American Airways tri-motor "Christopher Columbus" to be used in opening the first air mail and passenger service between the United States and Central and South America.

After a welcoming speech by Juan Trippe, Mrs. Coolidge picked up a beribboned bottle and smashed it on the nose of a Ford Tri-Motor saying, "I christen thee Christopher Columbus." The plane took off, circled the field and left while the crowd waved farewell.

This may seem normal enough, as it did to the group engaged in the christening, but the humorous part is that the plane involved was a Colonial Western Airways Ford 4-AT-B (4-AT-41), when it was supposed to be a Pan

4-AT-10 on skis loading supplies for the rescue of the downed crew of the Bremen trans-atlantic plane in Newfoundland. Note the newsreel camera on the left. (Hudek)

American Airways Fokker tri-motor. The Fokker F-10, piloted by Max Holtzen, had been damaged the day before in a takeoff accident at Hasbrouck Heights, New Jersey. Rather than abandon the ceremonies PAA leased a brand new two month old Ford from Colonial for one day and painted the name "Christopher Columbus" on the nose. Colonial pilot Ed Weatherdon then flew it to Hoover Field, Washington, DC, where the ceremony took place. As soon as it was over the substitute plane returned to New York City.

The "Floyd Bennett", 4-AT-15, being pushed out for early trial flights before the nose engine had been changed to a Wright Cyclone. (Hudek)

First Flight Over the South Pole

Ford Tri-Motor 4-AT-15 (NX-4542) was destined to carry the first men to fly over the South Pole. With backing from the Fords Rear Admiral Richard E. Byrd selected a new Tri-Motor for the task. Assigning his pilot Bernt Balchen to test the plane at the factory Byrd soon received the report that it was underpowered and would be unable to achieve the mission because of the altitudes that would be necessary.

Increased power was achieved by replacing the 220 hp Wright Whirlwind in the nose with the new Wright Cyclone of 525 hp and a change to a three-blade propeller. Additional fuel tanks were added in a new wing extended five feet two inches to 74 feet. It appears that this was so successful that it became standard for all 4-AT-B models. The extra 252 pounds added by the nose engine change was offset to some extent by the installation of lighter (thinner) skin, celluloid in place of glass in the cabin windows and removal of the cabin trim and wicker seats.

After extensive testing on skis in cold weather, in the Northern United States and in Canada, the plane was loaded aboard ship and on its way south. All of this planning and work paid off on the historic flight of November 28-29, 1929. Even with the additional power of the Cyclone the plane would not climb high enough to get over the 10,000 foot pass in The Hump on its way to the pole, so Byrd was forced to throw out 250 pounds of food to lighten the plane. There is a magnificent action painting by Birney Lettick in the January 1963 National Geographic magazine showing McKinley about to drop a bag through the trap door in the floor of the cabin.

This resulted in a lifting of the plane between 300 and 400 feet according to Byrd that allowed them to clear the pass by 500 feet. This clearance has been reported with all kinds of variations with the most dramatic, and imaginary, being "missed rocks by a yard" and "inches to spare."

After circling the pole the plane crossed back over the barrier between 11,500 and 12,000 feet and then landed at an advance base where gasoline had previously been

Co-pilot Harold June and pilot Bernt Balchen who flew the "Floyd Bennett" over the South Pole on November 28-29, 1929. (Hudek)

stored for this purpose. The total elapsed time for the flight was 17 hours and 59 minutes, covered 1,600 miles, and was the first time that man had flown over the South Pole. The crew consisted of Admiral Byrd, Bernt Balchen, Harold June and Capt. Ashley McKinley.

The plane was left at Antarctica when the expedition returned to the United States. When Byrd returned in 1934 he found the plane intact and almost buried in the snow. He was so impressed with its good condition that he made plans to return it the next Spring. So when the Second Expedition left in February 1935 the Ford was loaded on the stern of the "Jacob Ruppert", along with the Curtiss Condor. The Ford was returned to Dearborn and put on display at Greenfield Village where it can still be seen today.

The 1929 European Demonstration Flight

The first grand demonstration tour was carried out by Leroy Manning flying 5-AT-50 (NC-8412) to 21 European countries between July and November, 1929. He was such an accomplished diplomat, as well as superb pilot, that the Ford Motor Company sent him as their sales representative to the major capitols of Europe. This tour carried 3,750 passengers on 325 demonstration flights, a record for American aviation at the time and a tribute to

Below: The "Floyd Bennett" being dug out of its ice hangar at the South Pole after being buried over the winter prior to it's flight as the first plane over the South Pole. (Hudek)

the dependability of the Ford Tri-Motor. Between this and Perry Hutton's similar tour of Japan, Korea and China, it can be seen that thousands of people outside of the United States had a chance to see the Ford in action.

The following list of cities has been taken from the pilots logbook in the order in which they were flown between July 7th and November 8th, 1929: London, Paris, Cologne, Berlin, Danzig, Konigsburg, Riga, Smolensk, Moscow, Warsaw, Posen, Berlin, Dassau, Travemunde, Copenhagen, Malmo, Hamburg, Rotterdam, Amsterdam, Lyrupe, Hamble, London, Manchester, Brussels, Antwerp, Paris, Geneva, Zurich, Friedrichshafen, Munich, Prague, Vienna, Budapest, Belgrade, Bucharest, Constantinople, Sofia, Salonica, Athens, Brindisi, Naples, Rome, Venice, Milan, Munich and Prague. The total flying time for this tour was 146 hours and there are many published photographs of NC-8412 taken during this time. The tour ended in Prague as the plane was sold there to the Czechoslovakian State Airline and re-registered OK-FOR.

LeRoy Manning writes of some of his experiences on these flights in the April 1931 issue of Aviation magazine. Paperwork, forms and petty bureaucracy were commonplace with a typical experience in Brindisi, Italy. There the local customs authority demanded that the cowlings from all three engines be removed so that he could examine the name plates on the engine crankcases to determine if the engines were the same as those listed in the log books.

Leroy Manning, premier pilot and representative of the Ford Motor Company throughout Europe. (San Diego Aerospace Museum)

Below: 5-AT-50 at Amsterdam, Holland, during its 1929 European Tour. Leroy Manning flew it to 21 countries in five months. (H.C. Kavelaars)

5-AT-50 on exhibit at the International Aero Show in London during the 1929 Tour. It was visited by the King of Spain, the Prince of Wales and the Duke of York. (Peter M. Bowers)

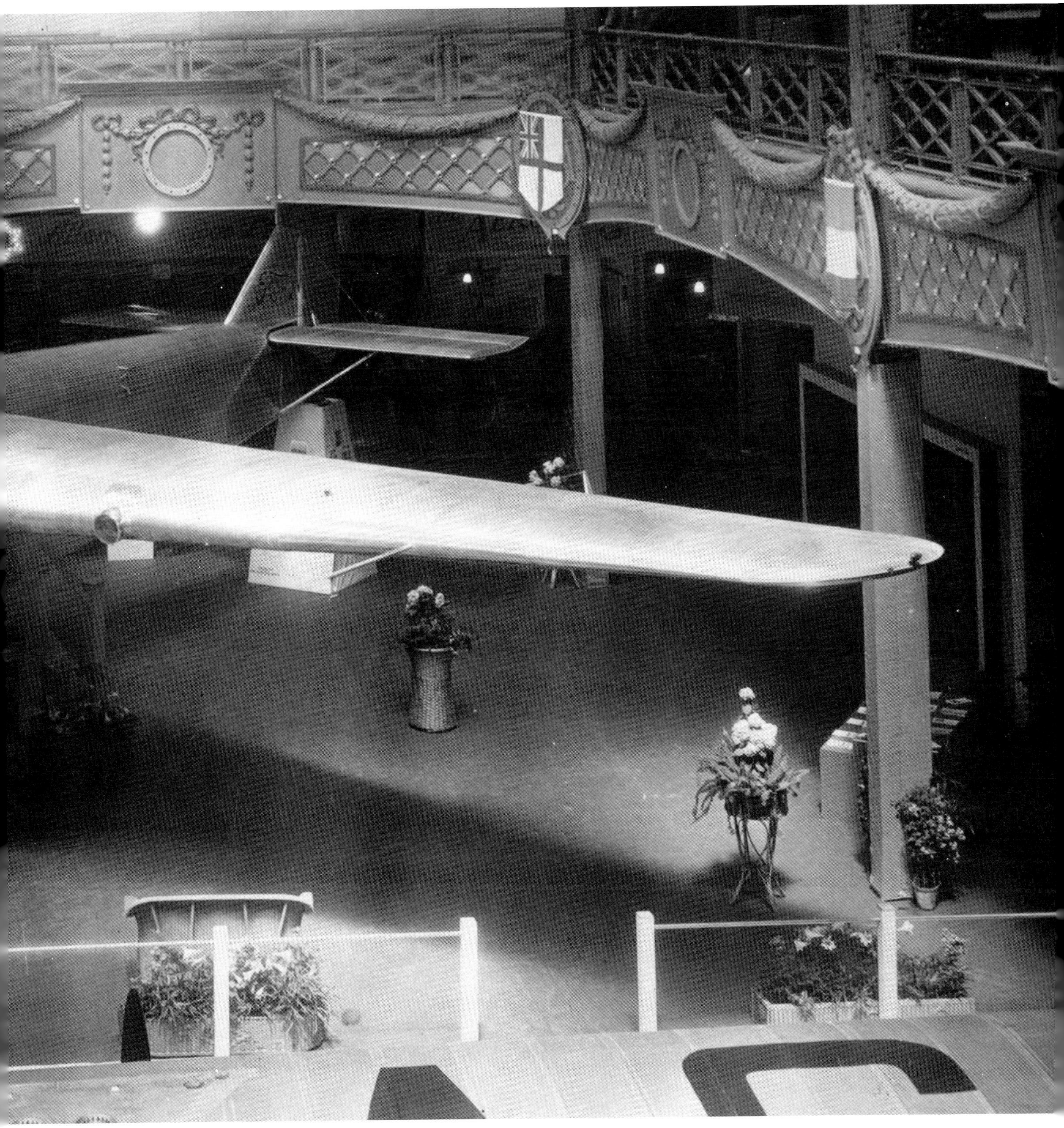

Demonstration Tour of Japan, Korea and China

5-AT-65 (NC-406H) was sent on an extensive sales tour by the company in 1930. Ford pilot Perry Hutton, accompanied by mechanic co-pilot Andrew Christian and salesman James H. Bear left the factory on February 1st and flew to Los Angeles. The plane was then disassembled and loaded aboard a ship at Long Beach harbor. Leaving via San Francisco the crew arrived at Yokohama in mid-March where the plane was unloaded and reassembled by Japanese employees of the Ford Motor Company. It was then flown to the Army base at Tatchikawa where a series of demonstration flights were begun.

After several weeks of carrying dignitaries and potential customers on scenic flights, with no results, they left for Korea. After a fuel stop at Osaka they flew across the Sea of Japan to Pusan, Korea. Here they were met by various civic officials including Count Kodama, Vice-Governor-General. During an overnight stay Mr. Shopaeff, acting manager of the Ford Company, "entertained some 70 representative citizens at a party by way of propagating the sterling worth of the Ford machine."

The following day they left for Mukden, Manchuria, where Hutton gave demonstration rides for several days. On one he was able to get Chang Hseuh-Liang, the "Young Marshall", to ride in the co-pilots seat. This so impressed him that he eventually bought the airplane.

On October 25th the Ford arrived at Hungjao Aerodrome, Shanghai, in a flight from Tsinanfu that lasted four hours and ten minutes. The 1930 reporters surprise at seeing the pilot confirmed the good judgement of the Ford Company officials in combining flying ability with good salesmanship as they had done with Leroy Manning and Perry Hutton. The Shanghai newspaper reported, "Mr. Hutton in no way approximated the popular conception of what a pilot should look like. No leather jacket, leather

5-AT-65 at Osaka, Japan, after being shipped there by boat. Photo from a Japanese photographer as all cameras on the plane were ordered sealed. General Tojo and others flew in the Ford during March and April 1930 while it was at the Tachikawa Army Air Base at Tokyo. (Perry Hutton)

The plane was then flown on to Seoul, Korea, arriving there on August 6, 1930. Perry Hutton is second from the left, and Andrew Kristian (his mechanic) is fourth from the left with the beret. The man on the right is probably Kyusaku Inada, Chief of the Sales Department of the Ford Motor Company in Japan. (Perry Hutton)

5-AT-65 at the Polo Grounds of the Tientsin Race Club in China. The two men standing on the right are Texaco employees. (Perry Hutton)

boots, khaki trousers, helmet and goggles for this pilot. He emerged from the plane in a blue lounge suit, as immaculate and calm as though he had spent the past hour at a tea dance."

By January 1931 the Ford had given rides to hundreds of officials and business men at Mukden, Tiensin, Shanghai and Nanking. Typical of these was one at Nanking in which the Minister of Foreign Affairs, Minister of Education, Chairman of Control and Vice Minister of Foreign Affairs were given a flight. By the end of 1931 NC-406H had flown 362 hours in China. Andrew Christian had returned to the U.S. and a new Ford mechanic, Carl Kjos, was sent as his replacement.

In 1932 T.V. Soong, the new Minister of Finance, was a passenger as was George Bernard Shaw who was on a tour of the Orient. In February 1932 Chang Hseuh-Liang had bought a second Ford Tri-Motor (5-AT-99). This new 5-AT-D was delivered with its U.S. Registration of NC-432H and flown by Perry Hutton in China with these markings.

5-AT-65 landing at Mukden in Manchuria in August 1930. The Mukden Arsenal is in the background. T.V. Soong, and Lord Litton of the League of Nations, flew in the Ford while it was in China. (Perry Hutton)

5-AT-57 with fuselage tanks installed to hold 1,800 gallons of gasoline for the purpose of aerial refueling of Jimmie Mattern's Lockheed 12A "The Texan." (John C. Mitchell)

Mechanic's Nightmare

One of the most fantastic items to be uncovered in the history of the Ford Tri-Motor is a photograph (*New York Times* rotogravure section, February 2, 1930 and *Western Flying*, April, 1930) showing James Terry, "inventor", hanging below the fuselage half way between the tail and the cain door demonstrating that, "it is possible to climb to the tail of a plane in flight and make repairs" during a flight 1,500 feet above Miami, Florida.

This action, titled "another step to greater safety in passenger flying" is graphically shown in the beautiful 8"x10" photograph in the New York Times. Just what repairs would be needed on a plane that is capable of flying straight and level enough to allow the mechanic, with no parachute, to attach his belt to a cable and slide to the tail and back, are not explained. This was the wrong month for an April Fool's joke so there is no real explanation for the whole story, thus it will have to be labeled preposterous but true. The plane used was 4-AT-35.

Aerial Refueling

Two Fords were modified for this unique service. The first was 4-AT-22 (NR-5493), a model 4-AT-B converted to a two-place aerial tanker to refuel the all-white Lockheed Vega named "Fort Worth" to be flown non-stop by Reg Robbins and H.S. Jones from Seattle, Washington, to Tokyo, Japan in July, 1931.

The Ford was flown by Jimmie Mattern and Nick Greener and five contacts were made. In one contact over Fairbanks, Alaska, 200 gallons were transferred at about one thousand feet altitude. Unfortunately bad weather was encountered and the planes became unmanageable attempting to fly close formation with their heavy loads. Robbins decided that it was too dangerous to attempt another in-flight refueling, abandoned the flight, and landed at Solomon near Nome, Alaska. Ironically the weather just a few hundred miles ahead was clear all the way to Tokyo. An interesting sidelight is that the engine in the Vega was a Wright J-5 (220 hp) which had been taken out of the Ford because of its lower fuel consumption of 11-1/2 gallons per hour.

The second instance also involved Jimmie Mattern, but this time it was Mattern's Lockheed 12-A "The Texan" that was to be refueled in flight. The Ford was a modified 5-AT-C (5-AT-57, NR-9648) with the seats taken out and the fuselage filled with tanks to hold 1,800 gallons of gas and 450 gallons of oil. The fuselage was so filled, in fact, that the only entrance to the plane was by ladder up to the top of the pilot's compartment on the right side of the fuselage and down through the escape hatch. The Lockheed 12-A was awaiting clearance papers to fly non-stop from Oakland, California to Moscow, Russia. While this was happening a reverse Russian flight had taken place and the plane was lost enroute. Jimmie Mattern

Franklin D. Roosevelt, his wife Eleanor, and sons Elliott and John alongside 5-AT-75 that took them from Albany, New York, to Chicago for the 1932 Democratic National Convention. In August 1964, Representative James Roosevelt, his wife and two children, flew in American Airline's restored 5-AT-39 from Washington DC, to the Democratic Convention in Atlantic City, New Jersey. (AA)

immediately took off to help in the search for the lost Russian flyers. Garland Lincoln followed in the Ford but ran into zero-zero weather at Fairbanks and had to land in the soup. He circled until all of his gas was used up (luckily the fuselage tanks were empty), gunned the engines, cut the switches and came down through the overcast. The plane was written off in the ensuing crash landing which turned it upside down in the ooze of the Alaskan tundra on August 21, 1937.

FDR Flies to Chicago

In the summer of 1932 Franklin Delano Roosevelt, then Governor of New York, flew from Albany, New York, to Chicago, Illinois. This sounds rather commonplace today, but at the time it was sensational, a stroke of political genius, and an act that captivated the attention of people all over the United States.

This was the first time that a candidate for the Presidency had ever flown to a national convention and the news broadcasts by radio had a startling effect on the delegates at the Democratic Convention. Between the newspaper and radio coverage of his flight FDR stole the thunder from the other nominees and won the party nomination for President.

The pilot of the Ford Tri-Motor was Ray Wonsey (1385), the co-pilot Fred D. Smith, and the Steward Max Pollet. The passengers, in addition to FDR, were Mrs. Eleanor Roosevelt, sons Elliott and John, Guernsey Cross, Samuel Rosenman, Marguerite Le Hand, Grace Tully, Gus Gennerich and Earl Miller.

For some years there was considerable disagreement over which Ford was used for this flight. Finally Fred Smith sent a copy of the page from his log book to the author which established its identity as 5-AT-75, NC-415H.

G.E. Ruckstell, Edith McManus and Irving Kravitz in front of 5-AT-8 of Grand Canyon Air Lines. (Irving Kravitz)

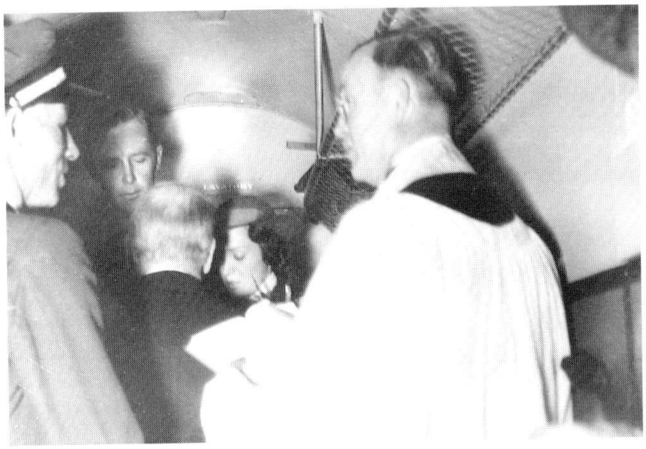

On October 7, 1935 Edith McManus and Irving Kravitz were married in flight in 5-AT-8 over the Grand Canyon. (Irving Kravitz)

Aerial Wedding Over Grand Canyon

On October 7, 1935, a unique aerial wedding took place 3,000 feet over the south rim of the Grand Canyon. In a fitting tribute to the airplane a Ford pilot and Ford stewardess were married in flight in Grand Canyon Air Lines 5-AT-8 (NC-9645) while flying over the Colorado River.

Irving S. Kravitz and Edith McManus, both of whom flew for Grand Canyon Air Lines, were married by the Rev. William S. Dando, with Rev. J.S. Doron assisting. Chief pilot G.E. Ruckstell turned the controls over to co-pilot Ernie Tissot so that he could participate in the ceremony.

The total of 2 pilots and 12 passengers was made up by the following additional people: M.R. Tillotson (Supt. of the Grand Canyon National Park), Mrs. Tillotson and her two children Denise and Harvey, Mrs. Ruckstell, Mrs. Doron, Mrs. Tissot and Harry Franse, a reporter for Associated Press.

In 1970, when the author discovered that the plane involved was the same one that William Harrah had just finished restoring, he asked Harrah to give Mr. & Mrs. Kravitz a ride in it. This was planned so that it took place on their 35th wedding anniversary and they were able to fly in the exact plane that they had been married in over Reno, Nevada, on October 7, 1970.

Harry Volpe, Edith Kravitz and Irving Kravitz posed in the position of the 1935 photo with Harrah's 5-AT-8. They flew in the same plane they were married in over Reno on their 35th wedding anniversary. (Harrah's Club)

A Ford at Wuadukwuadu

A famous explorer of the 192, Dr. Joseph F. Rock, spent a good deal of time in Yunan Province, China and southeastern Tibet. Many of his trips were arduous and

Right: Another aerial wedding took place over the Pitchfork Ranch in Wyoming, probably in 1937. Bill Monday, the "Flying Cowboy", was married aboard his 4-AT-46. (Larkins Collection)

lengthy, especially the five days on foot to cross the Yangtze gorge in the Likiang snow range. By 1934 the China National Aviation Company (CNAC) had established air service between Yunnanfu and Chungking so Dr. Rock, looking for a less strenuous way to reach this area, asked them if he could charter a plane.

Approval was received from the Shanghai office and the date set for February 3, 1936. In order to help pay expenses Dr. Rock invited two paying guests; Mr. Harding, Consul-General at Yunnanfu and Mr. Ezeghelian of the local branch of the Bank of Indochina. In addition to his guest Mrs. Byron O'Hara, he had two of his native Nakhi assistants and the Rev. Lankester of the Church Missionary Society of Yunnan in his party. The pilot was Byron O'Hara of CNAC and a co-pilot named Black.

Taking off at 7:45 am and climbing to 13,000 feet by 9:00 am they were at 14,400 feet and could see in the distance the peaks of Konkaling which are 22,000 feet high and first explored by Dr. Rock. Flying over the 12,000 foot deep gorge of the Yangtze river led to some dramatic comments by Rock. The altitude and performance of the 5-AT-D is remarkable as described in some of the following comments by him in *The North-China Daily News*: "The fierce wind which howled through the gorge caused our ship to flutter like a piece of paper in a gale. It drove us towards the peak of Haba, so that I feared

Harold Johnson performing his famous one-wheel landing with his 4-AT-B (4-AT-53). Johnson did 17 consecutive loops with this Ford Tri-Motor. (Dick Whittington)

Another view of the same maneuver at the 1936 All American Air Maneuvers at Miami, Florida. (Bill Sweet)

the wing of our plane would scrape the cliff which looked forbidding. My friend Lankester who sat opposite me shivered and looked queerly at me. He grabbed the spittoon with one hand and the camera with the other. I shuddered when I looked out at the cliffs, which it seemed I could touch, so close they were, one single glance into the depths below and I had enough and closed my eyes. We were tossed about, rising and dropping at the rate of 1,500 feet a minute; the ship swayed and every bump registered in our stomach. The roar of the engines seemed intensified, and we bumped and swayed and shook as we passed close to the ice-crowned vertical limestone cliffs and crags at an altitude of nearly 17,000 feet. Such a spectacle will for ever remain unforgettable. Serene and as if with contempt the mighty peaks looked down on us as we in our insignificant craft literally bumped through the virgin gorge. The heaving of my seat for moments made me forget the scenery, and made me hold on and close my eyes."

Reaching the southern end of the range they flew over the Likiang plain, where Dr. Rock had spent several years, and landed at 10:50 am at the 8,700 foot high plain called Wuadukwuadu. He described a friendly crowd surrounding the first airplane to be seen there, "some crawled underneath as if looking for eggs which the iron bird might have laid." They left at 1:35 pm, flying over the nearby town of Likiang, and with a tail wind arrived back at Yunnanfu in an hour and thirty minutes.

The four hours and thirty-five minute flight covered the same round trip that took fifty days by caravan. The photos taken were developed the next day and flown to Shanghai on the 6th, in comparison with a normal time of twelve days.

Harold Johnson and the National Air Races

No one who ever saw Harold S. Johnson fly his 4-AT-53 at the National Air Races at Cleveland will ever forget what he was able to do with that plane. Considering the fact that he was flying a standard 4-AT-B, with three Wright J-5's of 220 hp each, and not one of the hopped up post-war 4-AT's with BT-13 engines of 450 hp each, it is all the more remarkable. His skill and ability with the standard, unmodified, airplane was in the same category as that of Bob Hoover today flying his Aero commander.

Johnson bought his Ford in 1932 and flew it as part of his National Air Shows act until the start of World War II in December 1941 put an end to all air shows. During this time he toured the East and Middle West, as well as Florida, so that a lot of people were able to see him perform.

Bill Sweet, long-time airshow announcer, describes Johnson doing, "hammer-head stalls; Cuban eights; tail

6-AT-1 operating as a crop duster with the Royal Canadian Air Force in 1929. The WZ is part of the civil registration G-CYWZ and the plane was widely known as "WZ." The photo was probably taken at the start of operations at Duchibany Lake in Canada. (Hudek)

5-AT-74 at Choteau, Montana, shortly after Bob Waltermire flew it in from Guatemala in March 1950. The remains of the Empressa Guatemalteca de Aviacion (AVIATECA) airline insignia can be seen on the side of the fuselage. (Douglas D. Olson)

5-AT-74 with internal tanks and wing spray bars at Douglas, Wyoming, in July 1956. Diesel oil mixed with aldrin was used to combat a grasshopper plague. (Marion Havelaar)

Chuck LeMaster and Dale Glenn used 4-AT-69 as an agricultural sprayer. This excellent photo shows the spray bar installation and the thick chord of the wing on the Ford Tri-Motor. (Charles LeMaster)

4-AT-55 of Mamer Air Service at the Chamberlain Basin Meadows field in the Idaho National Forest with some of the supplies for the U.S. Forest Service fire fighters that were flown in from Spokane, Washington, in 1931. (Walter M. Jefferies Jr.)

4-AT-69 making a drop of fire retardant in 1957 in Idaho. The plane was equipped with two 275-gallon tanks in the fuselage. (U.S. Forest Service)

4-AT-55 was the second Ford to be modified as an Air Tanker to fight forest fires in 1957. It was tested on fires in Western Montana and Northern Idaho. (U.S. Forest Service)

spins, with a starting altitude at 1000 feet; snap rolls at 400 feet altitude; then plunge into three fast consecutive loops, his final loop starting at the 25 foot level. As a climax, he would land the three engine plane on one wheel as thousands cheered." Sweet states that Johnson taught his son Dwight to fly and that he soloed, at the age of 17, in the Ford Tri-Motor. Harold S. Johnson had Pilot's License No. 821, and he had no connection with the Johnson Flying Service of Missoula, Montana.

Several stories mention Johnson flying an air show on two engines. The claim is that his nose engine was not working at an air show at Daytona Beach, Florida, so he simply removed the nose prop and flew the act using the two wing engines. There are conflicting reports on his record of consecutive loops with the Ford. Bill Sweet claims it was twenty-seven, but Bob O'Hara gives a more conservative figure of seventeen. Johnson had a Continental special biplane for aerobatics, and had designs and plans to build a mount on the top of the Ford to carry the biplane to air shows in piggyback style. This would have been a spectacular sight and a precursor to the space shuttle atop the 747.

Johnson sold his Ford to Aubrey Loving in Richmond, Virginia, in October !942 and went to work flying Lockheed "Hudsons" across the Atlantic as a ferry pilot. After a year of this he became a production test pilot on the new Consolidated B-24's at the Ford Willow Run plant, and from there went to Lockheed as a test pilot on P-38's and the new P2V Neptune.

Fords in Agricultural Use

The first of several Ford Tri-Motors to be modified with tanks for agricultural use was 6-AT-1 in June 1929. Although "WZ" (short for G-CYWZ) was owned by the Royal Canadian Air Force it was used by the Civil Government Air Operations Division for experiments in forest dusting. For this purpose it was operated on Brewster floats from lakes and rivers. Operations stared on June 17, 1929, on the shore of Duchibany Lake in Canada.

Two previous attempts to control the Spruce Budworm infestation in the area, with smaller aircraft, had failed and it was thought that perhaps the large load carrying capabilities of the Ford would solve the problem. A great deal of difficulty was encountered in designing and building a hopper for the Ford that would work satisfactorily and carry loads of up to 1,400 pounds of dust on each flight. The dusting resulted in an estimated 90% kill on the caterpillar population in the dusted area despite rain and other difficulties.

After that job was finished WZ was flown to Ottawa, and then on to Manicouagan, on the north shore of the Gulf of St. Lawrence, to carry out a dusting operation for the control of a hemlock looper outbreak on the balsam fir stands in that area.

Johnson Flying Service used 5-AT-58 to carry Smokejumpers to fight forest fires. This photo was taken at their home base at Missoula, Montana, in September 1953. (Douglas D. Olson)

The Ford arrived July 4th and dusted all that month. 1,200 pounds per load was found to be the most effective, but trouble was still encountered with the hopper. The Ford flew twenty to forty feet above the tree tops during this operation. In dead calm air the swath was 250 feet wide. With calcium arsenate dust a better than 95% kill was established in the areas covered, at a total cost of about $6.00 per acre. Experiments with dusting operations continued through 1931. A new dust hopper with a form of vibratory agitator was designed and built, and improved, and finally in 1931 the dust cloud was considered to be satisfactory. The next activity seems to be after World War 2 when the Johnson Flying Service modified two 4-AT's as sprayers, 4-AT-58 and 4-AT-62. These were used on a massive Tussock Moth Control program in Northern Idaho in 1947. The two Johnson Fords were part of eleven planes used in this early project sponsored by the Potlatch Timber Protective Association, the Idaho State Forestry Department and the U.S. Department of Agriculture. Each Ford made 121 flights and sprayed a total of 96,527 gallons of spray mixture.

The Fords had two 215-gallon aluminum tanks installed in the fuselage. These were connected at the bottom with a 2-inch pipe, with a lead from the interconnecting tee to the pump. Spray fluid was drawn from these tanks with air-cooled, gasoline-motor-driven centrifugal pumps capable of delivering 60 gallons per minute. Two types of pumps were used, an Aurora HH4 (7 hp), and a Forester 2BW4 (5 hp), and both performed satisfactorily. From the pumps the spray flowed through a 2-inch oil-proof hose which led through the wings and down to the spray booms through an inspection plate. The booms were mounted on the underside of each wing and were made of 1-inch tubing, with evenly spaced 1/8-inch holes that pointed backward at an angle of 45 degrees. This system produced a swath 300 feet wide on each pass. This compares to a 100-foot swath for the Stearman PT-17, and a 400-foot swath for the Douglas C-47.

Three Fords were modified to be sprayers in 1950. Rex Williams 4-AT-69, Johnson's 4-AT-58 and the first 5-AT (5-AT-74) by Robert Waltermire of Northwest Agricultural Aviation Corporation at Choteau, Montana. 5-AT-74 was used to spray diesel oil mixed with aldrin to combat a grasshopper plague in Natrona County, Wyoming, in July 1956. The Ford carried a load of 700 gallons on each flight and sprayed at an average cost of 51 cents per acre. Northwest bought a second 5-AT in 1952 (5-AT-4) but it was lost in an accident less than a year later. Low level spraying is more hazardous than normal operations and three out of the seven Fords modified as sprayers were lost in accidents.

Fords and Fire Fighting

Because of the widespread publicity about the Johnson Flying Service in Missoula, Montana, most people today think that they were the only operator to use the Ford Tri-Motor to assist in fighting forest fires. However, the first was Nick Mamer who transported government crews of fire fighters and their equipment from Spokane, Washington, to the Nez Perce Forest in Idaho in the summer of 1931. Flying 4-AT-55 (NC-9612), Mamer carried 300 fire fighters and 60,000 pounds of equipment to the area. Most of it was delivered to the Chamberlain Basin Meadows field in the Idaho National Forest, and the remainder was flown into a 1,700 foot strip surrounded by high mountains and tall timber at Moose Creek in the Selway National Forest. The flights averaged two hours whereas four or five days would have been required for travel by land.

None of these were Smokejumpers (parachuting fire fighters) a concept developed by the U.S. Forest Service and first tested on live fires nine years later. Bob Johnson flew one of their two Fords in August 1940 on one of the first operational jumps. This would have been 4-AT-46 or 4-AT-58. The subject has been covered extensively in print and in a feature-length motion picture "Red Skies of Montana." Stan Cohen's *A Pictorial History of Smokejumping* is an excellent book on the subject and has good coverage of the Johnson Fords.

Instead of landing the plane to discharge the men, as was done in 1931, the trained fire fighters were parachuted from the air directly to the site of the fire. Once on the ground they acted as regular fire fighters, and when the blaze was put down they walked back to the nearest transportation. This can mean, at times, that the men will be dropped six or seven thousand feet up on the side of a mountain by slow flying Ford Tri-Motors. Even hot food is dropped by parachute to the men, and they are constantly supplied by air until they have been returned to their ground contact. Only the Ford had the performance and capacity to perform these flights so efficiently in the rugged mountain passes. The author was privileged to fly on a food drop in August 1952 with veteran Johnson pilot Jim Larkin flying 4-AT-58 out of McCall, Idaho.

Two Ford 4-AT's were tested as Air Tankers ("Borate Bombers") in 1957. 4-AT-69, a modified 4-AT-E with three BT-13 engines of 450 hp each, was being operated by the Aerial Service Company of Boise, Idaho for aerial spraying. It was converted by the addition of 19 x 20-inch free-swinging gates at the bottom of the two tandem 275-gallon tanks. Cable releases permitted emptying both tanks one at a time, or both at once. Five hundred gallons of water suspended sodium calcium borate was normally carried in the two tanks. This water and chemical slurry weighed approximately ten pounds per gallon resulting in the total exceeding 5,000 pounds.

Calibration tests showed a drop pattern roughly 70

The Johnson Flying Service 4-AT-55 with Smokejumpers at Porterville, California, on September 21, 1949. It is not well known that Johnson flew outside of Idaho and Montana. (Jeff Edwards)

feet wide and 700 feet long when both tanks were emptied at an altitude of 50 feet. The 4-AT-E was used on 74 drops on fires in the Boise and Payette National Forests with great success, much of this credited to the flying skill of its owner-pilot Glen Higby (Aircraft Service Company). U.S. Forest Service ranger Jim Butler wrote a fitting tribute to the plane: "The Ford was on this fire immediately and hit the head of the fire with a load of slurry that really flattened it. without this help, considering the 30 mph wind which prevailed, we would have been unable to control it at the 2 or 3 acres it burned."

Another report from a Payette National Forest fire officer said that as soon as the Profile Creek fire was reported, "Smokejumpers were dispatched from Idaho City and a Ford load of borate from Boise. When the jumpers arrived it was too windy to jump so they returned to Idaho City. The load of borate was dropped across the lead of the fire and the plane returned for another load . . . 50 men reached the fire by 1600 . . . Ranger Dahlgreen reported that if it hadn't been for the borate drop, the personnel on the fire could not have held it that day. The borate held the fire from spreading uphill until the ground personnel and jumpers arrived. Considering the burning conditions and fuel available for the fire to spread in, the borate undoubtedly prevented a large project fire."

The other Ford was Mamer's old 4-AT-55 then owned by William Hadden of Orofino, Idaho. It too had been modified to be an agricultural sprayer, but its 300 hp wright J-6's limited its load to 300 gallons. On August 8, 1957 the Northern Rocky Mountain Region of the USFS contracted to have three 100-gallon tanks installed, each with a separate dump valve and control. On August 9th test drops with water were made and following a training period the plane was dispatched on eight fires in Western Montana and Northern Idaho.

Flying time averaged one to two hours per fire with mixed results. The borate was ineffective in timber and in duff under trees but productive on a 1-1/2 acre fire of mill debris, grass and brush. In this case it hit the hot spots and was very effective in stopping the spread of the fire. These early tests were important in developing the now standard technique of dropping fire retardants ahead of a fire rather than on the fire itself.

Both Fords were sold to Johnson Flying Service, 4-AT-55 in October 1957 and 4-AT-69 in May 1958, but as far as is known neither was ever operated as an air tanker by Johnson who used them instead to transport smokejumpers and cargo.

TWA Anniversary Flight - 1949

Trans-World Airlines was the first to lease a Ford and fly it across the United States as publicity for an anniversary celebration. TWA leased 4-AT-55 in July 1949, painted it up as the "City of Los Angeles", and re-created the 1929 air-rail route from Los Angeles to New York. By this time few people knew the difference between a 4-AT and a 5-AT so the plane was accepted as one of the "airliners." It was then returned to Clinton Johnson in California where it remained until sold to William Hadden in Idaho.

Pioneer Maddux Ford pilot Felix Preeg points to 4-AT-55 for the benefit of the camera. TWA leased the plane for a transcontinental anniversary flight in 1949. (TWA)

A beautiful night photo showing 5-AT-58 leased by Northwest Airlines from Johnson Flying Service in 1956. They overhauled it, painted it white and flew it from New York City to Seattle. The photo was taken at the Minneapolis-St. Paul airport. (Northwest Airlines)

Northwest Anniversary Flight - 1956

Northwest Orient Airlines undertook an extensive program to commemorate its 30th Anniversary by leasing 5-AT-58, which had originally been delivered new to Northwest Airways, and flew it from New York City to Seattle in October 1956.

N-8419 was leased from Johnson Flying Service and sent to the Northwest shops for a complete overhaul, paint job and refinishing of the cabin interior. It was then flown on a leisurely trip from Idlewilde Airport to the Seattle-Tacoma Airport.

The Ford visited twenty cities; New York City, Washington, Pittsburgh, Cleveland, Detroit, Milwaukee,

The arrival of 5-AT-58 at Seattle on October 18, 1956 brought out an enthusiastic crowd in the rain. The Ford Tri-Motor has a magic appeal wherever it appears. (Northwest Airlines)

Madison, Rochester, Minneapolis-St. Paul, Chicago, Fargo, Bismark, Billings, Great Falls, Butte, Missoula, Spokane, Yakima, Portland and Seattle. Swarms of press photographers, TV cameramen and reporters met the plane at every stop and the resultant publicity gave the Ford the its greatest boost in twenty years.

American Airlines Operations 1962-1965

American Airlines undertook an extensive public relations program in September 1962 when they purchased 5-AT-39 (N-9683) from Aircraft Hydroforming in California. Before this national program was over in 1965 they had bought a second Ford, 5-AT-74, and gave the Ford Tri-Motor more public exposure in the United States than anyone has done since the 1930s.

"Frenchy" Savard, Vice President of Hayden Aircraft Corp., and American Airlines Captain Stanley J. Young, flew the plane from Gardena to AA's Tulsa Maintenance and Engineering Center in Tulsa, Oklahoma. There a dedicated crew of 22 mechanics, under the supervision of Floyd Tohline, completed the first phase of the restoration project in time for the Ford to fly to Washington, DC, to take part in the dedication of Dulles International Airport on November 17, 1962. When the airport opened officially

Walter Kollath (mechanic), Capt. Zeke Delong, Capt. Joe Kimm and Stewardess Coral Yahr were the crew that flew 5-AT-58 on its 30th Anniversary Flight across the United States. Captains Mel Swanson and Bob Bean flew an additional Twin Cities-Chicago-Twin Cities segment. (Northwest Airlines)

to commercial traffic on the 19th, the N-9683 was the first plane to leave.

The Ford then returned to Tulsa for the second phase of its rebuild and remained there until May 1963. It then started out on a national tour, primarily in 1963 and 1964,

Ford Tri-Motor specialists old and new. From left to right standing: Al Volk, Walt Kollath, Bill Frazier, Ted Sundberg, Manfred Boe, Emil Heideck, Russ Thiets, Ben Foster, Bud Winters, Bill Hoffman, Henry Walstrom, Nels Larson, Stanley Cady, John Vars, Joe Schuster, Leon S. DeLong. Left to right kneeling: Gene Roggeman, Lou Koerner, Clarence Magnuson, John Rosbach, Les Thiets, Roy Philblad, Reuben Peterson, Harold Hodgson, Chester Mahannah. (Northwest Airlines)

The dedicated crew that overhauled and re-built the interior of 5-AT-39 at the Tulsa, Oklahoma, overhaul facility of American Airlines. This November 1962 photo shows left to right: Floyd Tohline (Foreman, Airplane Overhaul), K.M. DeLong, L.D. Chappell, Bob Hanson (Project Coordinator), F.L. McCullum, J.G. Anderson, R.J. Fife, F.J. Caine, M.D. Watson, J. Hendricks, L.V. Roe, H.I. Terry, L.M. Yoakum, A.E. Morgan (Acting Foreman). Kneeling, left to right: J.F. Ross, R.F. Liebert, C.C. Stover, D.K. Grace, T.C. Partney, W.A. Olds, C.C. Cook, P.L. Jones, D.R. Laviness, E.J. Harris. (Hopkins photo via Floyd Tohline)

that resulted in an estimated three million people having a chance to see the plane in 32 states and Canada. An outstanding public relations program of advance publicity, display on the ground at local airports and guest flights allowed whole generations of people to see a plane that they had only heard about.

An example of the locations visited is shown by the following list of cities where the Ford was exhibited in 1963 during a flight from San Diego to Seattle: San Diego, Long Beach, Los Angeles, Santa Maria, Fresno, Monterey, San Jose, Oakland, San Francisco, Sacramento, Chico and Arcata, California; Medford, Eugene and Portland, Oregon; and Seattle, Washington.

The program ended in 1965 and the plane was stored pending its promised delivery to the new National Air and Space Museum upon completion of their new facility. For a short time in 1967 it was flown for special occasions, such as the 40th anniversary of Tinker Air Force Base, and Kelly Field's 50th anniversary.

American Airlines Captains that flew N-9683 during this time were James Adkins, Mel Burton, R.F. Carlin, R.C. Doverspike, William Hard, Ralph Long, Ed McNeil, H.C. Milton, Gordon Pierce, Sam Ridenour, Len Siemon, Frank Tosto and Stan Young. First Officers Harry Hargrove, Floyd Mace and Al Mitchell also piloted the Ford. Crew Chiefs were Gayle Collins, Carl Stover and Floyd Tohline.

A much less known part of this history is that American Airlines bought a second Ford, N-414H, in February 1965. The exterior was cleaned up and painted with American markings, but not given the overhaul that N-9683 had received, for static display at the New York World's Fair.

A New York City news story in July, 1965, said that juvenile delinquents had broken into the Fair grounds and wrecked N-414H. Ironically it turned out to be an exaggeration based on modern jet-age innocence; all of the "damage" turned out to be the collection of dents and bruises inflicted years before during its rough days of flying chicle in Guatemala.

Floyd Tohline went to New York in October, 1965, and supervised the removal of the plane. It was then flown back to Tulsa in a flight that took three days and 15 flying hours. It was put into storage until it was sold to Chuck LeMaster in October, 1972.

TWA's Second Anniversary Flight - 1963

On the occasion of the 25th Anniversary of the Civil Aeronautics Act, TWA leased 5-AT-74 (N-414H) from John Louck in Monmouth, Illinois, for a press flight from Los Angeles to Newark, New Jersey. Because TWA was trying to hold to the 1930 schedule there was not time for long stops on the way so, although there was some publicity at the time, this operation is not as well known as American's extensive public relations campaign.

Dave Runyon and Cecil Starner flew the Ford from Monmouth to Kansas City, Missouri, on June 9, 1963, to deliver it to the TWA maintenance base for a quick repainting. Louck's black and white paint was stripped off so that it would appear in its original aluminum finish, and a large red TWA was added to the side. The plane returned there on July 1st to have this reversed and Louck's colors put back on before the plane was returned to him. Starner was replaced by Jack Marshall, and Louck joined the group for the flight West. It was then flown to San Francisco via Omaha, Denver, Salt Lake City and Reno.

On June 18th it flew from San Francisco to Los Angeles with a group of newspaper reporters. Then early on the 20th it left Los Angeles with pilot Jack Marshall, co-pilot Dave Runyon, relief pilot John Louck, and veteran TWA Ford pilot Capt. Lee Flanagin as "TWA Command Pilot." The passengers were Jim Bishop, Newsweek; Eric Bramley, American Aviation; Bob Serling, United Press; Anne Chamberlin and Gordon Tenney, Saturday Evening Post; Paul J.C. Friedlander, New York Times; Stephen Kidd, Flying; Marvin Miles, Los Angeles Times; and Gordon Gilmore, VP public relations for TWA.

The first landing, unscheduled, was at Parker, Arizona, to replace a rocker box plug to stop an oil leak in the left engine. Then on to Albuquerque, Amarillo and overnight at Wichita. The next day to Kansas City, St. Louis, Indianapolis and overnight at Columbus. The last day had stops at Pittsburgh, Harrisburg, Philadelphia and Newark. The total flying time was 27 hours and 48 minutes, and a total elapsed time of 54 hours and 7 minutes.

Captain Edward McNeil and First Officer Harry Hargrove in front of 5-AT-39 at San Francisco on May 17, 1965. (W.T. Larkins)

After the trip had been completed the Ford went to Idlewilde Airport in New York, then to Washington, DC, where a crowd of 30,000 attended the FAA's celebration of the adoption of the Civil Aeronautics Act. Following this N-414H flew to Hartford, Connecticut, to take place in a celebration at the Pratt & Whitney factory. On the way home it visited Springfield and Boston, Mass., Williamsport, Penn., and Dayton, Ohio. Then to Indianapolis, Chicago, and back to Monmouth on June 29th.

Large crowds turned out all over the United States to inspect the beautifully restored 5-AT-39 operated by American Airlines. An estimated three million people saw it during 1963 and 1964, including a lucky few that were given rides at each stop. (American Airlines)

TWA Captain Lee Flanagin and TWA Stewardess Thelma Jean Harman (Hiatt) in front of 5-AT-74 during the June 1983 anniversary flight across the United States. Flanagin flew Fords for TWA and Harman started with TWA in 1934. Both were retired and were the honorary crew members for the transcontinental flight. (TWA)

5-AT-74, the second American Airlines Ford, next to the New York City Port Authority Heliport at the New York World's Fair in 1965. (American Airlines)

The author had the pleasure of flying from San Francisco to Los Angeles on June 18th and wrote the following at that time:

"They really scratched their heads in disbelief when TWA's anniversary Ford Tri-Motor pulled up to the terminal at Bakersfield. 'It's right out of the Twilight Zone' said one bewildered attendant. 'We may be 34 years late but we got here' answered one of the passengers with a broad grin.

"The nemesis of 1930s flying, bad weather, had caused the unscheduled stop for the Ford. The flight provided me with the opportunity of a lifetime, to ride in the Ford and a Boeing 707 between SFO and LAX on the same day.

"Speed and all-weather flying are the two big advances in air transportation demonstrated on this flight. Although the flying time in the Ford was its normal three hours and 20 minutes, as compared to the 707's 45-minute return trip, the Tri-Motor was the victim of fog and bad weather. In addition to being an hour late in leaving San Francisco we were on the ground an additional two and a half hours at Bakersfield waiting for better visibility in Los Angeles.

"Following the highway out of Bakersfield at an altitude of 6,000 feet was a vivid contrast in navigation to the 26,000 foot return over the top of total cloud cover. The 13-passenger Ford was very smooth riding in calm air. The ride in level flight was no different than the 707, and not a drop of coffee was spilled by TWA's first air hostess Mrs. Thelma Hiatt Harman who was wearing a 1934 white summer uniform for the occasion.

"The Ford had considerable sound proofing when built but pilot-owner John Louck had removed all of it from this plane. 'We did it to give the passengers a more realistic feeling of flying in the 1920s he said. He used the plane for barnstorming in the middle west, with over 17,000 passengers being carried in one eight-month season. To give his customers a genuine sensation of flying he kept the original Ford seats and removed the window curtains for a better view. The view of the ground was far better from the larger, single pane windows of the Ford than from the 707, but the low altitude flying of the Ford contributed an unfair advantage.

"Today's passenger would notice the sharp angle of the floor of the Ford while on the ground, quite different from 'conventional' tricycle-gear attitudes. The 707 had far more acceleration on takeoff and climb, as well as a definite feeling of deceleration on landing. Trim is very delicate on the Ford and one passenger walking up and down the aisle would throw it out of balance.

5-AT-74 at San Francisco International Airport on June 18, 1963, next to TWA's Boeing 707 N-754TW. It was leased from John Louck to make a 25th Anniversary transcontinental flight from Los Angeles to New York City. (W.T. Larkins)

5-AT-74 at Bakersfield, California, on the way from San Francisco to Los Angeles. Jack Marshall is running up the engines prior to departure and everyone is aboard except for the author who just had to have one more photo. (W.T. Larkins)

Although the Ford was once called 'a magnificent air yacht' its average speed of 100 mph was a sharp contrast to the 707's 600 mph. With ten times the range and three times the ceiling the Star-Stream had 95,000 hp as compared to the 1,350 hp of the Tin Goose."

A reporter wrote an outrageous story about the transcontinental flight entitled, "Last gasp of the Tin Goose; In a ramshackle museum piece, a dozen volunteers make a desperate journey down memory's airlane." A photo caption sets the tone with, "Copilot and terrorized passengers examine the right engine as the Tin Goose flies low and slow."

Since the *Saturday Evening Post* declined to print the authors letter to the editor following this it will be included here: "If Anne Chamberlin's article (Aug 10-17) is supposed to be funny it is pretty sick humor. I flew from San Francisco to Los Angeles on that 'ramshackle museum piece' and can guarantee that it was not a 'desperate journey' of 'terrorized passengers'. You have done a great injustice to a fine airplane that literally built the airline business in this country. Back in February 1939 there was an article 'Farewell, Tin Goose'; I am sure that your prophetic 'Last Gasp of the Tin Goose' will prove to be equally erroneous." In the ensuing 29 years N-414H has flown hundreds of satisfied passengers in Kansas and the middle west, at the EAA annual convention at Oshkosh, over the Grand Canyon innumerable times, and back across the United States in 1985 for a television documentary. It is in airworthy condition and regularly flying at Las Vegas in 1992 - quite a feat for an airplane described in 1963 as, "I calculated it had about six more miles to go before collapse."

TWA's Third Anniversary Flight - 1975

The least known of TWA's three cross country Flights with a Ford Tri-Motor is the one done in October and November, 1975.

Ken Roth, a Johnson Flying Service pilot with 10,000 hours in the Ford, and Jerry Casman, pilot for Harrah's Automobile Collection, flew 5-AT-8 (N-9645) from Reno to Newark to allow TWA to fly a transcontinental flight across the U.S. to commemorate their first all-air service in 1930. Following that itinerary it left Newark for Philadelphia. From there it made stops at Harrisburg, Pittsburgh, St. Louis, Kansas City, Wichita, Amarillo, Albuquerque, and ended at Los Angeles. Rides for the press and TWA officials were given along the way and the authentic TAT markings added to the reenactment by a plane that had been in TAT and TWA service.

N-414H Crosses the U.S. Again in 1985

Twenty-three years after it's TWA Anniversary crossing of the United States, 5-AT-74 did it again in fine style and with some spectacular additions.

After a year of preparation Scenic Airlines joined the United States Travel and Tourism Administration, in Frankfurt, Germany; a television crew from Saarlandischer Rundfunk, and TWA to film a seven day flight across the United States with the Ford Tri-Motor as the centerpiece. In order to accomplish this, Scenic flew one of their modified DeHavilland Twin Otters as a camera plane, photographing the Ford in flight from Long Beach,

California, to New York City. The 7-day, 3,000 mile flight was based on the 1929 TAT air-rail route, but to add spice to the travelogue side, trips were made to photograph interesting backgrounds.

Before the trip started Scenic spent $200,000 on the Ford, refurbishing the interior with soundproofing etc., and adding modern avionics to the cockpit such as dual communication, dual navigation, a glide slope and Loran-C. In addition to a general overhaul new cables and elevators were installed, as well as the horizontal stabilizer which had begun to show signs of corrosion. The work was so well done that the entire flight was made without a single squawk on the plane.

The planes left Long Beach on September 5, 1985, and flew to Scenic's headquarters at Las Vegas, Nevada. From there they headed for the Grand Canyon and some spectacular formation flying. The door had been removed from the Twin Otter and because they spent a good deal of time in steep banks, the German television crew literally sat on the edge of their seats, camera mounted on the floor, looking straight down at the Ford. Like gunners in military helicopters, there was nothing between them and the ground except for their safety belts. The Ford was filmed flying over Lake Mead, Hoover Dam and the length of the Grand Canyon. At Grand Canyon, Arizona, a helicopter was added for filming the Ford over the South Rim.

The planes followed the old TAT route with added stops, ending at Kennedy Airport in New York. TWA Vice President Ron Reynolds, who flew the Ford on the last leg from Lancaster, Pennsylvania, to Kennedy, flew it again for a tour of New York Harbor and the Statue of Liberty. Scenic Captain Fred Weir flew the first leg from Long Beach to Las Vegas, but the remainder of the trip was piloted by Bernie Godlove and his son Bryan, both United Air Lines pilots on vacation.

Unfortunately the hour-long documentary, produced and narrated by West German anchorman Otto Deppe, has not been seen in this country. It was made to encourage tourism to the U.S. by Germans, Swiss and Austrians. N-414H went on to East Hartford, Connecticut, to spend a month helping to celebrate Pratt & Whitney's 60th anniversary before returning to Las Vegas.

The author and John Louck in front of 5-AT-74 upon arrival at Los Angeles International Airport on 6-18-63. Louck must be given the credit for saving N-414H or it would not be still flying today. (Robert Hufford)

5-AT-74 flew across the United States again in September 1985 as part of a travelogue filming by a German TV crew. With side trips added for background scenery it took seven days to re-enact the 1929 air-rail route from Los Angeles to New York City. (Kathryn B. Creedy)

Chapter 8
Individual Histories of the Model 4-AT

4-AT-1; (TN)-2435, NC-1492; 4-AT-A
FF 6-11-26. Used by the Operations Division of the Stout Metal Airplane Division of the Ford Motor Company for research and development, and after rebuild to enclosed cockpit flown on the Ford Air Freight Lines for over 100,000 miles. Destroyed in a takeoff accident at the factory 5-12-28. (There were no aircraft registrations required before January 1927. Temporary Number 2435 was issued 5-3-27, and permanent registration NC-1492 was assigned about October 1927. Temporary Numbers were issued by the Department of Commerce, Bureau of Air Commerce, in early 1927 when they were faced with the massive task of licensing all aircraft and pilots in the United States for the first time. The Temporary Numbers were issued to allow the aircraft to operate while the formal paperwork for an airworthiness certificate was being prepared).

4-AT-2; (TN)-1039, NC-4309; 4-AT-A
FF 11-2-26. Delivered 11-2-26 to National Air Transport, Chicago, IL. 1-27-28 National Air Transport Flying Service, Chicago, IL. 5-2-29 Curtiss Flying Service, Chicago, IL. 6-3-30 Curtiss-Wright Flying Service, Glenview, IL. (Used during this time as a neon sign carrier). 8-24-31 E.B. Mulick and Elmer H. Leighton, Milwaukee, WI and reconditioned by the Hemilton Metalplane Company. 3-30-33 Georgia R. Bibby and Elmer H. Leighton, Milwaukee, WI. 6-16-33 Walter M. Blonski, Milwaukee, WI. 9-18-33 Nite Sky Advertising Company (W.M. Blonski, President), Milwaukee, WI. 3-25-35 E. B. Mulick, Milwaukee, WI. Flew with Temporary Number until 1-30-28 when it was changed to NC-4309.

4-AT-64, NC-8402. This interesting photo represents an equally fascinating puzzle. It is Ford Photo No. 7722, taken 8-28-30, of a spotless, polished 4-AT-E inside a large hall. It is probably the 10,000-seat Boardwalk Convention Hall at Asbury Park, New Jersey, which was opened for the first time three days earlier. There is no indication of any sale of this plane in the FAA files until 1933 when it went to Honduras, and the name New York Airways Inc. is not in the Index to the correspondence files of the Stout Metal Airplane Company. See also 5-AT-70. (Ford Archives)

NC 8402
NEW YORK AIRWAYS, INC.
NEW YORK AIRWAYS
NEW YORK ATLANTIC CITY WASHING
7722-8-28-30

4-AT-3; (TN)-3041, NC-3041, CF-AZB; 4-AT-A, 4-AT-B, 4-AT-E

FF 11-?-26. Put into service on 12-14-26 with the Ford Air Freight Line where it flew for five and a half years for a total of 4,000 hours or 400,000 miles. Modified to 4-AT-B standard with a new fuselage from Bulkhead #6 forward, and a new wing center section, in April 1929. In June 1929 300 hp Wright J-6's were installed to bring it up to 4-AT-E standard. 9-21-33 Roy W. Brillhart, Kansas City, KS. 1-27-34 Ben F. Gregory, Kansas City, KS. 2-24-34 Elizabeth Walker, Kansas City, MO. 1-9-35 Alton Walker, Kansas City, MO. In February wing engine cowls (speed rings), Bendix airwheels and an extra seat were added to license it as a threeplace freight carrier. 7-1-35 White Pass Airways, Skagway, AK. 3-30-36 British Yukon Navigation Company, Vancouver, B.C., Canada. In July 1940 it was being towed tail-first by a tractor on the airport at Whitehorse when a wingtip hit a hangar, wrenching the fuselage. An attempt to rebuilt it with parts from CF-BEP failed and so it was bulldozed into the ground as part of the construction of longer runways at Whitehorse. See 6-AT-1.

4-AT-4; A7526; 4-AT-A

FF 1-29-27. Delivered 3-9-27 to the U.S. Navy as model XJR-1. Stricken at the Naval Aircraft Factory 4-30-30.

4-AT-5; (TN)-3022, NC-1879, XA-DOL; 4-AT-A

FF 3-28-27. Delivered 6-23-27 to Stout Air Services, Detroit, MI where it flew as No. 3 on the Detroit-Cleveland Airlines. 5-12-31 Ford Motor Company, Dearborn, MI. It had been planned to place the plane on exhibit in the Edison Museum but instead it was dismantled and sold. 6-10-37 Milton Hersberger and R.N. Anderson, Put-In-Bay, OH. 7-10-41 Central Flying Service, Little Rock, AR. 2-19-43 Blanche Garbacz and Gladys Holbert, Little Rock, AR. 7-3-43 Charles H. Babb Company, New York City, NY. 8-4-43 Lights Inc., Alhambra, CA. 10-22-43 Charles H. Babb Company, New York City, NY. 7-19-44 International Aviation Enterprises, New York City, NY. 8-22-44 Transportes Aereos Mexicanos S.A. (TAMSA), Merida, Yucatan, Mexico. 330 hp Wright R-975-E's installed at this time. 2-10-47 Negociacion Aerea Mexicana S.A. (NAMSA), Ometepec, Guerrero, Mexico. Destroyed in a crash at Ometepec 5-12-47.

4-AT-6; NC-2492; 4-AT-A

FF 5-12-27. Delivered 5-18-27 to Standard Oil Company of Indiana, Chicago, IL. Named STANOLIND and first flew for the company on May 21, 1927, the day that Lindbergh landed in Paris. The plane flew 84,000 miles on company flights before it was replaced by a newer 5-AT. 3-1-29 Dale A. Seitz, Kansas City, KS. Destroyed in a crash at San Marcos, Texas, 2-8-30. There was a published rumor in 1966 that the remains had been found

4-AT-2, probably in 1933, after modifications but still showing the old half-moon windows of the 2-AT design. The lettering on the nose states American Aviation Corp., Lt. Walter M. Blake, Pilot. (Charles Kossack)

4-AT-3 on June 26, 1927 showing the wing engine exhaust pipes going up through the wing, and the elephant-ear ailerons. (Hudek)

4-AT-3 as modified and updated to 4-AT-E configuration. Plane No. 1 on the Ford Freight Line, probably in 1931. (William B. Stout)

4-AT-5 while it was being operated on sight-seeing tours of the Detroit area by Stout Air Services Inc., with the Temporary Number 3022. (Hudek)

4-AT-5 later when the registration NC-1879 had been assigned and it was being used on the Detroit-Cleveland route. Note the dolly under the tail skid for towing the plane. (Hudek)

4-AT-7 on its delivery flight to Maddux Air Lines in July 1927 as Temporary No. 3114. After reaching Los Angeles it was re-registered as NC-1102. (Peter M. Bowers)

4-AT-8 with its registration NC-880. It had previously been assigned the Temporary Number 3115. At Bettis Field, Pittsburgh, Pennsylvania in June 1928. (Kenneth M. Sumney)

4-AT-11 named "Remrand" for the Remington-Rand Corporation and registered to Marcell Rand in New York City. Posed at the factory with its propellers lined up properly on October 20, 1927. (Ford Archives)

in a barn in New Orleans and was being re-built but nothing has surfaced since then.

4-AT-7; (TN)-3114, NC-1102; 4-AT-A
FF 7-22-27. Delivered 7-26-27 to Jack L. Maddux, Los Angeles, CA. 11-16-27 Maddux Air Lines, Los Angeles, CA. (Maddux No. 1). 4-21-31 Transcontinental and Western Air (TWA), Wilmington, DE. After its license expired in September 1930 the plane was put on exhibit in the Pennsylvania Railroad Station in New York City. At some later date the plane was given to Henry Ford by the Pennsylvania Railroad Company and shipped disassembled by open flatcar to Dearborn. In 1938 the left wing was sold to Arthur Davis to repair 4-AT-42.

4-AT-8; (TN)-3115, NC-880; 4-AT-A
FF 8-1-27. Delivered 10-1-27 to Royal Typewriter Company, New York City, NY. Special interior for storage and cargo hatch for dropping typewriters by parachute. Temporary Number 3115 in use for one month only. 2-18-28 Stout Air Services, Dearborn, MI. Rebuilt back to passenger configuration with 14 seats, new engines installed and put into service on the Detroit-Cleveland Air Line. Crashed at Detroit on 10-13-28.

4-AT-9; NC-1076; 4-AT-A
FF 8-22-27. Delivered 10-6-27 to Stout Air Services, Dearborn, MI. Destroyed in an accident near Toledo, OH, 1-16-29.

4-AT-10; NC-1077, G-CARC, N-6077C; 4-AT-A
FF 9-10-27. Kept at the factory when new. This is the plane in which Bill Stout and Lindbergh's mother flew to Mexico City in December 1927. 5-21-28 Sky View Lines, Detroit, MI. Named "Niagara." Registered G-CARC in Canada on 6-11-29 with their affiliate Sky View Lines Ltd., Chippawa, Ontario. Used for sightseeing flights over Niagara Falls from the Canadian side. 1-19-35 United Air Transport, Edmonton, Alberta. 4-17-36 Northern Airways Ltd., Carcross, Yukon Territory, Canada. Registration cancelled 512-41 and plane put into storage. Sold 10-24-56 to Jim E. Kofahl, Kofahl-Davison Inc., Burbank, CA. 11-26-56 Eugene 0. Frank, Caldwell, ID.

4-AT-11; NC-1780, R-131; 4-AT-A
FF 10-11-27 .Delivered 10-20-27 to Marcell N. Rand, Rand Kardex Company, Tonawanda, NY. 9-1-28 Tri-Motor Safety Airways, Garden City, Long Island, NY. 3-8-29 New York Safety Airways, New York City, NY. 6-12-29 New York, Rio and Buenos Aires Line, New York City, NY. Names "Rio de la Plata." Destroyed in an accident at Cordoba, Argentina, 3-2-30.

4-AT-12; NC-1781; 4-AT-A
FF 10-26-27. Delivered 10-29-27 to Jack L. Maddux, Los Angeles, CA. 5-2-28 Maddux Air Lines, Los Angeles, CA. 1-16-29 G.E. Flaherty, Los Angeles, CA. 6-6-30 Mary Flaherty and Harold J. Flaherty, Los Angeles, CA. Photos taken at this time show the name Golden State Airways painted on the side. File cancelled 1-16-32 as plane went to Mexico. No further information.

4-AT-13; (ID)-3444, 28-348; 4-AT-A
FF 11-17-27. Delivered to the U.S. Army Air Corps on 2-15-27.It was flown with the Identified civil registration

A rare photo of 4-AT-13 showing its civil registration 3444 before it became Air Corps 28-348. It is in front of the airport terminal at Ford Airport in December 1927. (Ford Archives)

until officially received as model XC-3, AC 28-348, on 2-8-28. The registration 3444 was still visible in March 1928 when it was reported to the Department of Commerce for low flying. Scrapped at Wright Field as worn out in service "with fair wear and tear" 7-9-32.

4-AT-14; NC-3443; 4-AT-A
FF 12-14-27. Delivered 2-15-28 to The Texas Company, New York City, NY. Flown by Frank Hawks for TEXACO public relations work. Destroyed in a crash at Floresville, TX, 12-29-28.

4-AT-15; NX-4542; 4-AT-B
FF 3-20-28. Ownership remained with the Ford Motor Company while flown over the South Pole etc. See Chapter 7. Currently on exhibit at the Henry Ford Museum, Dearborn, MI.

4-AT-16; NC-4532; 4-AT-B
FF 3-30-28. Delivered 3-31-28 to Maddux Air Lines, Los Angeles, CA. 9-23-30 Consolidated Air Lines, Sacramento, CA. 1-28-31 Western Pacific Aviation Corporation, San Francisco, CA. 4-24-31 Pony Express Company, Seattle, WA. Registration cancelled 12-26-34 due to no reply from owner. Believed scrapped in 1932.

4-AT-17; NC-4805; 4-AT-B
FF 4-12-28. Delivered 4-20-28 to Gray Goose Air Lines, Chicago, IL. 10-26-29 Chicago Air Service, Chicago, IL. 12-5-30 United Aviation Corporation, Chicago, IL. 4-28-31 Skyway, Blackwell, OK. Destroyed in a hangar fire at Blackwell, along with seven other aircraft, on 3-15-32.

4-AT-18; NC-4806; 4-AT-B
FF 5-1-28. Delivered 5-10-28 to Stout Air Services, Dearborn, MI. 11-7-30 Ford Motor Company, Dearborn, MI. 6-16-33 Frank Free, Managua, Nicaragua. May have been involved in an accident at Managua on 10-18-33. License expired 7-1-34 as no renewal was requested. No further information.

4-AT-19; NC-5092; 4-AT-B, 4-AT-E
FF 4-28-28. Delivered 5-9-28 to Standard Oil Company of California, San Francisco, CA. Returned to the factory in March 1929 and rebuilt to 4-AT-E standard. 8-13-31 Jack W. Thornburg, Grand Canyon, AZ. 8-14-31 Ruckstell Corporation, Glendale, CA. 10-9-31 Grand Canyon Airlines, Grand Canyon, AZ. 5-25-34 Vernon Bookwalter, Seattle, WA. 11-24-34 White Pass Airways, Skagway, AK. The plane was destroyed when it hit a hangar while landing at Carcross, Yukon Territory, Alaska on 1-30-40. (The wings from Max Conrad's 5-AT, which had been damaged in a ground fire, had been purchased to put on NC-5092 but as the center section had 46 inches more span only the outer panels were useable so they were

Texaco Oil's 4-AT-14 was flown by Frank Hawks in the 1928 Ford Air Tour. It was lost in an accident one year after it was built. (Hudek)

4-AT-15 on March 27, 1928 before it's nose engine was changed for the Byrd Antarctic Expedition. It was already registered in the Experimental category because of internal changes made for its intended use. (Ford Archives)

Gray Goose Airlines took delivery of the new 4-AT-17 in April 1928. It is posed in its new paint scheme, with its propellers properly aligned, in front of the factory just eight days after it was built. (Ford Archives)

4-AT-17 in late 1931 while in use by Skyway Inc., of Blackwell, Oklahoma. The small Cessna GC-1 racer (NR-144V) is posed alongside for contrast. (Kenneth M. Sumney)

4-AT-20 at the factory when it was five days old. It was piloted by Clyde W. Ice (Transport License No. 1598) for Rapid Air Lines of Rapid City, South Dakota. The Blackfoot Indian name WAMBLEE OHANKO meant Swift Eagle, a much better name than Tin Goose. A photo taken in Mexico about 1928 shows a large map painted on the rear of the fuselage with a projected route from Canada to Panama. Rapid Air Lines had grand ideas of becoming an international airline before they went bankrupt in 1934. (Ford Archives)

4-AT-20 in the 1930s when it was flown by Ben Gregory and named "The Ship of Flame" for its spectacular nighttime advertising stunts described in the text. (Peter M. Bowers)

offered for sale at Skagway in April 1940). The left wing ended up on 5-AT-34.

4-AT-20; NC-5093; 4-AT-B
FF 5-10-28. Delivered 5-15-28 to Rapid Air Lines, Rapid City, SD and named "Wamblee Ohanko." 3-16-31 Thurmond Aircraft Corporation, Kansas City, MO. 6-3-31 Ben F. Gregory and J.E. Herndon, Kansas City, Kansas. 2-1-32 Ben F. Gregory, Kansas City, MO. Restricted license NR-5093 issued 12-31-36 for Aerial Lighting Advertising with 27 searchlights and power unit installed. At this time it had the name SHIP FROM MARS on the side of the fuselage and inside the cabin door, and THE SHIP OF FLAME on the nose. 3-25-42 Aircraft Exporting Corporation, New York City, NY. 4-8-42 H. W. Robinson, Ossining, NY. While on a delivery flight to sell it to Star Airlines, Anchorage, Alaska, it crashed near Metz, MO seriously injuring Ben Gregory.

4-AT-21; NC-5492; 4-AT-B
FF 5-18-28. Delivered 6-22-28 to Air Cruises, Detroit, MI. 5-29-31 Belle Fourche Air Lines, Belle Fourche, SD. 6-17-32 Air Cruises, Detroit, MI. 9-12-32 Clyde W. Ice, Rochester, MN. (Clyde Ice had been the Chief Pilot of Rapid Air Lines). 6-22-33 Government of Peru. Shipped on a Grace Line steamer, and still flying with the Peruvian Air Force in 1940.

4-AT-22; NC-5493, NR-5493, NC-5493; 4-AT-B
FF 6-1-28. Delivered 6-5-28 to Scenic Airways, Grand Canyon, AZ. 11-8-29 Col. Reg L. Robbins, Fort Worth, TX. Assigned Restricted license 7-1-31 to be used as two-place refueling plane for the Lockheed Vega "Fort Worth" on an attempted Seattle to Tokyo flight. 7-19-34 O.W. Robbins, Everman, TX, and Jesse Bristow, Fort Worth, TX. 1-25-35 Robertson Airplane Service Company, Robertson, MO. 5-3-35 Vernelle Irwin, Hallsville, IL. In March 1937 airwheels and aerial struts were installed, parts taken from Vernon Johns 4-AT-48. 8-25-40 Frank W. Clugston, Avon, IL. 10-29-40 George W. McCauley, Mineola, NY. 11-1-40 Atlantic Airmotive, Roosevelt Field, Mineola, Long Island, NY. Destroyed after a power dive into the ground at West Orange, NJ, on 6-10-42.

4-AT-23; NC-5577; TI-?; 4-AT-B
FF 6-16-28. Delivered 6-23-28 to Maddux Air Lines, Los Angeles, CA. 7-12-29 Curtiss Flying Service of California, Los Angeles, CA. After a crash at McCook, Nebraska, on 9-14-29 it was returned to the factory, rebuilt and released with new engines on 12-31-29. 3-9-33 Mac's Air Palace (W.H. McAfee), Uniontown, PA. 4-22-33 Harold L.

Maddux Air Lines 4-AT-23 shortly after delivery and before the letters "NC" were added to the registration. (EAA Library)

McAfee, Lamont Furnace, PA. 2-5-34 Paul E. Miller and Robert N. Matthews, Dunbar, PA. 6-26-34 Arthur Inman, Coffeyville, KS. 12-2-35 Rodger Inman (Inman Brothers Flying Circus), Coffeyville, KS. 2-27-39 Oscar W. Nichols, Newark, OH. 11-30-42 U.S. Government (Pan American Highway Project), Los Angeles, CA. Used by the U.S. Army Engineers in San Jose, Costa Rica together with Ford 4-AT-D NC-7583 and Bach T-11-P NC-34998. Reported as sold in Costa Rica in 1943. May be TI-61 or TI-64.

4-AT-24; NC-5578, HC-SBC; 4-AT-D
FF 6-16-28. Delivered 6-23-28 to Scenic Airways, Grand Canyon, AZ. The price was $3,000 more for a special 78-foot wing, bringing the total to $48,000. 9-14-29 Continental Air Express, Los Angeles, CA. 11-6-30 Samuel C. Rudolph, Los Angeles, CA. 11-19-30 Russell Reed and

Eugene Clemm, Glendale, CA. 10-1-37 Charles H. Babb, Glendale, CA. 12-8-37 J.A. Finklea and Jesse Bristow, Leland, MS. 6-20-38 St. Louis Flying Service, Robertson, MO. 7-21-38 John Leonard Yingst, Sheridan, PA and William S. Kirkpatrick, Easton, PA. 10-29-38 Aviation Credit Corporation, St. Louis, MO. 1-19-39 Louise A. Chamberlain, East Orange, NJ. 5-4-39 Robert P. Salter, Eutaw, AL. 3-10-41 Jesse Bristow, Columbus, OH. 3-13-41 Wichita Engineering Company Aviation School, Wichita Falls, TX. 8-12-43 Charles H. Babb Company. New York City, NY. 4-7-45 Shell Company of Ecuador, Quito, Ecuador. Crashed, Ayuy Airfield, Ecuador, 4-5-46.

4-AT-24, a modified 4-AT-D with a longer wing span, for Scenic Airways to fly over the Grand Canyon. (J. Roger Bentley)

4-AT-25; NC-5809; 4-AT-B
FF 7-2-28. Delivered 7-5-28 to Jefferson Airways, Minneapolis, MN. 4-13-29 The Embry-Riddle Company, Cincinnati, OH. 5-6-32 Robertson Airplane Service Company, Robertson, MO. 11-21-36 Robertson Aircraft Corporation, Robertson, MO. 6-14-37 Oral K. Southwick, Springfield, MO. 9-17-40 Dill M. Teel, Odessa, TX. 1-4-41 Hangar Six, San Antonio, TX. Washed out in a landing accident at Yoakum, Texas, on 6-14-41. The wreck was sold to Oscar W. Nichols, Reynoldsburg, Ohio, on 10-17-41 who took out all salvageable parts for his 4-AT-23 and sold the remainder as scrap.

4-AT-26 with B.C. Airways name under the right wing. G-CATX was previously NC-5810. J. Ernest Eve was President, Cecil Eve was Vice President, and Gordon Cameron was Secretary of the airline. This photo was taken on July 23, 1928 at the start of its first official flight from Victoria to Vancouver, British Columbia. The plane was lost in an accident just one month later. (G.R. Hearn)

4-AT-26; (TN)-5810, G-CATX; 4-AT-B
FF 7-14-28. Delivered 7-18-28 to British Columbia Airways, Victoria, B.C., Canada. Destroyed in a crash in Puget Sound 8-25-28. A Temporary Number 5810 was assigned 6-12-28 to ferry the plane to Canada. (Photo in *Airway Age*, August 1930, page 1082).

4-AT-27; NC-5811, NR-5811, NC-5811; 4-AT-B
FF 7-24-28. Delivered 7-26-28 to Queen City Air Lines, Cincinnati, OH. NR license issued 7-1-32 for advertising purposes (neon sign under the wing). 9-7-34 Ervin Saltzgaber, Canal Winchester, OH. Probably destroyed in a crash at Hundred, West Virginia, on 8-8-36.

4-AT-28 with the seldom seen markings of the Sundorph Aeronautical Corporation of Cleveland, Ohio. (William F. Yeager)

4-AT-28; NC-6892; 4-AT-B
FF 7-31-28. Delivered 8-17-28 to Stout Air Services, Dearborn, MI. 11-7-30 Ford Motor Company, Dearborn, MI. 9-27-33 E.C. Sundorph and Donald Patrick, Cleveland, OH. 7-1-38 Elmer H. Leighton, Manitowoc, WI. 12-14-40 Herbert C. Holtz, Milwaukee, WI. 12-14-40 George W. McCauley, Mineola, NY. 2-1-41 Atlantic Airmotive Corporation, Garden City, NY. Destroyed in a crash at Billings, Montana, on 11-21-42 while on a delivery flight to the U.S. Army Engineer Corps at Edmonton, Alberta, Canada.

4-AT-29; NC-6893, HC-SBD; 4-AT-B
FF 8-3-28. Delivered 8-6-28 to Robertson Aircraft Corporation, Anglum, MO. 9-7-29 Universal Aviation Corporation, St. Louis, MO. 4-10-31 American Airways, Robertson, MO. 4-4-32 Long and Harman, Dallas, TX. 12-10-32 Hangar Six, San Antonio, TX. (At this time it was plane No.2, of two Fords operated by the Dallas Aviation School, and named "Air Transport." Photo in Aero Digest, May 1932, page 17). 10-20-33 Dale P. Smith, Springfield, MO. After an accident at Girard, Kansas, on 4-23-34 a replacement wing tip and aileron from a 5-AT was installed. 10-13-34 Fly With Dale Air Services, Springfield, MO. 9-7-35 Ray Finklea, Leland, MS. 1-12-36 Frank Reimers, Lafayette, IN. Another accident on 7-9-39, near the Decker Airport at Austin, Minnesota, resulted in damage to the left wing and center section. 2-7-44 sold, less engines, to Charles H. Babb

4-AT-31 in its original 4-AT-B configuration. (Larkins Collection)

4-AT-31 after modification to 4-AT-E standard. (Larkins Collection)

Company, New York City, NY. 2-28-45 Shell Company of Ecuador Ltd., Quito, Ecuador. Exported on Certificate E-427 and registered HC-SBD. Destroyed in a crash 11-15-46 when a tire blew out on landing at Ayuy, Ecuador.

4-AT-30; NC-6894; 4-AT-B
FF 8-10-28. Delivered 8-11-28 to Robertson Aircraft Corporation, Anglum, MO. 11-26-28 Northern Air Lines, Minneapolis, MN. 5-22-30 Universal Aviation Corporation, St. Louis, MO. 4-10-31 American Airways, Robertson, MO. 8-15-32 M.A. Caffarello and G.T. Burrell, Chicago, IL. 10-27-32 Blue Bird Air Transport, Chicago, IL. 4-3-33 Freeman Aircraft Sales, Minneapolis, MN. 7-2-38 Mel Swanson, Minneapolis, MN. 7-8-38 George Formico, Minneapolis, MN. 7-23-38 Mrs. Eleanor Kipp, Randolph, MN. 12-29-38 Ben F. Gregory, Kansas City, KS. Destroyed in crash at Old Staley Airport, 3 miles East of Wichita Falls, Texas on 11-15-41.

4-AT-31; NC-7117, NR-7117, NC-7117, IM-5; 4-AT-B, 4-AT-E
FF 8-15-28. Delivered 8-18-28 to Maddux Air Lines, Los Angeles, CA. Converted by Maddux in February 1930 to 4-AT-E with J-6 engines. 4-21-31 Transcontinental and Western Air (TWA), New York City, NY. 4-10-33 Blue Bird Air Transport, Chicago, IL. Approved 9-9-33 for Restricted license for acrobatics in connection with the American Air Races Tour. 9-14-36 J. Frederick Wood, Kenneth Fondren Starnes and E.Z. Newsom Jr., Memphis, TN. 1-8-37 Kenneth Starnes and Lester Massingham, Memphis, TN. 4-2-38 Kenneth Starnes, Memphis, TN. 4-16-38 St. Louis Flying Service, Robertson, MO. 4-24-38 David W. Kratz, Robertson, MO. 10-24-38 Wilson E. Stone, Lawrence, KS. 31-39 Tex-O-Can Flour Mills , Dallas, TX. Operated in 1939-1941 with sound equipment and smoke writer tanks. 12-1-42 Charles H. Babb Company, New York City, NY. 4-13-43 W. Clayton Lemon, Roanoke, VA. 9-21-43 Charles H. Babb Company, New York City, NY. 10-11-43 Air Transport Corporation, Richmond, VA. 3-18-44 Charles H. Babb Company, New York City, NY. 3-18-44 Expreso Aereo Inter-Americano S.A., Havana, Cuba.

4-AT-32; NC-7118; 4-AT-B
FF 8-22-28. Delivered 8-25-28 to Maddux Air Lines, Los Angeles, CA. 7-15-29 Curtiss Flying Service of California, Los Angeles, CA. 8-29 Curtiss-Wright Flying Service, Los Angeles, CA. Blown upside down and destroyed by heavy winds at Grand Central Air Terminal, Burbank, CA on 11-21-30.

4-AT-33; NC-7119; 4-AT-B, 4-AT-E.
FF 8-28-28. Delivered 9-7-28 to Maddux Air Lines, Los Angeles, CA. Converted to 4-AT-E standard by Maddux in February 1930. 4-21-31 Transcontinental and Western Air (TWA), New York City, NY. Destroyed in a crash at Oklahoma City, Oklahoma, 12-19-31.

4-AT-34; NC-7120; 4-AT-B
FF 8-31-28. Delivered 9-14-28 to Stout Air Services (Plane No.9), Dearborn, MI. 1-13-31 Ford Motor Company, Dearborn, MI. 1-20-33 Sumner B. Morgan, Tela, Honduras. 10-19-33 Morgan Air Lines, Hoboken, NJ. License cancelled 2-1-34, reported crashed in Honduras.

4-AT-35 landing at Union Air Terminal in Burbank while owned by United Air Services in the late 1930s. The odd shape of the propeller blades is caused by the moving slit of the focal plane shutter of a Graflex camera. (A.U. Schmidt)

4-AT-35; NC-7121; 4-AT-B
FF 9-5-28. Delivered 9-21-28 to Tri-Motored Air Tours, Port Clinton, OH. 6-2-38 Gilbert R. Minick, Richond, VA. 1-11-39 Columbia Pictures Corporation of California, Hollywood, CA. Used in movie "Only Angels Have Wings." 6-22-39 United Air Services, Burbank, CA. On

10-14-41 Paul Mantz Air Services (United Air Services) notified the CAA that the plane had been dismantled and sold for scrap.

4-AT-36; NC-7582, CU-???; 4-AT-B, 4-AT-E
FF 9-7-28. Delivered 9-25-28 to Maddux Air Lines, Los Angeles, CA. (Photos show Maddux No.8 and the name "The Glendale"). Converted to 4-AT-E standard with J-6 engines by Maddux about September 1929. 4-21-31 Transcontinental and western Air (TWA), Wilmington, DE. 5-5-33 Pan American Aviation Supply Corporation, New York City, NY. Leased to Compania Nacional Cubana de Aviacion and probably sold to them in 1934. License cancelled by CAA 11-15-34.

4-AT-37; NC-7583, TI-?; 4-AT-B, 4-AT-D
FF 9-10-28. Delivered 9-14-28 to Universal Flyers, Washington, D.C. 6-11-31 Ray Loomis, Washington, D.C. 7-6-34 Ralph Barron, Hapeville, GA. 8-27-35 Dorothy Loomis, c/o Universal Flyers, Washington, D.C. Converted in June 1936 to 4-AT-D (Memo 2-322), further modified in June 1937 to use a Wright R-975-D of 300 hp in the nose. 8-11-38 Ray Loomis, Washington, D.C. 12-20-38 Reginald A. Dawson, Washington, D.C. 2-9-42 Archie Ray Loomis, Toledo, OH. 1-13-43 U.S. Government Engineering Division, Los Angeles, CA, for use in construction work on portions of the Pan-American Highway in Costa Rica. Operated by the U.S. Army Corps of Engineers. 6-5-44 Public Roads Administration, Federal Works Project, San Jose, Costa Rica. Probably became TI-61 or TI-64.

4-AT-38; NC-7584; 4-AT-B
FF 9-13-28. Delivered 9-26-28 to Robertson Aircraft Corporation, Anglum, MO. 9-7-29 Universal Aviation Corporation, St. Louis, MO. 4-10-31 American Airways, Robertson, MO. 11-21-31 C. Hahn, Pittsburgh, PA. 11-15-32 Air Service of Pittsburgh, Pittsburgh, PA. 11-4-36 R.N. Anderson and Milton Hersberger, Put-In-Bay, OH. 11-18-36 Air Tours, Put-In-Bay, OH. The WW2 surplus N3N engines (Wright R-760-8, 235 hp) were installed in May 1949. 8-31-53 Milton Hersberger, Put-In-Bay, OH. 8-31-53 Travelair Taxi, Sandusky, OH. Crashed at South Bass Island, Ohio, 7-1-77. Rebuilt by Kal-Aero and first flown again in March 1980. Crash at South Bass Island 7-1-77. Rebuilt by Kal-Aero and flown in March 1980. 8-12-85 Mercury Aviation Companies, Richmond Heights, OH. 10-18-85 Allan Thomas Chaney, Newark, OH. 10-6-91 Kermit Weeks, Miami, FL.

4-AT-39; NC-7585, NX-7585, NC-423H, TI-43; 4-AT-B, 9-A
FF 9-17-28. Kept at the factory until 1934. Used as a freight carrier in 1929-1930. Experimental license issued 9-15-30 to test Pratt & Whitney Wasp Junior engines with s/n 1 being installed in the nose. Model designation

4-AT-35 painted as an airliner for the motion picture "Only Angels Have Wings." The registration and name Barranca Airways are both fictitious. (Lee Enich)

4-AT-36 is a Ford that is seldom seen in photos with the Maddux Air Lines markings. (E.T. Smallwood)

4-AT-38 in an early 1928 photo when it was delivered to Robertson Aircraft Corporation in Anglum, Missouri. (Hudek)

4-AT-38 with Universal Air Lines logo on the side in 1930. NC-7584 is best known for its long years of service with Island Airlines. (Hudek)

changed to 9-A and registration changed to NC-423H in December 1930. Standard Ford Hi-Speed equipment added in 1931 and 1932. 1-26-34 Harold A. White, Tegucigalpa, Honduras. Sold (date unknown) to ENTA Costa Rica. Photos of a spectacular one wheel landing at San Jose, Costa Rica (*Popular Aviation*, October 1940, pg. 54) show it to be using a three blade prop on the nose engine.

4-AT-40; NC-7586; 4-AT-B
FF 8-22-29. Delivered 8-22-29 to Universal Flyers, Washington, D.C. See Chapter 4). 7-20-32 Ray Loomis, Washington, D.C. (Ray Loomis was President of Universal Flyers). CAA cancelled the license after an accident at Lima, Ohio, on 7-1-34. (Photo in Airway Age, April 1930, pg. 549).

4-AT-41; NC-7683; 4-AT-B
FF 9-22-28. Delivered 9-28-28 to Colonial Western Airways, New York City, NY. Destroyed in what was called at the time "The worst accident in the history of heavier-than-air aeronautics in this country" at Newark, New Jersey, on March 17, 1929.

4-AT-42; NC-7684; 4-AT-B
FF 9-26-28. Delivered 9-28-28 to Sky View Lines, Buffalo, NY. 1-27-31 W.F. Long and C.E. Harman, Dallas, TX. 3-11-37 Arthur J. Davis, East Lansing, MI. (As a result of an accident on 9-15-37 the left wing was replaced by the left wing of 4-AT-7 resulting in a 4-AT-A left wing and a 4-AT-B right wing. In October 1942 this was corrected by replacing it with the left wing from 4-AT-25). 8-19-38 Lew E. Tipper, Detroit, MI. Mike Murphy, Murphy Flying Service, Findlay, OH. 10-9-41 Air Tours, Put-In-Bay, OH. 8-31-53 Milton Hersberger, Put-In-Bay, OH. 8-31-53 Travelair Taxi, Sandusky, OH. Written off after a crash at Port Clinton, Ohio, on 8-21-72 but reappears on the civil register in the 1980s as sold to Allan T. Chaney, Hebron, Ohio. 1-92 "Sale Reported."

4-AT-43; NC-7685; 4-AT-B
FF 10-1-28. Delivered 10-16-28 to Nekoosa-Edwards Paper Company, Port Edwards, WI. 6-3-31 Major Leslie G. Mulzer, Wisconsin Rapids, WI (He had been the pilot for Nekoosa-Edwards). 11-2-32 Mulzer Flying Service, Wisconsin Rapids, WI. Destroyed in a tornado at Columbus, Ohio, on 6-22-34 when 75 mph winds turned it upside down, breaking off the tail and damaging the wings. Useable parts were salvaged and the remainder cut up for scrap. (See 4-AT-32).

4-AT-44; NC-7686; 4-AT-B
FF 10-3-28. Delivered 11-2-28 to Jesse M. Kenyon, Kenyon Transportation Company, Morris, MN. 4-13-32 J.H. O'Brien, Morris, MN. Destroyed in a crash near Neodesha, Kansas, on 3-31-33.

A very rare photo of 4-AT-45 of Spokane Airways. The plane was delivered on November 9, 1928 and crashed on December 10th. (Peter M. Bowers)

4-AT-45; NC-7687; 4-AT-B
FF 10-8-28. Delivered 11-9-28 to S.J. Wilson, Spokane Airways, Spokane, WA. Destroyed in a crash near Spokane, Washington, 12-10-28.

4-AT-46 while owned by William "Bill" Monday, the "Flying Cowboy" of Cody, Wyoming. (Gary Farrar)

4-AT-46; NC-7861; 4-AT-B, 4-AT-E
FF 10-9-28. Kept at the factory and rebuilt to 4-AT-E configuration with Wright J-6 engines in June 1929. A photo in U.S. Air Service magazine for December 1928 shows it being towed to the Philadelphia Aircraft Show. 4-30-30 Union Electric Light and Power Company, St. Louis, MO. 3-18-37 William A. Monday, "Flying Cowboy", Cody, WY. 9-19-39 Johnson Flying Service, Missoula, MT. 5-69 Dexter D. Coffin Jr., Palm Beach Florida. Donated in the 1970s to the Naval Aviation Museum, Pensacola, FL.

4-AT-47; NC-7862; 4-AT-C
FF 10-12-28. Delivered 10-25-28 to Sunbeam Air Transport Company, Denver, CO. One P&W Wasp of 410 hp in the nose and two Wright J-5's of 220 hp in the wings. Destroyed in a crash at Spur, Texas, 12-1-28.

4-AT-48; NC-7863; 4-AT-B
FF 10-17-28. Delivered 11-28-28 to Reid, Murdoch and Company (Monarch Foods), Chicago, IL. Special interior as a flying display case, see Chapter Four. 4-22-31 Vernon N. Johns, Dearborn, MI. Destroyed in an accident at Gasden, Alabama, on 4-28-35. The remains were sold to Joe Musleh, Jacksonville, FL on 2-29-36 who used the parts to rebuild his 4-AT-50.

4-AT-48 in 1931 after its use by Monarch Foods. Vernon Johns, the Monarch pilot, bought the plane and used it to fly scenic flights in conjunction with the Dearborn Inn at the Ford Airport. The airwheels and painted cowls are unusual. As can be seen throughout this book the underside of the right wing of the Ford was used to great advantage for advertising. (Hudek)

4-AT-49 with an Experimental license while used by the Wright Aeronautical Corporation as the prototype of the 4-AT-E. This photo shows it in its new condition as it appeared when flown as an accompanying plane in the 1929 Ford Air Tour. The pilot was George F. Chapline. (Kenneth D. Wilson)

4-AT-49; NX-7864, NC-7864; 4-AT-B, 4-AT-E
FF 10-26-28. Delivered 11-24-28 to Wright Aeronautical Corporation, Paterson, NJ. A prototype 4-AT-E with Wright J-6 engines installed in 1928. Wright applied to the Bureau of Air Commerce in September 1930 to relicense the plane as a 4-AT-E stating that it conformed to the specifications of ATC-132. 8-31-31 Curtiss-Wright Flying Service, New York City, NY. (A photo in U.S. Air Services magazine, December 1931, page 24, shows the large lettering AIR FERRY on the side when C/W was operating the Metropolitan Air Ferry Service around New York City). 5-25-32 Transamerican Airlines Corporation, Detroit, MI. 4-1-33 American Airways, Chicago, IL. 10-7-33 Theodore E. Knowles, Knowles Flying Service, Detroit, MI. Destroyed in a crash at Flint, Michigan, 5-18-35.

4-AT-49 at a later date showing changes in the engine exhausts and cooling louvers in the nose engine compartment. (Kenneth D. Wilson)

4-AT-50; NC-7865; 4-AT-B
FF 10-30-28. Delivered 5-16-29 to Curtiss Flying Service, New York City, NY, with 27:30 hours flying time. 10-25-29 Curtiss Flying Service of New England, East Boston, MA. 12-8-32 George M. Keightley, Jacksonville, FL. 5-15-33 Joe Musleh and George M. Keightley, Greenville, SC. Accident at Ashville, North Carolina, on 6-16-35. 6-26-35 Joseph Musleh, Jacksonville, FL. (Parts from this plane and NC-7863 were shipped to Parks Air College in East St. Louis to make one complete airplane. The wings, tail assembly and landing gear were taken from NC-7865, and the front part of the fuselage and center section was taken from NC-7583). 12-7-36 Helen Ward Musleh, Greensboro, NC. 4-3-37 George Jaynes, Atlanta, GA. 4-3-37 Helen Ward Musleh, Greensboro, NC. 4-8-37 Blevins Aircraft Corporation, Atlanta, GA. 7-2-37 Helen Ward Musleh, Jacksonville, FL. Destroyed in a crash at Powellsville, NC, 10-20-38.

4-AT-50, probably when owned by Helen Ward Musleh of Greensboro, North Carolina. Ralph Wickford flew this Ford as an accompanying plane in the 1929 Ford Air Tour. (Jack McNulty)

4-AT-51 with the Curtiss Flying Service of New York in 1929. It was one of several Fords operated by this company throughout the United States. (John Stiles)

4-AT-51; NC-9608, NR-9608, NC-9608, IM-4; 4-AT-B
FF 11-2-28. Delivered 5-22-29 to Curtiss Flying Service, New York City, NY. 12-21-32 W.I. Marsalis, c/o Curtiss Wright Flying Service, Long Island, NY. 4-7-33 Carolina Air Transport, Burlington, NC.(Restricted license approved for 11-10-33 to 5-15-34 for the purpose of carrying a show horse on tour. Structural changes included a large

door manufactured by Ford). 7-1-36 John and Harold McClintock, Pittsburgh, PA. 7-31-39 Frank Reimers, Lafayette, IN. 6-9-42 Cleo Cecil Stratton, Ballinger, TX. 12-29-42 Charles H. Babb Company, New York City, NY. 1-18-43 Expreso Aero Inter-Americano, Havana, Cuba.

4-AT-52; NC-9609; 4-AT-B
FF 11-9-28. Delivered 6-4-29 to Curtiss Flying Service, New York City, NY. 1-13-30 Curtiss Flying Service of Florida, Miami, FL. 5-9-30 Curtiss-Wright Flying Service, Valley Stream, L.I., NY. 9-26-30 Curtiss-Wright Flying Service, Pittsburgh, PA. 12-3-32 Waitman W. Martin, c/o Fakes and Company, Dallas, TX. 6-6-33 E. L. Fulton, Dallas, TX. Destroyed when blown upside down in a hurricane on the beach near the Chamal Ranch, Boca Chica, Tamaulipas, Mexico It was being operated at the time by a Brownsville, Texas, fishing company.

4-AT-53; NC-9610; 4-AT-B
FF 11-13-28. Delivered 5-14-29 to Curtiss Flying Service, Garden City, L.I., NY. 11-1-29 Curtiss Flying Service of the Middle West, Chicago, IL. 10-10-30 Curtiss Flying Service, Chicago, IL. 10-21-32 Harold Sherman Johnson, Chicago, IL. 10-7-42 Aubrey E. Loving and Floyd G. Clark, Richmond, VA. 5-28-43 Charles H. Babb Company, New York City, NY. 5-29-43 C.W. Murchison, Dallas, TX. 12-7-44 Air Tours, Put-In-Bay, OH. Approval for installation of war surplus N3N engines and propellers 6-1-46. 8-31-53 Milton Hersberger, Put-In-Bay, OH. 8-31-53 Travelair Taxi, Sandusky, OH. Destroyed in a crash at Kelleys Island, Ohio, 7-3-54.

4-AT-54; NC-9611; 4-AT-E
FF 1-11-29. Delivered 3-13-29 to Pennsylvania Airlines, Pittsburgh, PA. 5-27-30 Pittsburgh Airways, Pittsburgh, PA. Destroyed in a crash at Jennerstown, Pennsylvania, 12-20-30. The first production 4-AT-E.

4-AT-55; NC-9612; 4-AT-E
FF 1-15-29. Delivered 3-30-29 to Mamer Flying Service, Spokane, WA. 10-14-36 Reginald Pattinson and Wayne Parmenter, St. Elmo and later Witt, IL. 8-7-40 K-T Flying Service (Robert Tyce and Charles B. Knox), Honolulu, T.H. (Was at Pearl Harbor on 12-7-41). 8-15-45 Lt. Clinton Arthur Johnson (USN), Mt. Shasta City, CA. Shipped by boat to San Francisco and assembled at Oakland Airport, then stored at Livermore Sky Ranch. Leased in July 1949 by TWA, painted in TWA and TAT markings, and flown across the U.S. for a 20th anniversary celebration. 1-28-52 William Hadden, Orofino, ID. Orofino, ID. In June 1952 modified to an agricultural sprayer. 10-28-57 Johnson Flying Service, Missoula, MT. 2-21-69 Jack Adams Aircraft Sales, Walls, MS. 2-21-69 Dolph Overton, Santee, SC. 4-9-81 Dolph Overton, Wings and Wheels, Orlando, FL.

4-AT-52 in 1930. Curtiss-Wright at Pittsburgh, Pennsylvania, offered a transcontinental aerial hearse service. (Kenneth M. Sumney)

4-AT-55 posed with cars of the Arnot Motor Company, a Los Angeles Ford Dealer. The auto license plates all show the date 1929. This may have been an extension of Mamer's barnstorming operation with NC-9612. (Ernest L. True)

4-AT-55 years later in the early morning mist at Orofino, Idaho, on August 14, 1952. The rare 5-AT-40 with the Wright engines is on the left. (W.T. Larkins)

4-AT-55 taking off from the Davis-Winters Airfield on May 11, 1947 during an air show at this former AAF field in California. It was owned at this time by Clinton A. Johnson of Mt. Shasta City, CA, and had recently come from Hawaii. (W.T. Larkins)

4-AT-56; NC-9613; 4-AT-E
FF 1-17-29. Delivered 7-11-29 to Sky View Lines, Buffalo, NY. 3-23-31 Jerry Wood, Mount Prospect, IL. 5-8-31 Air Tours, Chicago, IL. 4-29-37 Air Flights, Oak Park,

IL. 5-24-38 Louisville Flying Service, Louisville, KY. 7-23-38 Herman Hamer, Champaign, IL. 5-24-39 Charles Earl Bradbury Jr., Champaign, IL. Damaged in a hard landing in a field North of Marcus, Illinois, 9-21-39. Repaired by E.M. Laird Airplane Company, Chicago. 2-29-40 Herman Hamer, La Salle, IL. 5-31-41 William Vogel, La Salle, IL. 10-11-41 Aircraft Export Corporation, New York City, NY. Destroyed by a strong wind which turned it on it's back at Corpus Christi, Texas, on 3-8-42.

4-AT-57 when used for aerial advertising by the Plane Speaker Corporation. The man seated in the open door has a microphone in his hand and the "Voice of the Sky" was used to broadcast messages while flying low over a city. (Larkins Collection)

4-AT-57; NC-9614, NR-9614; 4-AT-E
FF 1-26-29. Delivered 5-29-29 to Firestone Tire and Rubber Company, Akron, OH. 10-4-29 Stout Metal Airplane Company, Dearborn, MI. Because of an accident at Hasbrouck Heights, NJ, on 9-14-29, it needed a new right wing so the plane was sent back to the factory. 1-27-30 Chalon E. Corson, Stratford, CT. 2-10-30 New England and western Air Transportation (C.E. Corson, President), Stratford, CT. 1-13-31 Chalon E. Corson, Stratford, CT. 6-21-32 Plane Speaker Corporation, New York City, NY. Restricted license issued about 9-15-32 for aerial broadcasting. The plane, equipped with generators and loud speakers was named "Voice of the Sky." Destroyed in a hangar fire at Roosevelt Field, Long Island, New York on June 2, 1933.

4-AT-57, the "Voice of the Sky", at a later date advertising Silver Dust. Lester W. Bryant was the pilot of this Ford when it was owned by Firestone and accompanied the planes in the 1919 Ford Air Tour. (Harold G. Martin)

4-AT-58; NC-9642, NR-9642, NC-9642, NR-9642; 4-AT-E
FF 1-29-29. Delivered 4-18-29 to Mohawk Airways, Schenectady, NY. (A 5-9-32 photo shows "United Air Service" on the side, and pilot Art Bussy who plans to fly the Atlantic in it). Restricted license approved 2-24-35 for night advertising with a Link Electric Skysign operating from the Albany, New York, airport. On 8-12-36 it was returned to NC status. 3-12-36 J.A. Haraden and John Kovacs, Schenectady, NY. 4-15-36 Link Aeronautical Corporation, Endicott, NY. 4-10-39 Johnson Flying Service, Missoula, MT. In May 1950 it was modified to a convertible insecticide sprayer and a second Restricted license was issued 6-9-50. Classified as destroyed in a crash near Townsend, Montana, on 6-19-56. 4-13-79 Evergreen Helicopters, McMinnville, OR. 4-13-79 Kal Aero, Kalamazoo, MI. Registration N-9642 reissued 7-10-80.

4-AT-58 on August 13, 1952. The wheels are just leaving the ground as Jim Larkin, pilot for the Johnson Flying Service, takes off on a U.S. Forest Service flight from Mc Call, Idaho. (W.T. Larkins)

4-AT-59; A8273; 4-AT-E
FF 2-12-29. Delivered 5-28-29 to the U.S. Navy as model JR-2. Stricken at San Diego 1-31-35.

4-AT-60; A8274; 4-AT-E
FF 2-18-29. Delivered 6-12-29 to the U.S. Navy as model JR-2. Stricken at Quantico 7-32-34.

4-AT-60, U.S. Navy Serial Number A8274, at the Marine Corps Air Station at Quantico, Virginia, in the early 1930s. (Larkins Collection)

4-AT-61; NC-9678, G-ABEF, VH-UDY, A-45-2; 4-AT-E
FF 2-22-29. Export Certificate E-338 issued 9-19-30,

4-AT-61 presents one of the remaining mysteries about Ford Tri-Motor ownership and use. There is no record of any sale between the time it was built in February 1929 and its transfer to the Ford Motor Company Ltd., in London, in October 1930 where it became G-ABEF (EF for Edsel Ford). The photo above clearly shows NC-9678 and the name United Air Transport Inc. Unfortunately there is no information as to when and where this photo was taken. It is an original Box Brownie 120 negative from the collection of the late Jack McNulty. There may be an omission in the FAA files on NC-9678 as the name United Air Transport is in the Index to the Customer Service and Sales correspondence files of the Stout Metal Airplane Company. (Jack McNulty)

4-AT-62 with advertising on the side for its owner the Curtiss Publishing Company. The photo was taken at the factory the day before it first flew in July 1929. (Gordon S. Williams)

ownership changed to Ford Motor Company Ltd., London, England on 11-14-30. Approved for NC on 9-10-30 and sent to England as a demonstrator in October 1930. 7-1-34 British Air Navigation Company, registered G-ABEF and named "Vagabond." 1935 Holden's Air Transport Services Ltd., Salamaua, New Guinea, with Australian registration VH-UDY issued 1-8-36. 7-15-37 Guinea Airways Ltd. 1942 impressed into service with the Royal Australian Air Force at Townsville, Queensland, and assigned RAAF Serial No. A-45-2.

4-AT-62; NC-8400; 4-AT-E
FF 4-13-29. Delivered 7-11-29 to Curtiss Publishing Company, Philadelphia, PA. 7-14-31 Arthur H. Kudner, 420 Lexington Avenue, New York City, NY. 7-6-33 Despatch Corporation, New York City, NY. 2-17-36 C.M. Ewan, New York City, NY. 6-13-36 Manitowoc Air Service, Manitowoc, WI. 11-14-36 Holland G. Bryan, Paducah, KY. 6-3-37 Keith G. Cantine, Detroit, MI. 6-20-38 Mary Cantine, Akron, OH. 3-31-41 Johnson Flying Service. Crashed near Boulder, Montana, 7-14-53. 4-13-79 Evergreen Helicopters, McMinnville, OR. 4-13-79 Kal Aero, Kalamazoo, MI. Registration N-8400 reinstated 3-18-80.

4-AT-63; NC-8401, NM-?; 4-AT-E
FF 4-16-29. Delivered 6-27-29 to Pitcairn Aviation, Philadelphia, PA. 10-1-30 Intercontinent Aviation, Jersey City, NJ. Operated by their affiliate Compania Nacional Cubana de Aviation Curtiss in Havana, Cuba, under Cuban registration together with 4-AT-69 and 4-AT-70.

4-AT-64; NC-8402; 4-AT-E
FF 4-17-29. Kept as a factory demonstrator and used as a test airplane for High Speed equipment with the outboard engines mounted six inches higher. August 1930 photo shows name "New York Airways Inc., NY-Atlantic City-Washington" on the side and Bird's Eye Finish on the wing nacelles. NX-8402 registration approved 1-2631, reverted to NC on 6-30-31. Stored at Ford Airport until rebuilt in 1933. 11-17-33 Harold A. White, Tegucigalpa, Honduras.

4-AT-65; NC-8403; 4-AT-E
FF 5-1-29. Delivered 7-10-29 to Mamer Flying Service, Spokane, WA. 5-5-34 Tom Marshall Kester and Edward H. Groenendyke, Pasadena, CA. While operating as Ptarmigan Airlines the plane was washed out in an accident at Flat, Alaska, on 10-26-34. Remains recovered by the Alaska Aviation Heritage Museum at Anchorage in the summer of 1989.

4-AT-66; 11-AT-1, 4-AT-66; NC-8404, NX-8404, NR-8404, NC-8404; 4-AT-E, 4-AT-G, 11-AT, 4-AT-B.
FF 7-10-29. Built as a 4-AT-E and kept at the factory as a test airplane. Ford applied to the CAA for an experimental license on 327-30 for a conventional 4-AT-E with Packard Diesel engines. It first flew with these engines on 4-2-30 and was briefly called model 4-AT-G, but then changed to model 11-AT. This remained in effect until July 1934 when Ford notified the CAA that it had been remodeled to 4-AT-B standard with wright J-5 engines of 220 hp. From 3-21-31 to 4-1-32 it was issued a Restricted license as a cargo plane, then reverted to NC certification. It is uncertain if it was rebuilt with the shorter "B" type center section or had the longer "E" wing but lower h.p. engines. 7-3-34 Mulzer Flying Service, Columbus, OH. 1-25-36 Oral K. Southwick, Springfield, MO. Crashed at Belleville, Illinois, 5-29-37 and remains shipped to Parks Air College for rebuilding. The cost of repairs proved to be too high so it was cut into three pieces and sold as scrap.

4-AT-69 at Phoenix, Arizona, in 1967 while owned by Dale Glenn. Note the modified, non-standard cabin door. (Brian R. Baker)

4-AT-67; NC-8405, IM-3; 4-AT-E
FF 8-2-29. Kept at the factory for five years. Used to test various experimental windshields in 1930. 9-26-34 Westchester Airways, Auburn, NY and Miami Beach, FL. 11-21-42 Expreso Aereo Inter-Americano S.A., Havana, Cuba. Delivered to Cuba in May 1943 with Cuban registration IM-3.

4-AT-68; NC-8406, EC-KKA, G-ACAK, VH-USX; 4-AT-E
FF 8-14-29. Delivered 12-9-29 to Concesionaria de Lineas Aereas Subvencionades S.A. (CLASSA), Madrid, Spain. 9-7-32 Ford Motor Company, London, England. 5-24-35 Holden Air Transport Services, Salamaua, New Guinea. 5-14-37 Guinea Airways Ltd., Lae, New Guinea. Destroyed by Japanese action in January 1942.

4-AT-69; NC-8407, (Cuba -), (Dominican Republic -), N-8407; 4-AT-E
FF 8-21-29. Delivered 11-5-29 to Eastern Air Transport, Brooklyn, NY. 10-1-30 Intercontinent Aviation, New York City, NY, for operation by Compania Nacional de Aviation Curtiss, Havana, Cuba. Date unknown - to Cuerpo de Aviacion Militar (Air Force), Dominican Republic. 2-1-50 Rex Williams, Phoenix, AZ. In May 1954 the engines were replaced by a 550 hp P&W wasp SIDI in the nose and two 450 hp Wasps in outboard positions, making it the highest h.p. 4-AT ever flown. In December 1954 the nose engine was replaced by a 450 hp Wasp Jr. 2-15-55 David Callender, Eagle, ID. 7-1-55 Aircraft Service Company, Boise, ID. 5-22-58 Johnson Flying Service of Idaho Inc., Cascade, ID. 3-29-63 LeMaster-Glenn Aerial Spraying, Ottawa, KS. 7-25-64 Ford Tri-Motor Inc., Ottawa, KS, (Dale Glenn, President). 2-16-66 Ford Tri-Motor Inc., Lawrence, KS. 7-6-73 EAA Air Museum Foundation, Hales Corners, WI. 2-27-85 EAA Air Museum Foundation, Wittman Field, Oshkosh, WI.

4-AT-70; NC-8408, NM-?; 4-AT-E
FF 8-28-29. Delivered 11-22-29 to Pitcairn Aviation (later Eastern Air Transport), Brooklyn, NY. 10-1-30 Intercontinent Aviation, Jersey City, NJ, to be operated by Compania Nacional de Aviacion Curtiss, Havana, Cuba. (Photo in 1932 *Aircraft Year Book*, page 50, shows Cubana markings with U.S. registration).

4-AT-69 at Orange County Airport, Santa Ana, California. It was operated by Tallmantz for a short period and flown by Frank Tallman. (Henry W. Arnold)

4-AT-71; (ID)-9656, EC-WIO; EC-RRA, 42-8, EC-BAB; 4-AT-F
FF 7-27-31. Delivered 8-7-31 to Concesionaires de Lineas Aereas Subvencionadas S.A. (CLASSA), Madrid, Spain. 10-31 Lineas Postales Aereas Espanoles, Madrid, Spain. It was impressed into service with the Spanish Air Force during the Civil War, and later registered EC-BAB for Compania Anonima de Lineas Aereas (IBERIA). Destroyed in a crash in 1948.

4-AT-72 to 4-AT-79 Not Used.

4-AT-80; 29-220; 4-AT-E
FF 5-29-29. Delivered 6-14-29 to the U.S. Army Air Corps as model C-9. Surveyed at Panama 8-2-35.

4-AT-81; 29-221; 4-AT-E
FF 6-3-29. Delivered 7-5-29 to the U.S. Army Air Corps as model C-9. Surveyed at Wright Field 5-25-36.

4-AT-82; 29-222; 4-AT-E
FF 6-7-29. Delivered 6-26-29 to the U.S. Army Air Corps as model C-9. Surveyed at Selfridge Field 8-6-34.

4-AT-83; 29-223; 4-AT-E
FF 6-14-29. Delivered 6-29-29 to the U.S. Army Air Corps as model C-9. Surveyed at Wright Field 2-13-36.

4-AT-84; 29-224; 4-AT-E
FF 6-18-29. Delivered 6-29-29 to the U.S. Army Air Corps as model C-9. Surveyed at San Antonio Air Depot 11-1-34.

4-AT-85; 29-225; 4-AT-E
FF 6-20-29. Delivered 6-29-29 to the U.S. Army Air Corps as model C-9. Surveyed at Barksdale Field 5-1-36.

4-AT-86; 29-226; 4-AT-E
FF 6-21-29. Delivered 6-29-29 to the U.S. Army Air Corps as model C-9. Surveyed at Barksdale Field 9-3-35.

Chapter 9
Individual Histories of the Model 5-AT

5-AT-1; X-6926, NC-6926, C-?; 5-AT-A, 5-AT-B
FF 7-21-28. Delivered August 22nd to Pratt & Whitney Aircraft Co., Bridgeport, CT. 4-1-29 E.A. Deeds (Chairman of the Board, P&W), Hartford, CT. 8-11-30 The United Airports Of Connecticut Inc., East Hartford, CT. 5-3-34 Interamerican Aerotravel and Supplies Inc., NYC. 5-4-34 exported to Sociedad Colombo-Alemana de Transportes Aeros (SCADTA), Barranquilla, Colombia.

5-AT-2, X-7416, NC-7416, 5-AT-A
FF 8-30-28. Delivered 8-31-28 to Northwest Airways Inc., St. Paul, MN. Crashed at St. Paul 6-24-29. Price new was $65,000.

5-AT-3, NC-7739, 5-AT-A
FF 9-29-28. Delivered 10-6-28 to Northwest Airways Inc., St. Paul, MN. Destroyed in a hangar fire at Chicago 6-25-30.

5-AT-4, NC-9606, AN-AAQ, N-9606, 5-AT-B
FF 10-24-28. Delivered 11-24-28 to TAT. The "City of Columbus" used by Charles Lindbergh as a flying office to lay out TAT trans-continental route. Later "City of New York." Changed to Transcontinental & Western Air 4-6-31. 2-14-35 William Keith Scott, Los Angeles, CA. 5-13-39 Fairchild Aerial Surveys, Los Angeles, CA. 5-14-40 Texas Petroleum Co., New York City, NY (used in Venezuela for oil development). TACA Nicaragua 1942-1945, 1946-1951 unknown but probably TACA, 7-31-48 James C. Pippinger and Allen A. Crane, Caracas, Venezuela. 10-3-51 Sky-Ads Inc. (Jesse Bristow), Miami, FL. 7-14-52 Northwest Agricultural Aviation Corp., Choteau, MT, total time 9,673 hours. Destroyed in takeoff accident at Choteau, Montana, 5-6-53.

5-AT-98 at Boeing Field, Seattle, about 1932 when it was flying the Pacific Air Transport (PAT) division of United Air Lines. The small packages from the Railway Express Company truck are being loaded into the double wing bins that were standard on the 5-AT-D. Each PAT 5-AT-D had an individual name painted on the rudder, this one being DAWSON. (Boeing Airplane Company)

UNITED
5001-B

5-AT-5, NC-9607, 5-AT-B
FF 11-8-28. Delivered 11-22-28 to TAT. Change 4-6-31 to TWA, Wilmington, DE. Destroyed in crash at Quay, NM, 8-29-33.

5-AT-6; NC-9643, F-31; 5-AT-B
FF 11-22-28. Sold to TAT 11-28-28 for $65,475, delivered 1-18-29. 4-6-31 changed to TWA. TWA No.612. 4-5-35 Servicio Aereo Colombiano (SACO), Bogota, Colombia. Destroyed 6-24-35 in a collision with a Ford 5-AT-D at Medellin, Colombia.

5-AT-7; NC-9644, XH-, LG-AAJ, AN-AAT, 5-AT-B
FF 11-27-28. Delivered 1-18-29 to TAT. 4-6-31 changed to TWA. 3-27-36 Grand Canyon Airlines, Grand Canyon, AZ. 2-23-37 Grand Canyon-Boulder Dam Tours, Boulder City, NV. 12-11-37 TACA, Honduras, Guatemala and Nicaragua.

5-AT-8; NC-9645, XH-, AN-AAS, XA-FUB, XB-NET, N-58996, N-9645; 5-AT-B
FF 12-1-28. Delivered 1-18-29 to TAT (TAT No. A-3, City of Wichita). 4-6-31 changed to TWA (TWA No. 608). 7-16-35 G. E. Ruckstell, Grand Canyon Airlines, Grand Canyon, AZ. 2-23-37 Grand Canyon-Boulder Dam Tours, Boulder City, NV. 12-11-37 TACA, Tegucigalpa, Honduras. Ricardo Nevarez Izurieta, Campeche, Mexico, January 1946 to July 1950 (XA-FUB issued 6-4-46). Arturo D'Argence, Campeche, Mexico, August 1950 to July 1953 (new registration XB-NET issued 8-17-50). In February 1951 XB-NET was completely overhauled by Torres Landa in the Servicios Aeronauticos de Mexico S.A. shops in Mexico City, and in late 1951 was flown again after major repairs. The corrugated skin was replaced with modern sheet dural and so since that time this plane has been known as "the smooth skin Ford." In July 1953 Arturo sold the plane to his brother Augusto D'Argence. In January 1954 it was damaged when a wheel locked, turning the ship off the runway and into a ditch. It was not repaired and the plane was sold as is to Frank D. Oergel, Burbank, CA in May 1955. 11-2-55 purchased by Eugene Frank, Caldwell, Idaho from Frank D. Oergel, Jr., Mexico City, and assigned registration N-58996. 7-29-64 Harrah's Club, Reno, NV (changed to N-9645 9-28-64). Sold at Harrah's auction for 1.5 million. 6-28-86 Gary Norton, Athol, ID. 7-10-86 Norton Aero Ltd., Athol, ID. 3-90 Evergreen Aviation, McMinnville, OR. 1-92 747 Inc., McMinnville, OR.

5-AT-9; NC-9646, YV-MGO, 5-AT-B
FF 12-4-28. Delivered 1-18-29 to TAT. 4-6-31 changed to TWA. 9-22-37 Gulf Oil Corp., Pittsburgh, PA. 10-30-37 Mene Grande Oil Company C.A., Maracaibo, Venezuela, a Gulf Oil subsidiary. Flown to Venezuela in Feb 1938 with insignia of MGO in circle.

5-AT-3 illustrates the round-top 4-AT-B style cabin windows that identify the model 5-AT-A. (Northwest Airlines)

5-AT-4 after its service with TAT/TWA when it was sold to William Keith Scott whose initials are under the right wing. Scott was President of Jimsco Oil Company, owner of Scott Motors and a sports flyer in Los Angeles. (Warren M. Bodie)

5-AT-5 shows unusual markings for National Air Transport with the airline name in small type as if AIR MAIL LIMITED was the name of the company. (Larkins Collection)

5-AT-8 with the rare Indian Head insignia and Western Air Express style airline logo on TAT's "City of Wichita" at Columbus, Ohio in November 1930. (Ken Blaney)

5-AT-11 with the registration N-1629M in 1949 when it was completely overhauled by Pacific Airmotive Corporation at Burbank. Approximately 60% of the original corrugated aluminum skin was replaced and BT-13 engines and props were installed along with new cowlings and engine nacelles. (Pacific Airmotive)

5-AT-11 in March 1961 after a second major overhaul by Pacific Airmotive at what was by now known as Lockheed Air Terminal in Burbank. Dave Coleman and Ralph Jones, who had worked on it in 1949, manufactured parts and replacement skin by handcrafting each part. (Pacific Airmotive)

5-AT-11 at Port Clinton, Ohio, on August 11, 1967. Island Airlines bought the plane to complement their 4-AT's but it proved to be too expensive to operate on their short routes. (John C. Barbery)

5-AT-10; NC-9636, 5-AT-B
FF 12-6-28. Delivered 1-4-29 to Maddux Airlines, Los Angeles, CA. Destroyed in crash at San Diego, CA, 4-21-29.

5-AT-11; NC-9637, NM-22, X-ABCC, AN-AAJ, HI-3, NX-1629M, N-1629M, XB-KUI, XA-HIL, N-1629M, N-9637, N-76GC, N-9637; 5-AT-B.
FF 12-10-28. Delivered 1-4-29 to Pan American Airways, New York City, NY. Special modification with five gas tanks in wings for 565 gallons to fly route between Havana and Santiago de Cuba. Sold to subsidiary Cia Mexicana de Aviacion, Mexico City, about May 1929. In 1947 it was owned by Compania Dominicana de Aviacion, Dominican Republic. 1-22-48 Jesse Q. Bristow, Miami Shores, FL for $1,000. 10-4-48 Norman Pinney Company, Burbank, CA. 12-1-48 San Luis Mining Company, San Francisco, CA (and Tayoltita, Mexico). Rebuilt by Pacific Airmotive Corp., Burbank, CA, with BT-13 engines, and licensed XB-KUI on 3-28-49. About 4-9-49 re-registered as XA-HIL to be operated by Transportes Aereos-Terrestres, S.A. at Tayoltita for the San Luis Mining Company. 3-20-66 Arizona Airmotive Corporation, Tucson, AZ. 6-20-66 Travel Air Taxi, Port Clinton, OH. 10-31-68 Jack Adams Aircraft Sales, Walls, MS. 11-4-68 Dolph Overton, Santee, SC, as N-1629M. 3-22-69 re-registered N-9637 by Dolph Overton, Wings and Wheels Museum, Santee, SC. 1-23-76 Commuter Investment Corporation, Las Vegas, NV, (John R. Seibold, President). 6-11-76 re-registered N-76GC for 1976 Bi-Centennial Year/Grand Canyon Airlines. 6-5-82 re-registered N-9637. 8-30-82 San Diego Aerospace Museum, San Diego, CA.

5-AT-12; N-9661, X-ABCB, X-ABCO; 5-AT-B
FF 12-12-28. Delivered 2-6-29 to Cia Mexicana de Aviacion S.A., Mexico City, Mexico. Identification Mark 9661 issued for 15 days to ferry plane to Mexico. Crashed near Amemeca, Mexico, 3-26-36.

5-AT-13; NC-9667,XH-?, AN-AAR, 5-AT-B
FF 12-14-28. Delivered 2-14-29 to Erle P. Halliburton, Southwest Air Fast Express (SAFEWAY), Tulsa, OK (Fleet No. 1). 10-11-30 changed to Southern Air Fast Express, Dallas, TX. 6-11-31 American Airways, Cincinnati, OH. 5-12-34 changed to American Airlines, Chicago. 4-18-36 Aviation Manufacturing Corp., Chicago, IL. 6-6-36 TACA, Tegucigalpa, Honduras.

5-AT-14; NC-9663, XH-?, LG-AAH, 5-AT-B
FF 12-19-28. Delivered 2-5-29 to Robertson Aircraft Corp., Anglum, MO. 11-18-29 Universal Aviation Corp., St. Louis, MO. 5-6-30 Colonial Air Transport, New York City, NY (remodeled to Hi-Speed configuration 9-30). 5-12-34 American Airlines, Chicago. 11-8-34 American Airways, Chicago. 6-3-35 A.B. and Kenneth C. Clark, Watsonville, CA. 1-10-37 Grand Canyon-Boulder Dam Tours, Boulder City, NV. 12-11-37 TACA, Tegucigalpa, Honduras.

5-AT-15; NC-9668, XH-TAW, 5-AT-B
FF 12-21-28. Delivered 2-25-29 to Stout Air Services, Dearborn, MI for $65,475. 10-1-30 National Air Transport (NAT), Chicago, IL. Remodeled in January 1931 with high speed configuration: outboard engines lowered

six inches, mail bins installed in wings, center section reinforced, wings reinforced in area over engines, ring cowls and wheel pants installed. 10-17-33 Pennsylvania Airlines, Pittsburgh, PA. 1-21-36 TACA, Tegucigalpa, Honduras. Ferried from Cleveland, OH, to Brownsville, TX, to Honduras as XH-TAW in July 1936.

5-AT-16; NC-9638, F-32, LG-AAL, 5-AT-B
FF 12-27-28. Delivered 1-16-29 to Maddux Airlines, Los Angeles, CA, for $65,475. 4-21-31 TWA, New York City, NY. 4-5-35 Servicio Aereo Colombiano (SACO), Bogota, Colombia. 3-39 TACA, Tegucigalpa, Honduras for TACA Guatemala.

5-AT-17; NC-9639, OA-AAA, CB-CAM; 5-AT-B
FF 12-29-28. Delivered 2-9-29 to Maddux Air Lines, Los Angeles, CA. 4-21-31 TWA, New York City, NY. 7-5-34 Pan American Grace Airways (Panagra), New York City, NY. Remodeled to Hi-Speed configuration in Jan 1931. Panagra installed a cargo hatch in the top rear of the fuselage. Operated with both cargo and passengers with 550 hp Wasps in the outboard positions. Operated by Aerovias Peruanas, an affiliate of Panagra, during the Parcoy Mine operations in June 1936 as OA-AAA (named "San Fernando"). 4-17-39 Compania Aramayo de Mines en Bolivie, Las Paz, Bolivia.

5-AT-18; NC-9640, LG-AAI, AN-AAL, XA-FUP; 5-AT-B
FF 1-8-29. Delivered 2-26-29 to Maddux Air Lines, Los Angeles, CA. 4-21-31 TWA, New York City, NY. 3-27-36 Grand Canyon Airlines, Grand Canyon, AZ. 2-23-37 Grand Canyon-Boulder Dam Tours, Boulder City, NV. 12-11-37 TACA Tegucigalpa, Honduras. 1938-1942 TACA Guatemala. 1-42 to 3-46 TACA Nicaragua. 6-6-46 Negociacion Aerea Mexicana S.A. (NAMSA).

5-AT-19; NC-9641, TI-51, 5-AT-B
FF 1-10-29. Delivered 3-5-29 to Maddux Air Lines, Los Angeles, CA. 4-21-31 TwA, New York City, NY. Modified to Hi-Speed configuration 5-31. 2-17-36 Leslie G. Mulzer, Columbus OH. 6-29-36 Mulzer Flying Service, Columbus, OH. 3-39 Aerovias Nacionales, San Jose, Costa Rica.

5-AT-20; NC-9649, 5-AT-B
FF 1-18-29. Delivered 6-14-29 to TAT, New York City, NY. Destroyed in crash on Mount Taylor near Albuquerque, NM, 9-3-29.

5-AT-21; ID-9662, NC-9647, 5-AT-B
FF 1-23-29. Identification Mark 9662 issued 2-16-29 for U.S. Army endurance tests. Returned to the factory and rebuilt to standard 5AT-B model, registered NC-9647 4-1-29 and sold 4-26-29 to Transcontinental Air Transport, New York City, NY. Brought back to the factory and

5-AT-15 in February 1929 when delivered to Stout Air Lines. (Ford Archives)

5-AT-15 in an interesting publicity photo with considerable lettering added and the name "The Spirit of Transportation" on the nose. The single-place Szekley "Flying Dutchman" is under the wing for a comparison of size. (Peter M. Bowers)

released again on 6-1-29. After an accident at Indianapolis, IN, on 12-22-29 it was completely rebuilt and modified to Hi-Speed configuration. 4-6-31 TWA, New York City, NY. Destroyed in a crash at Harrisburg, Pennsylvania, 1-27-31.

5-AT-22; ID-9672, X-ABCA, NC-9672, C-205; 5-AT-B
FF 1-25-29. Delivered 3-5-29 to Cia Mexicana de Aviacion S.A., Mexico City, Mexico. (Identification Mark 9672 issued for 15 days to ferry plane to Mexico). 7-19-32 Pan American Airways, New York City, NY. 8-22-32 Pan American Grace Airways, New York City, NY. Panagra remodeled plane in its Lima, Peru, shops for 13,750 lbs. gross weight with 550 hp outboard engines. In January 1939 the 450 hp Wasps were re-installed. 3-15-39 South American Gulf Oil Company (SAGO), New York City, NY. Operated in Colombia as C-205, probably by Colombian Petroleum Company, after 8-12-40. Reported sold to AVENSA Venezuela in World War II. To the Shell Company of Ecuador in May 1946.

5-AT-23; NC-9664, 5-AT-B
FF 1-31-29. Delivered 3-25-29 to Pan American Airways, New York City, NY. Destroyed in crash at El Aceituno near San Lorenzo, Honduras 10-2-32.

5-AT-24; NC-9665, 5-AT-B
FF 2-7-29. Delivered 3-1-29 to Erle P. Halliburton, Southwest Air Fast Express, Tulsa, OK. 2-10-30 South-

ern Air Fast Express, Dallas, TX. 3-2-31 TwA, New York City, NY. Modified to Hi-Speed configuration at the factory in June 1931. Destroyed in crash at Pittsburgh, PA, 8-19-31.

5-AT-25; NC-9666, 5-AT-B
FF 2-11-29. Delivered 3-5-29 to Erle P. Halliburton, Southwest Air Fast Express, Tulsa, OK. 10-11-30 Southern Air Fast Express, Dallas, TX. 3-2-31 TWA, New York City, NY. Destroyed on the ground, after an emergency landing caused by a fire in flight, at Bakersfield, CA, 2-10-33.

5-AT-26; NC-9669, LG-AAG, 5-AT-B
FF 2-19-29. Delivered 4-24-29 to Stout Air Services, Dearborn, MI for $55,000. Stout Air Service No.11. 10-1-30 National Air Transport, Chicago, IL. Hi-Speed modification made in December 1930. 7-10-33 Pennsylvania Airlines, Pittsburgh, PA. 1-21-36 TACA, Tegucigalpa, Honduras. Operated by TACA Guatemala as LG-AAG.

5-AT-27; ID-9670, X-ABCD, NC-9670, XA-BCU, NM-25; 5-AT-B
FF 2-21-29. Delivered 3-7-29 to Cia Mexicana de Aviacion S.A., Mexico City, Mexico. Identification Mark 9670 issued 3-8-29 for 15 days to ferry plane to customer where it was assigned X-ABCD. 12-2-29 Pan American Airways, New York City, to operate in the Canal Zone. 7-19-32 back to Cia Mexicana as XA-BCU. 10-21-36 Pan American Airways. 11-30-36 Compania Nacional Cubana de Aviacion S.A., Havana, Cuba. 7-26-46 Remains sold as scrap to Air Tours, Putin Bay, OH together with 5-AT-40. Probably cannibalized for parts as it was never registered in the U.S. after 1936.

5-AT-28; NC-9671, XH-TAX, LG-AAE; 5-AT-B
FF 2-26-29. Delivered 3-19-29 to Erle P. Halliburton, Southwest Air Fast Express, Tulsa, OK. 10-11-30 Southern Air Fast Express, Dallas, TX. Modified to Hi-Speed configuration in June 1931, and for modified gross weight of 13,750 lbs. in October 1932. 12-17-32 American Airways, Chicago, IL. (12/34 to 1/36 leased to Central Airlines, Pittsburgh, PA). 4-21-36 Aviation Manufacturing Corp., Chicago, IL. 6-6-36 TACA, Tegucigalpa, Honduras as XH-TAX. Later operated by TACA Guatemala as LG-AAE.

5-AT-29; NC-9662; 5-AT-B
FF 2-28-29. Delivered 3-19-29 to Erle P. Halliburton, Southwest Air Fast Express, Tulsa, OK. 10-11-30 Southern Air Fast Express, Dallas, TX. Modified to Hi-Speed configuration in June 1931. 6-18-31 American Airways, Robertson, MO. Destroyed in crash at Cincinnati, OH, 8-9-31.

5-AT-30; NC-9685, AN-?; 5-AT-B
FF 3-5-29. Delivered 3-25-29 to Pan American Airways, New York City, NY. Flew the first commercial air mail from the U.S. to Central America. Modified to operate with a gross weight of 13,750 lbs. in December 1933. Sold 12-31-37 to the Nicaraguan Government.

5-AT-31; ID-9673, X-ABCE, NC-9673, XA-BCV, XH-?, TI-44, AN-AAE, XA-FOH; 5-AT-B.
FF 3-8-29. Delivered 3-28-29 to Cia Mexicana de Aviacion, Mexico City, Mexico. Identification mark 9673 issued for 15 days for ferry flight to Mexico where it became X-ABCE. 5-19-30 Pan American Airways, New York City, NY. 7-6-33 Cia Mexicana de Aviacion as XA-BCV. 8-27-37 Pan American Airways, New York City, NY. Modified to operate at gross weight of 13,750 lbs. in 1937. Sold to the Nicaraguan Government 12-31-37 (Nicaraguan National Airways?). TACA Costa Rica as TI-44 in 1939. 1-42 to 1-46 TACA Nicaragua. 1-46 Juan Tilghman Gallo (operating as SAN, Servicios Aereos Nacionales S.A.), Mexico. Crashed and written off 6-13-46 near Actopan, Hidalgo, Mexico.

5-AT-32; NC-9674; 5-AT-B
FF 3-14-29. Crashed five days later at the factory 3-19-29. Prospective customer unknown. Aircraft salvaged for parts.

5-AT-33; NC-9675; 5-AT-B
FF 3-20-29. Delivered 3-30-29 to Colonial Air Transport, New York City, NY. Destroyed in crash at Boston, MA, 6-5-30.

5-AT-34; NC-9651, NX-9651; 5-AT-B
FF 3-22-29. Delivered 5-16-29 to TAT, New York City, NY. 4-6-31 TWA, Wilmington, DE. Modified to Hi-

5-AT-34 when owned by the Radio Corporation of America at Camden, New Jersey. David S. Little and Halden Emrick flew it for extensive tests with then secret projects involving TV transmitters and drone control, the first airborne Radio (FM) Altimiter, and the first plane to carry an Omni-Directional Radiobeacon Receiver. (Gaylord Moxon)

Speed configuration in July 1931, for 13,750 pounds. gross weight in April 1932., 3-11-36 R.C.A. Manufacturing Company, Camden, NJ (NX Experimental license issued 8-3-36 for developing and testing radio apparatus). 1-30-41 Aircraft Exporting Corp., New York City, NY. 4-10-41 Star Air Lines, Anchorage, AK. In August 1943 the left engine quit on takeoff at Fairbanks and the ship ground looped and stood on its nose. It was dismantled and stored until it was sold on 4-18-52, by what by then had become Alaska Airlines, to Clyde Sampson, Compton Airport, CA. The plane remained in crates in Alaska until 7-21-53 when it was sold to Eugene O. Frank, Caldwell, Idaho, who brought the crates back down the Alcan Highway on a flatbed truck. 6-26-64 Mox-Air, Los Angeles, CA. 11-1-68 G.E. Moxon, Los Angeles, CA. 10-22-69 Irving B. and Janice Perlitch, Morgan Hill, CA.

5-AT-35; NC-9677, XH-?; 5-AT-B
FF 4-3-29. Delivered 4-12-29 to Colonial Air Transport, New York City, NY for $55,475. (See photo in 1930 *Aircraft Year Book*, page 31, showing the Colonial markings and unusual tail design). 11-2331 American Airways, New York City, NY. 6-25-36 Aviation Manufacturing Corp., Chicago, IL. 7-23-36 TACA, Tegucigalpa, Honduras.

5-AT-36; NC-9681, LG-AAF; 5-AT-B
FF 3-28-29. Delivered 4-6-29 to Colonial Air Transport, New York City, NY. Modified to H-Speed configuration 7-22-31 and to 13,750 lbs. gross weight 4-20-33. 4-4-33 American Airways, New York City, NY. 4-18-36 Aviation Manufacturing Corporation, Chicago, IL. Sold same day to TACA, Tegucigalpa, Honduras. Operated by TACA Guatemala as LG-AAF.

5-AT-37; NC-9650; 5-AT-B
FF 3-26-29. Delivered 5-22-29 to Transcontinental Air Transport, New York City, NY for $55,475. Destroyed in crash at Amarillo, Texas, 12-14-32.

5-AT-38; 29-219; 5-AT-B
FF 4-5-29. Delivered 6-9-29 to U.S. Army Air Corps as model C-4. Stricken at March Field 4-29-35.

5-AT-39; NC-9683, XH-TAK, AN-AAP, XA-FUE, XB-WAR, N-1124N, XB-YIT, N-7791B, N-9683; 5-AT-B
FF 4-6-29. Delivered 4-13-29 to Erle P. Halliburton, Southwest Air Fast Express, Tulsa, OK. 10-11-30 Southern Air Fast Express, Dallas, TX. 5-16-31 Colonial Air Transport, Newark, NJ. Modified to Hi-Speed configuration on 3-30-31. 4-3-33 American Airways, Chicago, IL. 4-18-36 Aviation Manufacturing Corporation, Chicago, IL. 6-6-36 TACA, Tegucigalpa, Honduras as XH-TAK. 1-42 TACA Nicaragua as AN-AAP. 3-46 Miguel A. Zuniga, Mexico City, Mexico who in turn sold it to Carlos Davalos, operating as TAJSA, and registered XA-FUE. 8-53 Raul Fierro Villalobos, Guadalajara, Jalisco, Mexico. 11-12-53 Robert W. Waltermire, Choteau, MT. Assigned N-1124N by the U.S. Government but he had to use XB-WAR to ferry it out of Mexico. 5-27-55 Gerald D. Wilson, Orofino, ID. 1955-56 (date uncertain) Jack Adams Aircraft Sales, Memphis, TN. 9-22-56 E.W. Brown III, Orange, TX. 10-22-56 Minerales de Zaragoza S.A., Torreon, Mexico as XB-YIT. 4-12-57 Edgar W. Brown III, Orange, TX as N-7791B. 11-18-57 Jack Adams Aircraft Sales, Memphis, TN. 12-9-57 Aircraft Hydroforming, Gardena, CA. 9-27-62 American Airlines, New York City, NY. 11-12-73. National Air & Space Museum, Smithsonian Institution, Washington, D.C.

5-AT-40; NC-9684, M-SCAN(?), X-ABCF, NC-9684, NM-25, N-69905; 5-AT-B.
FF 4-9-29. Delivered 5-1-29 to Cia Mexicana de Aviacion, Mexico City, Mexico. 11-1-36 Pan American Airways, New York City, NY. 6-15-38 Cia Nacional Cubana de Aviacion S.A., Havana, Cuba. 7-26-46 Air Tours, Put-in-Bay, OH. Modified to use three 420 hp Wright R-975-28 engines (all other 5-AT's had Pratt & Whitney engines), P-47 Oleo struts, Lockheed 18 wheels and other structural changes. 1-28-52 Charles F. Frensdorf, Orofino, ID. 8-1-53 Johnson Flying Service, Missoula, MT. Destroyed in crash in Flathead Forest, Montana, 8-17-53.

5-AT-40 at Orofino, Idaho, on August 14, 1952. This is the only Ford 5-AT to ever have three 420 hp Wright engines. It was lost in an accident after being sold to Johnson Flying Service. (W.T. Larkins)

5-AT-41; NC-9686; 5-AT-B
FF 4-11-29. Delivered 4-20-29 to Maddux Airlines, Los Angeles, CA. 4-21-31 Transcontinental and Western Air, Wilmington, DE. Modified to H-Speed configuration 9-4-31. Modified to sloping windshield and 13,750 lbs. gross weight 4-9-32. 2-3-36 Fred Kane and Jack Piersch, Kansas City, KS. 10-15-37 Fred Kane and George M. Prescott, Kansas City, KS. 10-8-38 Charles H. Babb, Glendale, CA. 11-28-38 Guinea Airways, Lae, British New Guinea. Dismantled and shipped 11-28-38. Fuselage and parts used to rebuild 5-AT-60.

5-AT-42; NC-9676, PH-AKE, PK-AKE; 5-AT-B
FF 4-19-29. Delivered 5-7-29 to Standard Oil Company of Indiana, Chicago, IL. Fuselage broken in two, left wing damaged, landing gear pushed into fuselage and tail damage in a windstorm at Wichita, Kansas, 6-2-29. Returned to the factory and rebuilt, test flown 7-11-29 and

returned to Standard Oil 7-18-29. 10-27-31 Northwest Airways, St. Paul, MN. Hi-Speed configuration and new cockpit emergency roof installed 11-25-31. 2-4-35 Northwest Airlines, St. Paul, MN. 4-27-35 Royal Dutch Airlines (KLM) New York City, NY and The Hague, Holland. Shipped from New York City in May 1935. 9-35 Royal Netherlands Indonesian Airways (KNILM), Amsterdam, Holland. 8-26-36 N.V. Bataafse Petroleum Maatschappij.

5-AT-43; NC-9682, TI-15, AN-AAG; 5-AT-B
FF 4-23-29. Delivered 5-8-29 to Southwest Air Fast Express, Tulsa, OK. Plane named "Wichita Falls" and Fleet No. 9. 10-11-30 Southern Air Fast Express, Dallas, TX. Modified to H-Speed configuration 631. 7-3-31 Colonial Air Transport, Newark, NJ. 10-4-32 American Airways, St. Louis, MO.(12/34 to 1/36 leased to Central Airlines, Pittsburgh, PA). 2-15-36 Aviation Manufacturing Corporation, Chicago, IL. Overhauled in AA's Chicago shops and sold 2-15-36 to Empressa Nacional de Transportes Aereos S.A., San Jose, Costa Rica. 1-42 to 3-46 TACA Nicaragua as AN-AAG.

5-AT-44; NC-9687, Colombian Army #2; 5-AT-B
FF 4-25-29. Delivered 5-14-29 to Southwest Air Fast Express, Tulsa, OK. 10-11-30 Southern Air Fast Express, Dallas, TX. 6-23-31 American Airways, Cincinnati, OH. Modified by AA in 1932 to operate at 13,750 lbs. gross weight, wing mail bins installed, stabilizer chord increased six inches, heavy duty wheels and axles installed, wing spars reinforced, outboard engine mounts lowered six inches and anti-drag cowlings (speed rings) installed on wing engines. 2-7-36 Aviation Manufacturing Corporation, Chicago, IL. 2-20-36 Republic of Colombia. This Ford and three others were ferried from Chicago to New York to Colombia by Colombian Army pilots under the direction of Roger Q. Williams.

5-AT-44 on wheels at Roosevelt Field, Long Island, New York. It was flown to Bogota by Colombian Army pilots. (Larkins Collection)

5-AT-45; NC-9688, XA-BCW; 5-AT-B
FF 4-26-29. Delivered 5-20-29 to Pan American Airways, New York City, NY for use in the Canal Zone. 11-1-34 Cia Mexicana de Aviacion, Mexico City, Mexico. Destroyed in crash near the San Martin volcano, Mexico, 3-5-40.

5-AT-46; NC-9689; 5-AT-C
FF 5-18-29. Delivered 5-31-29 to Maddux Airlines, Glendale, CA. Destroyed in a crash at Oceanside, California, 1-19-30.

5-AT-47; NC-9690, Colombian Army #3; 5-AT-C
FF 5-23-29. Delivered 6-3-29 to Southwest Air Fast Express, Tulsa, OK. 10-11-30 Southern Air Fast Express, Dallas, TX. 5-27-31 American Airways, Robertson, MO. Structurally modified in January 1933 to operate at 14,000 lbs. gross weight. 3-25-36 Aviation Manufacturing Corporation, Chicago, IL. 3-31-36 Republic of Colombia. One of four Fords flown by Colombian Army officers from New York to Colombia.

5-AT-47 at the factory on December 10, 1930, possibly for upgrading and overhaul for Southwest Air Fast Express in Dallas, Texas. (Ford Archives)

5-AT-48 flying for Northwest Airways in 1930. The rectangle on the top of the wing says WALK HERE and is the reinforced area for standing while putting gas in the tanks. (Paul Matt)

5-AT-48; NC-8410; 5-AT-C
FF 6-5-29. Delivered 6-14-29 to Northwest Airways, St. Paul, MN.
Repaired after being blown over in a windstorm at Chicago 9-27-30 and modified to Hi-Speed configuration at

the same time. 4-22-36 Charles H. Babb, Glendale, CA. 6-1-36 Chester G. Brown, Nome, AK. 3-5-37 Star Air Service, Anchorage, AK. Fell through the ice on Lake Spenard, Alaska, 4-1-37 and reported as being cannibalized for parts. 8-15-38 Henry D. Thrall and E.L. Williams, Minneapolis, MN. CAA file cancelled 2-23-39.

5-AT-49; NC-8411; 5-AT-C
FF 6-8-29. Delivered 6-18-29 to Scenic Airways, Phoenix, AZ for $55,475. 3-30 United Aviation Corporation, Chicago, IL. 4-18-30 Transcontinental Air Transport, New York City, NY. Modified to Hi-Speed configuration in December 1930. 1-30-31 Transcontinental and Western Air, New York City, NY. 7-30-37 St. Louis Flying Service, Robertson, MO. 9-27-37 Garland E. Lincoln, North Hollywood, CA. 6-20-38 Sought American Gulf Oil Company (SAGO), New York City, NY. In September 1938 Aero Trades of Roosevelt Field, NY, converted the plane to a cargo carrier and installed a Panagra type hatch in the top of the fuselage, heavy duty wheels, axles and brakes and wheel fenders for mud control. Destroyed in crash in mountains of Colombia 4-15-39.

5-AT-50; NC-8412, OK-FOR; 5-AT-C
FF 6-4-29. Used by the Ford Motor Company as a demonstrator and displayed at the Olympia Show in London from July 16th to 23rd, 1929. On August 3rd it left Croydon on a demonstration tour of twenty-one different countries including France, Germany, Russia and Italy. During this tour the plane carried 3,750 passengers on 325 demonstration flights. Upon the conclusion of the tour, about 1-10-30, it was sold to the Government of Czechoslovakia for use on their state-operated airline. Destroyed in a crash near Friederichdorf, Moravia, 8-22-30.

5-AT-51; NC-8413; 5-AT-C
FF 6-13-29. Delivered 6-24-29 to Maddux Airlines, Glendale, CA for $55,475. 4-21-31 Transcontinental and Western Air, Wilmington, DE. Used by TWA later as a cargo carrier. 9-2-37 Max Conrad, Winona, MN. Destroyed by fire in a ground accident at Mankato, MN 8-11-38.

5-AT-52; NC-8414, XH-?, LG-AAC, AN-AAO; 5-AT-C
FF 6-17-29. Delivered 6-29-29 to Stout Air Services, Dearborn, MI. 10-1-30 National Air Transport, Chicago, IL. 6-29-33 Pennsylvania Airlines, Pittsburgh, PA. 1-26-36 TACA Tegucigalpa, Honduras. Operated by TACA Guatemala as LG-AAC. 1-42 to 1-44 TACA Nicaragua as AN-AAO.

5-AT-53; NC-8415, XH-?; 5-AT-C
FF 6-21-29. Delivered 7-8-29 to Stout Air Services, Dearborn, MI. 10-1-30 National Air Transport, Chicago, IL. 6-27-33 Pennsylvania Air Lines, Pittsburgh, PA. 1-21-36 TACA, Honduras.

5-AT-48 at Boeing Field, Seattle, in 1937 after its flight from Alaska. It was landed on the grass on skis as the snow had melted before it arrived. (Gordon S. Williams)

5-AT-49 at the San Francisco Bay Airdrome, Alameda, California in 1938. Note the fuselage radio mast installed by TWA for two-way voice radio communication. (W.T. Larkins)

5-AT-51 is unusual because of the use of cowlings on all three engines while in service by TWA. It was at Los Angeles Metropolitan Airport to be measured for a Hollywood studio. (Walter M. Jefferies Jr.)

5-AT-54; NC-8416, OA-AAC, NC-8416, C-204, YV-?; 5-AT-C
FF 6-24-29. Delivered 7-2-29 to Pan American Grace Airways, New York City, NY. (Panagra had five Fords in South America, all modified with Hi-Speed equipment and cargo hatches in the top of the fuselage). 10-31-35 Aerovias Peruanas S.A., Lima, Peru. 10-21-38 Pan American Grace Airways, New York City, NY. 10-31-39 Aerovias Ramales Colombianas, Llanos Orientales, Colombia. Reported to have been operated by South American Gulf Oil in Colombia until 1940 (no record of such in

CAA files), who in turn sold it to AVENSA. To the Shell Company of Ecuador in May 1946.

5-AT-55; NC-8417, R-130, NC-8417; 5-AT-C
FF 6-25-29. Delivered 6-26-29 to New York, Rio and Buenos Aires Line, New York City, NY. 9-15-30 Pan American Airways, New York City, NY. 7-21-31 Pan American Grace Airways, New York City, NY. Destroyed in crash at Junin, Argentina, 6-11-34.

5-AT-56; NC-8418; 5-AT-C
FF 6-26-29. Delivered 7-11-29 to Pan American Grace Airways, New York City, NY. Destroyed in crash at Ovalle, Chile, 4-1-31.

5-AT-57; NC-9648, NR-9648; 5-AT-C
FF 6-27-29. Delivered 7-3-29 to Transcontinental Air Transport, New York City, NY. 4-6-31 Transcontinental and Western Air, Wilmington, DE. Modified to Hi-Speed configuration 1-9-31, converted to a cargo plane 10-13-36, re-converted to passenger interior 3-25-37. 7-19-37 Republic Oil Company, Pittsburgh, PA. Modified with fuselage tanks to hold 1,800 gallons of gasoline, and 450 gallons of oil, for aerial re-fueling of James Mattern's Lockheed 12-A "The Texan." When the Russian polar fliers were lost in August 1937 the plane was rushed into use to assist in the aerial search. Written off after a landing accident at Anchorage, Alaska, 8-21-37. The remains were purchased by Wien Alaska Airlines for parts.

5-AT-58; NC-8419; 5-AT-C
FF 6-29-29. Delivered 7-11-29 to Ford Motor Company, Dearborn, MI. Modified to Hi-Speed configuration 10-22-30. 1-31-31 Northwest Airways, St. Paul, MN. 9-6-35 Northern Air Transport, Fairbanks, AK. 11-24-36 Wien Alaska Airlines, Fairbanks, AK. 6-24-40 Kenneth Neese, Anchorage, AK. 6-24-40 (same day) Star Air Lines, Anchorage, AK. In August 1943 the left wing was replaced by a spare. 6-21-45 Monroe Airways, Monroe, MI who did a complete overhaul. 11-10-46 G and G Airlines, Tucson, AZ. 6-5-51 Johnson Flying Service, Missoula, MT. Leased to Northwest Airlines in 1956 for commemorative flight. Crashed 8-4-59 at Moose Creek, ID. 4-13-79 Evergreen Helicopters, McMinnville, OR. 4-13-79 Kal Aero, Kalamazoo, MI. Fuselage rebuilt by Oct 1982, flown 7-15-91.

5-AT-59; NC-400H, OA-AAD; 5-AT-C
FF 7-5-29. Delivered 7-18-29 to Pan American Grace Airways, New York City, NY. 10-31-35 Aerovias Peruanas S.A., Lima, Peru (a Panagra affiliate). 5-27-38 Pan American Grace Airways, New York City, NY. 4-17-39 Compania Aramayo de Mines en Bolivie, La Paz, Bolivia.

5-AT-60; NC-401H, G-ABHO; VH-UBI, RAAF A45-1; 5-AT-C
FF 7-5-29. Used as company demonstrator in England. Sold to Lord Lovelace in 1931, see Chapter 6. 1934 British Air Navigation Company for charter flying and named "Voyager." 5-35 Guinea Airways, Australia (Registered VH-UBI on 10-26-35). Officially written off due to a crash in July 1938. The fuselage of 5-AT-41, and other parts, were used to rebuild it. 2-6-42 impressed into service with the Royal Australian Air Force as A45-1 and delivered to the RAAF Unit at Townsville, Queensland. Crashed in the Lake Myola lakebed, New Guinea, the same year. Fuselage recovered by RAAF helicopter in 1979 for the National Museum at Papua.

5-AT-61; NC-402H, R-176, OA-AAB, C-206; 5-AT-C
FF 7-12-29. Delivered 7-22-29 to New York, Rio and Buenos Aires Line, New York City, NY for $55,000. 9-15-30 Pan American Airways, New York City, NY. 7-21-31 Pan American Grace Airways, New York City, NY. Operated initially under Argentine registration R-130 or R-176). 10-10-35 Aerovias Peruanas S.A., Lima, Peru. 10-21-38 Pan American Grace Airways, New York City, NY. 11-15-38 South American Gulf Oil Company, New York City, NY. Overhauled 9-1-39 by the Pan American base at Brownsville, Texas, including the change to a rectangular entrance door and the windows aft of station #2 covered with metal skin. Floor rails were installed to make it a two-place cargo plane with a 14,000 lbs. gross weight approval. SAGO transferred the plane to Colombian registration C-206 in 1940 while operating with its affiliate COLPET (Colombian Petroleum Company) until 1943. Reported sold to AVENSA in Venezuela, probably for parts.

5-AT-58 in the Minnesota winter snow. Note the large U.S. MAIL on the top of the left wing, not seen in the photo of 5-AT-48. (Northwest Airlines)

5-AT-62; NC-403H; 5-AT-C
FF 7-15-29. Delivered 7-31-29 to Pan American Airways, New York City, NY. Operated by Panagra and destroyed in an accident at Santiago, Chile, 7-16-32.

5-AT-63; NC-404H, R-148; 5-AT-C
FF 7-16-29. Delivered 7-31-29 to New York, Rio and Buenos Aires Line, New York City, NY for $55,000.

Crashed 4-8-30 at Buenos Aires, Argentina. CAA file cancelled 9-1-30.

5-AT-64; NC-405H, XH-? , AN-AAN, XA-FUO; 5-AT-C

FF 7-18-29. Released from Flight Test 7-31-29 as a Club model. (Probably used as a sales demonstrator). 11-15-29 Parks Air College, East St. Louis, IL. (Advertised in February 1930 as a, "Leviathan of the air. Only tri-motored plane in America used exclusively for student instruction." Photo with Parks Air College markings in Aviation magazine 1-11-30). 5-16-30 Southwest Air Fast Express, Tulsa, OK. 10-11-30 Southern Air Fast Express, Dallas, TX. 11-18-30 Erle P. Halliburton, Los Angeles, CA. 8-1-34 Compania Minera Agua Fria S.A., Tegucigalpa, Honduras. Modified by Timm Aircraft in August 1934 with reinforced cabin with cargo hatch in top rear and adjustable props. Sold to TACA Honduras (date unknown). 1-27-42 to 10-15-42 TACA Nicaragua as AN-AAN. 1943-1945 unknown. 4-8-46 M. A. Zuniga, Mexico City, Mexico, who in turn sold it to Ricardo Nevarez I., Campeche, Mexico. Mexican registration XA-FUO issued 414-46. Operated by Nevarez until July 1950.

5-AT-64 when it was owned by Erle P. Halliburton of Los Angeles in 1931. It was named "Cementer" as it was used as an executive plane for the Halliburton Oil Well Cementing Company of Duncan, Oklahoma. (George Copeland)

5-AT-65; NC-406H; 5-AT-C

FF 7-19-29. Released from Flight Test on 8-29-29 and used as a company demonstrator. Export License issued 1-29-30 for Japan and China. Disassembled and crated by the O'Donnell Aircraft Corporation, Long Beach, California and placed on a ship which left 2-15-30. It was re-assembled in Tokyo, Japan, and used for a six month demonstration tour of the Orient under the direction of pilot Perry Hutton. Sold in July 1931 to Marshal Chang Hseuh-Liang in China. See Chapter 6. Destroyed 10-24-35 by Japanese bombing at Hankow, China.

5-AT-66; ID-407H, (Chile), NC-407H; 5-AT-C

FF 7-26-29. Delivered 12-30-29 to the Chilean Government. Crashed in Chile (date and location unknown) and remains sold to Pan American Grace Airways. The Ford factory built a forward fuselage section, complete to station No.7, in November 1932 and delivered it to Panagra in Peru. In December Panagra bought a wing center section, two used wing tips and parts for a rear fuselage section. These were assembled in their Lima, Peru, shop and on 5-21-33 the area U.S. Dept. of Commerce Inspector test flew the plane, now known as "P-24 San Rafael", and approved it as NC-407H on 5-22-33. It was destroyed in an accident at Lima, Peru, on 3-22-34.

5-AT-67; NC-408H, Colombian Army No.1, HC-SBK; 5-AT-C

FF 7-27-29. Released from flight test on 8-9-29 and retained by the Ford Motor Company. 5-23-30 Southwest Air Fast Express, Tulsa, OK. 10-11-30 Southern Air Fast Express, Dallas, TX. 6-3-31 American Airways, Cincinnati, OH. (12/34 to 1/36 leased to Central Airlines, Pittsburgh, PA). 1-27-36 Aviation Manufacturing Corporation, Chicago, IL. Prior to export it was completely overhauled in the American Airlines shops at Chicago and modified to add reinforcements for float installation. 1-29-36 to the Government of Colombia. In October 1946 it was reported to be registered to the Shell Company of Ecuador as HC-SBK. It was destroyed in an accident on July 16, 1947.

5-AT-68; NC-409H, G-ABFF; G-ABHF; VH-UTB; 5-AT-C

FF 8-3-29. Released from flight test on 8-13-29 as company demonstrator of the Club model. Transferred 11-14-30 to the Ford Motor Company Ltd., London, England and registered G-ABFF. An exception to the normal progressive allocation of British civil registrations was made so that the plane could be re-registered G-ABHF (HF for Henry Ford). 12-10-34 Guinea Airways, Australia,. Operated 1935-1941 including use in the New Guinea gold fields. Destroyed in a crash at Wau, New Guinea, 10-23-41.

A beautiful publicity photo of 5-AT-68 with a Lincoln and Ford Model A at the factory on September 11, 1930. The registration NC-409H was short-lived as it went to England and became G-ABFF three months later. (Ford Archives)

5-AT-69; NC-410H, C-?; 5-AT-C, 5-AT-CS
FF 8-7-29. Released from flight test 8-20-29. 5-7-30 New England and Western Air Transportation Company, Stratford, CT. 10-16-30 Eastern Air Transport, Brooklyn, NY. 4-26-33 Transcontinental and Western Air, Kansas City, KS. (Approved for operations on floats by TWA from Downtown Skyport in lower Manhattan 8-29-35). 2-11-36 SCADTA, Baranquilla, Colombia, with sale including floats.

5-AT-70; NC-411H, TI-33; 5-AT-C
FF 8-10-29. Delivered 8-26-29 to Stout Air Services. 9-29-30 National Air Transport, Chicago, IL. 9-11-34 Long and Harman Airlines, Dallas, TX. 12-31-34 Braniff Airways, Oklahoma City, OK. 6-25-37 Alfred Frank, Salt Lake City, UT. Leased to National Parks Airways and operated for Western Air Express for scenic flights over Yellowstone Park. 6-24-38 Charles H. Babb, Glendale, CA. 6-24-38 (same day) sold to Empresa Nacional de Transportes Aereos (ENTA), San Jose, Costa Rica.

5-AT-70 with one of the many experimental cowling arrangements tried by Ford. This was one of the efforts made by Ford engineers to improve the performance and speed of the 5-AT. (Hudek)

5-AT-70 with the rare markings of New York Airways. This is part of the puzzle described in the caption for 4-AT-64. The FAA ownership records for NC-411H show it to be owned by National Air Transport in 1931. (Hudek)

5-AT-71; NC-412H, XH-FAB?, TI-42; 5-AT-C
FF 8-17-29. Retained at the factory until sold 6-12-30 to New England and Western Air Transportation Company, Springfield, MA. 9-2-30 Linden Associates, Springfield, MA. 10-2-30 Springfield Airport and Aeronautical School, Springfield, MA. 10-21-31 American Airways, New York

5-AT-68 taking off in England with the registration G-ABFF. (Hudek)

City, NY. 10-15-34 TACA, Tegucigalpa, Honduras. The TACA pilots took delivery in Chicago and flew it to Honduras. Operated by TACA in Costa Rica as TI-42 in December 1939.

5-AT-72; A8457; 5-AT-C
FF 8-26-29. Delivered 10-3-29 to the U.S. Navy as model JR-3. Stricken 10-6-34. See Chapter 5.

5-AT-73; NC-413H, LG-AAD, AN-AAM; 5-AT-C
FF 8-30-29. Delivered 9-29-30 to National Air Transport, Chicago, IL. 11-29-33 Pennsylvania Airlines, Pittsburgh, PA. 1-21-36 TACA, Tegucigalpa, Honduras. Operated by TACA Guatemala as LG-AAD. 1-27-42 to 10-15-42 TACA Nicaragua as AN-AAM.

5-AT-73 at the factory on September 26, 1930. It was delivered three days later to National Air Transport. (Gordon S. Williams)

5-AT-73 a month earlier on 8-15-30. Note the differences in the wing engine exhaust, landing gear struts, pants, cowlings and nose engine vents. Why were so many changes made just before delivery? Or is this proof of the stories that NC numbers were switched around on Ford airplanes? (Ford Archives)

5-AT-74; NC-414H, XA-BCX, NC-414H, NX-414H, NC-414H, XA-BKS, LGAFA, N-414H; 5-AT-C, 5-AT-CS

FF 9-4-29. Operated by Ford Motor Company as a demonstrator until 1932 including many flights on twin floats. Operated under an Experimental license in the first half of 1931. 11-4-32 Pan American Airways, New York City, NY. 3-5-35 Cia Mexicana de Aviacion, Mexico City, Mexico (XA-BCX). 11-10-36 Pan American Airways, New York City, NY. 3-26-40 Cia Mexicana de Aviacion, Mexico City, Mexico (XA-BKS). 5-41 Cia Guatemalteca de Aviacion (AVIATECA), Guatemala City, Guatemala (LG-AFA). 3-11-50 Robert W. Waltermire, Choteau, MT 3-21-50 Northwest Agricultural Aviation Corporation, Choteau, MT. 4-30-56 Lawrence L. Alzheimer, Collins, MT. 10-17-56 Jack Adams Aircraft Sales, Memphis, TN. 4-29-58 Jack A. Adams, Memphis, TN.4-29-58 C.M. Dunham, Haines City, FL. 4-2-59 Mary Jane Bergerson, Crystal River, FL. 10-21-59 John M. and Katherine M. Louck, Monmouth, IL. 2-24-65 American Airlines, New York City, NY. 10-11-72 John E. Burkdoll and Charles A. LeMaster, Ottawa, KS. 7-23-73 Burkdoll-LeMaster Inc., Ottawa, KS. 9-10-73 Charles LeMaster, Ottawa, KS. 10-6-73 LeMaster Inc., Ottawa, KS. 88-77 Commuter Investment and Development Corporation, Las Vegas, NV, (John R. Seibold, President). 9-12-85 Scenic Airlines, Las Vegas, NV, (John R. Seibold, President).

A beautiful photo of 5-AT-74, probably taken on September 6, 1931 while at the Detroit River Boat Races. With the large Ford logo on the side it provided impressive advertising as it took off and landed on the river. The hand holds built on the rear fuselage allowed a crew member to reach the top of the wing for refueling when the plane was on floats. (Gordon S. Williams)

5-AT-75; NC-415H, XH-TAH, AN-ABO, XA-GIJ; 5-AT-C

FF 8-23-29. Released from flight test 8-27-29 and used as a company demonstrator with the special "Bird's Eye" burnished finish. Delivered 10-3-29 to Firestone Tire and Rubber Company, Akron, OH. for $55,475 less $1,200 for time used. In addition $29,275 credit was given for the

A rare photo showing 5-AT-74 with a modified triangular tail and an Experimental license. The plane under the wing is a Heath Parasol registered 942N. (John Underwood)

5-AT-74 in Panama while flying for Pan American Airways. (Gene Risedorph)

5-AT-74 with American Airways markings for the New York World's Fair. The ever observant B.C. Reed noticed the one square wing tip in 1979. He continued to ask everyone about it from then on but did not get an answer until Bernie Godlove provided a copy of the Form 332 in 1991. The exact cause of the damage is unknown but on May 12, 1951 George F. Kreitzberg, A&E, completed the repairs that consisted of a new 7-foot rear spar, outboard aileron hinge, new ribs and new skin on the outboard 5 feet of the wing and the installation of a Grumman/Eastern FM-2 "Wildcat" wing tip. Bernie reports that it flies better with one square tip than 5-AT-11 did with its normal round tips. (American Airlines)

5-AT-75 at the factory on 8-25-29 when just two days old. It was used as a company demonstrator until delivered to Firestone Tire and Rubber Company in October 1929. (Ford Archives)

turn in of 4-AT-57 by Firestone. An Export License was issued in March 1931 for the Government of Chile but the sale did not take place. 10-23-31 American Airways, New York City, NY. On 5-6-32 a larger stabilizer with an additional six inches of chord was installed. 2-19-35 TACA, Tegucigalpa, Honduras. 6-1-44 TACA, Nicaragua, as AN-ABO. 3-19-47 Miguel Zuniga, Mexico City, Mexico. 4-47 Lineas Aereas Guerrero Oaxaca S.A., (LAGOSA), Puebla, Mexico. Destroyed in an accident at Putla, Oaxaca, Mexico 8-16-49.

5-AT-76; ID-416H, (Chile); 5-AT-C
FF 9-5-29. Delivered 12-30-29 to the Government of Chile. Shipped disassembled by boat to Valpariso, Chile in January 1930 under Export Certificate E-252 of 1-2-30.

5-AT-77; NC-417H, CB-?; 5-AT-C
FF 10-8-29. Delivered 10-10-29 to Bell Telephone Laboratories, New York City, NY. 12-26-39 Frank Ambrose, Whitestone, NY. 1-25-40 Compania Aramayo de Mines en Bolivie, La Paz, Bolivia. Both it and the Bell Laboratories Fairchild 71-A (NC-952V) were flown to Bolivia to be used to carry freight and passengers to the mines.

5-AT-78; NC-418H, TI-41; 5-AT-C
FF 9-13-29. Operated by the Ford Motor Company until 1930. Sold 10-1-30 to Phillips Petroleum Company, Bartlesville, OK and named "Wollaroc II." 5-22-34 Hanfords Tri-State Airlines, Sioux City, IA. 7-1-36 Hanford Airlines, Kansas City, MO. 12-3-1-36 DePonti Aviation Company, Minneapolis, MN. 8-12-37 Louis P. Quinn, Denver, CO. 9-26-39 Aerovias Nacionales, San Jose, Costa Rica. Flown to San Jose by Eddie DeLarm and Roman Macaya, arriving 10-1-39.

5-AT-79; NX-419H; 5-AT-C
FF 10-29. Used as an experimental test plane at the factory. Changes in the nose engine cowling, raised wing to be used later on the 5-AT-D, and a fuselage widened by ten inches. Destroyed in a crash at Dearborn, MI, 11-24-30.

5-AT-79 also had the nose engine mount tilted downward and the high wing placement of the 5-AT-D. Although it is identified as a model 5-AT-C by the factory it is probably the 5-AT-D prototype. It lasted one year before being lost in a crash in the center of the Ford Airport on November 24, 1930. (Gordon S. Williams)

5-AT-79A; NC-8485; 5-AT-C
See 6-AT and 7-AT. Rebuilt by the factory in February 1931 to ATC165 standard for the 5-AT-C. Flight tested 6-30-31 by LeRoy Manning. Sold 8-20-31 to American Airways, Chicago, IL. 3-26-36 Aviation Manufacturing Corporation, Chicago. American Airlines overhauled the plane and engines prior to ferrying to California for crating and shipment to China. About 4-4-36 Central Aviation School, Hangchow, China.

5-AT-80; NX-420H, NC-420H, C-208, CP-?; 5-AT-C
FF 11-5-29. Used for tests at the factory of the installation of the outboard engines in the wings. Delivered 10-20-30 to National Air Transport, Chicago, IL. 12-27-34 United Air Lines, Chicago, IL. 2-12-35 Hanford Airlines, Sioux City, IA. 4-8-35 Hanford's TriState Airlines Sioux City, IA. 8-19-36 W.F. Niedernhofer and Alvene Litzenberger, Pittsburgh,, PA. 11-10-36 Pittsburgh Aeronautical Service (W.F. Niedernhofer and E.G. Ashbaugh), Pittsburgh, PA. 4-28-37 Carl R. Litzenberger, Pittsburgh, PA. 6-638

5-AT-79 in a view that shows the fuselage widened ten inches. This little-known experiment was made to study the effects of a wider fuselage blanketing out the nose engine airstream, and the results of a double skin on sound deadening. In order to accomplish this a second layer of skin was placed approximately four to five inches out from the original, but faired in at the nose and tail. (Jack McNulty)

5-AT-80 with the combined markings of NAT and UAL. This is the plane that, as the 5-AT-E, had the engines mounted in the wings. This photo, taken about 1934, was after it had been rebuilt as a standard 5-AT-C. (Charles W. Kossack)

5-AT-80 at Pittsburgh, Pennsylvania, in 1936. Note the unusual addition of the word AIRLINER under Ford Tri-Motor on the fin. (A.R. Krieger)

Becker Aircraft Sales Company, Dravosburg, PA. 5-13-39 Colombian Petroleum Company, New York City, NY. 6-27-39 South American Gulf Oil Company, New York City, NY. Converted to a cargo carrier in June 1939 by Timm Aircraft Corp., Glendale, CA. Operated by SAGO in Colombia as C-208 in 1940. In 1941 sold to Compania Aramayo de Mines, Bolivia. Destroyed in a crash in the Andean Challhuani Range, Bolivia, 9-26-41.

5-AT-81; NC-421H; 5-AT-C
FF 12-18-29. Operated by Stout Air Services and then rebuilt by Ford with Hi-Speed equipment (wheel pants, engine cowlings, lowered engine mounts etc.) before delivery 10-4-30 to National Air Transport, Chicago, IL. Destroyed in a crash at Elyria, OH 4-29-31.

5-AT-82; A8598; 5-AT-C
FF 12-27-29. Delivered 5-10-30 to U.S. Marine Corps as model JR-3. Crashed in Nicaragua 8-4-30.

5-AT-83; A8599; 5-AT-C
FF 4-2-30. Delivered 5-21-30 to U.S. Marine Corps as model JR-3. Crashed Virginia Beach, VA, 3-22-33.

5-AT-84; A8840; 5-AT-C
FF 10-31-30. Delivered 11-8-30 to U.S. Navy as model RR-4. Stricken 4-23-37.

5-AT-85; NC-425H, (Chile); 5-AT-C
FF 11-10-30. Delivered 11-21-30 to the Government of Chile. Export License E-355 issued 11-19-30.

5-AT-86; NC-426H, C-207, HK-1501; 5-AT-C
FF 11-20-30. Delivered 11-28-30 to National Air Transport, Chicago, IL. 10-1-34 Long and Harman Airlines, Dallas, TX. 4-8-35 Braniff Airways, Oklahoma City, OK. 4-30-37 Akron Airways, Akron, OH. 4-13-38 E.M. Van Devere, Akron, OH. 6-20-38 South American Gulf Oil Company (SAGO), New York City, NY. Modified 8-28-38 by Aero Trades Company, Roosevelt Field, NY, with cargo hatch, heavy duty wheels etc. 2-15-40 registered C-207 in Colombia. Operated by COLPET, an affiliate of SAGO, from 1938 to 1947. Sold in 1947 to SCOLTA, a Colombian company. Sold in 1948 to a private owner (name unknown) who washed it out in a crash on the approach to the airport at Villavicencio, Colombia.

5-AT-87; NC-427H; 5-AT-C
FF 11-21-30. Delivered 11-26-30 to National Air Transport, Chicago, IL. Destroyed in accident at Ashley, Indiana, 10-27-31.

5-AT-88; NC-428H, CV-FAI; 5-AT-C
FF 1-20-30. Released from flight test 1-21-30 and used as a company demonstrator for the 5-AT-C Club model. In October 1930 the outboard engine mounts were lowered six inches and wheel pants were added. Sold to Romania through the Ford Motor Company of England in March 1931. The purchaser was Prince Bibesco, President of the Federation Aeronautica Internationale. The Club interior included leather upholstery and a galley etc. It carried both civil and military Romanian markings, the last three letters of the civil registration standing for the initials of the F.A.I. It was assembled at the Ford plant at Hooton, England, christened on 3-27-31 and left on a lengthy tour of European airports. Destroyed in a crash landing after a mid-air collision with a vulture at Benares, India on 4-17-31.

5-AT-89; NC-429H, Colombian Army #4, AN-AAD; 5-AT-C
FF 2-10-30. Delivered 2-12-30 to H.H. Timken, Timken Roller Bearing Company, Canton, OH. 11-6-30 Modified to Hi-Speed configuration by the factory. 7-12-33 Shell Aviation Corporation (Shell Oil), St. Louis, MO. 11-8-35 Government of Colombia, Bogota, Colombia. Export Certificate E-1903 issued on 4-1-36. From 1-15-42 to 10-15-42 operated by TACA Nicaragua as AN-AAD.

5-AT-90; NC-430H, XH-?, TI-46, AN-AAC.
FF 3-28-30. Delivered 6-21-30 to Continental Oil Company, Ponca City, OK as an 11-PCLM Club model with

5-AT-90, a Club Model, photographed on the first day it flew – March 28, 1930. It has the Bird's Eye Finish on the engine nacelles and large wheel pants. It was purchased by the Continental Oil Company as an executive corporate aircraft. (Ford Archives)

Birds Eye finish overall. . 3-6-33 Transcontinental and Western Air, New York City, NY. 4-19-33 modified to standard TWA configuration by addition of wing mail bins and standard passenger seats. 7-29-35 Compania Nacional Aviacion, c/o W.W. Hodkinson, Los Angeles, CA for operation in Guatemala. 2-20-36 TACA, Tegucigalpa, Honduras. In December 1939 it was operated by TACA Costa Rica as TI-46. From 1-15-42 to 10-15-42 it was operated by TACA Nicaragua as AN-AAC.

5-AT-91; 31-401; 5-AT-D
FF 12-27-30. Delivered 1-9-31 to the U.S. Army Air Corps as model C-4A. Surveyed at San Antonio Air Depot 5-26-38.

5-AT-92; 31-402; 5-AT-D
FF 1-30-31. Delivered 2-5-31 to the U.S. Army Air Corps as model C-4A. Surveyed at Wright Field 7-9-38.

5-AT-93; 31-403; 5-AT-D
FF 2-5-31. Delivered 2-11-31 to the U.S. Army Air Corps as model C-4A. Destroyed in a crash at Oscoda, Michigan on 6-11-34.

5-AT-94; NC-8486; 5-AT-C Special
FF 6-25-30 as model 6-AT-3 (See Chapter 2). Converted to model 5-AT-C by the factory in July 1930. (Listed as "5-AT-C Special No.3" in many references). The plane operated under CAA Memo 2-240 after conversion rather than ATC-165. 2-20-30 Colonial Air Transport, New York City, NY. 12-16-32 American Airways, St. Louis, MO. 5-12-34 American Airlines, Chicago, IL. 4-1-36 Aviation Manufacturing Corporation, Chicago, IL. 4-36 Central Aviation School, Hangchow, China (see 5-AT-79A). The plane and engines were overhauled by American Airlines prior to its flight to California for shipment by boat to China.

5-AT-95; 31-404; 5-AT-D
FF 2-12-31. Delivered 2-19-31 to the U.S. Army Air Corps as model C-4A. Surveyed at Chanute Field 9-30-38.

5-AT-96; NC-422H; 5-AT-C
FF 12-19-30. Delivered 12-22-30 to National Air Transport, Chicago, IL. 12-27-34 United Air Lines, Chicago, IL. 2-5-35 Hanfords TriState Airlines, Sioux City, IA. 7-14-36 Hanford Airlines, Kansas City, MO. 12-19-36 DePonti Aviation Company, Wold Chamberlain Airport, Minneapolis, MN. Destroyed in a hangar fire at Sioux City, Iowa, 1-20-37.

5-AT-97; NC-424H; 5-AT-D
FF 2-24-31. Delivered 7-2-31 to National Air Transport, Chicago, IL (Fleet No. 101). 6-24-33 Pacific Air Transport, Oakland, CA. 5-14-34 United Air Lines, Chicago, IL. 2-28-35 E. Palacio and Company. United records have a pencilled note stating, "sold 5-29-36 to the Government of Honduras."

5-AT-98; NC-431H; 5-AT-D
FF 3-25-31. Delivered 4-4-31 to Pacific Air Transport, Oakland, CA for $58,141 and named "Dawson." PAT handled the San Francisco to Seattle route for NAT, both later becoming what is today United Air Lines. Destroyed in an accident at Eugene, Oregon, 1-24-33.

5-AT-99; NC-432H; 5-AT-D
FF 4-6-31. Released from flight test 4-7-31. Ford Motor Company demonstrator for the 5-AT-D model. Flown from New York City to Washington, D.C., to Baltimore and Dayton in May and June 1931. Further flights to St. Louis, Indianapolis, Cincinnati, Atlanta, Norfolk etc., in August, piloted by LeRoy Manning. Sold 3-14-32 to Marshall Chang Hseuh-Liang, Peiping, China. Export Certificate No. E-498 issued 2-5-32. Plane shipped disassembled by boat from California.

A rare photo of 5-AT-94, the 6-AT-3 rebuilt back to 5-AT standards in July 1930. Colonial Air Transport became the Colonial Division of American Airways. The airline Fords flew low over town in the 1930s and a young enthusiast, Don Ives, kept track of them to see if they were on schedule etc. He could tell which pilot was flying by the sound of the propeller synchronization as each pilot flew his Ford with slight variations. (Donald M. Ives)

5-AT-99 was the company demonstrator for the 5-AT-D model. It is seen here on January 25, 1932 after being overhauled at the factory prior to going to China. (Ford Archives)

5-AT-100; NC-433H; 5-AT-D
FF (9-32); Rebuilt to 5-AT-D standards from the 13-A in August and September 1932. In addition to the P&W Wasp engines it had wing tip fuel tanks added bringing the fuel capacity to 499 gallons. The model designation was changed from 13-A to 5-AT-D, and the factory serial number from 1 to 5-AT-100. Sold 9-14-32 to Pan American Grace Airways, New York City, NY. In September 1935 P&W Wasp SlDl engines of 550 hp, with controllable pitch props, were installed in the outboard wing positions. Destroyed in a crash 12-24-35 at Lima, Peru.

5-AT-101; NS-1, ID-15551; 5-AT-D
FF 5-1-31. Delivered 5-13-31 to the U.S. Department of Commerce, Bureau of Air Commerce (later CAA and FAA), Washington, D.C. Club model sometimes referred to as "Model 5-D" it was fitted for a crew of two and nine passengers. Total flying time by Bureau of Air Commerce was 1366 hours. 7-15-35 Beech Aircraft Company, Wichita, KS.(Trade-in to Beech as partial payment on a new Beechcraft 17 for the Bureau of Air Commerce/ CAA). 7-26-35 Pan American Aviation Supply Corporation, New York City, NY. Identification Mark 15551 assigned 7-23-35 for the ferry flight to California for shipment to China. Nosed up on landing at Clover Field, Santa Monica, CA, when the brakes locked causing damage to about 20% of the plane. 10-23-35 sold to China National Aviation Corporation (CNAC), Shanghai, China.

5-AT-102; NC-435H; 5-AT-D
FF 4-17-31. Delivered 5-20-31 to Pacific Air Transport, Oakland, CA. 3-7-32 National Air Transport, Chicago, IL. 4-29-33 Pacific Air Transport, Oakland, CA. 5-14-34 United Air Lines, Chicago, IL. 9-5-34 Robert Johnson, Johnson Flying Service, Missoula, MT. Destroyed in an accident at Big Prairie, Montana, on 9-3-38.

5-AT-103; NC-436H, XH-TAO, AN-AAK, XA-FON; 5-AT-D
FF 5-31. Delivered 6-4-31 to National Air Transport, Chicago, IL. 615-33 Pacific Air Transport, Oakland, CA. 5-14-34 United Air Lines, Chicago, IL. 12-27-34 United Air Lines Transport Corp., Chicago, IL. United records state, "sold to E. Palacio & Company 2-28-35." 1936 (?) TACA Honduras. 1-24-42 TACA Nicaragua. 1-17-46 sold through Miguel Zuniga (agent for the Babb Company in Mexico City) to Carlos Davalos Guzman, Guadalajara, Jalisco, Mexico who operated it as Transportes Aereos de Jalisco S.A. It was flown by TAJSA until October 1949 on a route from Guadalajara to Talpa to Mascota to Puerto Vallarta on the Pacific Coast. In September 1948 it was flown to Los Angeles and modified to use three BT-13 engines, cowlings and controllable pitch props. 10-27-49 accident at Pinotepa Nacional, Mexico and rebuilt with the original 420 hp Wasp engines. 1-50 Lineas Aereas Guerro-Oaxaca S.A. (LAGOSA). 6-51 Servicios Aereos de Chiapas S.A. (SACSA). It did not fly much between 1951 and 1955 and was then brought dismantled to Mexico City. It was completely rebuilt and covered with the same type of "smooth skin" (non-corrugated) as XB-NET, and three old 420 hp Wasp engines were installed. Destroyed in an accident in the Sierra de San Adreas mountains 7-3-55.

5-AT-104; NC-437H; C-?; 5-AT-D
FF 5-1-31. Delivered June 1, 1931 to Pacific Air Transport, Oakland, CA. 5-14-34 United Air Lines, Chicago, IL. 12-27-34 United Air Lines Transport Corporation, Chicago, IL. 3-12-35 George Biederman, New York City, NY. 5-29-35 Sociedad Colombo-Alemana de Transportes Aereos (SCADTA), Barranquilla, Colombia. Flight tested at Oakland, CA, 4-11-35 and when Export Certificate E-1421 was issued on 4-26-35 the plane was flown to Colombia via Brownsville, Texas.

5-AT-105; A9206; 5-AT-D (RR-5)
FF 9-25-31(?). Delivered 2-17-32 to NAS Anacostia. Stricken 7-11-40.

5-AT-106; NC-439H, C-?; 5-AT-D
FF 4-15-31(?). Delivered 4-17-31 to Pacific Air Transport, Oakland, CA. 5-14-34 United Air Lines, Chicago, IL. 12-27-34 United Air Lines Transport Corp., Chicago, IL. 3-12-35 George Biederman, New York City, NY. 4-19-35 Sociedad Colombo Alemana De Transportes Aereos (SCADTA), Barranquilla, Colombia. Ferried to Colombia via Brownsville, Texas, together with NC-9657.

5-AT-106 in front of the passenger terminal at Boeing Field. The airline insignia on the side has been retouched, possibly to make it more readable for public relations purposes. This 5-AT-D was named PUGET. (Gordon S. Williams)

5-AT-107; NC-440H, G-ACAE, RAF X5000; 5-AT-D
FF 7-31. Delivered 8-31 to Ford Motor Company, London, England. Club model with special interior. 1932-1940 Honorable A.E. Guiness, Dublin, Ireland as G-ACAE. 6-40 Impressed into service with the Royal Air Force as X5000 and assigned to No. 271 Troop Transport Squadron at Doncaster civil airport in Yorkshire. The

radio equipment was changed to RAF standard at that time. Flown between England and Norway, and used for a few flights to the continent during the Dunkerque retreat. Believed to have been written off at Limavady Airport in Ireland as a result of running into a ditch on takeoff. Date and further details unknown.

5-AT-107 at the factory on August 18, 1931. It only carried the U.S. registration NC-440H for about two months as it went to England and became G-ACAE. This is the Ford that served with the Royal Air Force in World War II. (Gordon S. Williams)

5-AT-108; NC-9653, C-?; 5-AT-D
FF 5-27-31. Delivered 5-27-31 to Pacific Air Transport, Oakland, CA and named "Abbot." 5-14-34 United Air Lines, Chicago, IL. 7-31-34 Boeing School of Aeronautics, Oakland, CA. 5-1-35 United Air Lines Transport Corporation, Chicago, IL. 7-31-35 George Biederman, New York City, NY, (probably operating as Interamerican Aerotravel and Supplies). 8-16-35 Sociedad Colombo-Alemana De Transportes Aereos, (SCADTA) Barranquilla, Colombia. Flown to Colombia by Pan American Airways on its route, co-pilot Wilbur W. Lynch, Jr.

5-AT-109; A9205; RR-5 (5-AT-D)
FF 12-15-31. Delivered 12-23-31 to NAS Anacostia. 1931-1935 U. 8. Marine Corps. Stricken 8-31-37.

5-AT-110; NC-9655; 5-AT-D
FF 6-9-31. Delivered 6-10-31 to Pacific Air Transport, Oakland, CA and named "Glacier." 5-14-34 United Air Lines, Chicago, IL. 6-12-34 Hanfords Tri-State Airlines, Sioux City, IA. Accident at Cochrane, WI, 9-2-34. License revoked 11-30-34.

5-AT-111; NC-434H, C-?; 5-AT-D
FF 7-31. Delivered 11-12-31 to National Air Transport, Chicago, IL. NAT increased the baggage capacity and reduced to 11 passenger seats. 5-23-34 Interamerican Aerotravel and Supplies, New York City, NY. 8-4-34 Sociedad Colombo-Alemana de Transportes Aereos (SCADTA), Barranquilla, Colombia. Ferried by NAT to Brownsville, Texas, and by PAT to Colombia.

5-AT-112; NC-438H, C-31; 5-AT-D
FF 3-32. Sold 9-27-34, with a total time of only 9 hours and 15 minutes, to Sociedad Colombo-Alemana de Transportes Aereos (SCADTA), Barranquilla, Colombia. This 5-AT-D/5-D had a special Club interior, a modified triangular vertical tail surface, and wheel pants. It was ferried to Colombia in October 1934 under the registration C-31 and was destroyed 6-24-35 in a ground collision with Ford F-31 at Medellin.

5-AT-112 was special in two ways; it had the triangular tail used on the XB-906 Bomber, and it was finished in the unusual "White Gold" paint scheme. It was built in March 1932 and sold to SCADTA in Colombia in September 1934. (Gordon S. Williams)

5-AT-113; NC-9654, CB-?; 5-AT-D
FF 3-31-32. In a September 15, 1932 letter to the CAA the Ford Motor Company requested cancellation of the license because it had been sold and exported to South America. The only clues to its identity were the engine serial numbers which eventually identified it as the 5-AT-D that went to Bolivia in September 1932. Destroyed in a crash at Villa Montes, Bolivia, on 10-26-32.

5-AT-114; NC-9657, NR-9657, C-?; 5-AT-D
FF 3-17-32. Delivered 3-19-32 to National Air Transport, Chicago, IL. 6-15-33 Pacific Air Transport, Oakland, CA. 5-14-34 United Air Lines, Chicago, IL. 12-27-34 United Air Lines Transport Corporation, Chicago, IL. 2-16-35 George Biederman, New York City, NY. 6-5-35 Sociedad

5-AT-114 at North Beach Airport, New York, prior to the installation of the additional left hand door. After flying for United Air Lines it was sold to SCADTA airlines in Colombia. (Larkins Collection)

Colombo-Alemana de Transportes Aereos (SCADTA), Barranquilla, Colombia. United Air Lines modified the plane at their overhaul hangar at Oakland Airport to conform to Group 2-504 specifications. This included an additional door on the left hand side (possibly the only Ford to have a door on both sides), and a hostess jump seat. It was then flew it to Long Island, New York, to have Edo 43-14060 floats installed at their factory. An additional 126 gallon gas tank was mounted in the cabin for the ferry trip and it was flown with a new Restricted registration on 5-3-35. The ferry flight to Colombia was done by a Pan American crew.

5-AT-115; NC-9658, China; 5-AT-D
FF 4-25-33. Delivered 5-1-33 to Pan American Airways, New York City, NY. In April 1934 the engines were changed to 450 hp and controllable pitch props were installed. 2-3-35 China National Aviation Corporation (CNAC), Shanghai, China. Destroyed in a crash at Yunnan, China, 3-5-36.

5-AT-115 passing through Texas in February 1935. It had been sold by Pan American Airways and was on its way to the West Coast to be shipped to CNAC in China. (R.O. Moore)

5-AT-116; NC-9659, China; 5-AT-D
FF 6-7-33. Delivered 6-17-33 to Pan American Airways, New York City, NY. Assigned to PAA's Western Division at Brownsville, TX. In May 1934 the engines were changed to 450 hp Wasp C's, approved for use in South America, Central America and Mexico only. 8-12-35 China National Aviation Corporation (CNAC), Shanghai, China. It was disassembled and shipped on the steamer SS Nora Maersk from San Pedro, California. This was the last Ford Tri-Motor manufactured.

5-AT-113 was a second 5-AT-D with the unusual placement of the Ford Tri-Motor logo inside a colored oval on the fin. 5-AT-112 also had this change which may have only been on these two planes. (Gordon S. Williams)

Chapter 10
Accidents, Incidents and Big Winds

This listing of accidents, by calendar date, is genealogical in nature and intended to provide further information about the life and death of each individual Ford Tri-Motor. In addition it documents the same information about the lives of human beings for two purposes: first, to assist readers in identifying a specific occurrence when the only information available may be a person's name; second, as an aid to the genuine genealogist who is seeking information about a relative. In both cases the Index will locate this information easily.

Several accidents are listed that may not be a Ford, but because of the location, date and other information it is a possibility. By listing the known information perhaps a reader will be able to add the missing link. The other problem lies with accidents where it is known without a doubt that the plane is a Ford but the identity of the specific airplane is unknown.

The Ford was a rugged, dependable airplane used at times under impossible conditions on a job for which it was never designed. Engine failure and weather were the two major causes of Ford accidents, with the Johnson bar system of brakes contributing to a long chain of embarrassing nose-ups.

There was, however, some criticism of tri-motor designs in the late 1930. Despite heavy advertising promoting the extra safety of three engines some experienced pilots, such as Clarence Chamberlain, felt they were, "not nearly as safe as a single-motored airplane."

A studied analysis of the problems involved were discussed by Otto C. Koppen, Associate Professor of Airplane Design at the Massachusetts Institute of Technology, and former Ford Motor Company engineer, in a letter to the editor of Aviation magazine in September 1930. He stated, "After the recent accident at the Boston Airport when one engine of a three-engine transport plane stopped on the take-off and the airplane landed straight ahead in the harbor like any single-engine airplane would with a dead engine, no one raised the point, in the newspapers at least, that three-engine airplanes were supposed to be able to fly on two engines and by 'fly' is meant to have enough performance to get out of the usual

4-AT-85 (C-9, 29-225) from Barksdale Field, Louisana, on its nose in a typical Ford Tri-Motor accident. It was being flown by 2nd Lt. Ben Kelsey who was later to become famous for landing the XP-38 on a golf course. (Peter M. Bowers)

BARKSDALE FIELD
-10:00A) CRASH. C-9 A.C. NO.29-225

field. In fact, according to the same newspaper accounts the pilot and co-pilot were congratulating each other because they happened to be taking off toward the harbor rather than the densely populated area of East Boston. It would seem from the pilots' reaction that they do not expect the machines to do much when one wing engine is dead.

It is not sufficient that a three-engine plane be able to fly level or even climb slightly with one motor throttled after a safe climb has been reached. Anybody can do that. The trick is to keep climbing out of a field after one of the motors has unexpectedly stopped and the 'unexpectedly' part of it has a great deal to do with the difficulty of taking care of the situation. In the case of the single-engine airplane, the airplane at least goes straight ahead after the engine has stopped. In the case of the multi-engine ship you not only loose power but also must be able to take care of the eccentricity of thrust.

In the usual test of a three-motored airplane, the pilot climbs to a safe altitude, throttles one engine and then demonstrates the ability of the plane to fly level or even climb slightly. Under these conditions control is not very difficult. In the case of engine failure during take-off a pilot is not interested in maintaining an altitude of a few feet or even climbing at the speed of best 'rate' of climb as he faces the immediate problem of getting over an obstruction, so he automatically pulls the nose up to the speed of best angle of climb. Then since the propeller thrust increases, at full throttle, as the airspeed decreases and since the rudder is not usually placed in the slipstream, the rudder control decreases as the square of the airspeed and the turning moment due to the thrust increases more rapidly than the control moment due to the rudder as the airspeed decreases. There is then an airspeed below which the pilot cannot control the airplane, so even if the angle of climb with one motor dead is sufficient to clear the obstruction on account of his inability to hold the airplane straight at the speed of best angle of climb.

If the cases when one engine of a three-engine airplane stopped on take-off are analyzed it is found that in every case when the airplane was fully loaded, if the pilot was unable to land straight ahead, a serious accident occurred. This makes the three-engine airplane at least twice as dangerous as the single-engine craft during the most hazardous part of a flight.

Sooner or later it will be necessary for the Department of Commerce to require that a three-engine airplane be able to take off with a full load with any one engine dead with the same minimum performance required of a single-engine airplane at present. The allowable gross load should be limited on this basis for the present day ships rather than on the basis of structural strength." This is in sharp contrast to the official policy of the Ford Motor Company as stated in the following advertisement in the aviation trade magazines of the period: "Cut Any Engine On A Ford Plane And You Still Have Plenty Of Power; Safety demands reliability of power plant – and that's why the Ford plane's power is divided into three units, any two of which will keep it going. Three engines for safety. Three engines, too, for regularity. A choked jet, or a dirty distributor can't force the Ford plane down.

Transport pilots undergoing advanced training on Ford tri-motors at Dearborn soon learn what it means to have a plane that will carry on with a dead engine. For their training includes the cutting of any engine, by the chief pilot, in a steep climb, in a sharply banked turn.

Another thing about this power. With three engines working the power load with the 5-AT is 10.6 pounds, which is enough power to pull you out of a small field – to climb quickly over obstructions. It helps the pilot in those slight mistakes in judgement where only a world of power will carry the plane through safely. Even with only two engines you have more power for your load than many a plane possesses. The power load then is only 15.9. Still plenty of margin, plenty of reserve.

With the Ford plane a reasonable altitude can be maintained on two engines. This is particularly important in mountainous sections. With two engines the 4-AT will maintain an altitude of 10,000 feet fully loaded, the 5-AT, 8,900 feet, the 7-AT 6,300 feet."

The reader can balance these two opposing points of view in reading the following chapter and it can be seen that engine failure on takeoff has always been a problem – right up to the Island Air Lines crash of July 1977.

One of the best kept secrets in this area is the fact that at least six Fords have had an engine fall off in flight, plus one additional in which the engine fell off during landing.

It is interesting that those involving a safe landing were not given much publicity, and the airlines no doubt did not want to frighten prospective passengers with such horror stories, so that they have been very difficult to uncover. Two surfaced only because the pilots Mal Freeburg and James Carmichael Jr., were given Air Mail Flyer's Medals of Honor by the President of the United States. It seems to be a matter of semantics whether or not these constitute "structural failure." The one phrase that has been repeated more often than any other by all writers is, "There has never been a structural failure in a Ford Tri-Motor." Perhaps. For those interested in this subject it is recommended that the following accident reports be studied: 8-19-26, 1-21-30, 8-8-31, 4-12-32, Mid-Jan-33, 8-30-33, 9-20-33, 4-21-35, 1944 (XH-TAN) and 6-15-56.

One final note of warning. For better or worse newspapers are often the only source of readily available historical material. Unfortunately they are often in error, particularly in regard to the spelling of peoples names.

A good example of a garbled newspaper story is that of a Marine Corps JR-2, U.S. Navy serial number A-8273, flown by Major Roy S. Geiger USMC, which was involved in an accident at San Julian, Cuba, in July 1932.

The *New York Times* story states: "The U.S. Army plane NR-8273, piloted by R.S. Geisger, was forced down late this afternoon at San Julian . . ."

Thus the branch of service was changed from the Marine Corps to the Army, the Navy Serial Number A-8273 to a civil Restricted registration of NR-8273, and Major Geiger became Geisger.

In fairness to the newspapers it must be pointed out that they were often dependent on cablegrams based on telephone conversations with government or airline representatives in a foreign country and there is no luxury of time available in the newspaper business for double checking and written documentation. The reader should therefore weigh the evidence available and think of the possibility of similar sounding names. If any doubt remains it is suggested that the accident report from Mexico, for March 26, 1936, be read to someone on the phone and then see what they have written down!

Accident References

AB: Air Britain, *Central America and the Caribbean Civil Aircraft Registers* (England 1978).

AHC: Aircraft History Card. Individual aircraft histories kept by the Army and Navy.

AV: Ing Adolfo Villasenor M.

DH: Dan Hagedorn.

FF: File Folder on individual aircraft by registration number kept by the Dept. of Commerce/CAA/FAA.

Forero: Col. Jose I. Forero, "Historia de la Aviacion en Colombia."

HY: Harry Yerex interviews of TACA and other Central American pilots.

KCR: Kenn C. Rust, "Early Airlines; Accidents List 1926-1941", *American Aviation Historical Society Journal*, Fall 1987, pp 213-223.

LAT: Los Angeles Times.

LL: Lloyds of London accident reports via the late H.J. Nash who was a specialist on airline accident reports.

NYT: New York Times.

REGD: R.E.G. Davies, "Airlines of Latin America."

SFC: *San Francisco Chronicle.*

SD319: 71st Congress, 3rd Session, Senate Document 319 (Aircraft Accidents between May 20, 1926 and May 16, 1930).

5-AT-11 (XA-HIL) at Mazatlan, Mexico, after a groundloop accident while being flown by a mechanic/co-pilot that folded its landing gear and pushed it into a barbed wire fence. (Larkins Collection)

Accidents and Incidents

August 19, 1926
Near Nova, Ohio
(No registration, became 2435/NC-1492)
While flying in the 1926 Ford Reliability Tour with the new 4-AT-1 a defective propeller caused such heavy vibration that the right engine tore loose from its frame and fell from the plane, tearing away part of the landing gear, and in turn damaging the tip of the propeller on the opposite wing engine. The pilot, Major R.W. Schroeder, landed in a farmer's field without injury to passengers Harry Russell, Kenneth Boedecker, Ernest Greenwood and H.J. Wymer. (*Aviation* 8-17-29 pg. 341; The Ford Air Tours pg. 27)

November 18, 1927
Washington, DC
A7526
The new Navy XJR-1 was hit by a tornado at NAS Anacostia crushing the tail and breaking the right wing. It was returned via the Naval Aircraft Factory to the Ford Motor Company for repair.(AHC)

May 12, 1928
Dearborn, Michigan
NC-1492
William Munn and Earl Parker, pilots for Ford Air Freight Lines, were killed when their 4-AT-A stalled on takeoff for Buffalo from the Ford Airport, hit on the left wing and burned. Munn was making his first flight over the regular Ford schedule and was a former test pilot for the Hess Airplane Company. The plane was carrying 1,200 pounds of freight. (SD319; *NYT* 5-13-28 pg. 24)

August 25, 1928
Puget Sound, Washington
G-CATX
This British Columbia Airways 4-AT-B left Victoria, B.C., at 10:30 a.m. on the 25th for a flight to Seattle and was never seen again. It presumably flew into the water in fog but the only trace ever found was an oil slick near Port Townsend. Pilot Harold Walker, copilot R.L. Carson. Passengers Dr. D.B. Holden, Thomas E. Lake and Mr. & Mrs. Scott of England. (*NYT* 8-26-28 pg. 21; *CAHS Journal*, Fall 1965, pg. 68)

October 13, 1928
Detroit, Michigan
NC-880
Stout Air Service 4-AT-A hit a tree during a night landing and nose-dived into the ground. Pilot Ralph Reed, passengers Peter Berger and Harold Conroy. (SD319; *NYT* 10-14-28, pg. 3)

November 23, 1928
Spokane, Washington
NC-7687
Pilot William H. Williams and passengers L.N. DeBuger, Kenneth J. Dunlop, Arthur G. Enarson, Rex Heath, D.R. Mitchell. Three were killed when this Spokane Airways 4-AT-B crashed on Moran Prarie while attempting to land in dense fog. (SD319; *NYT* 11-24-28, pg. 19; 12-2-28 photo)

December 1, 1928
Spur, Texas
NC-7862
Homer D. Ballard, owner of the 4-AT-C and President of the Sunbeam Air Transport Company, was killed as well as pilot Mathew Watson and passengers Willis Washburn, James O'Banion and Mr. Quinter. The probable cause listed by the Department of Commerce was, "Plane caught fire in the air causing gas tank to explode." (SD319; *NYT* 12-2-28, pg. 25)

December 2, 1928
Jacksonville, Florida
NC-7684
This Sky View Lines 4-AT-B was forced to make an emergency landing when the engines failed due to water in the gas. Pilot Major John O. Leach and nine passengers. (SD319)

December 22, 1928
Floresville, Texas
NC-3443
Pilot Matt Nieminen, flying the TEXACO 4-AT-A, with passengers J.W. Royal, J.E. Wright and P.J. Clausen, had landed because of a heavy fog at his destination inside the half-mile race track at Floresville. After the weather cleared the pilot attempted to take off from the field inside the track but a cross wind and the muddy field prevented the plane from attaining sufficient altitude so that it went through two small fences and into a small house. No one was injured but the plane was damaged beyond repair. (SD319)

January 13, 1929
Newark, New Jersey
NC-1780
The left wing of this Tri-Motor Safety Airways 4-AT-A was damaged when hit while on the ground by a Waco 10. (SD319)

January 16, 1929
Near Toledo, Ohio
NC-1076
A fire in the mail compartment of this Stout Air Service 4-AT-A caused a forced landing after which the plane

4-AT-9 after an in-flight fire at Toledo, Ohio, on January 16, 1929. (Robert F. Pauley)

burned. Pilot James L. Brandon, passenger Arthur Z. Gruitch. (SD319)

January 18, 1929
Santa Rosa, California
NC-4532
This Maddux Airlines 4-AT-B hit a soft spot on landing and the plane nosed up to a sudden stop buckling the rear fuselage and crushing two bulkheads. Pilot Marino J. Guglielmetti and passengers B. Erich, F. Lenceoni, Armond Score, J. Shanks, and J. Shryver. (SD319, FF)

February 24, 1929
Cleveland, Ohio
NC-1879
One wing of this Stout Air Lines 4-AT-A hit a tree during a forced landing due to engine failure. Photos show the plane near houses on a snow covered field at West 65th Street and Denison Avenue with the name Stout Air Lines hastily painted out. Pilot Samuel J. Taylor and passengers Mrs. M.T., Dykena, M.F. Dykena, Mrs. M. Hayden, Jim McIntyre, George Mociejewski, Mr. & Mrs. H.R. Peterson, Mr. & Mrs. A.G. Poppins, R.H. Redfield, Walter Simmelink, Lawrence Simmelink. (SD319)

March 5, 1929
Cojimar, Cuba
NC-7684
During a forced landing due to bad weather this Sky View Lines 4-AT-B hit some rocks damaging the landing gear. Pilot H.P. Hublitz. No passengers listed. (SD319)

March 17, 1929
Newark, New Jersey
NC-7683
The first big Ford Tri-Motor crash, labeled at the time by the newspapers as, "the worst accident in the history of heavier-than-air aeronautics in this country." The pilot, Lou Foote was the only person not killed of the 15 aboard. This Colonial Western Airways 4-AT-B was flying sight seeing trips on a sunday afternoon. The final flight took off at 5 p.m. and at about 500 feet the left engine quit, then the center engine. With a full load the plane crashed into a gravel car in a rail yard and was cut in half. Passengers Joseph Bauer, Auton Boele, Raymond Helestetter, Thomas Henderson, Walter F. Hentschel Jr., Frank Hogmasi, Steven Hogmasi, Patrick M. Jannuzzi, William Marquette, Gertrude McSteever, W. Clifton McSteever, Delmont Parsons, Reginald D. Woodward, William Ziser. (SD319; *NYT* 3-18-29 pg. 1, 324-29 a 15-inch photo in the rotagravure section; *Boston Evening Transcript* 3-18-29 pg. 7 with photo).

There is much additional information in the *NYT* during the trial for damages. 3-25-31 pg. 18, Mr. H.I. Wells, with 1100 hours in tri-motors, testifies that a tri-motor is not safe to turn under 1000 feet; 3-26-31 pg. 56 and 3-27-31 pg. 16, Clarence Chamberlain states that, "tri-motors are not nearly as safe as single engine airplanes" (ordered stricken from the record of the trial); 3-28-31 pg. 13, Lou Foote describes the crash; 4-2-31 pg. 25, Wright Aeronautical expert finds the engines to be in good condition; 4-3-31 pg. 2, Bernt Balchen testifies in defense, once took off in a similar plane (Byrd's 4-AT-15) at a gross weight of 14,500 pounds while the crashed plane weight was estimated at 9500 lbs. 4-11-31 pg. 14, damages of $89,000 awarded to six persons; 11-24-31 pg. 11; 11-26-31 pg. 33, Chamberlain testifies again; 12-6-31 pg. 2, further damages of $71,000 awarded to two surviving relatives.

March 19,1929
Dearborn, Michigan
NC-9674
A Mysterious crash of a 5-AT-B at the factory that persistent rumors claim was kept out of the newspapers because there was a woman aboard. Believed to have been a test flight for TAT. A wing hit the ground during landing and engine failure prevented recovery. Pilots Dennis Taylor and H.L. Russell, with passengers Harold Gray and "one other unknown." FAA file states plane crashed during flight tests, not to be rebuilt, registration NC-9674 cancelled. The plane was only five days old. (SD319, FF)

March 21, 1929
Sherman, Texas
NC-1781
License cancelled 1-16-32 as plane was operating in Mexico. No further data but believed to have been in an accident and disposed of in Mexico.

March 28, 1929
Buffalo, New York
Unknown
Nosed up on landing in soft ground. Pilot K.L. Whitsett, no passengers. (SD319)

March 31, 1929
Sherman, Texas
NC-1781
The fuselage of this 4-AT-A was broken after landing in a cross wind which lifted the tail. Pilot Clarence Bragunier and 10 passengers, no injuries. Fuselage caved in between stations 8 and 10, repaired at the factory. (SD319, FF)

April 21, 1929
San Diego, California
NC-9636
A Maddux Airlines 5-AT-B on its way from San Diego to Phoenix was hit in mid-air by Air Corps Boeing PW-9D, Serial No. 28-37, which turned from right to left directly in front of the airliner. Pilot Howard W. Keefer of the 95th Pursuit Squadron was killed when his half-opened parachute caught on the tail of the fighter. All aboard the Ford were killed when the plane hit the ground upside down at a 45 degree angle. Pilots Maurice H. Murphy and Louis Pratt. Passengers Arturo and Amelia Guejardo, Cecilia Kelly. (SD319; *NYT* 4-22-29 pg. 1; SFC 4-22-29, pg. 1)

April 25, 1929
Eastport, Maryland
NC-7121
An outboard prop of this Tri-Motored Air Tours 4-AT-B hit a telephone pole on takeoff from a soft field in poor terrain. Pilot O.M. Goodsell, no passengers listed. (SD319)

June 2, 1929
Wichita, Kansas
NC-9676
Damaged in wind storm. Fuselage broken in two, left wing spars broken, landing gear broke and pushed into fuselage. Repairs completed at the factory in July 1929.

June 24, 1929
St. Paul, Minnesota
NC-7416
This Northwest Airways 5-AT-A crashed and burned near Indian Mounds Park about one minute after takeoff from Hollman Field enroute to Minneapolis. All three engines quit at once at about 500 feet altitude and the resultant crash killed the pilot Eddie Middaugh. The co-pilot Robert Johnson and passengers Halbert Ames, Paul Ames, Kendall Clough, Mr. & Mrs. Henry Foote Jr., and J. Bryant McCosker were injured. (SD319; *NYT* 6-25-29 pg. 35)

July 9, 1929
Clovis, New Mexico
NC-9646
During the inaugural air-rail flight the 5-AT-B "City of Los Angeles" was taking off when engine failure caused the plane to ground loop across plowed land into the hangar. Pilot J.B. Stowe. Passengers James Bryant, E. Greiner, Mrs. John T. Litch, Miss M. A. Salamon. (SD319, *LAT* 7-10-29 II pg. 1)

July 16, 1929
Brooks Field, Texas
29-225
This Army C-9 assigned to the 62nd Service Squadron was landing on soft ground when after a 100 yard run the wheels locked and the plane nosed up, tilting over on the right wing tip and back down on the landing gear. Pilot Capt. Claire L. Chennault. (AHC)

September 4, 1929
Mt. Taylor, New Mexico
NC-9649
This TAT 5-AT-B "City of San Francisco" hit a mountain in full flight during a severe thunderstorm, killing all eight aboard. First reports stated that the plane had been hit by lightning but these later proved to be untrue. The crash took place about 60 miles west of Albuquerque at 11:01

a.m. Pilot J.B. Stowe, co-pilot E.A. Dietel. Passengers W.H. Beers, M.M. Campbell, C.F. Canfield, H. Livermore, A.B. McGuffey, Mrs. Corina Raymond. (SD319; *NYT* 9-5-29 pg. 1, 9-9-29 pg. 1, 9-15-29 photo in rotagravure section)

September 14, 1929
McCook, Nebraska
NC-5577
The landing gear of this Curtiss Flying Service 4-AT-B collapsed on landing causing the fuselage and center section to be twisted. "Forced landing, probably due to engine failure." Rebuilt at the factory. Pilot Carlos L. Reavis. Passengers Pinkney F. Denver, W.H. Garrison and 9 others. (SD319)

September 14, 1929
Hasbrouck Heights, New Jersey
NC-9614
This Firestone Tire and Rubber Company 4-AT-E had to have its right wing replaced after being hit on the ground by a landing Fokker "Universal" being flown by Max Holtzen. (SD319)

November 2, 1929
Chicago, Illinois
NC-5492
Transport Pilot Perry Hutton (No. 547) was the pilot of this non injury accident involving a Air Cruises 4-AT-B. No details other than a bent propeller, cowling and minor parts. (FF)

December 22, 1929
Indianapolis, Indiana
NC-9647
This TAT 5-AT-B arrived from St. Louis at 5:05 p.m. and ran into a snow storm. While landing the pilot, Dean Burford, hit a snow covered stump tearing away the left engine and ripping a six-foot long gash in the bottom of the cabin. Co-pilot H.J. Zimmerman. Passenger D.C. Law, of Warner Brothers Pictures, was killed. The other passengers were Jon B. Bowman, C.M. Cline, W.S. Edwards, Mary Fearnow, Mr. Klemeyer, B.G. Leighton, J.H. Lunneman, Russell McFarland, Dorothy O'Brien, M. Stearns and F.J. Walsh. (SD319), *NYT* 12-23-29, pg. 1)

5-AT-21, TAT's "City of Indianapolis" after landing in a heavy snow storm in December 1929. (Edward Peck)

January 1, 1930
Pacasmayo, Peru
NC-400H
A sudden downdraft caused this Pangra 5-AT-C to make a hard landing which damaged the fuselage. Pilot Homer V. Farris. Passengers H.R. Harris, Maurice Nathan, Jose Pleza, Richard Tennel, J.W. Van Low. (SD319)

January 6, 1930
Montevideo, Uruguay
NC-8418
Panagra 5-AT-C "damaged." No details. (LL)

January 16, 1930
St. Louis, Missouri
NC-9650
This TAT 5-AT-B skidded on an icy runway and ran through a fence on landing. Pilot Earl W. Fleet. Passengers G.H. Covert, J.T. Mitchell, W.A. Murray, George Nevenger, Miss Noftvger, L.F. Oliver, P. Siggemeyer, Mrs. P. Siggemeyer. (SD319)

January 19, 1930
Oceanside, California
NC-9689
This Maddux Airlines 5-AT-C was en route from Agua Caliente, Mexico, to Los Angeles when it encountered a sudden line squall at 6:23 p.m. The pilot, Basil Russell, attempted to turn back but was so low that his left wing hit the ground. All 16 persons aboard were killed in the ensuing crash and fire, labeled, "the greatest disaster in American air transportation" by the newspaper reports. The plane hit at San Clemente, near Oceanside, and was Fleet No. 15. Co-pilot F.L. Walker, passengers Hanna Bolstein, Edward Bower, Edla Bower, Cedric Brown, Sadie Brown, Doris Cantilion, Frances Jameson, B. Miller, Addie McGlover, William Paddon, Charles Robard, Edward J. Small, Elizabeth Squibb. (SD319; *NYT* 1-26-30, photo is roto section; SFC 1-20-30 pg. 1)

An unreported "accident" involving 5-AT-74. Details are lacking but it may have been that someone left the rear inspection plates off the floats so that they filled with water. (Hudek)

January 21, 1930
Miami, Florida
NC-415H
A fuselage brace on this Firestone Tire & Rubber 5-AT-C collapsed while taxying. Structural failure of diagonal bracing and possibly too hard a landing. Pilot William M. McConnell. Passengers C.F. Deidenich, Helen Evans, W.H. Graham, W.H. Murphy, Mrs. W.H. Murphy, J.G. Peeler, B.P. Rafters, J.B. Rice, W.R. Southerland, Clyde L. Smith, Grace Wans. (SD319, FF)

January 23, 1930
Dayton, Ohio
29-223
Air Corps C-9 piloted by 1st Lt. R.W. Warren. No details. (HC)

February 2, 1930
Near Alba, Michigan
29-222
Air Corps C-9 piloted by 1st Lt. Harry A. Johnson. After the center engine quit and the right engine was loosing power the pilot made an emergency landing seven miles SE of Alba. The plane hit a stump with the right ski knocking off the engine nacelle and damaging the right wing and fuselage. Engine failure was caused by water in the fuel. Plane No.22 of the 94th Pursuit Squadron at Selfridge Field, Michigan. (HC)

February 8, 1930
San Marcos, Texas
NC-2492
This early 4-AT-A owned by Dale Seitz was being flown by Ben F. Gregory nosed up on landing due to gear failure. Wings loose and fuselage broken. Passengers Mr. & Mrs. Paunds, Mr. & Mrs. Walker, Miss Walker and Mr. Zimmerman. (SD319, FF)

February 20, 1930
Columbus, Ohio
Unknown
This TAT 5-AT struck another plane while taxying. The other plane was being turned around and there was not sufficient room on the runway. Pilot George C. Price. No passengers listed. (SD319, FF)

March 2, 1930
Cordoba, Argentina
NC-1780 (R-131)
This NYRBA 4-AT-A crash is listed by the Lloyds of London insurance register as taking place on March 2, 1930 with the plane's name being "Rio de la Plata." The FAA file folder says the plane was washed out in South America between August 1 and 16, 1929, but this seems to be in error. (LL, FF)

5-AT-34 after an emergency landing at LaLande, New Mexico, in May 1930. The plane was repaired and flown back to the TAT shops. The underwing markings are rare in showing the combined TAT-MADDUX name. (Robert E. Gardyne Jr.)

March 3, 1930
Mitchel Field, New York
29-221
Air Corps C-9 being flown by 1st Lt. Newton Longfellow. While taxying a strong gust of wind got under the tail and put the ship up on its nose damaging the prop, fuselage and right wing tip. Plane No. 53 from Bolling Field, Washington D.C. (HC)

April 8, 1930
Buenos Aires, Argentina
R-130
NYRBA 5-AT "Santiago" damaged. No details. (LL)

May 22, 1930
LaLande, New Mexico
NC-9651
This TAT 5-AT-B damaged its landing gear and props in an emergency landing. It was repaired and flown out. (FF)

June 5, 1930
Boston Harbor, Massachusetts
NC-9675
This Colonial Air Transport 5-AT-C named "Nacomis" crashed on takeoff from the East Boston Airport on a flight to New York City on the afternoon of the 5th. Although 15 people were aboard all escaped the crash, but one drowned while swimming away. The accident was caused by the failure of the right wing engine on take-off, causing the crash landing in eight-foot deep water off the end of the runway. The fuselage settled below the water, with most of the passengers escaping through the pilot's roof hatch. In the NYT story a state aviation inspector blamed the crash on the engines being allowed to idle too long, causing them to become "loaded up." Pilot Owen O'Connor, co-pilot Val Chick. Passengers H.D. Beaton, Simon DeVaulchier, H.S. Ford Jr., Mr. & Mrs. Charles H. Jacobson, L.H. Morrison, M.H. Shapiro, W.H. Sheafer, W.A. Stayton, Pearl S. Thorsen, Henry Wallace and Mrs. H.E. Webster. (*NYT* 6-6-30 pg. 1, 6-8-30 pp 1, 18; *Boston Evening Transcript* 6-5-30, pp 1, 5.)

June 25, 1930
Chicago, Illinois
NC-7739
Northwest Airways 5-AT-A destroyed in a hangar fire. (FF)

August 4, 1930
Ocotal, Nicaragua
A8598
U.S. Marine Corps JR-3 destroyed by fire after the wing and nose hit the ground during landing. Gunnery Sgt. Greer, the pilot, escaped unhurt. (*NYT* 8-5-30 pg. 14; AHC)

August 22, 1930
Jihlava (Iglau), Czechoslovakia
OK-FOR
Twelve persons were killed when this regularly scheduled service of the Czechoslovak State Airplane Service crashed

on the afternoon of the 22nd near Jihlava (Iglau) in west Moravia. It was flying on its regular airline route from Prague (Praha) to Vienna (Wien), Austria. The 5-AT-C was flying low because of mist, encountered a storm, and while attempting to land crashed into a brick yard and burned. The London Times reported that it crashed, "on a house top in the middle of town." (NYT 8-23-30 pg. 3; *London Times* 8-23-30 pg. 9)

September 9, 1930
Montreal, Canada
NC-415H
Firestone Tire & Rubber Company 5-AT-C. No details. (FF)

September 27, 1930
Chicago, Illinois
NC-8410
This Northwest Airways 5-AT-C was "blown over by the wind" and repaired at the factory. (FF)

November 21, 1930
Glendale, California
NC-7118
This Curtiss-Wright Flying Service 4-AT-B was destroyed when it was flipped upside down and broken by a severe wind storm while tied down at the Grand Central Air Terminal.

November 24, 1930
Dearborn, Michigan
NX-419H
Myron Zeller, Chief Pilot of the aircraft division of the Ford Motor Company, and Carl Wenzel, Chief Test Mechanic, were killed in the crash of this experimental 5-AT-C. After having been up for nearly an hour witnesses saw a sudden rush of smoke from one of the engines. Zeller headed for the field at about 1,000 feet altitude, passed over the home of Henry Ford, across Michigan Avenue just over the trees and landed in the center of the airport. In braking for the fast landing the plane nosed up, stood poised on its center prop for a few seconds and then went over on its back and burned. (*NYT* 11-25-30 pg. 1)

November 24, 1930
Greencastle, Indiana
NC-9606
Pilot Howard E. Hall nosed up in landing in bad weather, in TWA No. 614, resulting in the nose engine mount and propellers being replaced. (FF)

December 20, 1930
Jennerstown, Pennsylvania
NC-9611
Pittsburgh Airways 4-AT-E. No further info. Remains probably junked. (FF)

4-AT-32 at Glendale, California, after a severe storm with Santa Ana Winds that picked it up and threw it upside down across the field at Grand Central Air Terminal in November 1930. (Joe Barry)

December 22, 1930
Chile
Unknown
A Linea Aerea Nacional crash of a Ford. (REGD)

January 2, 1931
Tripoli
G-ABHO
5-AT-C damaged in landing accident. (LL)

March 30, 1931
Columbus, Ohio
NC-8411
TWA No. 616. Damage to right wing, prop, landing gear and engine mount after a Jack slipped from under the plane in the shop. (FF)

April 1, 1931
Ovalle, Chile
NC-8418
A Pan American Airways inspection party walked away from a crash landing in this 5-AT-C at a one-way Chilean government airport, bounded by high cliffs of the Andes mountains and strong cross winds. The pilot elected to dig a wing into the ground and cartwheel the plane rather than crash into the base of a cliff. "All three engines were torn off and the fuselage crumpled like paper, but Clifford Travis, the pilot, saved the lives of the six persons in the cabin, all of whom were out of the plane within 30 seconds of final impact, climbing through the windows, which splintered as the metal sides of the fuselage collapsed." The party continued their tour in a Lockheed "Vega" . . . from a first hand description by New York Times reporter Leo A. Kieran who was aboard the plane. The co-pilot was Alec C. Knothe. (*NYT* 4-2-31 pg. 10, 4-3-31 pg. 16, 4-4-31 pg. 11)

April 17, 1931
Mihinia, India
CV-FAI
The short-lived 5-AT-C "Comte de la Vaulx" had been christened only March 27th at the start of its inspection tour. The plane hit a vulture in flight, damaging the engine cowl, and landed at Bamrauli airport in India. The decision was made to refuel and continue on to Calcutta. The plane took off at 1:00 p.m. and about an hour later hit another vulture with the left wing, damaging the plane so badly that an immediate landing was considered necessary. This was done in a plowed field near the village of Mihinia, about 45 miles east of Benares. In landing on the rough ground the plane turned over, ruptured an overhead gas tank and the plane caught fire. All four people, including Prince Bibesco, escaped with various injuries. (*London Times* 4-20-31 pg. 13; *The Aeroplane* 4-22-31)

April 29, 1931
Elyria, Ohio
NC-421H
Seven passengers and three pilots lived through this serious crash of a NAT 5-AT-C bound from Chicago to Cleveland. First the right engine quit, then the nose engine. In the crash landing the plane scraped a tree and barn roof, but landed upright in a farmyard and did not burn. The nose engine and landing gear were torn away. Pilot Sam Taylor, co-pilot Allen McDiarmid. Passengers Raymond Bjorkolm (another NAT pilot riding as a passenger), Lynch Dordon, Harry Fisher, P.G. Gadunbusch, G. Jones, E. Taylor, T.W. Walsh and William Weber. (*NYT* 4-30-31 pg. 13)

July 29, 1931
David, Panama
NC-9664
PAA 5-AT-B, no details. (FF)

August 8, 1931
Cincinnati, Ohio
NC-9662
All six persons were killed in the crash of this Cincinnati to Atlanta 5-AT-B of the Embry-Riddle Division of American Airways. About one minute after take-off from Lunken Airport, at 8:40 a.m., and less than 500 feet up, the right hand prop was torn loose and fell from the engine causing it to revolve as such a speed that it too was torn loose from the wing, landing 1500 feet from the wreckage. Pilot Marvin T. Odell headed for a sand bar on the bank of the Little Miami River but the plane turned over on its back in the soft mud. The baggage and mail was all that was saved. Both pilots were considered experts and this crash caused considerable discussion among the anti-tri-motor pilots. Odell had 4,000 hours and co-pilot William J. Dewald was a former flight instructor with 3,000 hours. Passengers V.B. Baum, William P. Brimberry, Gwenna D. Hughes and William E. Keith. (*NYT* 8-10-31 pg. 1)

August 14, 1931
Harrisburg, Pennsylvania
NC-9647
Pilot Ralph W. Ritchie landed TWA No. 609 short and hit an embankment off the runway. The right wing and engine were torn loose and the right landing gear washed out. (KCR)

August 19, 1931
Pittsburgh, Pennsylvania
NC-9665
TWA No. 618 destroyed in a landing accident. Pilot A.D. Smith overshot the runway in a storm, attempted a ground loop to stop the plane but it slid off the wet runway injuring five. (KCR)

September 19, 1931
Dearborn, Michigan
NX-9652
Leroy Manning, Chief Test Pilot of the Ford Motor Company, and L.H. Garriott, mechanic, were killed when the experimental Ford bomber XB-906-1 crashed and burned after a power dive at South Field and Van Born Roads at 10:30 a.m. (*NYT* 9-20-31 pg. 29; *Detroit Free Press* 9-20-31 pg. 1)

October 10, 1931
Ilo, Peru
NC-403H
Panagra 5-AT-C, no further info. (FF)

October 12, 1931
St. Louis, Missouri
NC-7861
Union Electric 4-AT-B, no further info. (FF)

October 21, 1931
North Beach, New York
NC-8400
Arthur Kudner 4-AT-E. (FF)

October 27, 1931
Ashley, Indiana
NC-427H
NAT 5-AT-C. No information. Pilot Ralph Reed. (FF, KCR)

November 27, 1931
Harrisburg, Pennsylvania
NC-9647
TWA 5-AT-B "washout." (FF)

December 19, 1931
Oklahoma City, Oklahoma
NC-7119
TWA 701, a 4-AT-B, crashed and burned on take-off. When one engine would not start pilot George C. Price attempted to take off on two engines. The co-pilot N.C. Morse was killed. The plane crashed about 500 yards south of the Oklahoma City Airport while flying from Tulsa to Amarillo. It was a ferry flight and there were no passengers. (*KCR, NYT*, FF)

January 10, 1932
Dallas, Texas
NC-434H
NAT 5-AT-D . Nose-up, no further info. (FF)

January 28, 1932
Biscoe, Arkansas
29-225
Army Air Corps C-9 had to make a forced landing due to bad weather. The right wheel hit a hole in the ground putting the plane up on its nose damaging the prop and engine mount. The plane was No. 550 from the 53rd School Squadron at Randolph Field, Texas, and being flown by 2nd Lt. James L. Daniels Jr. (AHC)

February 16, 1932
Port Columbus, Ohio
NC-9607
TWA. No info. 5-AT-B. (FF)

February 28, 1932
Beaumont, Texas
NC-9613
Air Tours 4-AT-E. No info. Plane repaired by PAA at Brownsville. (FF)

April 12, 1932
Wabasha, Minnesota
Unknown
A Northwest Airways 5-AT was flying between St. Paul and Chicago when one blade of the right propeller broke off, causing the engine to break loose. Pilot Mal B. Freeburg, and co-pilot Joe Kimm, managed to fly the plane to a sand bar in the Mississippi River, rock the plane so that the engine would fall free, and then fly the plane to a safe landing at the emergency field at Wabasha, NNE of Rochester. Despite a damaged landing gear on the right side they were able to save the plane, passengers and mail. On December 13, 1933, President Franklin D. Roosevelt presented Freeburg with the Air Mail Flyer's Medal of Honor at a ceremony at the White House. See 2-10-33 accident report regarding Eddie Bellande. (*NYT, National Geographic*, May 1933, pp. 590-591.

May 8, 1932
Amarillo, Texas
NC-8413
A ground fire destroyed the center engine and entire pilots compartment of TWA No. 601 due to a broken gas line to the carburetor. Pilot M.E. Bowen. The plane was rebuilt and replaced in service only to be destroyed in another ground fire on 6-19-38. (FF)

May 19, 1932
Cerro Azul, Peru
NC-402H
Panagra 5-AT-C. No info. (FF)

June 5, 1932
Bushland, Texas
NC-9651
TWA 5-AT-B suffered $10,368 damage to the leading edge of the wing and the top of the wing, cowls, stabilizer and fuselage from a hail storm. Pilots Ralph Montee and J.E. Bowen reported that the plane flew "normally" after

5-AT-108, Pacific Air Transport's ABBOTT, at Seattle in July 1932. (Boeing Airplane Company)

the hail storm. A photo showing the after effects was used by the Ford company in one of their advertisements (see ad in August 1932 Aero Digest "BASHED IN BY FIST-SIZE HAIL ALL-METAL FORD COMPLETES TRIP"). The plane, Fleet No. 605, had 3,340 flying hours at the time. (FF)

June 16, 1932
Chicago, Illinois
NC-9676
This Northwest Airways 5-AT-B was hit on the leading edge of the right wing by a taxying Stinson Tri-motor. (FF)

July 1, 1932
San Julian, Cuba
A-8273
A Marine Corps JR-2, being flown by Major Roy S. Geiger, was forced down late in the afternoon at San Julian on the west end of Pinar del Rio Province, buckling the fuselage and damaging the engine mounts. (*NYT* 7-2-32 pg. 8; AHC)

July 11, 1932
Seattle, Washington
NC-9653

5-AT-108 six months later at Weed, California, after a successful emergency landing. The wings have been removed and the fuselage is being prepared to tow down the highway. It was re-assembled at the Dunsmuir airport and flown back to the UAL shops at Oakland. (Philip T. Sharp)

This Pacific Air Transport (United Air Lines) 5-AT-D was taking off from Boeing Field when the left en gine quit at an altitude of about 100 feet. The pilot, Heber C. Miller, elected to make a forced landing off the runway in the undeveloped part of the field. Stewardess Alice Powers was thrown over a seat but there were no injuries. (FF, Seattle Times 7-11-32, Vic Seely letter 1-65)

July 16, 1932
Santiago, Chile
NC-403H
This Pan American Grace Airways 5-AT-C was lost in a severe snowstorm while crossing the Andes Mountains from Santiago, Chile, to Buenos Aires, Argentina. It was found 20 months later in a high Andean valley near Mt. El Plomo, close to Puente del Inca, a Transandean railway station. All nine were killed but the plane did not burn. Pilot Charles J. Robinson, co-pilot C.W. Myers. Two passengers were Edward Camus and J.C. Sabater. (*NYT* 7-17-32 pg. 2, 7-18-32 pg. 15, 7-19-32 pg. 10, 3-23-34 pg. 17)

September 4, 1932
Fort Worth, Texas
NC-413H
NAT 5-AT-C, no further info. (FF)

October 2, 1932
Near San Lorenzo, Honduras
NC-9664
A Pan American Airways 5-AT-B crash-landed in a jungle swamp at El Aceituno between Managua, Nicaragua, and San Lorenzo, Honduras. It was one hour out of San Lorenzo when it turned back due to bad weather. There were no injuries reported to the passengers or crew but the plane was destroyed. The passengers and mail were rescued by Marine Corps airmen led by Capt. F.P. Mulcahy. There are no names of the crew or passengers in the NYT. (*NYT* 10-3-32 pg. 6, 104-32 pg. 8)

October 26, 1932
Villa Montes, Bolivia
"Cruz del Sur" (5-AT-113)
A Ford 5-AT-D which arrived in Bolivia 9-26-32 was destroyed in a crash while in the military service of Bolivia. Aircraft destroyed and pilot Donald Duke and German mechanic Willy Kettman killed. (USN Office of Naval Intelligence report, DH)

December 7, 1932
Burbank, California
NC-5578
4-AT-D of Reed and Clemm. No data. (FF)

December 14, 1932
Amarillo, Texas
NC-9650
Pilot Ralph Montee, and co-pilot John E. Bowen, were killed in the crash of TWA No. 610, a 5-AT-B, while attempting to land in a blinding snowstorm. There were no passengers. (*KCR*, LL)

December - 1932
Weed, California
NC-9653
Although not an accident this emergency landing is of interest. Pacific Air Transport's 5-AT-D was caught in a snow storm and pilots Grover Taylor and Kenneth Householder were forced to land on a small emergency field at Weed in Northern California near Mt. Shasta. The plane was partially dismantled and towed several miles south down the highway to the Dunsmuir Airport where it was reassembled and flown out. (J.R. Smith)

Mid-January, 1933
Chicago, Illinois
Unknown
A remarkable safe landing was made by this United Air Lines 5-AT after the right engine fell off in flight between Chicago and Moline. A propeller blade flew off, causing the engine to vibrate so badly that it fell from the plane. The pilot E. "Mike" Matucha, and co-pilot W. Ray Allemang, were able to turn the plane around and return to Chicago Airport and land with no injuries and slight damage to the plane. The right wheel structure had been damaged and it caused the plane to veer to the right on rollout. They were extremely lucky; see the 8-8-31 American Airlines fatal crash at Cincinnati. (W.R. Allemang)

January 24, 1933
Eugene, Oregon
NC-431H
Pacific Air Transport's 5-AT-D "Dawson" left Portland for Seattle after cancelling the passenger reservations, but landed at Eugene in bad weather. After a delay the flight was cancelled and the mail put on the train. On takeoff to return to Portland the left engine quit, the plane careened into a landing light, then hit a telephone pole and finally plowed into a vacant house. The plane and house burned killing pilot Harold R. Adams and co-pilot Kenneth Householder. Stewardess Cornelia Pederman escaped with minor injuries. Adams was an experienced Army pilot who had flown in France in World War I. (*KCR, Portland Oregonian* 1-25-33 pg. 1)

February 10, 1933
Bakersfield, California
NC-9666
A remarkable landing, after an in-flight fire, saved all of the nine crew and passengers of TWA No.617. On its regular night flight from San Francisco to Los Angeles, via Fresno and Bakersfield, "sparks from the motor ignited fuel in the gasoline line" about ten miles out from the Bakersfield Airport. Pilot Eddie Bellande managed to land on the airport and evacuate the plane, with Mrs. Adelaide Helwig being the last to get out with burns on her face and hands. Airline officials were quoted as saying, "Only the ships all-metal construction prevented its destruction in mid-air and the death of all nine occupants."

5-AT-25 after its emergency landing at Bakersfield, California, in February 1933, that earned pilot Eddie Bellande the Air Mail Pilots Medal of Honor. (Larkins Collection)

The co-pilot Lynn Berkenkamp was killed in a TACA Ford crash in Nicaragua in 1941.

Other reports state that the fire was caused by the floor heater which operated from an exhaust stack on the nose engine. An interesting comment on this is that the heating element leading to the pilots compartment burned through on the Marine Corps RR-4, A8840, at Anacostia on 11-3-1. (*SFC* 2-11-33 pg. 1)

On October 29, 1935, Eddie Bellande was one of seven air mail pilots to receive the Air Mail Fliers Medal of Honor (authorized by Congress in 1931) from President Franklin Roosevelt in Washington, DC. The award with the medal read, "Edward A. Bellande, who on the night of February 10,1933, while flying from San Francisco to Los Angeles, landed safely seven passengers after his plane caught fire in the air. One passenger was slightly burned and some of the mail was destroyed."

As copilots were not eligible for the medal Lynn Berkenkamp was given a letter of recommendation, "for checking the flames and keeping them from the passengers compartment while the pilot made the safe landing." (*NYT* 10-30-35 pg. 7)

5-AT-83 at Virginia Beach, Virginia in March 1933. (Peter M. Bowers)

March 22, 1933
Virginia Beach, Virginia
A-8599
Marine Corps JR-3 wrecked beyond repair near Norfolk. See photo (AHC)

March 23, 1933
Chanute Field, Rantoul, Illinois
29-222
Air Corps pilot 1st Lt. E.E. Partridge attempted a take-off in a C-9 with soft snow on the wings which did not blow off. After a long run the ship got 50 feet in the air and then stalled and fell off on the left wing at the edge of the field. The plane was from the 57th Service Squadron at Selfridge Field. (AHC)

March 28, 1933
Scott Field, Illinois
29-225
Pilot 2nd Lt. Ben S. Kelsey of the 77th Pursuit Squadron at Barksdale Field nosed up on soft ground during a landing roll. The C-9 was plane No. 56 of the 71st Service Squadron at Barksdale Field. (AHC)

March 31, 1933
Near Neodesha, Kansas
NC-7686
The owner of this 4-AT-B, J.H. O'Brien of Morris, Minnesota, and six members of a group of young Canadian athletes were killed when the left engine quit and the plane made a forced landing in a soggy, narrow plowed field. The passengers were members of the Winnipeg Toilers, basketball champions of Canada, on their way home after a series of games with the Tulsa Oilers. Photos indicate the forward fuselage destroyed by fire but no mention of this is made in the news story. Pilot Alvis H. Hakes, co-pilot H.E. Eggens. Passengers R.H. Bonynge,

Andry Brown, Bruce Dodds, Joe Dodds, Hugh Penwarden, Lander Phillips, Allan Sampson, Mike Shea, T.A. Silverthorne and Ian Wooley. This unfortunate accident happened on the anniversary of the Knute Rockne crash. (*NYT* 4-1-33 pg. 3)

April 24, 1933
Bolling Field, Washington, DC
31-402
This C-4A, Bolling Field No. 51, was damaged when two men ran into the path of the landing plane. 1st Lt. F.V.H. Kimball, the pilot, landed fast after having to give more throttle to go over them, hit a soft spot in the field and ground looped. The tail came up and then dropped down, buckling the fuselage. (HC?)

May 27, 1933
Port Columbus, Ohio
31-403
Air Corps C-4A piloted by 1st Lt. R.L. Williamson. The plane hit a hangar with its wing tip while taxying causing $7,028 worth of damage. It was plane No. 3 from the 57th Service Squadron at Selfride Field. (AHC)

June 2, 1933
Mineola, L.I., New York
NR-9614
The 4-AT-E "Voice of the Sky" was destroyed in a disastrous hangar fire at Roosevelt Field along with 27 other aircraft. The 10:00 pm fire, the second in four months, was watched by 2,000 people. (*NYT* 6-3-33, pg. 7)

July 1, 1933
Chicago, Illinois
NC-420H
NAT 5-AT-C, no information. (FF)

July 2, 1933
Chicago, Illinois
NC-9610
Harold S. Johnson and his 4-AT-B, no further info. (FF)

August 29, 1933
Quay, New Mexico
NC-9607
This TWA 5-AT-B hit the south end of Mesa Mountain, 60 miles from Clovis, at night in a bad storm killing all five aboard. The plane had left Amarillo at 11:35 p.m. for the flight to Albuquerque. Pilot H.R. Morgan, co-pilot W.G. Barcus, passengers Mr. & Mrs. Ralph Gore and their 3-year old grandchild Evelyn Gore. (*NYT* 8-30-33 pg. 15)

August 30, 1933
Chicago, Illinois
NC-8419
Northwest Airways 5-AT-C. While taxying the right wheel hub broke and the ship nosed up and fell back down on the tail buckling the fuselage. (FF)

September 20, 1933
LaCrosse, Wisconsin
NC-9676
This Northwest Airways 5-AT-B had to make a forced landing after the left prop broke off and the engine was torn loose from its mount near West Salem, WI. The engine did not drop off and pilot Mal Freeburg landed the plane on one wheel with no injuries to the passengers. Co-pilot Martin. (FF, ALPA newsletter)

5-AT-58 after breaking its back at Chicago in August 1933. (Larkins Collection)

September 26, 1933
Lakeland, Maryland
NS-1
The Lloyds of London list states a, "U.S. Commerce Department tri-motor radio-plane crashed near Lakeland." NS-1 was the only Department of Commerce tri-motor at that time and it was used for radio tests. No further information but this was no doubt the Bureau of Air Commerce 5-AT-D. (LL)

October 18, 1933
Managua, Nicaragua
NC-4806?
Either this plane or NC-8266 (not a Ford) was involved in an accident resulting in fatal injuries to pilot William Davis and passengers Jack Lafferty and Mr. Hansel. Owner/operator Frank Free of Manugua. Registration cancelled 7-1-34. (FF)

December 15, 1933
Perry, Florida
NC-6894
Freeman Aircraft Sales 4-AT-B. No further info. (FF)

March 22, 1934 (21?)
Lima, Peru
NC-407H
Both pilots and a passenger were killed in this crash which involved two Panagra Vice Presidents and an Ambassador. The 5-AT-C crashed on takeoff from Lima on its way to Santiago when the left engine quit at 150 feet altitude and then the center engine sputtered and lost power - the most critical phase of flying for the Ford Tri-Motor. The pilot Homer V. Farris, the co-pilot (reported as radio operator) Lawrence A. Wagner, and a passenger Frank Large were killed. Among the injured were John D. McGregor Panagra VP from New York City, Capt. Harold Harris, Panagra VP in charge of South American operations, Manuel Trucco Chilean Ambassador to the United States, his daughter Grace Trucco and Carmela Bustamente. (*NYT* 3-23-34 pg. 17)

March 24, 1934
Toledo, Ohio
31-401
Minor damage to the tail wheel fork while the Air Corps C-4A was flying the mail. Pilot 2nd Lt. Paul W. Blanchard Jr. Plane No.19 from Wright Field. (AHC)

April 23, 1934
Girard, Kansas
NC-6893
Dale Smith's 4-AT-B had an accident which involved replacing a wing tip and aileron. (FF)

June 11, 1934
Oscada, Michigan
31-403
After the right engine, and then the center engine, quit on takeoff this Air Corps C-4A struck the tops of some trees at the edge of the field at Camp Skeel. The plane was demolished but there were no injuries. The pilot was T/Sgt Frank J. Siebenaler and the plane was assigned to the 38th Pursuit Squadron. Photos show the No.3 on the fin. (AHC)

June 11, 1934
Junin, Argentina
NC-8417
This Panagra 5-AT-C was flying in heavy rain when it had to make a forced landing in Mar Chiquita, a shallow lake near Junin, Buenos Aires Province, Argentina. Five were killed and five injured. The survivors sat on the wings for four hours until rescued. Pilot Carl F. Lindenberg. (*NYT* 6-12-34 pg. 2, KCR)

July 1, 1934
Lima, Ohio
NC-7586
The registration file on this 4-AT-D of Ray Loomis was cancelled as a result of an accident. No further details. (FF)

September 2, 1934
Cochrane, Wisconsin
NC-9655
Hanfords Tri-State Air Lines evidently only had this 5-AT-D for three months when it was lost in an accident. No details, but the license was cancelled 11-30-34.

October 14, 1934
Winchester, Kentucky
NC-7583
No further information. 4-AT-D owned by Ralph Barron. (FF)

October 26, 1934
Flat, Alaska
NC-8403
The 4-AT-E "Ptarmigan II" was damaged beyond economical repair in a ground loop accident at this airstrip near a mine. (FF)

October 29, 1934
Near La Cerba, Honduras
Unknown
TACA Ford destroyed. (LL)

November 2, 1934
Fort Crockett, Texas
29-226

4-AT-65 "Ptarmigan II" after a ground-loop accident at Flat, Alaska, in October 1934. (Gordon S. Williams)

This Army Air Corps C-9 of the 60th Service Squadron was parked when a 50 mph wind gust broke the tie downs, pushing the wing against gasoline storage tanks. Damage to the right wing and aileron. (AHC)

December 10, 1934
Near Palma Soriano, Cuba
NM-7
This Cia Cubana de Aviacion 4-AT-E crashed in a wooded, mountainous area about 20 miles SW of Palma Soriano on a flight from Santiago to Havana. Four were killed and four injured. Although there was such heavy rain that the injured could not be brought out for two days the manager of Pan American Airways stated that he suspected a bomb in the mail sack. Pilot Torres Navarro, copilot Emeterio Zorrilla, and Steward Cardenas. Passengers George H. Bunker (VP and general manager of the Guantanamo Sugar Company), Cesario Ariola and Jose Coll (inspectors of the Cuban Treasury Department), Jose de Cabus (Managing Editor of the Havana morning paper ACCION), and Manuel Rodriguez (Manager of the company airport Rancho Boyeros just outside of Havana). Two days later a group armed with machine guns and pistols raided the newspaper office and kidnapped six employees. They were forced to drink large amounts of castor oil and then released. (*NYT* 12-11-34 pg. 13, 12-12-34 pg. 14, 12-13-34 pg. 5)

January 10, 1935
Jacksonville, Florida
31-401
Air Corps C-4A ground looped at night into a row of Boeing P-12's parked 28 feet off the runway. Pilot Major Victor H. Strahm. (AHC)

January 14, 1935
Fairbanks, Alaska
NC-8499
The single-engine 8-AT struck a hangar while landing in a ground fog. The left wing and fuselage were damaged. A replacement wing and aileron were purchased from TWA for repairs. (FF)

April 21, 1935
Near Hancock, Maryland
Unknown (NC-408H?)
This Central Airlines 5-AT left Washington, DC, on a midnight flight with six passengers. About 85 miles out one of the wing engines broke off its mounts and fell from the plane damaging the landing gear in the process. Pilot James H. Carmichael Jr., (later President of Capital Airlines) turned back and radioed ahead to Bolling Field as he felt the Air Corps crash facilities there were the best available. He made a perfect one wheel landing and ground-looped to a stop with no injury to passengers or crew. Copilot R. H. "Bat" Taylor. One of the passengers was Dr. J.A. Jennings. (*NYT* 4-23, pg. 1)

On October 29th President Roosevelt awarded him the Air Mail Flyer's Medal of Honor (at the same time as Eddie Bellande) with the statement, "James H. Carmichael Jr., who while flying on April 21, 1935, from Washington to Detroit lost a motor from his plane, manoeuvred the craft safely back to Washington and made a landing on one wheel without injury to his passengers or loss of the

4-AT-49 destroyed in a crash at Flint, Michigan, in May 1935. This photo is rare because it shows the Knowles Airways logo. (Robert L. Cavanaugh)

mail." A letter of commendation was given to R.H. Taylor, "for his cooperation in helping handle the plane after a motor had been lost." (*NYT* 10-30-35, pg. 7 ills)

April 28, 1935
Gadsden, Alabama
NC-7863
Vernon Johns 4-AT-B washed out, no details. The remains were sold to Joe Musleh who combined parts from 4-AT-50 to rebuild it. (FF)

May 7, 1935
Lake Izabel, Guatemala
Unknown
Ken R. Meinard escaped when the plane he was piloting crashed near Lake Izabel, killing co-pilot W. Bruenersten. The plane was reported to be carrying a heavy load of chicle. (This may not have been a Ford Tri-Motor but is presumed to be because of the load and the fact that it had a co-pilot. Neither pilot flew for TACA) (*NYT* 6-12-34 pg. 2)

May 18, 1935
Flint, Michigan
NC-7864
Pilot Theodore E. Knowles (President of Knowles Flying Service) and two others were killed, and nine injured, when this 4-AT-E carrying passengers on five minute sight seeing hops crashed on take-off during the dedication of the Bishop Municipal Airport. A pilot witness stated that, "at 100 feet the right wing engine quit, then the nose engine, the ship went into a spin and nosed into the ground with one wing down." Newspaper accounts stated that there was no fuel in the tanks after the crash. (*NYT* 5-19-35

June 16, 1935
Ashville, North Carolina
NC-7865
Joe Musleh's 4-AT-B, no further info. (FF)

June 24, 1935
Medellin, Colombia
F-31
Seventeen persons were killed when two Ford Tri-Motors collided and burned at Olaya Herrera airport, Medellin, in the worst accident to that date in the history of Colombian aviation. Ernesto Samper Mendoza, famous Colombian pilot and co-founder of the Colombian airline SACO, was piloting one of their Fords. For reasons unknown in the middle of the takeoff run it suddenly veered off the runway and hit a SCADTA 5-AT-D that was waiting to leave. Carlos Gardel, famous Argentine singer and movie star, and musicians accompanying him were also killed. It is unclear as to which passengers were in which Ford but it is probable that the following were in F-31: Jose Aguilar, Alfredo Azalf, Estanislao Zuleta Ferrer, Carlos Gardel, Alfredo Lepera, Jorge Moreno Olano, Celedonio

Palacios, Jose Plaza, Domingo Rivera and Guillermo Escobar Velez. Samper had left Roosevelt Field in New York only a month earlier when he and Stan Harvey, an American pilot flying for SACO, ferried F-31 and F-32 to Colombia. (*NYT* 6-25-35 pg. 1; *Chicago Daily Tribune* 6-25-35 pg. 1; *Forero* pp 276-277)

June 24, 1935
Medellin, Colombia
"Manizales" (5-AT-112)
The SCADTA 5-AT-D that was hit by F-31 taking off. Pilot Hans Thomas. Passengers believed to be Grant Flynt, William B. Forster, H. Fuerst, Lester W. Strauss and H. Schwartz. The names of the two co-pilots are not identified and thus may be included in these two lists of passengers names. Four of these individuals were identified as Americans. (*NYT* 6-25-35 pg. 1; *Forero* pp 276-277)

August 13, 1935
Santa Monica, California
NC-15551
This 5-AT-D was being ferried from Brownsville, Texas, to Long Beach, California, for shipment to China. While landing at Clover Field the brakes locked and the ship nosed up causing considerable damage to the nose section and wing. Pilots Bill Winston and Wilbur W. Lynch, Jr. (FF)

5-AT-101 on its nose at Santa Monica, California, in August 1935. It is particularly rare because it shows the registration NC-15551 that was only used for three months. (John W. Caler)

September 8, 1935
Solola, Guatemala
NC-430H
5-AT-C owned by Compania Nacional de Guatemala crashed on takeoff. No details. (LL)

November 9, 1935
Near Jutiapa, Honduras
Unknown
A TACA tri-motor crashed and burned injuring seven persons. The plane was en route to La Ceiba. (No names,

5-AT-6, one of the two 5-AT's that collided on takeoff at Medellin, Colombia, in June 1935. (Daniel P. Hagedorn)

may not be a Ford) (*NYT* 11-10-35 pg. 42)

December 24, 1935
Lima, Peru
NC-433H
The original model 13-A, converted back to a model 5-AT-D and operated by Panagra, crashed in the fog during a test flight. Named "San Felipe", and piloted by Harold McMickle and engineer Russell Petch, the plane hit a house, killing a woman and boy, one half mile from the airport at Limatambo. Cause believed to be either a stall or engine failure , or both. (*NYT* 12-25-35 pg. 2)

February 1, 1936
Quantico, Virginia
A-8840
This Marine Corps RR-4, assigned to VJ-6M, nosed up on takeoff damaging the prop, engine, cowl and fuselage. (AHC)

March 9, 1936
Lansing, Michigan
NC-9668
TACA 5-AT-B in the U.S. (FF)

March 5, 1936
Near Pengyi, China
Unknown
While flying the route from Chungking to Kweiyang this CNAC 5-AT-D crash-landed in snow, sleet and fog in the mountain area of Tzukung, 30 miles East of Yunnanfu. Amazingly there were no injuries although the Ford was demolished with two engines torn off and the tail section broken off and folded under the wing. The pilot, Byron G. O'Hara, had to walk 30 miles to Pengyi to send a telegram reporting on the crash site. Co-pilot P.H. Thom, Radio Operator N.A. Chen, and three passengers. (*The China Press*, 3-736, pg. 1, 8; 3-21-36, pg. 1, photos)

March - 1936 (?)
Nanking, China
Unknown
This CNAC 5-AT caught fire on the approach to Nanking. The pilot, C.L. Sharp, was able to land the plane but it was subsequently destroyed by fire.

March 26, 1936
Near Amecameca, Mexico
XA-BCB
This Cia Mexicana de Aviacion 5-AT-B had been chartered by the Hamburg-American Line to carry a group of German tourists from Mexico City to Guatemala City. All 14 aboard were killed when the plane crashed in a 12,000 foot pass between the two volcanoes Ixtaccihuatl (17,343 feet) and Popocatepetl (17,883 feet). The probable explanation given at the time is that the plane was flying close to the volcanoes so that the tourists could take pictures (Cameras then, unlike today, had to be opened and a folding bellows pulled out and locked in order to take a picture. Many cameras were found in this open position). It is believed that the pilot stalled with all three throttles wide open in a high altitude turn and spun into the ground, burning on impact. The clock on the instrument board was stopped at 11:06 a.m. Pilot Adrian Borchers, co-pilot Preciado Acosta, steward Daniel Madrigal, radio operator Rodolfo Limon. Passengers Adolf Prince of Schaumburg-Lippe and his wife Princess Elisabeth, Siegmund Baron von Stieber, Mrs. Dora Thein, Victoria Thein, Marie Margarethe Harder, Elizabeth Schroer and Liesbeth Pust from Germany; Adolf Igler from Austria; and Elmer von Rohenczy from Hungary. (*NYT* 3-27-36 pg. 1, 3-28-36 pg. 7)

July 15, 1936
Teller, Alaska
NC-8410
No info. 5-AT-C owned by Chester Brown. (FF)

August 8, 1936
Hundred, West Virginia
NC-5811
Ervin Saltzgaber's 4-AT-B. Believed to have been destroyed in this accident. License expired 5-15-37 and was not renewed.

September 22, 1936
Norwich, New York
NC-7121
No info. Tri-Motored Air Tours 4-AT-B. (FF)

October 3, 1936
Puerto Cabezas, Nicaragua
Unknown
TACA aircraft, may not be a Ford. Crash reported to be due to engine trouble with the plane destroyed. The pilot who was killed was Robert B. Ewalt, former Marine Corps pilot and manager of the Nicaraguan Division of TACA. The co-pilot and two passengers were not injured. (*NYT* 10-5-36 pg. 6)

April 1, 1937
Slippery River, Alaska
NC-8410
Star Air Service 5-AT-C. No info. (FF)

May 29, 1937
Belleville, Illinois
NC-8404
Oral K. Southwick's 4-AT-E washed out in accident, no details. Remains were moved to Parks Air College for

rebuilding but the cost of repairs was found to be too expensive so the owner had the fuselage cut into three pieces and sold as junk. (FF)

July 13, 1937
Kannapolis, North Carolina
NC-7865
Helen Musleh's 4-AT-B. No info. (FF)

August 21, 1937
Fairbanks, Alaska
NR-9648
This 5-AT-C turned over on its back in the Alaskan tundra after an emergency landing in zero-zero weather. The pilot Garland Lincoln gives a vivid narrative description in the first "I Learned About Flying" department of *Popular Aviation*. Co-pilot Frank Tomick, passenger motion picture photographer Charles Marshall. (*Popular Aviation*, May 1939, pp 18-19, ills)

September 15, 1937
Lansing, Michigan
NC-7684
4-AT-B owned by Arthur Davis. As a result of this accident (no further information) the left wing was replaced by the left wing of 4-AT-7. It in turn was replaced by the left wing of 4-AT-25 in 1942. (FF)

September 28, 1937
Near La Cumplida, Nicaragua
LG-AAE
No details. (AB)

October 3, 1937
Puerto Cabezas, Nicaragua
Unknown
The wreckage of a TACA tri-motor was found in the jungle 25 miles southwest of Puerto Cabezas. The pilot was Lynn Shepard. (*NYT* 10-4-37 pg. 12)

May 10, 1938
Chile
Unknown
A Ford of Linea Aerea Nacional (LAN), no info. (REGD)

July 6, 1938
Coffeyville, Kansas
NC-5577
A new rudder and right elevator were needed after the propeller of an Aeronca hit the tail of this 4-AT-B owned by Rodger Inman. (FF)

August 11, 1938
Mankato, Minnesota
NC-8413
Max Conrad was attempting to start his 5-AT-51 when the left engine backfired and started a carburetor fire. By the time he and his mechanic retrieved the hand extinguisher it was too late and the plane burned to the ground in fifteen minutes. Some parts were salvaged and the two wing panels were shipped to Alaska where the left panel eventually wound up on 5-AT-34. (FF, *Plane and Pilot*, January 1975, pg. 59)

September 3, 1938
Big Prarie, Montana

5-AT-102 of the Johnson Flying Service at the U.S. Forest Service strip at Big Prarie, Montana, in September 1938. This was Johnson's only 5-AT-D and it was not rebuilt. (Penn Stohr Jr.)

NC-435H
The Johnson Flying Service 5-AT-D was being flown by Dick Johnson when downdrafts during landing broke one landing gear and the plane swerved into trees at this landing strip. (Extensive details and photos in *Fly The Biggest Piece Back*, pp 138-141)

October 20, 1938
Powellsville, North Carolina
NC-7865
Destroyed in a crash near Ahoskie, killing pilot Joe Musleh.(FF)

November 20, 1938
Cleveland, Tennessee
NC-8400
Mary Cantine's 4-AT-E. No info. (FF)

1938
Near Quibdo, Colombia
C-60
SCADTA 5-AT-D. No further data. (REGD)

March 2, 1939
Vancouver, B.C., Canada
CF-BEP
"Old WZ", the 6-AT, was destroyed while parked on the Sea Island Airport by a Royal Canadian Air Force Hawker "Hurricane." Sgt R. L. Davis was taking off on his first solo flight in a "Hurricane" when the fighter swerved to the left off the runway and headed for the Ford. When a collision appeared imminent the pilot tried to zoom over the parked tri-motor but his landing gear hit the Ford's right wing. The "Hurricane" cartwheeled, burst into flames and was totally destroyed. Fortunately the pilot escaped with minor injuries. The remains were purchased by White Pass and Yukon Airways who failed in an attempt to rebuild a plane from it and the parts of CF-AZB. Both were buried as fill in a gully at the end of a new runway at Whitehorse.

March 14, 1939
Unknown
"Leticia"
SCADTA 5-AT crash. No further info. (REGD)

March - 1939
Tegucigalpa, Honduras
LG-AAH
Destroyed by fire. No further details. Registration cancelled 3-31-39. (AB)

April 15, 1939
Near El Carmen, Colombia
NC-8411
Capt. James Drummond and co-pilot Lawrence Smith were killed when their 5-AT-C crashed into a mountain in the Catatumbo jungles of Colombia. The wreck was found ten miles northeast of the village of El Carmen in the State of Santander del Norte. The plane left the Tarra airfield with a $20,000 payroll for the Ayachuco workers of the South American Gulf Oil Company and the money, although scattered about the wreckage, was all recovered. (*NYT* 4-19-39 pg. 3)

July 9, 1939
Austin, Minnesota
NC-6893
This 4-AT-B suffered engine failure on takeoff 1/4 mile East of the Decker Airport at Austin. The center section and left wing were damaged. (FF)

6-AT-1 (CF-BEP), "Old WZ" after being hit by a Royal Canadian Air Force Hawker Hurricane in March 1939. (RCAF)

September 21, 1939
Near Marcus, Illinois
NC-9613
Hard landing in a field north of Marcus, possibly flown by owner Charles Bradbury Jr. The 4-AT-E was repaired by the E.M. Laird Company of Chicago. (FF)

October 22, 1939
Hickory, North Carolina
NC-9608
The leading edge of the right wing tip of this 4-AT-B was damaged. No further information. (FF)

November 1, 1939
Parrita, Costa Rica
TI-40
The left brake locked on this Aerovias Nacionales 5-AT during landing causing it to ground loop into an eight-foot ditch alongside the runway. Pilot Frank H. Jerdone, co-pilot Perez. (*Pilot of Fortune*, pp 192-193)

November - 1939
Guatemala City, Guatemala

LG-AAG
Destroyed by fire at La Aurora Airport. No further details. (AB)

January 30, 1940
Carcross, Yukon Territory, Canada
NC-5092
This 4-AT-E hit a hangar while landing. Pilot Vernon Bookwalter of White Pass Airways. (FF)

February 20, 1940
Near Prinzapolka, Nicaragua
Unknown
A TACA transport, carrying freight to the mines on the East coast of Nicaragua, crashed in flames. Pilot A. Sleeppey and the co-pilot were taken to the hospital. (*NYT* 2-22-40 pg. 8)

February 25, 1940
San Isidro, Costa Rica
TI-33
TACA 5-AT-C. No details. (AB)

March 5, 1940
Near San Martin, Mexico
XA-BCW
While flying on its regular run to Chetumal, Quintana Roo Territory, this Cia Mexicana 5-AT-C ran into bad weather. The pilot, Capt. Sanchez Cardenas, came out of the overcast right on top of a heavy forest. Unable to go around due to low speed and downdrafts from the mountains, the Ford stalled into the trees on a mountain side near the San Martin volcano between Veracruz and Minatitlan. The only injury was the co-pilots broken arm and everyone spent the night on some mattresses that were being carried as cargo. Search planes found the crash site the next day by spotting Very flares shot up through the overcast. (AV)

August 2, 1940
Liberty, New York
NC-8405
The left and center engines quit due to vapor lock on this Westchester Airways 4-AT-E while on a sight-seeing flight. The resultant forced landing resulted in damage to the left landing gear and wing tip. (FF)

August 8, 1940
Whitehorse, Yukon Territory, Canada
CF-AZB
While being towed by a tractor attached to the tail the right wing struck a hangar doorway and the rear fuselage crumpled when the tail swung and hit the hangar wall. The aircraft, together with CF-BEP, was buried as fill under the new runway at Whitehorse airport. (*CAHS Journal*, Spring 1970)

October 7, 1940
Near Colon, Costa Rica
Unknown
A TACA plane flying in clouds and rain on the evening of the 7th crashed on the Cerro Cedral near the village of Colon. The pilot Enrique Malek was a Panamanian of long experience in transport flying. He and the five passengers were killed (This may not be a Ford as TACA had other planes that would carry eight). (*NYT* 10-9-40 pg. 7)

5-AT-73 on its back, presumably in Nicaragua. No further information. (Harry Yerex)

5-AT-71 in an accident at Puenta Arenas, Costa Rica, in 1940. (Harry Yerex)

The TACA air service in Costa Rica was partially paralyzed on December 13th when the heirs of six victims of the crash obtained a judicial embargo on six of the company's planes, causing them to be grounded. Control of TACA had been recently obtained by American Export Lines. (*NYT* 12-15-40 pg. 32)

. . . 1940?
Puenta Arenas, Costa Rica
TI-42
An ENTA 5-AT groundlooped (?) onto railroad tracks with minimum damage. No information, photo only.

. . . 1940
San Jose, Costa Rica
TI-43
The 9-AT being operated by ENTA made a spectacular and excellent landing with the left landing gear broken. (*Popular Aviation*, October 1940, pg. 54)

January 20, 1941
Near Kian, China
Unknown
CNAC 5-AT crashed in the mountains near Kian in Kiangsi Province. Bernard Wong, pilot.

April 4, 1941
Nicaragua
Unknown
This TACA freighter took off from Puerto Cabezas for Alamicambra, loaded with cargo for the mines. The wreckage, and bodies of the pilots Usher Rousch and Lynn Berkenkamp, was found on April 20th in the mountains on the East coast of Nicaragua. (*NYT* 4-6-41 pg. 8, 4-22-42, pg. 11)

April 21, 1941
Putumayo, Colombia
FAC 641
Colombian Air Force 5-AT No. 641 crashed near Putumayo near the Brazil-Colombian border. It was operating on floats at the time. (*Forero* pg. 302)

June 14, 1941
Yoakum, Texas
NC-5809
This Hangar Six 4-AT-B was washed out in an emergency landing. Sold as is to Oscar W. Nichols who took out all the salvageable parts for his 4-AT-23 and sold the remainder for scrap metal. (FF)

Presumably the other side of 5-AT-71 before it had been removed from the railroad tracks. One of the frustrations in finding such rare photos in an album is the lack of good information. This print merely said, "Ford that thought it was a train." (Eddie DeLarm)

One of a spectacular series of photos taken by TACA pilot Bob Edgerton of TI-43 (9-AT-1). It is landing at San Jose, Costa Rica, with the left wheel folded under the fuselage. The ENTA transport had eight passengers and there were no injuries. (Harry Yerex)

August 15, 1941
Palanquero, Colombia
FAC 642
Crash with one fatality at this Colombia Air Force base. Pilot Capt. Hector Arango. Another report lists four killed and 13 survivors. (*Forero* pg. 302)

August 27, 1941
Near Tarapaca, Colombia
FAC 644
Colombian Air Force crash killing 4 crew and 6 passengers. Pilot Capt. Alvaro Almeida, co-pilot Jacob Wiesner. Fire in flight. (*Forero* pg. 302)

September 26, 1941
Andes Mountains, Bolivia
CB-CAM
Pilot William Brooks, geologist Frank Burgess, and three Bolivians were killed when this Ford belonging to the Aramayo Mining Company crashed in the Andean Challhuani Range while flying from Tupuani to La Paz. The accident was reported at the time to have been due to engine failure. Major Bill Brooks was famous for having flown with the Gates Flying Circus, the Nicaraguan Air Force, and was said to have headed the Honduras Air Force in 1939. (*NYT* 10-2-41 pg. 3, 10-4-41 pg. 6)

October 23, 1941
Wau, New Guinea
VH-UTB
This 5-AT-C had made a forced landing at Wau and after repairs attempted a takeoff. At this time the wing swung around and the aircraft turned off the runway and went over the cliffs to rocks 100 feet below. Pilot I.J. Hosie. A slightly different account states, "Just as the tail was lifting from the ground, the plane was hit by a high gust of wind and took a sudden turn to the right. Instead of continuing down the runway, it shot across the 'drome, careened across the road and finished up over the almost sheer drop into Little Wau valley. When the Ford reached the rocky banks of the creek, the wings hit outcrops of stone with such force that the plane stopped abruptly, disconnecting the cockpit and engines which plunged forward free of the machine. This no doubt saved the life of the pilot. As helpers arrived, they were astonished to find Mr. Hosie, uninjured, standing beside the plane!." The Ford was carrying a load of lumber. (Dept. of Civil Aviation, Australia 3-52; *Pacific Islands Monthly*, November 1941, pg. 21)

November 15, 1941
Near Wichita Falls, Texas
NC-6894
Pilot Ben Gregory was flying his 4-AT-B when the right engine quit on takeoff resulting in its destruction at the Old Staley Airport, 3 miles East of Wichita Falls. The engines and props were salvaged and the airframe sold to a local junk yard. (FF)

March 8, 1942
Corpus Christi, Texas
NC-9613
Although staked down with the engines removed this 4-AT-E was blown over on its back by a strong wind. Dismantled and sold for scrap. (FF)

April 17, 1942
Near Metz, Missouri
NC-5093
This 4-AT-B was destroyed on its delivery flight to Star Airlines. During a forced landing, caused by failure of the left engine, the plane hit a tree with the left wing and cartwheeled. The pilot Ben Gregory was seriously injured. (FF)

June 10, 1942
West Orange, New Jersey
NC-5493
This 4-AT-B owned by Atlantic Airmotive entered a power dive from which it failed to recover, crashed and burned. The pilot, Richard A. Behrens, who was flying alone was killed. The nose engine was buried ten feet deep in the earth at the edge of the Pleasantdale Cemetery. Behrens, a Transport Pilot, was conducting some radio experiments for Atlantic Airmotive, a unit of the Aerial Radio Corp. (*NYT* 6-11-42, pg. 15)

November 21, 1942
Billings, Montana
NC-6892
This 4-AT-B crashed near the southwest boundary of the airport at Billings at 8:11 a.m. The pilot Albert T. Mitten was seriously injured and the co-pilot Ralph L. Swanson was killed. The plane, registered to Atlantic Airmotive, Roosevelt Field, New York, was in the process of being transferred to the U.S. Army Engineer Corps at Edmonton, Alberta, Canada. It had been flown from New York and stopped overnight at Billings. The plane was tied down outside with the temperature at 15 to 20 degrees above zero at takeoff. After a run of between 3,500 and 4,000 feet the aircraft was airborne at an altitude of about twenty feet when it settled in a turn and the tail hit the boundary fence. The Ford bounced across a highway, hit a tree, slid over the rimrocks and crashed to the ground 100 feet below. The accident was caused by heavy frost on the wings and reduced power from improper warmup of the engines. (CAB File No. 3033-42; *NYT* 11-22-42 pg. 49)

August 1943
Fairbanks, Alaska
NC-9651
While being operated by Star Air Lines, the left engine quit during the takeoff roll causing the plane to groundloop and stand on its nose. The left wing was damaged and replaced by the left wing of 5-AT-51. This was confirmed by B.C. Reed in 1965 when he was examining the Ford being overhauled by Gaylord Moxon at Santa Monica. Even though paint has been stripped from alclad it always leaves a faint outline and if viewed under the correct lighting conditions it can be seen years later. "BC" was able to see the outline of NC-8413 on the left wing of Moxon's airplane. (Letters from Rex Williams 2-54, and Boardman C. Reed 7-65)

. . . 1944
Near Tegucigalpa, Honduras
XH-TAN
Pilot Rusty Bodemer and 13 others were killed when the wing came off this TACA 5-AT-D in flight about 15 minutes after leaving Tegucigalpa. Believed to be crystallization of the metal in the wing spars from vibration, turbulence and constant operation from rough fields. TACA pilot Bob Anson recalls, "The problem we had at the end was that the wing spars would break. This was because of rough fields, overloads, bad weather, forces on the wing from normal vibration etc. You wouldn't notice it because they had two or three spars, you couldn't really tell on the ground, but you could tell in flight because the airplane didn't fly level – they were all out of trim. I flew a couple of them out of trim and they found one of the spar caps broken." (HY, R.L. Taylor)

July 3, 1944
Nicaragua
Unknown
Frederick Broham of Union City, PA, killed in the crash of a TACA aircraft when it hit a mountain in rain and fog near Matagalpa. Had been reported at first as a Pan American a/c. This may not be a Ford. (*NYT* 7-5-44 pg. 10, 7-6-44 pg. 7)

. . . 1944
Honduras
Unknown
This TACA 5-AT had been fueled and ready to go but the weather turned bad so pilot Grant Spillman waited until the next day to fly. He took off and flew for 45 minutes when suddenly all three engines quit on top of the overcast. He spiraled down, coming out over an 1800 foot strip where he was able to land. Someone had deliberately drained the gas in the tanks. There were also instances of someone putting sugar in the fuel in Honduras in 1944. (HY)

April 5, 1946
Ayuy, Ecuador
HC-SBC
Shell Oil of Ecuador 4-AT-D damaged beyond repair at the Ayuy airfield, 80 miles east of Shellmera, after nosing over on landing. (*AAHS Journal,* Summer 1986)

June 13, 1946
El Arenal, Mexico
XA-FOH
During a flight from Tuxpan, Veracruz, to Pachuca, Hidalgo, pilot-owner Juan Tilghman Gallo (operating as Servicios Aereos Nacionales) ran into bad weather while flying at 14,000 feet over the top. As he was descending, at an altitude of 9,500 feet, the right engine quit and almost immediately the left engine also quit. He was at this time over 7,800 foot mountains and tried to stretch his power glide with one engine to reach the Actopan airfield. This was not possible and he was forced to make a crash landing four miles short of the airport, sliding along a ridge and ground looping to the right. The crew and passengers were unhurt. The probable cause was determined to be a broken gasoline feeder line. The remains of

the 5-AT-B were disassembled and stored for parts. (Villasenor 4-57)

September 7, 1946
Near La Esperanza, Cuba
Unknown
A 4-AT of Expresso Aero Inter-Americano was flying from Santa Clara to Havana. Unable to find Havana at night in the fog and bad weather they flew until they ran out of gas and then crashed on a farm killing all seven aboard. Pilot Jose Prado, copilot Marcelino Vazquez, stewardess Carolina Fuentes. Company inspector Henry W. Mabry, formerly of Lockheed Aircraft Company, was aboard as were passengers Mr. & Mrs. Pedro Loranza Fernandez and Domingo Perez. (*NYT* 9-8-46 pg. 32)

September 10, 1946
Tiputini Airstrip, Ecuador
HC-SBI
Shell Company of Ecuador 5-AT destroyed after running off the end of the runway with a load of cement. Pilot Tandiis and two passengers. (LL, *AAH8 Journal*, Summer 1986)

November 15, 1946
Ayuy, Ecuador
HC-SBD
This Shell Oil of Ecuador 4-AT-B had the left tire blow out while landing at the drilling site at Ayuy, resulting in the plane hitting a pile of rocks at the end of the runway. The pilot, John Spiller from England, was killed and three workmen were injured. (LL, *AAHS Journal*, Summer 1986)

November 15, 1946 (1948?)
Ecuador
HC-SBJ
A fourth Shell Oil of Ecuador accident involving a Ford in eight months. The propeller of the right hand engine broke in flight causing the engine to come off while landing. Fuselage badly damaged. (LL)

November - 1946
Mexico
XA-FUP
Damaged in Mexico. Being operated by NAAM, Negociacion Aerea Abastecedora Mexicana, of Mexico City. No further information. (LL)

December 6, 1946
Mexico
XA-FUQ
Total loss in Mexico. Being operated by NAAM, no further details. (LL)

. . . 1946
Near Puerto Cabezas, Nicaragua
Unknown
TACA 5-AT freighter with pilot . . . Baldenberg and a crew of two. While approaching Puerto Cabezas with a heavy load one engine quit. With two engines wide open they settled into the 150-foot high trees of the jungle, tearing off the wings, tail and nose engine. The fuselage settled against the trees and they stepped out with no injuries. All three walked out safely after taking the compass out of the Ford. (HY)

May 12, 1947
Ometepec, Mexico
XA-DOL
This NAMSA 4-AT-A ground looped during takeoff in strong, gusty winds. The two-man crew was unhurt but the fuselage was broken in two. (AV)

July 16, 1947
Ecuador
HC-SBK
Shell Oil 5-AT. No details.

. . . 1948
San Martin, Colombia
HK-1501-E
This 5-AT-C was involved in a non-injury accident during an approach to the San Martin Airport, Los Llanos Orientales, Colombia. No further details. (Director General of Aviation, Colombia, 3-52 and W.H. Hightower, Colombian Petroleum Co., 1-56)

August 16, 1949
Putla, Oaxaca, Mexico
XA-GIJ
This LAGOSA 5-AT-C was taking off when the left tire blew out 600 feet down the runway, causing the plane to crash into a bank at the side of the runway. The plane, carrying 2,680 pounds of coffee, was nearly demolished but the two-man crew was uninjured. (AV)

October 27, 1949
Pinotepa Nacional, Mexico
XA-FON
The uninjured crew was very lucky in this ground loop accident as the plane was hauling gasoline as cargo. The plane was rebuilt and the BT-13 engines were replaced by the original 420 hp Wasps. (AV)

July 26, 1951
Mazatlan, Mexico
XA-HIL
The 5-AT-B with BT-13 engines ground looped off the runway and through a barbed wire fence which folded up the landing gear and damaged all three props. (Photos)

The remains of 5-AT-4, the famous "City of Columbus", at Choteau, Montana in July 1952. (Douglas D. Olson)

May 6, 1952
Choteau, Montana
N-9606
The famous 5-AT-B "City of Columbus" met its final end while flying for the Northwest Agricultural Aviation Corporation. During takeoff it was caught in a sudden gust of wind, drifted off the runway and over a small embankment. The jolt ruptured a gas line and sprayed gasoline on the hot exhaust, burning the plane to the ground shortly after the two pilots got out. (R. Waltermire 8-53)

July 14, 1953
Boulder, Montana
N-8400
This 4-AT-E, being used by the Johnson Flying Service to spray Spruce Budworms, hit a static cable that was strung about 150 feet above a powerline and could not been seen from the air. The cable broke and pieces were hanging on the nose engine, propeller and tail surfaces. As the pilot attempted an emergency landing in an open field near the edge of town the cable on the tail whiplashed around a power pole, tearing the tail surfaces from the Ford, and bringing it to the ground on its nose, completely demolishing the plane and killing the two pilots Jim Dillon and Dick Duffield. (R. Johnson 8-53)

August 17, 1953
Hungry Horse, Montana
N-69905
This second Johnson Flying Service Ford was on a U.S. Forest Service trip to drop six smoke jumpers on a fire in the Spotted Bear area of the Flathead Forest at the height of the summer fire season. While taking off from the Spotted Bear airstrip the left engine quit. Although the pilot was able to restart it all three engines then quit resulting in a crash landing in the timber. Although there were only minor injuries the Ford was almost completely demolished. Two of the Smokejumpers aboard were B. Fred Nolfrum and David L. Owen. The plane had been purchased only two weeks previously and was the modified 5-AT-B with 450 hp Wright engines. (R. Johnson)

July 31, 1954
Kelleys Island, Ohio
NC-9610
Sky Tours (Island Air Lines) 4-AT-B destroyed with injuries to 2 passengers and pilot Hugo M. Rosendahl. The plane took off at 7:23 pm with a full load in 83 degree temperature, and immediately started a climbing turn to the left. After passing over a barn the plane stalled with all three engines running. The left wing hit the tops of some 60-foot high trees, then hit the ground and the aircraft cartwheeled over its nose to the left. At least two, and possibly more, of the passengers were pilots. Total time on the aircraft was 4,733 hours. The pilot's time in Fords was 1,315 hours. Passengers David E. Benjamin, David Clark, John Donahey, Oliver T. Duck, Kae Finley, Joan L. Hrubec, Sandra Leland, Lloyd F. Noss, Paul Roby, Frederick J. Schrenck Jr., Eugene R. Smith, and William E. Strauss. (FAA General Aviation Accident Report No. 542161)

July 3, 1955
Near San Martin, Mexico
XA-FON
During the rebuilding of this 5-AT-D, following its 1949 accident, the 450 hp BT-13 engines were removed and the old standard 420 hp Wacp "C" engines were installed. In July 1955 the plane left Mexico City for Tuxtla via Veracruz and Minititlan. At 9:05 a.m. it had to make a crash landing when two engines quit near the Sierra de San Andres Tuxtla (close to where XA-BCW had crashed in 1940). None of the four persons aboard were injured but the plane was destroyed. (AV)

. . . 1955
Mexico
XB-NET
The Mexican Government cancelled the private registration of this 5-AT-B owned by Frank Oergel on 12-5-55 due to an accident. Possibly a Jan 1954 accident? No further information. (AV)

June 15, 1956
Middletown, New York
N-9651
While on an aerial crop control flight near Middletown the left engine of this 5-AT-B became rough and although the ignition was immediately turned off, it shook free and fell from the aircraft. The pilot E. A. Phillips had difficulty maintaining level flight but after experimenting discovered that he could regain lateral control by reducing power on the nose engine. He continued to Middletown and landed safely. Co-pilot Eugene O. Frank. (Resume of U.S. Civil Air Carrier and General Aviation Accidents, Calendar Year 1956, Civil Aeronautics Board, pg. 26)

June 19,1957
Near Townsend, Montana
NC-9642
This Johnson Flying Service 4-AT-E was lost while spraying a herbicide and oil mixture to control sagebrush for the U.S. Forest Service. It was loaded with 400 gallons but had made an earlier trip with 450 gallons. The weather was calm, temperature 60 degrees and the altitude 6,500 feet. The left wing tip hit the side of a 20-degree slope, while the plane was turning away from a hill, causing the Ford to cartwheel and land inverted 350 feet from the point of impact, where it was destroyed by fire killing the pilots Penn Stohr and Bob Vallance. Stohr was a well known bush pilot who had been with Johnson Flying Service for over 25 years and had 12,000 hours flying time. (*The Swath*, January 1958, pg. 16)

August 4, 1959
Moose Creek, Idaho
NC-8419
While landing at the Moose Creek Ranger Station in the Selway National Forest this 5-AT-C of Johnson Flying Service crashed killing one crew member and three smoke jumpers. The pilot, Bob Culver, and one passenger survived. No further details. (LL)

12-6-70
Bedminster, New Jersey
N-9637
This 5-AT-B nosed up on landing bending the prop.

8-21-72
Port Clinton, Ohio

5-AT-11 after nosing up on landing at the small field at Bedminster, New Jersey. Note the bent nose prop blades. This was not a Pan American plane but Dolph Overton's Wings and Wheels Museum Ford in December 1970. (John C. Barbery)

NC-7684
The right engine of this Island Air Lines 4-AT-B failed on takeoff, as the plane was about 200 feet in the air, resulting in the plane crashing off the end of the runway at the Port Clinton Airport. The pilot, Dave St. Clair, attempted to turn back to the field and the left wing hit the ground in a steep turn. The wing and nose were destroyed and one passenger was injured. There were 9 adults and 6 children on board including four-year old Deborah Wilson. The other passengers were Bernard, Jacqueline and David Brobst; Robert and Rose Dravetz; Mrs. Kay Sutton and Dan, Deborah and Cynthia Sutton; George and Helen Szahler; Willard, Pamela and Kimberly Wilson. Ralph Dietrich, President of Island Air Lines, stated that it would be too costly to rebuild the plane and that it would be salvaged for parts. (*Cleveland Press State News* 8-22-72 pg. B7 (ill); *The Blade* 8-22-72, Sec. II pg. 21 (ills); *The Monroe Evening News* 8-22-72 pg. 9A)

8-23-73
Peachtree City, Georgia
N-9637
Nosed up at an air show after trouble with the brakes.

6-16-73
Burlington, Wisconsin
N-8407
Dale Glenn's 4-AT-E was at the 3rd All-American Air Show benefit for the EAA Air Museum when a sudden violent thunderstorm with heavy rain and 75 mph winds hit the field. A total of 12 aircraft were damaged or destroyed including the Ford. Although tied down the large wing of the Ford created so much lift that it tore the tiedowns out of the ground, rolled the plane backwards into a trailer and bus, and then lifted some 50 feet into the air before crashing to the ground on its nose and then onto its back. gasoline was pouring from the ruptured tanks there was no fire. The plane was sold as is and where is by the insurance company to the EAA Air Museum. (*The Vintage Airplane*, August 1973, pp 14-15)

Dale Glenn's 4-AT-69 after a severe wind storm at Burlington, Wisconsin, demolished it in June 1973. After the tie downs let go it rolled backwards for a hundred feet, then rose some 50 feet into the air before nosing down to hit the ground. It was sold "as is" to the Experimental Aircraft Association who had it rebuilt to flying status. (Dick Stouffer)

The remains of Island Airlines 4-AT-38 after it crashed on South Bass Island, Ohio, in July 1977. Although it seems impossible, this plane was rebuilt by Kal-Aero and is flying in 1992. (E.J. Payette)

2-6-77
Las Vegas, Nevada
N-76GC
This Scenic Airlines 5-AT-B veered off the runway and crashed into a ditch on takeoff. The right landing gear, prop and wing tip were damaged. Onc of the 15 passengers was injured. (*LAT* 2-8-88 ill)

7-1-77
South Bass Island, Ohio
N-7584
This Island Air Lines 4-AT-B crashed on the Put-in-Bay airport when it lost power on takeoff in 15 knot winds. The plane hit the top of a telephone pole (one paper states two utility poles) and hit on its nose and right wing. The cockpit was demolished and the right engine and part of the wing were ripped away. The pilot, David Martin, was seriously injured. There were only two passengers, Russell L. Childers (a vintage airplane buff) and his wife Ramona, and they were not injured. They did, however decline to fly back and took the ferryboat to Catawba Island. (*The Plain Dealer* 7-2-77 pg. 8A; *The Cleveland Press* 7-2-77)

8-10-81
Las Vegas, Nevada
N-76GC
A severe wind storm broke the tie downs and blew 5-AT-11 upside down and then into a ditch causing the "destruction" of the airplane (see photo). The plane was then given to the San Diego Aerospace Museum and is being rebuilt over a several year period.

5-AT-11 after a severe wind storm rolled it into a ditch at Las Vegas, Nevada, in August 1981. It was donated to the San Diego Aerospace Museum and a dedicated crew of volunteers has been at work rebuilding it. Their plans are to fly it in 1992 or 1993. (Larkins Collection)

Chapter 11
The Bushmaster

Still a dreamer and enthusiastic promoter in 1953, Bill Stout announced in December that, "At least 100 of the famous Ford Tri-Motor all-metal transports will be built under new production plans . . . by a group of California businessmen setting up a company on the West Coast." In addition he announced from Detroit that, "The new Tri-motor transports are planned for bush operations since they will be able to take off from short strips carrying 4,000 lb. payloads. Price will be approximately $100,000."

Early in 1954 the Ford Motor Company, through the efforts of Henry Ford II, gave Bill Stout the exclusive rights to the full use of the original Ford Tri-Motor blueprints, flight test data, stress analyses and basic load data to be used in the design of a new airplane.

Preliminary design studies were done by Bill Stout, Don Alder, Colin Simpson and a dozen other engineers to determine the exact nature of the desired engineering changes to be incorporated into the new design. This required complete and exhausting analysis and correlation of the bushels of drawings received from the Ford Company along with the accompanying volumes of engineering and test data. It also involved research into the past, and 1954 users, of the Ford Tri-Motor to determine the desired modifications they had to recommend from experience.

The Hayden Aircraft Corporation was incorporated January 15, 1955, at Bellflower, California, for the purpose of building the "Stout Bushmaster." Robert E. Hayden was announced as President and Chairman of the Board; William B. Stout, Director of Engineering; and W.B. Thompson, Raymond Moore, Albert Moody, Donald H. Alder, Frank Endow, E.H. Cooper and Walter Unsell as Directors. In addition Commander George O. Noville and test pilot Gene May were named as Advisors.

Following this action Bill Stout, Bob Hayden and Ray Moore went to the Ford Archives to study and secure additional engineering information made available to Hayden Aircraft which included wind tunnel data, load data and stress analysis.

Then, in the jargon of the aerospace industry, "Design studies, new layouts, new detail drawings and organization of major assemblies were continued. Much time was also spent in absorbing the basic high strength-weight ratio design philosophy used throughout the Ford Tri-

Bushmaster 2000, s/n 2, N-750RW, at one of its first public appearances at the 28th Annual Antique Fly-In at Merced, California, on June 8, 1985. It was unpainted at the time. (W.T. Larkins)

Except for the three-bladed props there is a distinct similarity between the Bushmaster 2000 and the Ford Tri-Motor in this closeup view taken at Concord, California, on January 31, 1970. (W.T. Larkins)

Motor. To this philosophy was added the adaptability of new and improved material alloys for further weight reduction and added strength and environmental resistance. New component designs were made such as spring-oil struts for easier landings and take-offs and reduced maintenance."

In January 1956 a more comprehensive market analysis was conducted for Alaska, Canada and Australia. During the following month the results were compiled indicating that 100 aircraft could be sold in those areas alone:

> "Based on one hundred aircraft a thorough budget analysis was undertaken to determine the total facilities, labor, material and parts needed to design and produce a prototype aircraft and a subsequent 99 additional aircraft. Learning curves were applied and break-even points were established. The results were checked and double-checked against independent industry norms and estimates, and adjusted (for 1956 labor and material cost) Ford figures for 1932, and all agreed within plus or minus five percent."

Once again dreams and enthusiasm clashed with reality. Before the first aircraft had been built and flown the company projected a "potential" of 1,000 Bushmasters being sold. Unfortunately the harsh glare of historical accuracy shows a total of two being built by 1985. A third fuselage was started and may yet be completed in the future.

In one of the strangest stories in the history of aviation a company was formed to build a modified version of an airplane (the 5-AT-D) 24 years after the design first flew. It then took 11-1/2 years before the first plane flew, and 30 years from the time the company was incorporated until the second plane was built!

The original design configuration showed a plane very similar to 5-AT-D (5-AT-112) with the triangular shaped tail, with the addition of a large square cargo door on the left side. When the first Bushmaster was built this was moved to the right side, and major changes were made in the size and shape of the vertical and horizontal tail surfaces.

The original Stout Bushmaster became the Hayden Bushmaster 15-AT in an attempt to continue the line of Ford Tri-Motor model designations. This was dropped when it became the Aircraft Hydroforming Bushmaster. An attempt was made to sell the plane to the Army in 1957 and the words "28 Troop Seats" were painted over the door.

The Aircraft Hydroforming Bushmaster was granted Type Certificate No. A19WE on October 8, 1968. It was approved for three Pratt and Whitney R-985-AN-14B or AN1 engines, and the use of three-blade Hartzell controllable pitch propellers. This original certification was for a maximum weight of 12,500 lbs., a crew of one, one passenger and 3,380 lbs. of baggage. The approved fuel capacity was 366 gallons.

An interesting comparison between the 5-AT-D and two plans for the Bushmaster shows the following:

	5-AT-D	1957	1971
Span	77'10"	79'4"	77'10"
Length	50'3"	50'3"	49'6"
Height	12'8"	13'7"	13'9"
Tread	18'7"	20'	21'
Weight, Gross	13,500	12,500	12,500
Weight, Empty	9,100	6,500	7,500
Payload	3,403	6,000	4,000
Maximum Speed	150	145	130+
Stalling Speed	64	45*	60
Range (Miles)	560	500	460
Wing Area (Sq Ft)	835	843	900
Cabin Width	4'6"	6'5' avg	
Cabin Height	6'0"	6' avg	7' avg
Cabin Length	18'9"	20'	20'
Cabin Volume (Cu Ft)	529	720	720

* This figure was given for a design incorporating flaps.

The company sales brochure, issued in 1971, states that the plane with a 12,500 lb. gross weight will take off over a 50-foot obstacle in 850 feet of unimproved surface, and that with two pilots and only 600 gallons of fuel it will clear the same obstacle in only 600 feet of runway. Improvement over the Ford Tri-Motor include trim tabs, a larger and more effective fin and rudder for engine out control with the rudder and elevators interchangeable. The cockpit has almost twice the window area, the control

The fuselage for the second Bushmaster at Long Beach on July 10, 1971. It was completed in January 1985. If it was started about the time that serial number 1 was completed it took 20 years to be built. A third fuselage was being assembled alongside. (W.T. Larkins)

cables have been moved inside and a 51"x46" inch cargo door replaces the original small passenger entrance.

An October 1971 letter from the Bushmaster Aircraft Corporation offered the Model 2000 for sale for $175,000 F.O.B. Long Beach, with payments of 20% down on signing the contract and four additional payments prior to delivery.

The most interesting part of the letter is the statement, "Our production rate is one-per-month and the delivery date depends upon the date-of-purchase, which determines the position on our production line."

Charles LeMaster advertised his Bushmaster 2000 for sale for $350,000 in December 1978. Bushmaster #2 sold for $250,000 at the Museum of Flying auction in May 1990.

The aircraft nameplate showing the date of manufacture. Taken through the window with a telephoto lens while the photographer was balanced on a chair held by the author. (Milo Peltzer)

Bushmaster 2000
s/n 1, Bushmaster 2000, N-7501V

The date built and date first flown is uncertain. Ralph williams, President of Aircraft Hydro-Forming applied to the FAA for an aircraft registration on 7-7-65. An Experimental Certificate was issued on 8-25-66 for 30 days for taxi tests only. On 10-7-66 an Experimental Certificate for flight was issued for Research and Development and stipulated that the first flight must take off on Runway 12 at Long Beach Airport and all further flights to be made at Chino Airport.

On 11-7-69 it was sold to the Whittaker Corporation, Los Angeles. The next day, 11-8-69, it was sold to American Air Museum Society, Ralph Johnson – President, Richmond, CA. On 3-27-70 six Beech seats were installed by Rep-Air at Oakland Airport. At this time it was changed to Normal Category and no longer Experimental. Total time as of 5-22-70 was 120 hours. On 2-2-73 sold to Bushmaster Aircraft Corporation (Ralph Williams, President and Walter D. Greer, Vice President) Long Beach, CA.

On 12-17-73 it was sold to Stephen C. Cowper, Fairbanks, Alaska. Sold 9-30-77 to LeMaster Inc., Ottawa, Kansas (Charles A. LeMaster, President). On 3-24-78 13 seats, Brownline rail, carpet and new lower wall covering were installed by Maurice Dooley at Olathe, Kansas. Sold

The Bushmaster 2000, serial number 1, N-7501V, taking off from Crissy Field at the Presidio of San Francisco on August 13, 1972. The Federal prison, Alcatraz Island, is in the background to the left. At this time it was painted yellow with black trim. It is now silver with Pan American markings in the Owl's Head Museum at Owl's Head, Maine. (W.T. Larkins)

4-9-80 to Thomas J. Watson Jr., Stowe, Vermont. On 5-20-83 two additional brake master cylinders were installed by Northeast Airmotive in Portland, Oregon.

Donated 6-4-85 to the Owls Head Transportation Museum, Owls Head, Maine. Registration cancelled 10-11-88.

s/n 2, Bushmaster 2000, N-750RW

(RW = Ralph Williams)

Again the dates built and first flown are uncertain. The FAA lists a Certification Date of 5-4-84, but the aircraft nameplate states the date of manufacture is 1-18-85.

On the 1-5-85 microfiche for the Civil Register the owner is given as Bushmaster Aircraft Corporation, Long Beach, CA. By 6-3-89 the ownership had changed to Repatria Inc., Reno, Nevada although at the time the plane was at the Donald Douglas Museum at Santa Monica, California, and being flown by Mina Houserman.

Sold at the Museum of Flying Auction on 5-20-90 for $250,000. Registration 2-2-91 listed as "Sale Reported" in San Clemente, California. Registered 8-31-91 to Philip S. Young, Trustee, at San Clemente. In 1991 it was operated by Michael Lauver and Patrick O'Hare as "California Wings Air Tours" in San Diego. In early 1992 it was repainted for Denali Wings Air Tours and will fly scenic tours of the Denali National Park in Alaska in the summer of 1992.

A Pilot's Comparison of the Ford Tri-Motor and the Bushmaster 2000

by Bernie Godlove

The Ford Tri-Motor and the Bushmaster 2000 certainly have a close resemblance to one another, especially at first glance. In fact the Bushmaster is more often than not mistaken for a Ford. They appear to be near twins. However, the differences are much more extensive than just old and new. I have had the rare opportunity to have extensively flown and instructed in four different old Ford Tri-Motors and the second Bushmaster built. This experience has led to the opportunity to express some observations and comments relating to the flying characteristics of these aircraft.

The Ford 5-AT and the Bushmaster 2000 require pilot's to have type ratings whereas none are required on the smaller Ford 4-AT. The ratings are different, and they appear on the airman's certificate as F0-5 and BU-2000.

The Bushmaster incorporates a number of changes, some quite obvious and others much more subtle. Although the wing appears to be the same on the Bushmaster, it is different. The Bushmaster has Pratt & Whitney Wasp Jr. R-985 engines of 450 hp each. Over the years many of the larger flying Fords (the 5-AT's) have had their power plants retro-fitted to these same lighter weight Pratt & Whitney engines.

The Bushmaster incorporates the three-blade constant speed full-feathering Hartzell propellers making it considerably quieter than the Ford Tri-Motor, while at the same time greatly enhancing the performance especially with an inoperative engine. The Bushmaster has a large rudder which is almost twice as large as the rudder on the Ford, plus the addition or a large dorsal fin. These features greatly enhance the flying characteristics of the Bushmaster. In the three-point position the tail sits up much higher due to the longer vertical arm attached to the tail wheel. These improvements cut down on the shielding by the fuselage of the airflow over the rudder giving the Bushmaster superior ground handling characteristics. The airplanes are similar on take-offs. The tail wheel on the Bushmaster is either full swivel or locking. On the Ford it is neither lockable nor steerable but has bungee cords that tend to keep it in trail and at the same time acting as a shimmy damper. Starting the take-off roll the Bushmaster is a simpler task as the rudder is much more positive at the lower airspeeds. With the aid of a locking tail wheel there is a greater assistance to keep the aircraft aligned with the runway especially in cross-wind conditions.

On an engine-out operation the VMC is significantly lower on the Bushmaster at 58 mph, whereas, it is considerably higher on the Ford at 75 mph, a quantum leap forward for the Bushmaster. On climb-out the Bushmaster performance is quite an improvement over the Ford primarily due to the NACA cowlings on the enginges, the wing, and a whole cleaner airplane in general.

In cruise the Bushmaster is a little faster, somewhere in the area of 3-4 mph, maybe a little more. One of the main problems with the old Ford was that it just didn't have enough rudder for engine-out and cross-wind operations. On the Ford Tri-Motor the elevator and rudder cables run down the exterior of the fuselage which makes them very accesible for pre-flight inspection. However, there is additional drag making the Ford an even more rudder airplane. Ailerons are heavy on the Ford. It is obvious that the aileron boost on the Bushmaster does assist in its aileron pressures. The addition of the rudder trim on the Bushmaster does make it considerably easier for engine-out operations as all of the control pressures can be trimmed out. In the case of the Ford, if it were necessary to fly some distance, it would be mandatory to apply extreme rudder pressure. The only aid in getting relief for the pilot's leg would be to put both feet on the same rudder pedal. Honestly, that's the way the old-timers used to do it. Both aircraft are heavy on the controls and sluggish in response. This sluggishness is magnified in turbulent air conditions creating a considerable amount of wallowing around. Again, the Ford takes second place.

On landings, if the option is for wheel landing, both airplanes are comparable. However, as the air speed decays to around 25 mph or so, just after the tail starts to come down, there is considerably more rudder control available with the Bushmaster. Also, the rudder is not blanked out as much on the Bushmaster as on the Ford. Three-point landings are easier in the Bushmaster. Again, the main reason is more positive rudder control throughout the final stages of the flare. During the rollout the combination of the locking tail wheel and the larger rudder gives much more positive control to the Bushmaster in tracking down the runway, especially during a cross-wind condition.

In the cockpit the Bushmaster has an adjustable seat. In the Ford the seat is fixed and the rudder pedals cannot be adjusted. Thus, the shorter pilots will need to bring along pillows.

All the instrumentation in the Bushmaster is positioned on the inside. The Ford came with the outboard engine instruments which included the tachometer, oil pressure and oil temperature gauges located out on their respective pods. The interior of the Bushmaster is a little more spacious than the Ford. It is about a foot and a half wider and a foot higher.

The Fords left Dearborn with a Johnson bar for brakes. However, over the years most have been converted to toe brakes. Of those that have been converted to toe brakes, they will work the same as the Bushmaster. The ones that retained the Johnson bar are a world apart. The Bushmaster has significantly less drag than the Ford, however, you can tell only minimal improvement in cruise speed. Both planes are nearly identical in stall characteristics, both are very docile. In all other ways there is a noted improvement especially in climb and engine-out performance. In single engine operation the Bushmaster will hold altitude. At the lower density altitudes it will even register a positive rate of climb. The Ford, however, will not do as well. On approach the Ford takes appreciably more power than the Bushmaster and has a poorer glide ratio.

In comparing the two aircraft the Bushmaster is a definite improvement over the world famous Ford Tri-Motor. These improvements were developed over many decades since the Ford first entered service in 1926. However, no matter how you compare them the Bushmaster is simply not a Ford. It can never overshadow the Ford's glamorous history and its significant place in the annals of aviation history. The authentic Tin Goose will live in all its glory, forever.

(Bernie Godlove is the only FAA Designated Pilot Examiner, at the ATP level, for pilot Type Ratings in the Ford Tri-Motor and the Bushmaster. He has 1,450 hours in Fords and 60 in the Bushmaster. He is a United Air Lines Captain currently rated in the 747).

Chapter 12
Survivors - 1992

The following list of Ford Tri-Motors still officially in existence is arranged by their date of manufacture. Thus it may be seen that Gene Franks 4-AT-10 is the oldest Ford, and 5-AT-74 is the newest, in terms of length of life. Three of the planes listed, 4-AT-42, 4-AT-58 and 5-AT-62, are the remains of crashed airplanes but because they are on the U.S. Civil Aircraft Register as aircraft acknowledged by the FAA they are included. Often this involves more paperwork than airplane, i.e. the legal title to an aircraft that has not been declared destroyed. As with the current warbird scene anything can be rebuilt into a flyable airplane if enough money is spent on it. Of the 17 airplanes listed 8 are capable of flight, but of that number only 5 are currently flying.

9-10-27, 4-AT-10, 4-AT-A, N-1077
Registered Owner 6-92: Eugene O. Frank, Caldwell, Idaho.
Gene Frank has had 4-AT-10 since 1956 and had originally intended to rebuild it as a non-flying museum exhibit. As of January 1992 the fuselage was near completion and the wing spars were spliced. He now intends to make it flyable and take it to air shows where enthusiasts can appreciate such a rare plane. In addition to being the oldest Ford in existence, it is the plane in which Lindbergh's mother flew to Mexico City and back with Bill Stout in 1927. He intends to have authentic wicker seats made in the Philippines and is looking for three Wright J-4 engines in order to make it as authentic as possible.

3-20-28, 4-AT-15, 4-AT-B, NX-4542
Owner 6-92: Henry Ford Museum, Greenfield Village, Dearborn, Michigan.
Admiral Byrd's Ford, the first plane to fly over the South Pole, is in excellent condition and on public exhibit at Greenfield Village.

9-13-28, 4-AT-38, 4-AT-B, N-7584
Registered Owner 6-92: Kermit A. Weeks, Miami, Florida.
This former Island Airlines Ford has been owned and operated by Allan T. Chaney for six years and is a familiar sight in the Mid-west and Southeast portion of the U.S., particularly in Florida. His barnstorming operations have been widely covered by the local newspapers and some magazines. Chaney ended this operation in 1991 and put the plane up for sale at the second Museum of Flying auction in Santa Monica on October 6, 1991. He flew the

4-AT-15 at the Henry Ford Museum in Greenfield Village at Dearborn, Michigan. It is kept in good condition and is on public display. (Henry Ford Museum)

NX
OYD BENNETT
BYRD ANTARCTIC
EXPEDITION

4-AT-10 in 1964 when Gene Frank trucked it to his field at Caldwell, Idaho. (Ed Wojtas)

plane there where it was bid on and sold for $650,000 to Kermit Weeks for his Weeks Air Museum in Miami, Florida, where it is now on display. Thus still another Ford crossed the U.S. in recent years.

9-26-28, 4-AT-42, 4-AT-B, N-7684
Registered Owner 6-92: Sale Reported, Hebron, Ohio. Allan Chaney has owned the remains of this crashed Island Airlines Ford since August 1972. The FAA records indicate a sale in progress and it is probable that it is being sold to Kermit Weeks for parts.

10-9-28, 4-AT-46, 4-AT-B/E, N-7861
Owner 6-92: Naval Aviation Museum, Pensacola, Florida. This 4-AT-E has been in the Naval Aviation Museum since the 1970s when it was donated to them by Dexter Coffin. It still has the Pratt & Whitney R-985 engines, and is painted in the markings of the NAS Pensacola 5-AT-D, so its appearance is deceptive. On public display at the museum.

A beautiful photo of two rare tri-motors in formation in August 1980. Gene Coppock is flying the Stinson A and Harold Hauck is flying Island Airlines 4-AT-38. (Dick Stouffer)

4-AT-46 at the Naval Aviation Museum, Pensacola, Florida, on May 10, 1986. This 4-AT has three 450 hp Wasp engines and is painted to represent Pensacola's 5-AT-D. (Robert L. Lawson)

12-1-28, 5-AT-8, 5-AT-B, N-9645
Registered Owner 6-92: 747 Inc., McMinnville, Oregon. Harrah's magnificent restoration that was sold by Gary Norton in March 1990 to Evergreen Aviation, McMinnville, Oregon. Penn Stohr Jr., has been flying it for Evergreen to several small airshows and gatherings such as a smokejumpers reunion in Missoula, Montana. It is kept in pristine condition at Portland, Oregon, and may be seen flying during the summer months.

12-10-28, 5-AT-11, 5-AT-B, N-9637
Registered Owner 6-92: San Diego Aerospace Museum, San Diego, CA. This Ford was given to the San Diego Aerospace Museum by Scenic Airlines in August 1982 after it was nearly totally destroyed in a severe windstorm at Las Vegas, Nevada. The museum staff of volunteer workers has been repairing and rebuilding it ever since, and as of January 1, 1992 they had contributed 52,832 hours of work. Under the direction of Tim Cunningham, the museum Shop and Restoration Supervisor, and Charles Wheeler, Ford Rebuild Supervisor, the airplane is now about 70% complete. It is still in the basement of the museum in Balboa Park, and work is now progressing on the interior. In order to get historically accurate metal and leather seats they had to go into the business of manufacturing them and so extras were made for Kal Aero and Scenic Airlines. The Ford is being rebuilt to fly and when the time comes it will have to be disassembled and removed from the basement to be trucked to Gillespie Field for re-assembly. Hopefully this will be some time in 1993.

1-15-29, 4-AT-55, 4-AT-E, N-9612
Registered Owner 6-92: Dolph D. Overton, Orlando, Florida.
This Ford has been under renovation for a number of years and is currently in Smithfield, North Carolina. It is reported as being finished except for the wings and even includes an original wash basin obtained from long-time Ford supervisor Bob Baron before his death. In 1979 it was being worked on at the Peachtree City Airport in Georgia for the then operating Wings and Wheels Museum in Florida. It was offered for sale for $500,000 at the Museum auction in 1982 but the highest bid was $320,000 and so it was not sold. Hopefully this will be another "new" Ford in mint condition and flying in the 1990s.

5-AT-8 in September 1964 at Reno, Nevada. This view shows the "smooth skin" rebuilding done in Mexico City. (L.S. Smalley)

Harry Volpe, on the left, supervising the rebuilding of 5-AT-8 in Harrah's Aircraft and Boat Shop at Sparks, Nevada. (Harrah's Club)

The author speaking at the dedication of the "new" 5-AT-8 on May 31, 1970. Tennessee Ernie Ford was Master of Ceremonies, and Lee Flanagin was an honored guest. The nose prop is turned because the plane was rolled out at a dramatic moment to stop just behind the speakers podium. (Harrah's Club)

5-AT-8 on Virginia Street in Reno on September 13, 1983. For two years, at the start of the National Championship Air Races, the main street was blocked off by the casinos to exhibit the Ford and other planes. The Ford was dismantled and trucked to the site and then re-assembled. It was a magnificent sight at night with theatrical lighting plus the neon signs on both sides of the street. (W.T. Larkins)

An earlier August 1970 photo pf 5-AT-8 in an unusual pose. It is taking off from Crissy Field, San Francisco, with the Golden Gate Bridge and a typical fog layer in the background. The three hour wait for this precise combination was completed in 1/400th of a second. (W.T. Larkins)

1-29-29, 4-AT-58, 4-AT-E, N-9642

Registered Owner 6-92: Kal Aero Inc., Kalamazoo, Michigan.

One of the Johnson crashes that was picked up by Evergreen when they bought the Johnson Flying Service in 1979. It was sold to Kal Aero for a possible re-build and the parts are in Kalamazoo awaiting an interested buyer.

3-22-29, 5-AT-34, 5-AT-B, N-9651

Registered Owner 6-92: Irving B. Perlitch, Morgan Hill, California.

Irv Perch's 5-AT-B has been on public display at his facility at Morgan Hill, California, since 1971. It was a frequent visitor to local air shows in the summer, and has been filmed for two feature films and two documentaries. In 1975 it was flown for the movie "The Fortune", a Columbia Pictures farce about con artists starring Jack Nicholson and Warren Beatty. In 1984 it was seen for a short sequence in "Indiana Jones and the Temple of Doom" with Harrison Ford. In this film a model, thank goodness, crashes into the side of a mountain demolishing the airplane.

It was also featured in a TV documentary on disasters with Glen Ford as the narrator, an advertisement for the Michigan Automobile Club, and finally in James Culp's forthcoming film on the Ford Tri-Motor with Tennessee Ernie Ford being interviewed in front of N-9651 shortly before his death.

The plane is on public display at the Hill Country Transportation Museum at Morgan Hill, next to the Flying Lady Restaurant full of aircraft models and memorabilia. It is open Tuesdays through Sundays. Irv has had this plane listed for sale for $1,250,000 since 1978. He took it to the first Museum of Flying auction in May 1990 where it sat alongside the second Bushmaster 2000. The Bushmaster sold but the highest bid for the Ford was $1,000,000 so it was not sold and returned to Morgan Hill.

4-6-29, 5-AT-39, 5-AT-B, N-9683

Registered Owner 6-92: National Air & Space Museum, Washington, DC.

The Ford that American Airlines flew all over the United States in 1963-1965 was rebuilt back to 1929 standards by them and given to the Smithsonian Institution in 1973 upon the opening of the new facility. It had been in storage at Dulles International awaiting completion of the new museum.

If the numbers of people that saw this plane during the American Airlines publicity campaign are added to those that have seen it hanging from the ceiling of the NASM since then the total must be several million. Certainly more people have seen this Ford than any other in the 66-year history of the Tri-Motor. Unfortunately some of the modernizations of this plane, such as the engine cowls, wheel pants, engines and engine pods, propellers, windshield etc., remain and unsuspecting artists and plastic model manufacturers have dutifully copied the errors and further muddied the waters for future generations.

5-1-29, 4-AT-65, 4-AT-E, N-8403

Owner 6-92: Alaska Aviation Heritage Museum, Anchorage, Alaska.

The remains of N-8403 sat out in the Alaskan weather for 55 years until a group of volunteers from the museum recovered the damaged fuselage in 1989. It had been known for some time that it was still in existence. Art Walker, who had flown it for Mamer in the early 1930s, told the author that he overflew it in world War 2 while flying a C-47, approximately 60 to 70 miles west of Fairbanks and that, "it was lying on her belly in the muskeg with a stovepipe protruding through the center section, the registration 8403 was plainly visible on the top side of the right wing."

5-AT-11 landing at Santee, South Carolina, on May 3, 1969. It was giving rides to patrons of the Wings and Wheels Museum at Santee. (Jim Sullivan)

5-AT-11 at Long Beach in January 1977 with the short-lived markings of Grand Canyon-Scenic Airways. The registration N-76GC represented the Bi-Centennial Year 1976 and the name Grand Canyon. (Harry Gann)

5-AT-34 at Watsonville, California, in May, 1975. It is painted a cream color with dark red trim and the TAT/TWA lettering in black. Irv Perch wanted to honor the air-rail route that this plane took part in as the "City of Philadelphia." (Jerry L. Edwards)

A memorable flight with 5-AT-34 took place at San Jose, California, on January 2, 1970. From left to right: The author, Larry Fritz, Jan Perch, Irv Perch and John Guglielmetti. Both Fritz and Guglielmetti flew Fords for Maddux Air Lines and both took turns at the controls of N-9651 on this flight. The photo was taken with the author's trusty 616 Kodak Monitor on a tripod with a self timer. (W.T. Larkins)

The two pilots that have flown 5-AT-34 for Irv Perch over the years. Left to right in costume for the movie "The Fortune" are, Transport Pilots Raymond Stevens and Lennert Von Clemm. (Irv Perch)

5-AT-39 as it was when found in Mexico. Bob Waltermire is on the left looking at the remains of XB-FUE. Photo taken at Guadalajara on October 24, 1953. (Calvin Southard)

4-AT-65, Ptarmigan II, at Anchorage, Alaska in August 1989. The Alaska Aviation Heritage Museum recovered it from Flat and hopes to restore it as a static exhibit. (Jim "Jet" Thompson)

5-AT-58 has the first fully feathering propellers ever installed on a Ford Tri-Motor. This August 1991 photo shows the left engine shut down and the prop feathered. The pilots on this first flight were Bernie Godlove and John Ellis. (Bernie Godlove)

6-29-2, 5-AT-58, 5-AT-C, N-8419

Registered Owner 6-92: Kalamazoo Aviation History Museum, Kalamazoo, Michigan.

First of the three Johnson wrecks to be re-built by Kal Aero. After several years of slow work a decision was made to complete it for the 1991 EAA convention at Oshkosh. With three crews working overtime it was completed and flown with the paint hardly dry by Penn Stohr Jr., from Kalamazoo, Michigan, to Oshkosh, Wisconsin. A decision had been made to finish it in Army Air Corps markings based on the C-9 ambulance plane. The beautiful restoration was admired by many but the EAA judges disqualified it from the warbird category in which it had been entered because 5-AT-58 had never been in Army service. Instead a Special Award was given to Kal Aero.

A sale was arranged in January 1992 which led to its donation to the Kalamazoo Aviation History Museum, where it will be properly maintained in flying condition. It will be on public display and flown in the 1990s.

7-5-29, 5-AT-60, 5-AT-C, RAAF A45-1

Owner 6-92: National Museum, Papua, New Guinea.

This Royal Australian Air Force ambulance plane lay on the Lake Myola lakebed in New Guinea for 37 years

The beautifully restored 5-AT-58 just out of the Kal-Aero shop and on its way to the EAA Convention at Oshkosh in August 1991. It was finished in the markings of the C-9 ambulance plane but was disqualified from entering the Warbird Category because it has never been in the Army. It was instead given a Special Award for excellence. (Kal-Aero)

The new 1991 instrument panel on 5-AT-58 (N-8419). The three controls for the full-feathering propellors are in the top center of the photo, as are additional modern instruments for flight safety. (Bill Barbre)

The final product; 5-AT-39 hanging in the National Air and Space Museum, Smithsonian Institution, Washington, DC. Additional work by NASM was done on the plane before it was put on exhibit. (NASM)

before it was recovered in a spectacular operation with an RAAF helicopter.

The fuselage and parts are now at the National Museum in Papua and when and if funds become available plans are to rebuild it as a museum static display.

Plans for the recovery started in August 1979 but it was October before the operation took place. An RAAF Chinook lifted the fuselage, wing center section and outboard engines. A second Chinook attempted to lift the wings and nose engine but ran into difficulties and had to drop them. It landed and picked up the engine only, and another Chinook retrieved the wings in June 1980.

One of the interesting historical aspects of this Ford is its correct identity. Because it, like many airplanes, had been rebuilt with parts from another plane, presented a dilemma. The recovered fuselage turned out to have a home-made nameplate stating that it was 5-AT-41. This led to the following letter by the author to Air Enthusiast magazine in England in November 1979:

"The news that RAAF A45-1 turns out to have a nameplate for 5-AT-41 is even more interesting and poses a problem in ethics for all of us. The solution to the puzzle over '41' is simple, what to do about it is the real problem.

"This story clearly starts with the crash or ground accident to 5-AT-60 on July 21, 1938. Whatever this was, it was so serious that the plane was unlicensed for two years, being renewed as VH-UBI on June 5, 1940. On November 28, 1938, Guinea Airways Ltd., bought 5-AT-41 from Charles Babb in Glendale, California, and it was dismantled and shipped in parts

5-AT-39 as it appeared at Long Beach on August 30, 1959. Note the square door that, along with much of the rest of the plane, had to be rebuilt in the American Airlines shops. (L.S. Smalley)

4-AT-69 after its complete reconstruction. It is painted in light blue markings of Eastern Air Transport. This photo was taken at the EAA Convention at Oshkosh on July 27, 1985. Paul Poberezny has a number of hours in it and Jimmie Leeward, Jim Barton and Dick Hill are regular pilots flying it for EAA. (J.M.G. Gradidge)

5-AT-74 at Oshkosh in August 1973. It was being barnstormed by Charles LeMaster who named it "The Kansas Clipper." (John C. Barbery)

4-AT-55 being rebuilt at the Peachtree City Airport in Georgia in October 1978. It is reported to be 75% complete and in North Carolina in 1992. (Ed Taylor)

5-AT-11 being rebuilt in the basement of the San Diego Aerospace Museum on November 15, 1989. (W.T. Larkins)

to Sydney, Australia. It was never licensed in Australia and was obviously used for parts to repair 5-AT-60. Since the nameplate now reads 5-AT-41 it is obvious that at least the forward part of the fuselage was used, and almost certainly the entire fuselage.

"In the United States, and I assume in most other countries, the legal basis for ownership and identification of an aircraft is determined by the fuselage, all other parts being components. Thus under the above circumstances, which are quite common, the wrecked 5-AT-60 ended its career in July 1938. The reports and paperwork should have been filed to show 5-AT-41 being imported and either now being registered as VH-UBI or a new registration requested. Obviously this was not done and as a result all of the official records and subsequent historical writings show 5-AT-60 as continuing to this day.

"So now what to do? Forget the whole thing and leave the records as is? Upset the Australian Department of Civil Aviation over a 40-year old 'historical problem?' Or quietly explain the real story on a museum plaque?"

The museum has decided to identify the plane as 5-AT-60 and that is its identity as given in subsequent publications.

7-6-29, 4-AT-62, 4-AT-E, N-8400

Registered Owner 6-92: Kal Aero Inc., Kalamazoo, Michigan.

Third of the ex-Johnson Flying Service wrecked airplanes purchased from Evergreen Helicopters. Restored to the U.S. Civil Register in 1980. A potential "new" Ford that may be added to the airshow scene some day.

8-21-29, 4-AT-69, 4-AT-E, N-8407

Registered Owner 6-92: EAA Aviation Foundation Inc., Oshkosh, Wisconsin.

The EAA bought the remains of N-8407 after it was destroyed in the terrible wind storm of June 1973. At first it was intended to rebuild it as a non-flying museum display but as work progressed plans changed to a complete restoration. It first flew, again, on July 20, 1985 and

An interesting photo of 5-AT-74 painted in cream and green colors as a Boeing 80-A of United Air Lines. It was painted at Sequoia Field, Visalia, California and filmed at Auburn for a United Air Lines TV commercial shown during the 1984 Olympic Games. (Bernie Godlove)

5-AT-74 on the Conger Mesa plateau near Farmington, New Mexico in July 1991. The man in the foreground is playing the part of "Mr. Tabacco" in a film made for TV's "Unsolved Mysteries" series. He supposedly organized twenty flights in a Ford Tri-Motor in 1933 to carry 16 tons of gold from Mexico City to Conger Mesa where it is believed to be buried. (Bernie Godlove)

5-AT-74 painted as Adolph Hitler's Junkers Ju 52 for the Mel Brooks movie "To Be or Not to Be" in 1983. Left to right: Art Scholl, his mechanic and Bernie Godlove who flew it for some night landing scenes. Photo at San Fernando airport on April 28, 1983. (Bernie Godlove)

can be seen at the EAA antique field, known as Pioneer Airport, at Oshkosh, Wisconsin.

9-4-29, 5-AT-74, 5-AT-C, N-414H

Registered Owner 6-92: Scenic Airlines Inc., Las Vegas, Nevada.

Old 414 Hotel, mentioned so many times in this book, is alive and well and can be seen at the Grand Canyon, Arizona, airport most of the year. It is on display next to the airport terminal with a large sign identifying it. Those who wish to see it should contact Scenic Airlines in Las Vegas, Nevada, before visiting as it does fly frequently to provide a Ford Type Rating to a seemingly endless stream of pilots who wish to add it to their license.

Like 5-AT-29, it has been an actor in movies and TV specials. The wide-screen film "Flyers", shown at the NASM auditorium, features N-414H, but before this it was filmed for "The Amazing World", a 1979 American Express Company travel film on the Grand Canyon. In 1983 it was in disguise as Hitler's Junkers Ju 52 in the Mel Brooks film "To Be or Not to Be" starring Anne Bancroft and Jose Ferrer. In 1984 United Air Lines used it to represent a tri-motor Boeing 80-A in a TV commercial shown during the Olympic Games. In 1987 it was filmed as part of a BBC TV series to be shown in England. And, of course, it was the star of the hour-long German travel film made in 1985. It's most recent acting call was for the TV series "Unsolved Mysteries", in which it played the part of a 1933 Ford Tri-Motor that flew gold from Mexico to the U.S. The filming was done at Conger Mesa, near Farmington, New Mexico, in July 1991. The beautiful Scenic rainbow was painted out with women's silver hair spray by Bernie Godlove who flew it for the filming.

5-AT-8 as it appears in 1992 with the markings of its new owner Evergreen International. Penn Stohr Jr., is flying it in formation with Evergreen's B-17G. (Evergreen Aviation)

Serial No.2 in February 1992 about to fly to Alaska where it will operate scenic tours of the Denali National Park. (Michael Lauver)

Appendixes

Appendix 1
Model Designations

MODEL	SERIALS	ENGINE	REMARKS
1-AS	1	1-Curtiss OX-5 (90)	Stout "Air Sedan", three-place.
2-AT	1-11	1-Liberty (400)	"Air Pullman" re-designated "Air Transport."
3-AT	1	3-Wright J-4 (200)	Modified 2-AT, engines in wings.
4-AT-A	1-14	3-Wright J-4 (200)	New design, 12PCLM, 9200 lb. gross weight.
4-AT-B	15-53	3-Wright J-5 (220)	Increased wing span, weight, performance.
4-AT-C	47	1-P & W Wasp (400) 2-Wright J-4 (200)	4-AT-B modified with Wasp in nose. One only.
4-AT-D	24	3-Wright J-4 (200)	5-AT-A wing root with 4-AT-B wing tips and fuselage. (All three Ds have this enlarged wing). 12 PCLM
4-AT-D	37	1-Wright J6-9 (300) 2-Wright J-5 (220)	Larger engine in nose, 15 PCLM.
4-AT-D	40	3-Wright J-6 (300)	
4-AT-E	54-70, 80-86	3-Wright J6-9 (300)	Increased power and performance. 80-86 for U.S. Army as C-3A.
4-AT-F	71	3-Wright J6-9 (300)	Increased gross weight, refinements. Last 4-AT built.
4-AT-G	66	3-Packard Diesel (225)	4-AT-66 modified, re-designated 11-AT
5-AT-A	1-3	3-P & W Wasp (420)	13PCLM, 4-AT-B fuselage with increased wing span, Wasp engines.
5-AT-B	4-45	3-P & W Wasp C-1 or SC-1 (420)	15PCLM, increased gross weight.
5-AT-C	46-96	3-P & W Wasp (420)	17PCLM, increased gross weight.
5-AT-CS	69, 74, 75	3-P & W Wasp (420)	Seaplane, Aircraft Products No. A-27000 floats.
5-AT-D	97-116	3- P & W Wasp (420-450)	Increased weight, raised wing. Special "Club" models also known as "5-D."
5-AT-DS	114	3-P & W Wasp (420)	Seaplane, Edo 43-14060 floats.
5-AT-E	80	3-P & W Wasp (420)	5-AT experimentally flown with outboard engines in the wings.
6-AT-A	1-3	3-Wright J-6 (300)	5-AT-C with Wright J-6 engines.
6-AT-AS	1	3-Wright J-6 (300)	Seaplane, Brewster Floats.
7-AT-A	1	1-P & W Wasp (420) 2-Wright J-6 (300)	6-AT-2 modified. Wasp in nose.
8-AT-A	1	Various.	Single engine 5-AT-C cargo plane.
9-AT-A	1	3-P & W Wasp Junior (300)	4-AT-39 modified.
10-A	None	4-P & W Hornet (575)	Four engine design, 26500 lb. gross. Not built.
11-AT	1	3-Packard Diesel (225)	4-AT-66 modified.
12-A	None	1-Hispano Suiza (1000) 2-P & W Hornet (575)	Modified 10-A design, not built.
13-A	1	1-Wright Cyclone (575) 2-Wright J-6 (300)	5-AT-100 modified
14-A	1	1-Hispano Suiza (1100) 2-Hispano Suiza (715)	10-A design with 3 Hissos. Built and ground tested but not flown.
XB-906	1	3-P & W Wasp SR-1340 (450)	U.S. Army Air Corps bomber design. Gross weight 14,137 lbs. Modified 5-AT-D design.

Appendix 2
Characteristics and Performance

		2-AT	4-AT-A	4-AT-B	4-AT-E	F-AT-F	5-AT-A	5-AT-5	5-AT-C	5-AT-CS	5-AT-D	5-AT-DS	6-AT-S	7-AT-A	8-AT-A	8-AT-AS	9-AT-A	11-AT	13-AT	C-4A
WEIGHT	Gross	5790	9200	10000	10130	11000	10800	12650	13500	13500	13500	13500	12500	12910	11000	12500	10130	10130	13500	13500
	Empty	3790	5200	6000	6500	6700	6700	7650	7600	9100	7840	9100	8250	7280	6195	7267	6696	6500	8135	8434
LOAD	Disposable	2000	4000	4000	3630	4300	4100	5000	5900	4400	5660	4400	4250	5630	4805	5233	3434	3630	5315	5066
	Pay	1280			1725	2394			3643	2143	3403	2143	2344	3380	3596	3570		1774		
SPEED	Maximum	116		128	132	138	130	135	152.5	130	150	135	120	134	138	127	140	116		148
	Cruising (1700 rpm)	100	100	107	107	113	110	115	122	104	122	108	100	110	110	102	112	100		127
	Stalling	53		55	57	59	59	60	64	64	64	61.5	60	55	59	57	55		69	
RANGE	Radius of Action	500	500	500	570	580	440	500	560	490	560	490	535	615	550	510	570			
CLIMB	Rate at Sea Level ft./min.				920	960			1050	900	1050	900	650	880	750	500				770
	Climb from SL in 10 min.				7200	7000			8000	6800	6800	8000	6800	5000	6800					
CEILING	Service				16500	16300			18500	14200	18500	14200	11000	14100	14700	6500				18050
	Absolute				18600	18500	18000	20000	20500	16100	20500	16100		16000	17000	8000	18600			
	Absolute worst 2 engine combination				7100	7800			10500	6000	10500	6000		6300						
PLANE	Span	58'4"	68'10"	74'0"	74'0"	77'10"	77'10"	77'10"	77'10"	77'10"	77'10"	77'10"	77'10"	77'10"	77'10"	74'0"	74'0"	77'10"	77'11"	
DIMENSIONS	Length	45'8"			49'10"	49'10"	49'10"	49'10"	50'3"	51'4"	50'3"	51'4"	50'6"	50'3"	53'6"	49'10"	49'10"	50'3"	51'0"	
	Height	11'10"			11'9"	11'9"		13'8"	12'0"	14'6"	12'8"	14'6"	14'1"	12'0"	12'10"	15'11"	11'9"	12'8"	12'8"	12'7"
Tread				16'9"	16'9"	16'9"	18'7"	18'7"	14'9"	18'7"	14'9"	18'7"	18'7"	14'6"	16'9"	16'9"	18'7"			
CABIN	Width, Average				4'6"	4'6"	4'6"	4'6"	4'6"	4'6"	4'6"	4'6"	4'6"	4'6"	4'5"	4'5"	4'6"	4'6"	4'6"	
DIMENSIONS	Height, Average				6'0"	6'0"	6'0"	6'0"	6'0"	6'0"	6'0"	6'0"	6'0"	6'0"	5'11"	5'11"	6'0"	6'0"	6'0"	
	Length				16'3"	16'3"	16'3"	18'9"	18'9"	18'9"	18'9"	18'9"	18'9"	18'9"	19'2"	19'2"	16'3"	16'3"	18'9"	
	Volume (Cubic Feet)				461	461	461	462	529	529	529	529	529	529	552	552	461	461	529	
	Wing Area (Square Feet)	600			785	785	835	835	835	835	835	835	835	835	835	835	785	785	835	835
PASSENGER	Seats (Removable)	6	10	10	11	11	13	13-15	13	14	13	12	13	0	0	11	9-11	14	13	
	Baggage Space (Cubic Feet)				30	30		50	30	30	30	30	30	30			30	30		
FUEL	Gasoline, US Gallons		210	231	231	231	260	277-355	277-355	277	277-355	277	231	281	231	231	231	180		288-488
	Oil		15	15	24	24		34	34	34	34	34	24	30	15	15	24	18		37.5

Appendix 3
Approved Type Certificates

ATC	Date	Model	Type	Engines	Empty Weight	Useful Load	Gross Weight
87	11-19-28	4-AT	14PCLM	3-Wright (220)	6169	3961	10130
	r2-4-30	4-AT-B	14PCLM	3-Wright Jr. (220)	6169	3961	10130
132	3-30-29	4-AT-E	14PCLM	3-Wright R-975A (300)	6696	3434	10130
	r9-11-30	4-AT-E	14PCLM	3-Wright R-975 (300)	6696	3434	10130
	r11-14-30	4-AT-E	14PCLM	3-Wright R-975A (300)	6696[1]	10130	
	r6-23-31	4-AT-E	14PCLM	3-Wright R-975A (300)	–[2]	–[2]	10130
	r9-23-31	4-AT-E	14PCLM	3-Wright R-975A (300)	6696	3434	10130
156	6-4-29	5-AT-B	17PCLM	3-P & W Wasp (450)	7576	5674	13250
	r8-27-30	5-AT-B	17PCLM	3-P & W Wasp (420)	7576	5674	13250
	r10-11-30	5-AT-B	12-17PCLM	3-P & W Wasp (420)	7576	5674	13250
165	6-14-29	5-AT-C	17PCLM	3-P & W Wasp (450)	7500	6000	13500
	r7-12-30	5-AT-C	17PCLM	3-P & W Wasp (420)	7500	6000	13500
	r10-11-30	5-AT-C	17PCLM	3-P & W Wasp (420)	7500[3]	6000	13500
173	7-26-29	6-AT	15PCLM	3-Wright R-975 (300)	7048	5096	12144
	7-26-29	6-AT	15PCLM	3-Wright R-975 (300)	7009	4721	11730[4]
246	9-30-29	7-AT	15PCLM	2-Wright J6 (300) 1-P & W Wasp (450)	7230	5330	12560[5]
	9-30-29	7-AT	15PCLM	2-Wright J6 (300) 1-P & W Wasp (450)	7280	5630	12910[6]
	r9-16-30	7-AT	15PCLM	2-Wright R-975 (300) 1-P & W Wasp (450)	7280	5630	12910
296	2-12-30	5-AT-CS	15PCSM	3-P & W Wasp (450)	8675	4825	13500[7]
307	4-2-30	9-A	13PCLM	3-P & W Wasp Jr. (300)	6863	3267	10130
409	3-30-31	5-AT-D	16PCLM	3-P & W Wasp C1 (420) 3-P & W Wasp SC1 (450)	8320	5620	14000
431	6-22-31	13-A	16PCLM	2-Wright R-975 (300) 1-Wright Cyclone R-1820-E (575)	8135	5315	13500
	r6-30-31	13-A	16PCLM	2-Wright R-975 (300 1-Wright Cyclone R-1820-E (575)	7632	5368	13000
441	8-10-31	4-AT-F	14PCLM	3-Wright R-975 (300)	6929	4071	11000

Notes:

r - Indicates Revised
[1] - Approximate, will vary with fuel and cabin arrangement
[2] - Approximate, will vary with fuel and cabin arrangement
[3] - Approximate, will vary with fuel and cabin arrangement
[4] - With 231 gallons of fuel
[5] - Without center section tanks
[6] - With center section tanks
[7] - Aircraft Products No. A-27000 floats

Appendix 4
CAA memos - Letters of Approval

Memo	Date	Model	Type	Engines	Gross Weight	Serial No.
2-9	r9-25-28	4-AT-A	14PCLM	3-Wright Jr. (220)	9300	1 to 14
2-10			<< Superceded by ATC-87 >>			
2-11	10-27-28	4-AT-C	14PCLM	2-Wright Jr. (220) 1-P & W Wasp (450)	10000	47 only
2-12	2-16-29	5-AT-B	14PCLM	3-P & W Wasp (450)	12650	4 and up if built
			<< for NAT or TAT >>			
	r9-18-30	5-AT-B	14PCLM	3-P & W Wasp (420)	12650	4 and up
2-32	2-7-29	5-AT-A	14PCLM	3-P & W Wasp (420)	12150	1 to 3
	r10-6-30	5-AT-A	12-14PCLM	3-P & W Wasp (420)	12150	2 and 3
2-80	6-14-29	6-AT-S	2PCSM	3-Wright R-975 (300)	12500	2 and 3
	r-11-8-29	6-AT-Special	12PCSM	3-Wright R-975 (300)	12500	6-ATS-1[1]
2-97	7-23-29	6-AT	16PCLM	3-Wright R-975 (300)	12176	3 and up
	r7-23-30	6-AT	16PCLM	3-Wright R-975 (300)	12176	4 and up
2-240	7-26-30	5-AT-C Special	15PCLM	3-P & W Wasp (420)	13245[2]	4 and up
2-242	7-28-30	5-AT-C Special	15PCLM	3-P & W Wasp (420)	13500	70 only
2-322	1-23-31	4-AT-D	12PCLM	3-Wright j5 (220)	10130	24 only
2-485	8-16-34	8-AT, 8-ATS	2-13PCLSM	1-Wright Cyclone GR-1820F-1 (420)	–	–
2-504	5-28-35	5-AT-DS	12PCSM[3]	3-P & W Wasp S1D1 (420)	–	–
2-518	11-4-35	5-AT-CS	16PCSM	2-P & W Wasp B (420)	–	–
				1-P & W Wasp C (420)	–	–

Notes:

r - Indicates revised

[1] - Brewster floats.

[2] - Gross weight 13500 if wheel fairings and radio installed

[3] - 12-place without hostess, 13-place with hostess. Edo 43-14060 floats.

Appendix 5
Cross-Index by U.S. Registration

NC Number	Refer To	NC Number	Refer To	NC Number	Refer To
1	5-AT-101	8406	4-AT-68	9675	5-AT-33
880	4-AT-8	8407	4-AT-69	9676	5-AT-42
1039	4-AT-2	8408	4-AT-70	9677	5-AT-35
1076	4-AT-9	8410	5-AT-48	9678	4-AT-61
1077	4-AT-10	8411	5-AT-49	9681	5-AT-36
1102	4-AT-7	8412	5-AT-50	9682	5-AT-43
1492	4-AT-1	8413	5-AT-51	9683	5-AT-39
1780	4-AT-11	8414	5-AT-52	9684	5-AT-40
1781	4-AT-12	8415	5-AT-53	9685	5-AT-30
1879	4-AT-5	8416	5-AT-54	9686	5-AT-41
2435	4-AT-1	8417	5-AT-55	9687	5-AT-44
2492	4-AT-6	8418	5-AT-56	9688	5-AT-45
3022	4-AT-5	8419	5-AT-58	9689	5-AT-46
3041	4-AT-3	8485	6-AT-2	9690	5-AT-47
3114	4-AT-7	8486	6-AT-3	15551	5-AT-101
3115	4-AT-8	8499	8-AT-1	69905	5-AT-40
3443	4-AT-14	9606	5-AT-4	7791B	5-AT-39
3444	4-AT-13	9607	5-AT-5	6077C	4-AT-10
4309	4-AT-2	9608	4-AT-51	76GC	5-AT-11
4532	4-AT-16	9609	4-AT-52	400H	5-AT-59
4542	4-AT-15	9610	4-AT-53	401H	5-AT-60
4805	4-AT-17	9611	4-AT-54	402H	5-AT-61
4806	4-AT-18	9612	4-AT-55	403H	5-AT-62
5092	4-AT-19	9613	4-AT-56	404H	5-AT-63
5093	4-AT-20	9614	4-AT-57	405H	5-AT-64
5492	4-AT-21	9636	5-AT-10	406H	5-AT-65
5493	4-AT-22	9637	5-AT-11	407H	5-AT-66
5577	4-AT-23	9638	5-AT-16	408H	5-AT-67
5578	4-AT-24	9639	5-AT-17	409H	5-AT-68
5809	4-AT-25	9640	5-AT-18	410H	5-AT-69
5810	4-AT-26	9641	5-AT-19	411H	5-AT-70
5811	4-AT-27	9642	4-AT-58	412H	5-AT-71
6892	4-AT-28	9643	5-AT-6	413H	5-AT-73
6893	4-AT-29	9644	5-AT-7	414H	5-AT-74
6894	4-AT-30	9645	5-AT-8	415H	5-AT-75
6926	5-AT-1	9646	5-AT-9	416H	5-AT-76
7117	4-AT-31	9647	5-AT-21	417H	5-AT-77
7118	4-AT-32	9648	5-AT-57	418H	5-AT-78
7119	4-AT-33	9649	5-AT-20	419H	5-AT-79
7120	4-AT-34	9650	5-AT-37	420H	5-AT-80
7121	4-AT-35	9651	5-AT-34	421H	5-AT-81
7416	5-AT-2	9652	XB-906-1	422H	5-AT-96
7582	4-AT-36	9653	5-AT-108	423H	9-AT-1
7583	4-AT-37	9654	5-AT-109	424H	5-AT-97
7584	4-AT-38	9655	5-AT-110	425H	5-AT-85
7585	4-AT-39	9656	4-AT-71	426H	5-AT-86
7586	4-AT-40	9657	5-AT-114	427H	5-AT-87
7683	4-AT-41	9658	5-AT-115	428H	5-AT-88
7684	4-AT-42	9659	5-AT-116	429H	5-AT-89
7685	4-AT-43	9660	14-A-1	430H	5-AT-90
7686	4-AT-40	9661	5-AT-12	431H	5-AT-98
7687	4-AT-45	9662	5-AT-29	432H	5-AT-99
7739	5-AT-3	9663	5-AT-14	433H	5-AT-100
7861	4-AT-46	9664	5-AT-23	434H	5-AT-111
7862	4-AT-47	9665	5-AT-24	435H	5-AT-102
7863	4-AT-48	9666	5-AT-25	436H	5-AT-103
7864	4-AT-49	9667	5-AT-13	437H	5-AT-104
7865	4-AT-50	9668	5-AT-15	438H	5-AT-112
8400	4-AT-62	9669	5-AT-26	439H	5-AT-106
8401	4-AT-63	9670	5-AT-27	440H	5-AT-107
8402	4-AT-64	9671	5-AT-28	1629M	5-AT-11
8403	4-AT-65	9672	5-AT-22	1124N	5-AT-39
8404	4-AT-66	9673	5-AT-31		
8405	4-AT-67	9674	5-AT-32		

Appendix 6
Cross-Index to Foreign Registrations

Foreign Registration	Refer To	Foreign Registration	Refer To	Foreign Registration	Refer To
AN-AAC	5-AT-90	HC-SBQ	4-AT-	TI-64	4-AT-37?
AN-AAD	5-AT-89	HI-3	5-AT-11	VH-UBI	5-AT-60
AN-AAE	5-AT-31	HK-1501	5-AT-86	VH-UDY	4-AT-61
AN-AAG	5-AT-43	IM-3	4-AT-67	VH-USX	4-AT-68
AN-AAJ	5-AT-11	IM-4	4-AT-51	VH-UTB	5-AT-68
AN-AAK	5-AT-103	IM-5	4-AT-31	X-ABCA	5-AT-22
AN-AA1	5-AT-18	LG-AAC	5-AT-52	X-ABCB	5-AT-12
AN-AAM	5-AT-73	LG-AAD	5-AT-73	X-ABCC	5-AT-11
AN-AAN	5-AT-64	LG-AAE	5-AT-28	X-ABCD	5-AT-27
AN-AAO	5-AT-52	LG-AAF	5-AT-36	X-ABCE	5-AT-31
AN-AAP	5-AT-39	LG-AAG	5-AT-26	X-ABCF	5-AT-40
AN-AAQ	5-AT-4	LG-AAH	5-AT-14	X-ABCO	5-AT-12
AN-AAR	5-AT-13	LG-AAI	5-AT-18	X-ABCU	5-AT-27
AN-AAS	5-AT-8	LG-AAJ	5-AT-7	X-ABCV	5-AT-31
AN-AAT	5-AT-7	LG-AAL	5-AT-16	X-ABCW	5-AT-45
AN-ABO	5-AT-75	LG-AFA	5-AT-74	XA-BCX	5-AT-74
AN-ACM	4-AT-	M-SCAN	5-AT-40?	XA-BKS	5-AT-74
C-202	5-AT-104	NM-1		XA-DOL	4-AT-5
C-203	5-AT-108	NM-2		XA-FOH	5-AT-31
C-204	5-AT-54	NM-3		XA-FON	5-AT-103
C-205	5-AT-22	NM-4	4-AT-69?	XA-FUB	5-AT-8
C-206	5-AT-61	NM-5	4-AT-70	XA-FUE	5-AT-39
C-207	5-AT-86	NM-7	4-AT-63?	XA-FUO	5-AT-64
C-208	5-AT-80	NM-14	5-AT-?	XA-FUP	5-AT-18
C-210	5-AT-1	NM-18	4-AT-	XA-GIJ	5-AT-75
CB-CAM	5-AT-17	NM-22	5-AT-11	XA-HIL	5-AT-11
CF-AZB	4-AT-3	NM-24	5-AT-40	XB-KUI	5-AT-11
CF-BEP	6-AT-1	NM-25	5-AT-27	XB-NET	5-AT-8
CV-FAI	5-AT-88	OA-AAA	5-AT-17	XB-WAR	5-AT-39
EC-BAB	4-AT-71	OA-AAB	5-AT-61	XB-YIT	5-AT-39
EC-KKA	4-AT-68	OA-AAC	5-AT-54	XH-TAB	5-AT-71?
EC-RRA	4-AT-71	OA-AAD	5-AT-59	XH-TAH	5-AT-75
EC-WIO	4-AT-71	OK-FOR	5-AT-50	XH-TAI	
F-31	5-AT-6	PH-AKE	5-AT-42	XH-TAJ	
F-32	5-AT-16	R-130	5-AT-55	XH-TAK	5-AT-39
G-ABEF	4-AT-61	R-131	4-AT-11	XH-TAL	
G-ABFF	5-AT-68	R-148	5-AT-63	XH-TAN	
G-ABHF	5-AT-68	R-176	5-AT-61	XH-TAO	5-AT-103
G-ABHO	5-AT-60	TI-15	5-AT-43	XH-TAR	
G-ACAE	5-AT-107	TI-33	5-AT-70	XH-TAS	
G-ACAK	4-AT-68	TI-40	5-AT	XH-TAT	
G-CARC	4-AT-10	TI-41	5-AT-78	XH-TAW	5-AT-15
G-CATX	4-AT-26	TI-42	5-AT-71	XH-TAX	5-AT-28
G-CYWZ	6-AT-1	TI-43	9-AT-1	XH-TAY	
HC-SBC	4-AT-24		(4-AT-39)	XH-TAZ	
HC-SBD	4-AT-29	TI-44	5-AT-31	YV-AVB	5-AT
HC-SBI	5-AT	TI-46	5-AT-90	YV-MGO	5-AT-9
HC-SBJ	5-AT	TI-51	5-AT-19		
HC-SBK	5-AT-67	TI-61	4-AT		

Appendix 7
C/N Listing, Model 4-AT

Constructor's Serial Number	Original Registration	Constructor's Serial Number	Original Registration	Constructor's Serial Number	Original Registration
1	1492	28	6892	55	9612
2	4309	29	6893	56	9613
3	3041	30	6894	57	9614
4	A7526	31	7117	58	9642
5	1879	32	7118	59	A8273
6	2492	33	7119	60	A8274
7	1102	34	7120	61	9678
8	3115	35	7121	62	8400
9	1076	36	7582	63	8401
10	1077	37	7583	64	8402
11	1780	38	7584	65	8403
12	1781	39	7585	66	8404
13	28-348	40	7586	67	8405
14	3443	41	7683	68	8406
15	4542	42	7684	69	8407
16	4532	43	7685	70	8408
17	4805	44	7686	71	9656
18	4806	45	7687		
19	5092	46	7861	72-79	Not Used
20	5093	47	7862		
21	5492	48	7863	81	29-220
22	5493	49	7864	82	29-221
23	5577	50	7865	83	29-222
24	5578	51	9608	84	29-223
25	5809	52	9609	85	29-224
26	5810	53	9610	86	29-225
27	5811	54	9611	87	29-226

Appendix 8
C/N Listing, Model 5-AT

Constructor's Serial Number	Original Registration	Constructor's Serial Number	Original Registration	Constructor's Serial Number	Original Registration
1	6926	40	9684	79	419H
2	7416	41	9686	79A	8485
3	7739	42	9676	80	420H
4	9606	43	9682	81	421H
5	9607	44	9687	82	A8598
6	9643	45	9688	83	A8599
7	9644	46	9689	84	A8840
8	9645	47	9690	85	425H
9	9646	48	8410	86	426H
10	9636	49	8411	87	427H
11	9637	50	8412	88	428H
12	9661	51	8413	89	429H
13	9667	52	8414	90	430H
14	9663	53	8415	91	31-401
15	9668	54	8416	92	31-402
16	9638	55	8417	93	31-403
17	9639	56	8418	94	8486
18	9640	57	9648	95	31-404
19	9641	58	8419	96	422H
20	9649	59	400H	97	424H
21	9647	60	401H	98	431H
22	9672	61	402H	99	432H
23	9664	62	403H	100	433H
24	9665	63	404H	101	NS-1
25	9666	64	405H	102	435H
26	9669	65	406H	103	436H
27	9670	66	407H	104	437H
28	9671	67	408H	105	A9206
29	9662	68	409H	106	439H
30	9685	69	410H	107	440H
31	9673	70	411H	108	9653
32	9674	71	412H	109	A9205
33	9675	72	A8457	110	9655
34	9651	73	413H	111	434H
35	9677	74	414H	112	438H
36	9681	75	415H	113	9654
37	9650	76	416H	114	9657
38	29-219	77	417H	115	9658
39	9683	78	418H	116	9659

Appendix 9
C/N Listing, All Other Models

Constructor's Serial Number	Original Registration
6-AT-1	G-CYWZ
6-AT-2	8485
6-AT-3	8486
7-AT-1	8485
8-AT-1	8499
9-AT-1	7585
11-AT-1	8484
13-A-1	433-H
14-A-1	9660
XB-906-1	9652

Appendix 10
Ford Tri-Motor Owners

I. Airlines

Aerovias de Guatemala S.A.	Guatemala
Aerovias Ramales Colombianas	Llanos Orientales, Colombia
AVIANCA, Aerovias Nacionales de Colombia S.A.	Colombia
Aerovias Nacionales	San Jose, Costa Rica
Aerovias Peruanas S.A.	Lima, Peru
Air Tours	Chicago, Illinois and Put-In-Bay, Ohio
Akron Airways	Akron, Ohio
Alaska Airlines	Anchorage, Alaska
American Airways	St. Louis, Missouri
American Airlines	New York City, NY
Arctic Airways	Nome, Alaska
AVENSA, Aerovias Venezuela S.A.	Venezuela
AVIATECA, Empressa Guatemalteca de Aviacion	Guatemela
Bell Fouche Airline	Bell Fouche, South Dakota
Blue Bird Air Transport	Chicago, Illinois
Braniff Airways	Oklahoma City, Oklahoma
British Air Navigation Company	England
British Columbia Airways	Vancouver, Canada
British Yukon Navigation Company	Canada
Carolina Air Transport	Burlington, North Carolina
Central Airlines	Pittsburgh, Pennsylvania
Chicago Air Service	Chicago, Illinois
China National Aviation Corp.	Shanghai, China
Cia Cubana de Aviacion S.A.	Havana, Cuba
Cia Mexicana de Aviacion S.A.	Mexico City, Mexico
Colonial Air Transport	New York City, New York and Newark, New Jersey
Colonial Western Airways	New York City, New York
Compania Anonima de Lineas Aereas	Spain
Compania Nacional Cubana de Aviacion	Havana, Cuba
Compania Nacional de Aviacion Curtiss	Havana, Cuba
Consolidated Air Lines	Sacramento, California
Continental Air Express	Los Angeles, California
CLASSA, Concesionaires de Lineas Aereas	Madrid, Spain Subvencionadas S.A.
Detroit-Cleveland Airline	Detroit, Michigan
Eastern Air Transport	Brooklyn, New York
ENTA, Empressa Nacional de Transportes Aereos	San Jose, Costa Rica
Expreso Aereo Inter-Americano S.A.	Havana, Cuba
Ford Air Freight Lines (Ford Motor Company)	Dearborn, Michigan
G and G Airlines	Tucson, Arizona
Golden State Airways	Los Angeles, California
Gray Goose Airlines	Chicago, Illinois
Grand Canyon Airlines	Grand Canyon, Arizona
Grand Canyon-Boulder Dam Tours	Boulder City, Nevada
Guinea Airways	Lae, British New Guinea
Hanford Airlines	Kansas City, Missouri
Hanfords Tri-State Air Lines	Sioux City, Iowa
Holden Air Transport Services	Salamaua, New Guinea
Island Air Service (Island Air Lines)	Put-In-Bay, Ohio
Jefferson Airways	Minneapolis, Minnesota
Kenyon Transportation Company	Morris, Minnesota
KLM, Royal Dutch Airlines	New York City & Holland
LAGOSA, Lineas Aereas Guerrero-Oaxaca S.A.	Pueblo, Mexico
LAPE, Lineas Aereas Postales Espanoles	Madrid, Spain
Long and Harman Airlines	Dallas, Texas
McConachie Air Transport Company	Edmenton, Canada
Maddux Airlines	Los Angeles, California

Mamer Air Transport	Spokane, Washington
Metropolitan Air Ferry Service	New York City, New York
Mohawk Airways	Schenectedy, New York
Monroe Airways	Monroe, Michigan
Morgan Airlines	Hoboken, New Jersey
Nacional Cubana de Aviacion Curtiss	Havana, Cuba
NAMSA, Negociacion Aerea-Mexicana S.A.	Ometepec, Mexico
NAT, National Air Transport	Chicago, Illinois
New England & Western Air Transportation	Stratford, Conn., and Springfield, Mass.
NYRBA, New York, Rio & Buenos Aires Line	New York City, New York
New York Airways	New York City, New York
New York Safety Airways	New York City, New York
Nicaraguan National Airways Company	Nicaragua
Northern Air Lines	Minneapolis, Minnesota
Northern Air Transport	Fairbanks, Alaska
Northern Airways Ltd.	Carcross, Canada
Northwest Airways (Northwest Airlines)	St. Paul, Minnesota
KNILM, N.V. Koninklijke Nederlands-Indische Luchtvaart Maatschappij	Amsterdam, Holland
PAT, Pacific Air Transport	Oakland, California
Pacific Alaska Airways	Fairbanks, Alaska
PAA, Pan American Airways	New York City, New York
PANAGRA, Pan American-Grace Airways	New York City, New York
Panama Airways	Panama City, Panama
Pennsylvania Airlines	Pittsburgh, Pennsylvania
Pennsylvania Airlines & Transport Co.	Pittsburgh, Pennsylvania
Pittsburgh Airways	Pittsburgh, Pennsylvania
Queen City Airlines	Cincinatti, Ohio
Rapid Air Lines	Rapid City, South Dakota
SACO, Servicio Aereo Colombiano	Bogota, Colombia
SACSA, Servicios Aereos de Chiapas S.A.	Mexico City, Mexico
SAN, Servicios Aereos Nacionales S.A.	Huasteca, Mexico
SCADTA, Sociedad Colombo-Alemana de Transportes Aereos	Barranquilla, Colombia
Scenic Airways	Grand Canyon, Arizona
Scenic Airlines	Las Vegas, Nevada
Sky View Lines	Detroit, Michigan and Buffalo, New York
Southern Transcontinental Airways	Dallas, Texas
SAFE, Southwest Air Fast Express	Tulsa, Oklahoma
SAFE, Southern Air Fast Express	Dallas, Texas
Star Air Lines (Star Air Service)	Anchorage, Alaska
Stout Air Lines (Stout Air Service	Detroit, Michigan
Sunbeam Air Transport Company	Denver, Colorado
TACA, Transportes Aereos Centro Americanos	Costa Rica, Guatemala, Honduras and Nicaragua
TAJSA, Transportes Aereos de Jalisco S.A.	Jalisco, Mexico
TATSA, Transportes Aereos-Terrestres S.A.	Tayoltita, Mexico
Transamerica Airlines	Detroit, Michigan
TAT, Transcontinental Air Transport	New York City, New York
TWA, Transcontinental and Western Air	Delaware and New York
Travel Air Taxi	Put-In-Bay, Ohio*
Tri-Motor Safety Airways	New York City, New York
Tri-Motored Air Tours	Port Clinton, Ohio
Transamerican Airlines	Detroit, Michigan
Transportes Aereos Mexicanos	Merida, Mexico
Tropical Air Transport	Nicaragua
United Air Lines	Chicago, Illinois
Universal Airlines System	Robertson, Missouri
Western Air Express	Los Angeles, California
Westchester Airways	Grand Rapids, Michigan & Miami Beach, Florida, and Auburn, New York
White Pass Airways	Skagway, Alaska
Wien Alaska Airlines	Fairbanks, Alaska
Yukon Air Transport	Edmonton, Canada
Yukon Southern Air Transport	Edmonton, Canada

II. Companies

(Some may have operated as airlines)

Air Cruisers	Detroit, Michigan
Air Flights	Oak Park, Illinois
Air Service of Pittsburgh	Pittsburgh, Pennsylvania
Air Transport Corporation	Richmond, Virginia
Alaskan Aviation Heritage Museum	Anchorage, Alaska
Aircraft Exporting Corporation	New York City, New York
Aircraft Hydroforming	Gardena, California
Aircraft Service Company	Boise, Idaho
Atlantic Airmotive Corp.	Garden City, New York
Aviation Credit Corp.	New York City, New York and St. Louis, Missouri
Aviation Manufacturing Corp.	Chicago, Illinois
Charles H. Babb Co.	Glendale, California
Becker Aircraft Sales Company	Dravosburg, Pennsylvania
Beech Aircraft Company	Wichita, Kansas
Bell Telephone Laboratories	New York City, New York
Blevins Aircraft Corp.	Atlanta, Georgia
Boeing School of Aeronautics	Oakland, California
British Yukon Navigation Company	Vancouver, Canada
Carolina Air Transport	Burlington, North Carolina
Central Flying Service	Little Rock, Arkansas
Chicago Title & Trust Co.	Chicago, Illinois
COLPET, Colombian Petroleum Co.	Cucuta, Colombia
Colombian Petroleum Company	New York City, New York
Columbia Pictures Corp. of Calif.	Hollywood, California
Compania Aramayo de Mines S.A.	La Paz, Bolivia
Compania Minera Agua Fria S.A.	Tegucigalpa, Honduras
Compania Nacional Aviacion	Los Angeles, California
Continental Air Express	Los Angeles, California
Continental Oil Co.	Ponca City, Oklahoma
Curtiss Flying Service	Valley Stream, New York; Chicago, Illinois; Los Angeles California; Miami, Florida
Curtiss-Wright Flying Service	Valley Stream, New York; New York City, New York; St. Louis, Missouri; Pittsburgh, Pennsylvania; Boston, Mass, Glenview, Ill.
Curtiss Publishing Co.	Philadelphia, Pennsylvania
Dallas Aviation School and Air College	Dallas, Texas
DePonti Aviation Company	Minneapolis, Minnesota
Despatch Corporation	New York City, New York
Embry-Riddle Co.	Cincinnatti, Ohio
EAA Aviation Museum	Oshkosh, Wisconsin
Evergreen Aviation	McMinville, Oregon
Fairchild Aerial Surveys	Los Angeles, California
Firestone Tire and Rubber Company	Akron, Ohio
Ford Motor Co.	Dearborn, Michigan
Ford Motor Company of England	Ford Junction, England
Ford Tri-Motor Inc.	Ottawa, Kansas
Freeman Aircraft Sales	Minneapolis, Minnesota
Gulf Oil Corporation	Pittsburgh, Pennsylvania
Hangar Six	San Antonio, Texas
Harrah's Club	Reno, Nevada
Interamerican Aerotravel and Supplies	New York City, New York
Intercontinent Aviation	Jersey City, New York
International Aviation Enterprises	New York City, New York
Jack Adams Aircraft Sales	Memphis, Tennessee
Johnson Flying Service	Missoula, Montana
Kal-Aero	Kalamazoo, Michigan
Kenyon Transportation Company	Morris, Minnesota
Knowles Flying Service	Detroit, Michigan
K.T. Flying Service	Honolulu, Hawaii
LeMaster-Glenn Aerial Spraying	Ottawa, Kansas

Lights, Inc.	Alhambra, California
Linden Associates	Springfield, Mass.
Link Aeronautical Corp.	Endicott, New York
Long and Harman	Dallas, Texas
Louisville Flying Service	Louisville, Kentucky
Mamer Air Service (Flying Service)	Spokane, Washington
Manitowoc Air Service	Manitowoc, Wisconsin
Marcell Rand Company	New York City, New York
Mac's Air Palace (McAfee)	Uniontown Pennsylvania
Mene Grande Oil Company, C.A.	Maracaibo, Venezuela
Minerales De Zaragoza S.A.	Torreon, Mexico
Mox-Air	Los Angeles, California
Mulzer Flying Service	Wisconsin Rapids, Wisconsin and Delaware, Ohio
Murphy Flying Service	Findlay, Ohio
N.A.T. Flying Service	Chicago, Illinois
National Air & Space Museum	Washington, D.C.
National Museum of New Guniea	Papua, New Guinea
Naval Aviation Museum	Pensacola, Florida
Nekoosa-Edwards Paper Company	Port Edwards, Wisconsin
New England & Western Air Transportation	Stratford, Connecticut
Nite Sky Advertising Company	Milwaukee, Wisconsin
Northwest Agricultural Aviation Corp.	Choteau, Montana
N.V. Bataafse Petroleum	Maatschappij Holland
Pacific Finance Corp.	Los Angeles, California
Pan American Supply Corp.	New York City, New York
Parks Air College	St. Louis, Missouri
Phillips Petroleum Company	Bartlesville, Oklahoma
Plane Speaker Corporation	New York City, New York
Pony Express Company	Seattle, Washington
Norman Pinney Company	Burbank, California
Pitcairn Aviation Company	Brooklyn, New York
Pittsburgh Aeronautical Service	Pittsburgh, Pennsylvania
Pratt and Whitney Aircraft Co.	Bridgeport, Connecticut
R.C.A., Radio Corporation of America	Newark, New Jersey
Reid, Murdock and Company	Chicago, Illinois
Republic Oil Company	Pittsburgh, Pennsylvania
Robertson Airplane Service Co.	Robertson, Missouri
Robertson Aircraft Corporation	Anglum, Missouri
Royal Typewriter Company	Hartford, Connecticut
San Diego Aerospace Museum	San Diego, California
Ruckstell Corporation, Ltd.	Glendale, California
San Luis Mining Company	San Francisco, California
SCOLTA	Colombia
W.S. Shakleton, Ltd.	London, England
Shell Aviation Corporation	St. Louis, Missouri
Shell Company of Ecuador	Quito, Ecuador
Skyway	Blackwell, Oklahoma
South American Gulf Oil Co.	New York City, New York
Springfield Airport & Aeronautical School	Springfield, Mass. St. Louis Flying Service Robertson, Missouri
Standard Oil Company of California	San Francisco, California Standard Oil Company of Indiana Chicago, Illinois
Stout Metal Airplane Company	Dearborn, Michigan
TEXACO, The Texas Company	New York City, New York
Tex-O-Kan Flour Mills	Dallas, Texas
Thurmond Aircraft Corporation	Kansas City, Missouri
Union Electric Light and Power Co.	St. Louis, Missouri
United Air Services	Burbank, California
United Aircraft Corporation	Bridgeport, Connecticut
United Airports of Connecticut	East Hartford, Connecticut United Aviation Corporation Chicago, Illinois
Universal Flyers	Washington, D.C.
Western Pacific Aviation Corp.	San Francisco, California
Wright Aeronautical Corporation	Patterson, New Jersey

III. Individual Owners

Jack A. Adams	Memphis, Tenn.
Lawrence L. Alzheimer	Collins, Montana
Frank Ambrose	Whitestone, New YorkY
R.N. Anderson	Put-In-Bay, Ohio
Ralph Barron	Hapeville, Georgia
Mary Jane Bergerson	Crystal River, Florida
Georgia R. Bibby	Milwaukee, Wisconsin
Prince Bibesco	Romania
Walter M. Blonski	Milwaukee, Wisconsin
Vernon Bookwalter	Seattle, Washington
Abe Bowler	Orofino, Idaho
Charles E. Bradbury, Jr.	Champaign, Illinois
Roy W. Brillhart	Kansas City, Kansas
Jesse Bristow	Leland, Miss., & Miami, Florida
Chester G. Brown	None, Alaska
Edgar W. Brown III	Orange, Texas
Holland G. Bryan	Paducah, Kentucky
G.T. Burrell	Chicago, Illinois
M.A. Caffarello	Chicago, Illinois
David Callender	Eagle, Idaho
Keith C. Cantine	Detroit, Michigan
Mary Cantine	Detroit, Michigan, and Akron, Ohio
Louise A. Chamerlain	East Orange, New Jersey
Allan T. Chaney	Newark, Ohio
A.B. Clark	Watsonville, California
Floyd G. Clark	Richmond, Virginia
K.C. Clark	Watsonville, California
E. Clemm (Reed and Clemm)	Glendale, California
Frank W. Clugston	Avon, Illinois
Max Conrad	Winona, Minnesota
Chalon E. Corson	Stratford, Conn.
Arturo D'Argence	Campeche, Mexico
Augusto D'Argence	Campeche, Mexico
Arthur J. Davis	East Lansing, Michigan
Reginald A. Dawson	Washington, D.C.
Colonel C.W. Deeds	Hartford, Conn.
C.M. Dunham	Haines City, Florida
C.M. Ewan	New York City, New York
Alfred Frank	Salt Lake City, Utah
Eugene O. Frank	Caldwell, Idaho
Frank Free	Managua, Nicaragua
Ray Finklea	Leland, Miss.
Harold J. Flaherty	Los Angeles, California
Mary Flaherty	Los Angeles, California
George Formico	Minneapolis, Minnesota
Charles F. Frensdorf	Orofino, Idaho
E.L. Fulton	Dallas, Texas
Juan Tilghman Gallo	Huasteca, Mexico
Blanche Garbacz	Little Rock, Arkansas
Ben F. Gregory	Kansas City, Kansas
Edward H. Groenendyke	Pasadena, California
The Honorable A.E. Guinness	Dublin, Ireland
Carlos Davalos Guzman	Guadalajara, Mexico
William Hadden	Orofino, Idaho
C. Hahn	Pittsburg, Pennsylvania
Erle P. Halliburton	Duncan, Oklahoma & Dallas, Texas
Herman Hamer	La Salle, Illinois
J.A. Haraden	Schnectady, New York
C.E. Harman (Long and Harman)	Dallas, Texas
J.E. Herndon	Kansas City, Kansas

Milton Hersberger	Put-In-Bay, Ohio
Hans Hoffman	Colombia
Gladys Holbert	Little Rock, Arkansas
Herbert C. Holtz	Milwaukee, Wisconsin
Marshall Chang Hsueh-Liang	China
Clyde W. Ice	Rochester, Minnesota
Arthur Inman	Coffeyville, Kansas
Rodger Inman	Coffeyville, Kansas
Ricardo Nevarez Izurieta	Campeche, Mexico
George Jaynes	Atlanta, Georgia
Vernon N. Johns	Dearborn, Michigan
Clinton Arthur Johnson	Miami, Florida and Mt. Shasta, California
Harold Sherman Johnson	Chicago, Illinois
Robert S. Johnson	Missoula, Montana
Fred Kane	Kansas City, Kansas
Tom Marshall Kester	Pasadena, California
George M. Keightly	Jacksonville, Florida
Eleanor Kipp	Randolph, Minnesota
William S. Kirkpatrick	Easton, Pennsylvania
Jim E. Kofahl	Montrose, California
John Kovacs	Schnectady, New York
David W. Kratz	Robertson, Missouri
Arthur H. Kudner	New York City, New York
Elmer H. Leighton	Laredo, Texas and Milwaukee, Wisconsin
W. Clayton Lemon	Roanoke, Virginia
Garland E. Lincoln	North Hollywood, California
Alvene Litzenberger	Pittsburgh, Pennsylvania
Carl R. Litzenberger	Bettis Airport, Pennsylvania
W.F. Long (Long and Harman)	Dallas, Texas
Archie Ray Loomis	Toledo, Ohio
Dorothy Loomis	Washington, D.C.
Ray Loomis	Washington, D.C.
John M. Louck	Monmouth, Illinois
Katherine M. Louck	Monmouth, Illinois
Lord Lovelace	England
Aubrey E. Loving	Richmond, Virginia
Harold L. McAfee	Lamont Furnace, Pennsylvania
W.H. McAfee	Uniontown, Pennsylvania
George W. McCauley	Mineola, New York
Harold McClintock	Pittsburgh, Pennsylvania
John McClintock	Pittsburgh, Pennsylvania
G.W.G. McConachie	Edmonton, Canada
Jack L. Maddux	Los Angeles, California
James M. Markley, Jr.	Miami, Florida
W.I. Marsalis	Valley Stream, New York
Waitman W. Martin	Dallas, Texas
Lester Massingham	Poplar Bluff, Missouri and Memphis, Tennessee
James Mattern	Los Angeles, California
Robert N. Matthews	Dunbar, Pennsylvania
Paul E. Miller	Dunbar, Pennsylvania
Gilbert R. Minick	Richmond, Virginia
William A. Monday	Cody, Wyoming
Pedro Moreno	Jalisco, Mexico
Sumner B. Morgan	Tela, Honduras
Edward B. Mulick	Milwaukee, Wisconsin
Leslie G. Mulzer	Wisconsin Rapids, Wisconsin
C.W. Murchison	Dallas, Texas
Michael C. Murphy	Findlay, Ohio
Helen Ward Musleh	Greensboro, North Carolina and Jacksonville, Florida
Joe Musleh	Jacksonville, Florida
Kenneth Neese	Anchorage, Alaska
Oscar W. Nichols	Newark, Ohio
W.F. Niedernhofer	Pittsburgh, Pennsylvania
J.H. O'Brien	Morris, Minnesota

Frank D. Oergel Jr.	Los Angeles, California
Dolph Overton	Santee, South Carolina
Wayne Parmenter	St. Elmo, Illinois
Reg Pattinson	St. Elmo, Illinois
Don Patrick	Cleveland, Ohio
Irving B.Perlitch (Perch)	Morgan Hill, California
Jack Piersch	Kansas City, Kansas
George M. Prescott	Kansas City, Kansas
Louis P. Quinn	Denver, Colorado
Marcell N. Rand	Tonawanda, New York
R. Reed (Reed and Clemm)	Glendale, California
Frank Reimers	Layafette, Indiana
Reg L. Robbins	Fort Worth, Texas
O.W. Robbins	Fort Worth, Texas
Dan R. Robertson	Robertson, Missouri
H.W. Robinson	Ossining, New York
Samuel C. Rudolph	Los Angeles, California
Robert P. Salter	Eutaw, Alabama
Ervin #. Saltzgaber	Winchester, Ohio
Clyde Sampson	Compton, California
Dale A. Seitz	Kansas City, Kansas
William Keith Scott	Los Angeles, California
Dale P. Smith	Springfield, Missouri
Kenneth F. Starnes	Poplar Bluff, Missouri and Memphis, Tennessee
Wilson E. Stone	Kansas City, Kansas
Cleo Cecil Stratton	Ballinger, Texas
Oral K. Southwick	Springfield, Missouri
E.C. Sundorph	Cleveland, Ohio
Mel Swanson	Minneapolis, Minnesota
Dill M. Teel	Odessa, Texas
Jack W. Thornburg	Grand Canyon, Arizona
Henry D. Thrall	Minneapolis, Minnesota
H.H. Timken	Canton, Ohio
Lew E. Tipper	Detroit, Michigan
E.M. Van Devere	Akron, Ohio
Irwin Vernelle	Hallsville, Illinois
Raul Fierro Villalobos	Guadalajara, Mexico
William Vogel	LaSalle, Illinois
Alton Walker	Kansas City, Missouri
Elizabeth Walker	Kansas City, Missouri
Robert W. Waltermire	Choteau, Montana
Kermit Weeks	Miami, Florida
Harold A. White	Tegucigalpa, Honduras
E.L. Williams	Minneapolis, Minnesota
Rex Williams	Phoenix, Arizona
Gerald D. Wilson	Orofino, Idaho
Jerry Wood	Oak Park, Illinois
J. Frederick Wood	Memphis, Tennessee
John Leonard Yingst	Sheridan, Pennsylvania
Miguel A. Zuniga	Mexico City, Mexico

IV. Government Use

Chile (Government Airline)
Chinese Army
Colombian Air Force
Costa Rica; Public Roads Administration
Cuban Navy
Czecho-Slovakia State Airline
Dominican Republic Air Force
Nicaraguan Government
Peruvian Air Force
Royal Air Force, England
Royal Australian Air Force
Royal Canadian Air Force
Spanish Air Force
U.S. Army Air Corps
U.S. Army Corps of Engineers
U.S. Department of Commerce; Bureau of Air Commerce
U.S. Marine Corps
U.S. Navy

Appendix 11
Performance of Ford Aircraft in Reliability Tours

Year	Start	Finish	Miles	Start	Finish	Place	Model	Pilot	Points	Title-Remarks
1925	Sept. 28	Oct. 4	1900	17	15	–	2-AT	Hamilton	–	"Ford Reliability Tour." 11 out of 17 finished with perfect score so all were considered winners and their names engraved on the Edsel Ford Trophy.
1926	Aug. 7	Aug. 21	2599	25	18	17th	2-AT	Manning	1055.7	"Second Airplane Reliability Tour For Edsel Ford Trophy." Plane carried Race No.8 painted on fuselage under wing. The 4-AT-1 (Race #7) started tour but did not finish. Won by Walter Beech flying Travel Air.
1927	June 24	July 12	4200	14	13	4th	4-AT	Mulford	7609.8	"Third national Reliability Tour For The Ford Trophy." Ford airplane was a non-contestant for prize awards. Won by Eddie Stinson flying Stinson Detroiter.
1928	June 30	July 28	6300	24	24	2nd	4-AT	Hawks	24390.8	"Fourth National Air Tour." Ford was Race #2 (NC-3443). Won by John Wood flying a Waco.
1929	Oct. 5	Oct. 21	–	–	25	3rd 10th	7-AT 5-AT	Zeller Warner	38494.03 28090.60	"National Air Tour." 7-AT was Race #16 (painted on tail), and 5-AT was race #17 (also on tail). Won by Waco with 45672 points.
1930	Sept. 11	Sept.27	4800	18	18	1st 4th	7-AT 5-AT	Russell Zeller	58575.6 55016.2	"Sixth Annual National Air Tour." 7-AT was Race #6, 5-AT Race #5 (NC-401H), both numbers painted on the tail. 2nd and 3rd place by Waco airplanes.
1931	July 4	July 25	–	10	10	1st 2nd	13-A 5-AT	Russell Smart	63764.3 53813.0	"Seventh National Air Tour." No other large aircraft were entered. Trophy awarded permanently to Ford Motor Company and Tour ended.

References:
Aircraft Year Book, 1926, p.124, 126; 1927, p.177, pp.190-191; 1928, p.247, 490; 1929, p.159, 446; 1930, p.479, 587; 1931, p.550; 1932, p.504.
Aviation, October, 1930, 1930 pp.241-244; November, 1930, pp.278-279, 281.
Western Flying, November, 1930, p.51.

Appendix 12
Cross-Index to Military Ford Tri-Motors

I. U.S. Army

Military Serial Number	Refer To
28-348	4-AT-13
29-219	5-AT-38
29-220	4-AT-80
29-221	4-AT-81
29-222	4-AT-82
29-223	4-AT-83
29-224	4-AT-84
29-225	4-AT-85
29-226	4-AT-86
31-401	5-AT-91
31-402	5-AT-92
31-403	5-AT-93
31-404	5-AT-95
NX-9652	XB-906-1

II. U.S. Navy and Marines

Military Serial Number	Refer To
A-7526	4-AT-4
A-8273	4-AT-59
A-8274	4-AT-60
A-8457	5-AT-72
A-8598	5-AT-82
A-8599	5-AT-83
A-8840	5-AT-84
A-9205	5-AT-109
A-9206	5-AT-105

Appendix 13
Ford Tri-Motor Names

Name	Registration	Operator
Abbot	NC-9653	Pacific Air Transport
Air Express	NC-7684	Dallas Aviation School
Air Transport	NC-6893	Dallas Aviation School
Barranquilla	C-60	SCADTA
Cartagena	C-66	SCADTA
Cementer	NC-405H	Erle P. Halliburton
City of Albuquerque	NC-9643	TAT
City of Bridgeport	NC-9614	New England & Western
City of Columbus #1	NC-9606	TAT
City of Columbus #2	NC-9648	TAT
City of Indianapolis	NC-9647	TAT
City of Los Angeles	NC-9646	TAT
City of Los Angeles #2	NC-9612	TwA Lease (1949)
City of New York	NC-9606	TAT
City of Philadelphia	NC-9651	TAT (1929)
City of Philadelphia	NC-9651	Irv Pertch (1971)
City of Reno	NC-9645	Harrahs Club
City of Saint Louis	NC-9650	TAT
City of San Francisco	NC-9649	TAT
City of Washington	NC-9644	TAT
City of Waynoka	NC-9639	TAT
City of Wichita	NC-9645	TAT
Comte de la Vaulx	CV-FAI	Prince Bibesco/FAI
Dawson	NC-431H	PAT
Estrella Fugaz	XA-FON	TAJ
Floyd Bennett	NX-4542	CDR Richard E. Byrd
Glacier	NC-9655	PAT
Independence	NC-7863	Monarch Foods
Kingbird	NX-6926	Pratt & Whitney A/C
Kunming	23	CNAC
Leticia		SCADTA
Manizales		SCADTA
Marin	NC-437H	PAT
Mendoza	R130	Panagra
Miss Albany	NC-9642	United Air Service
Nacomis	NC-9675	Colonial Air Transport
Nemissa	NC-9681	Colonial Air Transport
Nonantum	NC-9677	Colonial Air Transport
Olympia	NC-435H	Pacific Air Transport
Ptarmigan II	NC-8403	Ptarmigan Airlines
Puget	NC-439H	PAT
Remrand	NC-1780	Marcell N. Rand
Quick Silver	NC-428H	Ford Motor Company
Royal Air Truck	NC-3115	Royal Typewriter Co.
Rio de la Plata	NC-1780	NYRBA
Salta	NC-402H	NYRBA
San Antonio	NC-9672	Panagra
San Cristobal	NC-8418?	Panagra
San Felipe	NC-433H	Panagra
San Fernando	NC-9639	Panagra
San Fernando	OA-AAA	Aerovias Peruanas
San Jose	NC-403H	Panagra
San Pablo	NC-402H	Panagra
San Pedro	NC-8417	NYRBA and Panagra
Santa Mariana	NC-400H	Panagra
Santa Marta	SCADTA	
Santa Rosa	NC-8416	Panagra
Santander	C-210	Avianca
Santiago	NC-8417	NRYBA
Santiago #2	NC-402H	NYRBA
Stanolind I	NC-2492	Standard Oil of Indiana
Stanolind III	NC-9676	Standard Oil of Indiana
Tanganyika Star	G-ABHO	Lord Lovelace
Tarapaca	C-62	SCADTA
The Glendale	NC-7582	Maddux Air Lines
The Golden Gate	NC-9686	Maddux Air Lines
The Kansas City	NC-9607	TAT
The Kansas Clipper	N-414H	Charles Lemaster
The Ship From Mars	NC-5093	Ben Gregory
The Ship of Flame	NC-5093	Ben Gregory
The Spirit of Transportation	NC-9668	Stout Air Lines
The Voice of the Sky	NC-9614	Plane Speaker Corp.
Tulsa	NC-9665	SAFE
Vagabond	G-ABEF	British Air Navigation
Voyager	G-ABHO	British Air Navigation
Wamblee Ohanko	NC-5093	Rapid Air Lines
West Wind (#1)	NC-9612	Mamer Flying Service
West wind (#2)	NC-8403	Mamer Flying Service
Wichita Falls	NC-9690	SAFE
Woolaroc II	NC-418H	Phillips Petroleum Co.

Appendix 14
Accident Summary

Date	Identification	Location
8-19-26	None	Nova, OH
11-18-27	A7526	Washington, DC
5-12-28	NC-1492	Dearborn, MI
8-25-28	G-CATX	Puget Sound, WA
10-13-28	NC-880	Detroit, MI
11-23-28	NC-7687	Spokane, WA
12-1-28	NC-7862	Spur, TX
12-2-28	NC-7684	Jacksonville, FL
12-22-28	NC-3443	Floresville, TX
1-13-29	NC-1780	Newark, NJ
1-16-29	NC-1076	Toledo, OH
1-18-29	NC-4532	Santa Rosa, CA
2-24-29	NC-1879	Cleveland, OH
3-5-29	NC-7684	Cojimar, Cuba
3-17-29	NC-7683	Newark, NJ
3-19-29	NC-9674	Dearborn, MI
3-21-29	NC-1781	Sherman, TX
3-28-29	Unknown	Buffalo, NY
3-31-29	NC-1781	Sherman, TX
4-21-29	NC-9636	San Diego, CA
4-25-29	NC-7121	Eastport, MD
6-2-29	NC-9676	Wichita, KS
6-24-29	NC-7416	St. Paul, MN
7-9-29	NC-9646	Clovis, NM
7-16-29	29-225	Brooks Field, TX
9-4-29	NC-9649	Mt. Taylor, NM
9-14-29	NC-5577	McCook, NB
9-14-29	NC-9614	Hasbrouck Heights, NJ
11-2-29	NC-5492	Chicago, IL
12-22-29	NC-9647	Indianapolis, IN
1-1-30	NC-400H	Pacasmayo, Peru
1-6-30	NC-8418	Montevideo, Uruguay
1-16-30	NC-9650	St. Louis, MO
1-19-30	NC-9689	Oceanside, CA
1-21-30	NC-415H	Miami, FL
1-23-30	29-223	Dayton, OH
2-2-30	29-222	Alba, MI
2-8-30	NC-2492	San Marcos, TX
2-20-30	Unknown	Columbus, OH
3-2-30	R-131	Cordoba, Argentina
3-3-30	29-221	Mitchel Field, NY
4-8-30	R-130	Buenos Aires, Argentina
5-22-30	NC-9651	LaLande, NM
6-5-30	NC-9675	Boston Harbor, MA
6-25-30	NC-7739	Chicago, IL
8-4-30	A8598	Ocotal, Nicaragua
8-22-30	OK-FOR	Jihlava, Czechoslovakia
9-9-30	NC-415H	Montreal, Canada
9-27-30	NC-8410	Chicago, IL
11-21-30	NC-7118	Glendale, CA
11-24-30	NX-419H	Dearborn, MI
11-24-30	NC-9606	Unknown
12-20-30	NC-9611	Jennerstown, PA
12-22-30	Unknown	Chile
1-2-31	G-ABHO	Tripoli
3-30-31	NC-8411	Columbus, OH
4-1-31	NC-8418	Ovalle, Chile
4-17-31	CV-FAI	Mihinia, India
4-29-31	NC-421H	Elyria, OH
7-29-31	NC-9664	David, Panama
8-8-31	NC-9662	Cincinnati, OH
8-14-31	NC-9647	Harrisburg, PA
8-19-31	NC-9665	Pittsburgh, PA
9-19-31	NX-9652	Dearborn, MI
10-10-31	NC-403H	Ilo, Peru
10-12-31	NC-7861	St. Louis, MO
10-21-31	NC-8400	North Beach, NY
10-27-31	NC-427H	Ashley, IN
11-27-31	NC-9647	Harrisburg, PA
12-19-31	NC-7119	Oklahoma City, OK
1-10-32	NC-434H	Dallas, TX
1-28-32	29-225	Biscoe, AR
2-16-32	NC-9607	Port Columbus, OH
2-28-32	NC-9613	Beaumont, TX
4-12-32	Unknown	Wabasha, MN
5-8-32	NC-8413	Amarillo, TX
5-19-32	NC-402H	Cerro Azul, Peru
6-5-32	NC-9651	Bushland, TX
6-16-32	NC-9676	Chicago, IL
7-1-32	A-8273	San Julian, Cuba
7-11-32	NC-9653	Seattle, WA
7-16-32	NC-403H	Santiago, Chile
9-4-32	NC-413H	Fort Worth, TX
10-2-32	NC-9664	San Lorenzo, Honduras
10-26-32	(5-AT-113)	Villa Montes, Bolivia
12-7-32	NC-5578	Burbank, CA
12-14-32	NC-9650	Amarillo, TX
12-32	NC-9653	Weed, CA
1-?-33	Unknown	Chicago, IL
1-24-33	NC-431H	Eugene, OR
2-10-33	NC-9666	Bakersfield, CA
3-22-33	A-8599	Virginia Beach, VA
3-23-33	29-222	Chanute Field, IL
3-28-33	29-225	Scott Field, IL
3-31-33	NC-7686	Neodesha, KS
4-24-33	31-402	Bolling Field, DC
5-27-33	31-403	Port Columbus, OH
6-2-33	NR-9614	Mineola, NY
7-1-33	NC-420H	Chicago, IL
7-2-33	NC-9610	Chicago, IL
8-29-33	NC-9607	Quay, NM
8-30-33	NC-8419	Chicago, IL
9-20-33	NC-9676	LaCrosse, WI
9-26-33	NS-1	Lakeland, MD
10-18-33	NC-4806?	Managua, Nicaragua
12-15-33	NC-6894	Perry, FL
3-22-34	NC-407H	Lima, Peru
3-24-34	31-401	Toledo, OH
4-23-34	NC-6893	Girard, KS
6-11-34	31-403	Oscada, MI
6-11-34	NC-8417	Junin, Argentina
7-1-34	NC-7586	Lima, OH

9-2-34	NC-9655	Cochrane, WI
10-14-34	NC-7583	Winchester, KY
10-26-34	NC-8403	Flat, AK
10-29-34	Unknown	La Cerba, Honduras
11-2-34	29-226	Fort Crockett, TX
12-10-34	NM-7	Palma Soriano, Cuba
1-10-35	31-401	Jacksonville, FL
1-14-35	NC-8499	Fairbanks, AK
4-21-35	Unknown	Hancock, MD
4-28-35	NC-7863	Gadsden, AL
5-7-35	Unknown	Lake Izabel, Guatemala
5-18-35	NC-7864	Flint, MI
6-16-35	NC-7865	Ashville, NC
6-24-35	F-31	Medellin, Colombia
6-24-35	(5-AT-112)	Medellin, Colombia
8-13-35	NC-15551	Santa Monica, CA
9-8-35	NC-430H	Solola, Guatemala
11-9-35	Unknown	Jutiapa, Honduras
12-24-35	NC-433H	Lima, Peru
2-1-36	A-8840	Quantico, VA
3-5-36	Unknown	Pengyi, China
3-9-36	NC-9668	Lansing, MI
3-36	Unknown	Nanking, China
3-26-36	XA-BCB	Amecameca, Mexico
7-15-36	NC-8410	Teller, AK
8-8-36	NC-5811	Hundred, WV
9-22-36	NC-7121	Norwich, NY
10-3-36	Unknown	Puerto Cabezas, Nicaragua
4-1-37	NC-8410	Slippery River, AK
5-29-37	NC-8404	Belleville, IL
7-13-37	NC-7865	Kannapolis, NC
8-21-37	NR-9648	Fairbanks, AK
9-15-37	NC-7684	Lansing, MI
9-28-37	LG-AAE	La Cumplida, Nicaragua
10-3-37	Unknown	Puerto Cabezas, Nicaragua
5-10-38	Unknown	Chile
7-6-38	NC-5577	Coffeyville, KS
8-11-38	NC-8413	Mankato, MN
9-3-38	NC-435H	Big Prarie, MT
10-20-38	NC-7865	Powellsville, NC
11-20-38	NC-8400	Cleveland, TN
1938	C-60	Quibdo, Colombia
3-2-39	CF-BEP	Vancouver, BC, Canada
3-14-39	Unknown	Unknown (SCADTA)
3-39	LG-AAH	Tegucigalpa, Honduras
4-15-39	NC-8411	El Carmen, Colombia
7-9-39	NC-6893	Austin, MN
9-21-39	NC-9613	Marcus, IL
10-22-39	NC-9608	Hickory, NC
11-1-39	TI-40	Parrita, Costa Rica
11-39	LG-AAG	Guatemala City, Guatemala
1-30-40	NC-5092	Carcross, Canada
2-20-40	Unknown	Prinzapolka, Nicaragua
2-25-40	TI-33	San Isidro, Costa Rica
3-5-40	XA-BCW	San Martin, Mexico
8-2-40	NC-8405	Liberty, NY
8-8-40	CF-AZB	Whitehorse, Canada
10-7-40	Unknown	Colon, Costa Rica
1940	TI-42	Puenta Arenas, Costa Rica
1940	TI-43	San Jose, Costa Rica
1-20-41	Unknown	Kian, China
4-4-41	Unknown	Nicaragua
4-21-41	FAC 641	Putumayo, Colombia
6-14-41	NC-5809	Yoakum, TX
8-14-41	FAC 642	Palanquero, Colombia
8-27-41	FAC 644	Tarapaca, Colombia
9-26-41	CB-CAM	Andes Mts, Bolivia
10-23-41	VH-UTB	Wau, New Guinea
11-15-41	NC-6894	Wichita Falls, TX
3-8-42	NC-9613	Corpus Christi, TX
4-17-42	NC-5093	Metz, MO
6-10-42	NC-5493	West Orange, NJ
11-21-42	NC-6892	Billings, MT
8-43	NC-9651	Fairbanks, AK
7-3-44	Unknown	Nicaragua
1944	XH-TAN	Tegucigalpa, Honduras
1944	Unknown	Honduras
4-5-46	HC-SBC	Ayuy, Ecuador
6-13-46	XA-FOH	El Arenal, Mexico
9-7-46	Unknown	La Esperanza, Cuba
9-10-46	HC-SBI	Tiputini, Ecuador
11-15-46	HC-SBD	Ayuy, Ecuador
11-15-46?	HC-SBJ	Ecuador
11-46	XA-FUP	Mexico
12-6-46	XA-FUQ	Mexico
1946	Unknown	Puerto Cabezas, Nicaragua
5-12-47	XA-DOL	Ometepec, Mexico
7-16-47	HC-SBK	Ecuador
1948	HK-1501	San Martin, Colombia
8-16-49	XA-GIJ	Putla, Mexico
10-27-49	XA-FON	Pinotepa Nacional, Mexico
7-26-51	XA-HIL	Mazatlan, Mexico
5-6-52	N-9606	Choteau, MT
7-14-53	N-8400	Boulder, MT
8-17-53	N-69905	Hungry Horse, MT
7-31-54	NC-9610	Kelleys Island, OH
7-3-55	XA-FON	San Martin, Mexico
1955	XB-NET	Mexico
6-15-56	N-9651	Middletown, NY
6-19-56	N-9642	Townsend, MT
8-4-59	NC-8419	Moose Creek, ID
12-6-70	N-9637	Bedminster, NJ
8-21-72	N-7684	Port Clinton, OH
8-23-73	N-9637	Peachtree City, GA
6-16-73	N-8407	Burlington, WI
2-6-77	N-76GC	Las Vegas, NV
7-1-77	N-7584	South Bass Island, OH
8-10-81	N-76GC	Las Vegas, NV

Appendix 15
Ford Factory Employees

An attempt has been made to find as many names of indiviuals whose work contributed to the production of the Tri-Motor. This has been difficult because of the traditional secrecy that was part of Henry Ford's style of management. As John Lee writes, in the AAHS Journal, "This organization in the 1924-1927 period was still a monolithic dictatorship, with Henry Ford at the top. Only two other men were ever mentioned; one was Henry's son Edsel, who was Vice President, and the other was William B. Mayo, Chief Engineer. Nobody else in the Company had a title." Harold Hicks, in a 1951 interview, remembered how George Prudden was fired for getting his photograph on page one of the Detroit Free Press as he was taking notes on the crash of the USS Shenandoah for Henry Ford.

Despite this, and because of letterheads, bills of sale, rememberences of individuals who worked in the plant and other items it has been possible to compile the following lists. It must be emphasized that this in not to be considered complete or official but on the other hand is more extensive than anything so far published.

The list of assembly and production workers turned up for the first time in 1991 due to the alertness and generosity of Ed Peck. It is from the estate of Edward Jackson who was employed by the Ford Motor Company for 42 years. It was labeled by him "Tri-Motor Days, Names of Fellow workers 1930." Jackson worked in the aircraft plant during the entire time of its existence from 1926-1933.

For the names of the Ford Motor Company pilots see Appendix 16.

1. Stout Metal Airplane Company - When Purchased by Ford.
William B. Stout, President
Glen Hoppin, Treasurer
George Prudden, Chief Engineer
Stanley Knauss, Shop Superintendent

2. Officers - Stout Metal Airplane Company (January 1930)
Edsel B. Ford, President
William B. Mayo, Vice President
B.J. Craig, Sectretary-Treasurer

3. Officers - Ford Motor Company, Airplane Division (October 1931)
Edsel B. Ford, President
P.E. Martin, Vice President
B.J. Craig, Secretary

4. Special Titles
Robert T. Walker; Assistant to W.B. Mayo (1925-1933).
G. Goin; Superintendent of Manufacturing (1925-1933).
Including maintenance, service and sales of parts.
Harold A. Hicks; Chief of Design and Development (1925-1933).
Leroy Manning; Manager of Ford Airport and Chief Pilot.
William F. Bliss; Ford Airways Division (1925-1928).
Edward C. Jackson; General Foreman on Assembly (1926-1933).
Alex Runkis; Floor Superintendent over all manufacturing of Tri-Motors (1926-1933).
Milton Beal; Chief Inspector.
Gilbert C. Peterson; Sales Manager (1929-1932).
J. Parker Van Zandt; Chief Pilot and Operations Manager 1926-1927, European Aviation Representative 1929-1930.

5. Engineers
Arthur Buchner, Dart, Al Esper (wind tunnel). Harold Hicks, Harry Karcher, Otto Koppen, John G. Lee, James S. McDonnell, Ross, Tom Towle, J. Parker Van Zandt, Horace E. Weihmiller, Wright.

6. Shop Supervisors
H. Fifield, Hull, Edwin Jackson, C. Johnson.

7. Production and Assembly Employees

R. Allen
C. Amerman
L. Anderson
Mark Assenmacher

Ball
Ballau
J. N. Barnabee
A. Barschoff
A, Beaton
R. Bennet
H. Bensen
Bibeau
Fred Bilbrough
F. Billbraugh
L. Bingham
H. Bird
H. Bishop
William Black
Bodger
W. Bonestelle
A. Bonstelle
J. Bowen
F. Bowein
W. Bowles
George Boyette
E. Bragg
J. Breejen
C. Brenninger
F. Brierton
William Brodie
R. Brooks
J. Brown
J. Brownville

J. Cain
L. Camen
Napoleon Carrier
Fred Chadwick
M. Chaowin
W. Chaowin
R. Charbonease
Mat Chowhan
R. Clay
W. Colberth
P. Cook
C. Cowan
R. Crambic
S. Crawford
R. Crine

Davis
D. Deely
M. Depriest
F. Dostert
A. Dowbrowski
W. Dowd
E. Duback
P. Dupont
L. Dylus

N. Edwards
E. Effeinger
K. Ehrheart
F. Elexy
Willard Ely
M. Esselin
H. Evans

D. Faust
Fiddler
A. Foder
R. Foster
H. Fowler
W. Foyer
Freeman
French
R. Friewald

E. Galke
Lawerence Galler
M. Galler
W. Galusha
Gardner
G. Garnett
B. Gayne
Peter Geary
Ray Gehrig
H. Gidson
C. Gilbert
F. Gildersleeve
Glumm
G. Gnebba
J. Gnibba
Sam Goldberg
George Goo
G. Goodfellow
Z. Goodrum
G. Gordon
V. Gorris
Merril Grix
Guein
G. Gundy

Haddow
T. Hale
G. Halgren
K. Hall
T. Halpin
J. Harding
J. Hargraves
H. Herbein
F. Heuttman
Hill
C. Hocking
F. Hoffman
G. Hoffman
C. Holland
J. Hunter
J. Hurley
Walter Hurst

Steve Jacobowski
F. James
O. Jarsel
Jennings
John Johnson
A. Jumelweg

A. Key
J. Kischell
Ed Kivari
F. Kornrumph
J. Koshtrzci
C. Kotcher

A. Labozik
C. LaCroix
Paul LaCroix
P. Lamar
R. LaMarr
M. Lample
L. Lapanya
A. Laschinsky
George Lavision
Henry Lavigne
J. Leverton
H. Lawrence

G. Lembeck
Fred Lemon
H. Levine
H. Lindemuth
C. Loftos
Louellar
C. Loyd
C. Lubs
Lucas
S. Lumm
A. Luther

S. Majewsky
W. Marker
H. Marshall
R. Martin
R. Martz
G. McArthur
R. McArthur
W. McBain
J. McCourtin
D. McDonald
K. McDonald
McEwin
J. McFee
A. McGill
J. McGurck
McMillan
Brent Meland
G. Meland
G. Melefant
Lynch Mercure
F. Mohn

Fred Monteith
F. Moore
Donald Morris
G. Morris
Ed Motle
V. Mudinger
C. Muir
A. Mulder
F. Munn

M. Nedin
H. Nelson
James Nelson
W. Nichol
Mark Norheim

F. Oklat
J. O'Reilly
D. Ort
T. Overall

F. Patrick
A. Payette
R. Paylitz
V. Pell
R. Pender
R. Peterson
E. Pitt
H. Plowman
W. Podsiadly
G. Pucareiv
Purkevich

D. Rache
A. Rankin
V. Raschke
Redcraft
Paul Renaud
A. Rickey
H. Ristow
J. Ritchie
J. Ross
L. Rozdoske

G. Sagan
Samson
F. Satchel
Ralph Saunders
H. Schuabelt
G. Schaufman
D. Schmank
U. Schemansky
A. Schoenfield
Clarence Scott
T. Seat
L. Sexton
H. Shepard
J. Slayton
Artemas Smith
C. Smith

E. Snyder
W. Spain
J. Spence
M. Spencer
Squires
W. Stack
N. Stanley
P. Staples
G. Sterling
W. Sterling
J. Stewart
C. Stoneking
F. Stoneking

E. Stratotanovich
Earl Stringer
J. Sweggles
M. Swiezer
S. Symes

Tackener
V. Taiple
H. Teague
Jerome Theisen
Charles Thomson
G. Thurlow
M. Todt

C. Trombly
George Tyle

D. Vallance
J. Valante
F. Van Pette
G. Van Sickle
E. Villaire
Oliver Vincient

Walker
N. Wallis
W. Wallis

C. Walters
H. Warner
H. Weingarten
F. West
J. Wickersham
H. Williams
Walter Witzawak
J. Woesti
Woolbraith
W. Wremm

A. Zarnowski

Appendix 16
Ford Tri-Motor Pilots

One of the goals involved in this Ford research over the years has been to document as many pilot's names as possible. This has turned out to be as difficult as obtaining information on the Tri-Motors themselves.

The following lists are as accurate and complete as it has been possible to make them after years of research. The major problem is that few airlines flew only Ford Tri-Motors at a given period, thus a list of the pilots flying for a given airline in 1930, for example, does not necessarily mean that they all flew Fords. And, in addition, the statement that "he flew trimotors in the 1930s" is insufficient since there were Boeing, Fokker and Stinson trimotors in use at the same time as the Fords. Several names are from correspondence with pilots of the 1930s and the extensive list of TWA pilots is the result of the generous contribution of information from TWA Captains Melvin Bowen and Ed Betts.

It seems probable that the majority of the individual owners of Fords, as listed in Table 10, also flew their planes. Additional names of pilots have been listed throughout the book and in photo captions.

It is important to give credit to these pioneers and to document as well as possible for the first time the names of those that are known.

Their pilot license numbers have been added, where known, to give an idea of their relative standing. It should be mentioned, however, that although these are good indications of the early status of pilots that it is important to understand how they were issued. There were no government licenses for aircraft, pilots or mechanics before January 1, 1927. There was not even a government agency to establish requirements and issue the licenses. When this came about as a result of the 1926 Air Commerce Act the Department of Commerce, Bureau of Aeronautics, was established in Washington, D. C. This eventually became the Civil Aeronautics Administration (CAA) and finally the Federal Aviation Administration (FAA).

At this point the usual thing happened, i.e. those who are in a position to issue license numbers give themselves the first numbers. So it should be understood that the lowest numbers did not go to those who at that time had been flying the longest. In some cases higher numbers were issued simply because some old time pilots were in no hurry to apply, fill out forms and be given a test.

Thus it was that License No.1 was issued to William P. McCracken, No. 2 to Clarence M. Young, No. 3 to Ralph G. Lockwood, and No. 5 to Frank H. Jerdone, all of the Bureau of Aeronautics. By comparison Charles A. Lindbergh was issued No. 69. Despite all of this it is still very impressive to the author to see these low numbers and realize that his license number of 107709 was issued in 1941.

American Airways/American Airlines
Herbert W. Anderson
Myron G. Beard (755)
Simon P. Bittner (2412)
Daniel L. Boone (1230)
Walter W. Braznell (2636)
J.H. Burns
Arthur L. Caperton (166)
Paul L. Carpenter (1135)
Erwyn M. Carson (8586)
Val Chick
William J. Dewald
A.H. DeWitt
Ernest E. Dryer (2706)
Joe B. Glass
Paul V. Gustine (1856)
T.J. Haire
Laurence W. Harris (5685)

Clyde M. Holbrook
L.P. Hudson
Walter J. Hunter (3703)
Robert M. Jewell (558)
M.M. Kay
Roscoe V. Kent (1254)
Durward W. Ledbetter (2424)
T.J. Lee
George M. McCabe (964)
Duncan McCallum (111)
R.C. Maguire
William A. McDonald (4255)
Wellington P. McFail (900)
Eoy L. Mitchell (662)
Byron C. Moore (2059)
Owen O'Connor
Marvin T. Odell
S.D. Page
Bledsoe Payne
Homer J. Rader (766)
R.J. Rentz
U.E. Rousch
Harold B. Russell (2517)
R.W. Sanford
Hiram W. Sheridan (4119)
Eyer L. Sloniger (432)
Fred D. Smith
Eugene R. Stotts (2521)
Paul A. Vance (523)
Warren R. Vine (671)
James H. Walker (923)
Howard H. West (6100)
Joe F. Westover (1668)
Sherman L. Willard (197)
Ray D. Wonsey (1385)
Gerald H. Woolweaver (7683)

Central Airlines
Al Brooks
Albert C. Carl
Walter J. Carr
James H. Carmichael
Bill Day
Jack Fife
Jim Gott
Mac McDonough
Merle Moltrop
Helen Richey
Trow Sebree
Duke Slimon
Horace Stark
Roger H. Taylor

China National Aviation Corp. (CNAC)
E.M. Allison
.... Black
Harold Chin
Arthur Kidder
Floyd Nelson
Byron G. O'Hara (29374)
Charles L. Sharp
P.T. Thom
Bernard Wong
Donald Wong

Cia Mexicana de Aviacion
Precidio Acosta
K.V. Beer
Adrian Borchers
W.W. Bradley
Sanchez Cardenas
G. Craigher
V.A. Dirrey
C.M. Drayton
A.D. Durst
H.E. Gray
A.J. Nieto
F.J. Nolan
H.T. Phels
E.A. E. Pratt
R. Torres Rico
H.W. Sheridan
W. Stone
S.F. Varian
W.R. Warren

Colonial Air Transport
(And Colonial Division of American Airways)
Edward C. Carrington (1894)
Frank Crowley
Harold W. Crowley (2704)
Carl A. Dixon
Walter Hughen
Bill Lester
Richard W. Mackie (2174)
Jesse T. Meneffee (1533)
Charles Moses
Owen J. O'Connor
Paul E. Reeder
Wallace M. Striker
"Pie" Swanson
E.H. Veblen
Earl Ward
Edwin T. Weatherdon (1911)
Kirby Whitsett
Ray D. Wonsey (1385)
Charles L. Wright

Eastern Air Transport
Frank B. Kern (639)
Gil Waller (1568)

Ford Motor Company
Paul F. Baer (1587)
Dean W. Burford (302)
Harry J. Brooks
John A. Collings (267)
Edward O. DeLarm (2844)
Lawrence G. Fritz (337)
Hylas H. Gallup (216)
Edward G. Hamilton (366)
Arthur K. Horner (1532)

Benjamin O. Howard (1083)
Perry G. Hutton (547)
Ross Kirkpatrick
Wharton E. Larned (1424)
Harold Little (333)
Leroy T. Manning (307)
Lester T. Munger (1656)
William A. Munn (814)
Carlyle LaMar Nelson (1203)
Earl Parker (128)
Harry L. Russell
Rudolph W. Schroeder (6988)
J.H. Smart
F.V. Tompkins (1272)
Byron S. Warner
Ray D. Wonsey (1385)
Roderick M. Wright
Myron E. Zeller

Island Air Service/Island Air Lines
R.N. Anderson
Ed Bush
Dave St. Clair
Ralph Dietrick
Harold Hauck
Milton Hersberger (4777)
Jack Marshall
David Martin
Dave Nehls
Hugo M. Rosendahl
Ed Rusch
Jan Shaffer
George Tyler
Newell Witte

Johnson Flying Service
Frank Borgeson
Merle "Abe" Bowler
Bob Culver
Hoyt DeMers
Jim Dillon
Dick Duffield
Warren Ellison
Bob Fogg
Ken Huber
Jack Hughes
Richard L. Johnson (6996)
Robert R. Johnson (2772)
Jim Larkin
Gil Musgrove
Swede Nelson
Ken Roth
Willis Penn Stohr (13743)
Earl Vance
Bob Vallance

Maddux Air Lines and TAT-MADDUX
George W. Allen (1634)
Henry G. Andy Andrews (914)
Amberse M. Banks
Edward A. Bellande (664)
"Ace" Bergundi
Ken Blaney
E.F. Brown
Arthur C. Burns (1290)
Dean Burford
Milo H. Campbell (883)
Jack Collier
Amos W. Collins
Paul F. Collins
Raymond C. Crawford (1679)
Edwin A. Dietel
Lawrence G. Fritz (337)
John A. Guglielmetti (221)
Marino J. Guglielmetti (5064)
Jessie Hart
Noble G. Heuter
Jack Hewson
William Houston
Ben O. Howard
Theodore R. Howe (2462)
T. Benson Hoye
Charles A. LaJotte (162)
Nick A. Laurenzana
Vernon R. Lucas
Tex Marley
Harry W. McGee
William Monday
John J. Montijo (7040)
Maurice H. Murphy (551)
Fred R. Pastorious (9747)
Louis Pratt
L.A. "Slim" Perrett
Felix F. Preeg (3625)
Richard Reynaldi
Les Rodda
Basil T. Russell (2067)
Paul P. Scott
Stephen R. Shore
Morley F. Slaght (5851)
Albert D. Smith
Ernest LeRoy Smith (2253)
Moye W. Stephens Jr. (1667)
J.B. Stowe
Daniel W. Tomlinson (764)
F.V. Tomkins (1272)
Fred (Floyd?) Walker (F.L.)
Goodwin "Ted" Weaver (2734)
Frederic "Doc" Whitney (1312)
Stuart Wilkinson
Al Wilson
Clarence Woods

Mamer Air Transport
Ben Beiber
Vernon Bookwalter (2530)
Lou Brennan
Ralph O. Daniel (4720)
George Hallett
John Hounsel
Nick B. Mamer (817)
Art Walker

National Air Transport/Pacific Air Transport/United Air Lines
Harold Adams
Walter J. Addems (965)
W. Ray Allemang
Frederick B. Angstadt
Clarence R. Beindorf
James Lamont Brandon (190)
Edward J. Brooks
Leland C. Brown
Robert E. Coulter
Robert F. Dawson
Richard L. Dobie (171)
Walter Eefsen
James N. Going
L.M. Gravis
Edwin B. Gray (6647)
George B. Grogan
John A. Herlihy (6002)
Lawrence H. Holsinger
Kenneth Householder
C.W. Hudson
James O. Johnson
Paul E. Johnson
A.F. Kalberer
Paul Kanuit
Willis H. Kennedy
Edward T. Kiessig (15095)
Harold L. Knoop
W.E. Larned (1424)
H.P. Little
Egbert P. Lott
Arthur C. Lybarger
Enery J. Martin
E. "Mike" Matucha
Everett L. McMillen
C.C. Melton
Frank Morton
Leigh R. Murphy
John G. Murray
Fred B. Novinger
John J. O'Brien
Paul B. Payne
Charles E. Peebles (1122)
R.W. Radell
Paul E. Reeder (2545)
Cameron T. Robertson (1666)
E.C. Rockwood
Samuel J. Sampson (1547)
Clarence Savage
Marion Sterling (50)
W.L. Smith
W.J. Spencer
Grover Taylor
Bill Williams
Warren D. Williams
J.F. Wolf

New York, Rio & Buenos Aires Line (NYRBA)
Nat C. Browne
Edward O. DeLarm (2844)
Edward C. Hamilton (366)
John K. Montgomery
Eduardo Olivero

Northwest Airways
Walter. R. Bullock (606)
Homer F. Cole (2489)
Leon. S. DeLong (2302)
Mal B. Freeburg (608)
Melvin. O. Fried (2236)
Charles W. Holman (1026)
Robert Johnson
Joseph E. Kimm (17892)
John F. Malone (2211)
Karl R. Martin (1106)
Eddie Middaugh
Russell J. McNown (2508)
Anthony R. Mensing Jr. (4096)
Joseph E. Ohrbeck (2233)
Chadwick B. Smith (1444)
Charles L. Smith (9460)
Robert L. Smith (4153)
Fred W. Whittemore (2554)

Pan American Airways/Pan American Grace
Charles B. Ames (4662)
"Kitty" Barrows
William F. Baxter (7646)
Gilbert B. Blackmore
Norvell O. Carmichael (5379)
Harry F. Colliver (7617)
Vernon A. Dorrell (2669)
William S. Doxey
Cornelius K. Dunbar (15006)
Homer V. Farris
Robert Henry Fatt Jr. (118)
James L. Fleming (31258)
Richard J. Grier (6104)
John J. Harris
Lewis H. Holman (8020)
Thomas F. Jardine (2909)
Benjamin F. Jones (7278)
Alexander C. Knothe (24665)
George Kraigher (404)
Henry C. Kristofferson (9071)
Carl F. Lindenberg
Wilbur W. Lynch (26558)
Arthur L. McCullough (2425)
Harold McMickle
C.W. Myers
Archie Paschal
Byron D. Rickards (3235)
Charles J. Robinson
Warren B. Smith (1724)
Frederick T. Sterling Jr. (19617)
John H. Tilton
Charles R. Titus (5597)
Clifford Travis
John E. Tremayne (3006)
John I. Wagner (3591)
Raymond Williams
Bill Winston

Scenic Airways/Grand Canyon Airlines (1928-1938)
Walter R. Ballard (2276)
Dean W. Burford (302)
Ed Campbell
George E. Johnsen (15942)
Irving B. Kravitz (8341)
J.B. Massick
Art Nelson
Carlyle LaMar Nelson (1203)
Loyal T. Penn (12864)
Richard H. Renaldi (2675)
Glover E. Ruckstell (10006)
Jack W. Thornburg (5125)
Ernie Tissot
J. Parker VanZandt (17)
Malcolm Wallace

Scenic Airlines/Grand Canyon Airlines (1976-1992)
Carl Allison
Art Blissitt
Hank Borgerding
Doug Buchanan
Hoot Gibson
Bernie Godlove
Bryan Godlove
Peter Mason
Jim Purcell
Gerald Schirmer
Jerry Terstiege

Southwest Air Fast Express (SAFE)
Robert W. Cantwell (1466)
Lawrence G. Fritz (337)
Maurice A. Marrs (2596)
Charles E. Norton

South American Gulf Oil Company
Richard A. Behrens (23341)
William C. Brown (32360)
William N. Craig (29391)
W. Myron Hightower (18689)
Edward S. Maloney (16075)

Stout Air Lines
James Lamont Brandon (190)
Leland C. Brown
L.W. Bryant
Arthur K. Horner (1532)
James O. Johnson
Wharton E. Larned (1424)
Lee R. Murphy
Ralph A. Reed (112)
Byron D. Rickards (3235)
Leon D. Sherrick
Samuel J. Taylor
Byron S. Warner

T.A.C.A.
Herbert W. Anderson
Robert E. Anson
.... Baldenberg
Dick Barker
Lynn F. Berkenkamp (13458)
Rusty Bodemer
Frederick Broham
Edward C. Brice
W. Bruenersten
Pete Clerenger
Clare Coe
Howard B. "Pete" Crawford (228)
Edward DeLarm (2844)
Bob Deuhl
Bob Edgerton
Robert B. Ewalt
Luis Alonso Fiallos
Robert C. Forsblade
Ron George
Bob Grundy
Charles J. Hirst
Henry E. Hix (28004)
Frank H. Jerdone (5)
Alfred Juul
Jack Keene
Wayne F. Lansing (274)
Bill Lyons
Roman Macaya
Enrique Malek
Ken Matheson
Charles E. Mathews
John Matthews
Ken R. Meinard
John Menefee
Paul Moore
Kendrick Murray
Pappy Norton
Henry Oakes
David W. Ohlwiler
Carl R. Overly (28225)
Samuel D. Penry (10943)
L.A. "Slim" Perrett
Louie Roppe
Herman Usher Rousch
George Schleppey
Thurston Schutz
Cornell N. Shelton
Lynn Shepperd (Shepard)
Ralph A. Shope
Grant Spillman
Harold A. White
Sherman "Snark" Wilson
Floyd Wright
Guillermo Xucla
Lowell Yerex
Fred Young

Transcontinental & Western Airlines (TWA)
Clifford V. Abbott (3317)
Henry G. Andrews
Theodore H. Ashford (4962)
Walter L. Avery
W. Glenn Barcus
Joseph S. Bartles (5378)

Edward A. Bellande (664)
Lynn Berkenkamp
Benjamin Billings
Lester Bishop
Ken Blaney
Lawrence Fred Bohnet
Dana Boller
Harvey F. Bolton
Edward Z. Boqua (20585)
John E. Bowen
Melvin O. Bowen (4562)
George W. Brill (2836)
Albion Brooks
J.R. Brooks
Otis F. Bryan (6968)
Dean W. Burford (302)
Arthur C. Burns (1290)
Harry E. Campbell (6336)
Milo H. Campbell (883)
William M. Campbell (6289)
Lawrence J. Chiappino (2940)
J.D. Christian
Floyd F. Church
Herbert Clark
John A. Collings (267)
Amos W. Collins (3329)
Richard G. Conover
F.O. Converse
O. William Coyle
C.D. Daily
William H. Devries
Russell J. Dick
Andrew Dixon
William H. Dowling
Harry Downes
Robert A. Eccles
James O. Eisheid (3658)
Otto Ferguson
S.M. Fergusson
Howard M. Fey (4503)
Lee Flanagin (1280)
Earl W. Fleet (530)
Paul S. Frederickson (5428)
L.G. Fritz (337)
Jack Fry (933)
Robert G. Fry
Hylas H."Pat" Gallup (216)
J.J. Garrigan
Hal George
Harvey C. Goakes
Waldon "Swede" Golien (5207)
Lewis W. Goss (1081)
Ormand M. Gove (8367)
John D. Graves
Kenneth H. Greeson
Howard E. Hall (4296)
Richard G. Hanson (2767)
John E. Harlin (6118)
Oscar R. "Ted" Heueter
Richard A. Heideman (2961)
Edgar Ted Hereford (5342)
Noble G. Heuter
Marion L. Hoblit (7884)
R.H. Hoffman
Halbert H. Holloway (2866)
George L. Houle
Harlan Hull
J.C. Hutchinson
Ellsworth A. Jaquish (12629)
Wallace W. Jones
Eugene O. Klose (1086)
Irving S. Kravitz (8341)
Robert M. Larson (397)
Royal T. Leonard (2627)
Robert S. LeRoy (1005)
Evan Lewis (18022)
Harry C. Lewis
J.H. Lewis
Charles A. Lindbergh (69)
Alvene A. Litzenberger
Rex Long
H.J. Lynch
Jessie Mathias
Daniel M. Medler (8774)
Raymond J. Merritt
Douglas L. Mesker
Glen Miller
Wilton "Red" Miller (8975)
R.T. Minor
Theodore M. Moffitt (1205)
William Monday
Silas A. Morehouse (399)
Ralph Montee
Harold P. Moon
Howard R. Morgan
Willard A. Morris
N.C. Morse
James M. Moser
Jack Moxness
Lester D. Munger (1656)
Harry Musick
C. Lamar Nelson (1203)
Frank E. Niswander (1305)
Earl J. Noe
Ivan R. Olson
Lloyd W. Olson (18621)
Alton N. Parker (852)
L.A. "Slim" Perrett
Wendell F. Peterson
Wesley F. Phillipi
William F. Piper Jr. (21562)
Felix F. Preeg (3625)
George C. Price
Carl W. Rach (830)
Peter M. Redpath (9749)
George K. Rice (572)
Fred G. Richardson (3014)
Paul E. Richter Jr. (501)
Ralph W. Ritchie
Charles E. Robey
James H. Roe (14114)
P.J. Russell

Percy T.W. Scott
Walter W. Seyerle
Stephen R. Shore (1203)
Robert L. Simons
Walton H. Smiley (9682)
Albert D. Smith (573)
Ernest L. Smith (2253)
Wesley L. Smith
Harold B. Snead
Stanley T. Stanton (3250)
Moye W. Stephens Jr. (1667)
R.E. Supple
Roger H. Taylor
Donald R. Terry (3364)
Jack Thornburg (5125)
D.W. Tomlinson (764)
Harvey Vence
Frank D. "Jack" Wade
Truman T. Wadlow
Don Walbridge
John G. Walsh
Waldo Waterman
Goodwin K."Ted" Weaver (2734)
Don Welbridge
St. Clair D. Welsh (739)
Frederick "Doc" Whitney
Ardell M. Wilkens
Frank E. Williams (1022)
Laurence L. Williams (23616)
Maurice C. Williams (23615)
Wayne C. Williams (6680)
Franklin Young (2832)
H.J. Zimmerman

Bibliography

(Listing by Date Published)

71st Congress, 3rd Session, Senate Document 319, ". . . Aircraft accidents which have occurred between the dates of May 20, 1926, and May 16, 1930, of which the department has a record." Lists Place and Date, Pilot and Passengers Names, Aircraft Model, Engine, and Cause. U.S. Government Printing Office, Washington, D.C., 1931.

Wilks, Russell, "When Ford Went Up", *Popular Aviation*, December 1927, pp. 7-10.

"Cancelled Aircraft Licenses", *Air Transportation*, September 22, 1928, p. 38.

Longenecker, Charles, "How Ford Planes are Built at Dearborn", *Heat Treating and Forging*, September 1928, pp. 1032-1035.

Air Transportation, August 18, 1928 to October 13, 1928. Weekly lists of Licensed and Identified Aircraft.

Barker, Fowler, "Barnstorming in a Ford Tri-Motor", *Aviation*, December 22, 1928, pp. 2036-2037.

Now That Man Has Wings, Ford Motor Company, Dearborn, 1928, 32 pages, 17 illustrations.

Air Transportation, January 26, 1929. Annual list of licensed and identified aircraft.

"Mexican Aircraft Licenses", *Air Transportation*, April 6, 1929, p.63.

Weekly List of Licensed Aircraft, June to December, 1929, Aeronautical Chamber of Commerce of America, NYC.

Weekly List of Licenses, Aircraft, Pilots, Mechanics and Students, Vol.3 Nos 1-53, January 1931 to January 1932, Aeronautical Chamber of Commerce of America, NYC, 1931-1932.

Air Commerce Bulletin, Vol.1, No.1 (July 1, 1929) to Vol.11, No.6 (December 15, 1939), U.S. Department of Commerce, Washington, D.C.

Book of Instruction, *Ford All-Metal Monoplane*, Ford Motor Company, Dearborn, 1929, 114 pages.

Lift Up Your Eyes, Ford Motor Company, 1929. Reprints of company advertisements, also contains front and side view factory drawings of the 4-AT on the inside covers.

1929 Register, American Bureau of Aircraft, NYC, 1929.

Nevill, John T., "Ford Motor Company and American Aeronautic Development", *Aviation*:
Part 1 - June 1, 1929, pp. 1870-1873
Part 2 - June 15, 1929, pp. 2073-2076
Part 3 - July 6, 1929, pp. 41-44
Part 4 - July 27, 1929, pp. 229-231
Part 5 - August 10, 1929, pp. 306-308
Part 6 - August 17, 1929, pp. 339-341
Part 7 - September 14, 1929, pp. 568-570
Part 8 - October 12, 1929, pp. 753-755

"Converted 5-AT Seaplane", *Aviation*, March 1, 1930, p.453. "Ford 5-AT Club Plane", Aero Digest, March 1930, pp. 124-126.

Stoll, Bert, "Air Transportation with Safety; A Brief History of a Million Miles of Flying on Stout Air Lines", *Aero Digest*, May 1930, pp. 55-56.

Russell, Harry L., "How I Flew The Tour", *Aviation*, November 1930, pp. 281-282. (Flying the 7-AT).

Ford News, November 15, 1930, p.257; December 15, 1930, p.279; December 1931, p.9.

Report on Civil Aviation and Civil Government Operations 1929, Canada, Department of National Defense, 1930, pp. 72-87, pg.97 ills.

General Description Ford All-Metal Transport Planes, Ford Motor Company, Dearborn, 1930.

Licensed and Identified Aircraft, annual 1930-1939, Aeronautical Chamber of Commerce of America, NYC.

"The Giant Ford Comes To China", *The Far Eastern Review*, January 1931, pp. 27-28. (Has four large photos).

Foreign Aeronautical News, Department of Commerce, Bureau of Foreign and Domestic Commerce, No.236, February 27, 1931.

Manning, LeRoy, "Touring Europe By Private Plane", *Aviation*, April 1931, pp. 232-235.

"Fifty-Five Miles Over New York For Five Dollars", *Airports and Airlines*, November 1931, pp. 16-17.

U.S. Army Air Corps Materiel Division, Technical Report No.3507, Performance Test of Ford XB-906.

Parts Price List, Ford Tri-Motor Airplane, Ford Motor Company, Dearborn, February 1932.

"The New Ford Airliner", *Aero Digest*, April 1932, pp. 64-68.

Wakefield, Newton. "Mine Development by Airplane", *Engineering and Mining Journal*, May 1932, pp 264-265.

Aircraft International Register 1933, Bureau Veritas, Paris, 1933.

Scheduled Airline Aircraft in Service and Reserve, 1933-1938 (annual), U.S. Department of Commerce, CAA (Departmental mimeographed report listing NC Number, ATC, Model, Type, Engine, Year Built and Airline).

"Complete Task Flying 735 Tons Over The Andes", Pan American Air Ways, September-October 1934.

"Planes Move 735 Tons of Equipment to Mine; Rise 16,000 Feet in Andes With 4,300 Pounds", *New York Times*, November 2, 1934, p.25.

Zalles, Robert I., "Trucking In The Clouds", *The Grace Log*, November-December 1934, pp. 571-577.

"TWA Ford Trimotors Retired", *Popular Aviation*, December 1934, p.353.

Ford Seaplane for River Service in Colombia", *Aviation*, May 1935, pp. 187-188.

"Douglas Aircraft", *Fortune*, May 1935, pp. 81, 83.

Van Dusen, William (PAA), "Mine Freight by Air in South America", *Engineering and Mining Journal*, November 1935, pp. 569-570.

Prouty, Roswell E., "Airplanes Aid Mining in Honduras", *Engineering and Mining Journal*, December 1935, p. 633.

Inspection Handbook of Approved Aircraft, Chapter XVIII, Department of Commerce, CAA, March 1936.

Rock, Joseph F., "By Aeroplane Over Yunnan", *The North-China Daily News*, March 2 and 3, 1936.

"Flying Machinery Into an Andes Mining Camp", *Compressed Air Magazine*, December 1936, pp. 5206-5207.

Semple, C. Carleton, "Peru's Gold-Mining Industry Grows", *Engineering and Mining Journal*, December 1936, pp. 609-612.

"Gold Mine Opened by Flying Freight", Pan American Air Ways, January 1938.

Deutsch, Hermann B., "Flying The Jungle Run", *The Saturday Evening Post*, September 3, 1938, pp. 10-11, 67, 69-70, 72.

Statistical Study of Registered Aircraft, January 1, 1939, CAA.

Certificated and Uncertificated Aircraft, February 1939 and February 1940 (annual), Aeronautical Chamber of Commerce of America, NYC.

Collings, John F., "Farewell, Tin Goose", *Popular Aviation*, February 1939, pp. 20-23.

Rand, Kurt, "Pacific To Atlantic – In 29 Minutes!", *Popular Aviation*, February 1939, pp. 28-30, 72.

Lincoln, Garland, "I Learned About Flying, No. 1", *Popular Aviation* May 1939, pp. 18-19, 74. (Includes large photo of NR-9648 upside down in the Alaskan tundra).

Winston, Robert A., "Barnstorming in the Modern Manner", *Sportsman Pilot*, September 15, 1939, pp. 12-13, 28.

Branch, Eyre, "Wings Over Central America, The Story of T.A.C.A.", *The Intava World*, Vol.2, No.1, October 1939, pp. 2-8.

Lansing, Wayne F., "I Learned About Flying From That! No.18", *Popular Aviation*, October 1940, pp. 31, 80.

Hancock, Ralph, "TACA . . . Jungle Air Freighter", *Aviation*, January 1940, pp. 30-31, 88.

Hancock, Ralph, "TACA: Gold Express", *The Intava World*, Vol.3, No.2, December 1940, pp. 38-40.

"Bill Stout", *Fortune*, January 1941, pp. 46-51.

Sheehan, William M., "Coming: A Merchant Aerine", *Flying*, August 1942, pp. 28-30.

Andrews, Paul, "Freedom of the Skies", *Air News*, May 1943, pp. 14-17.

Severin, Kurt, "South America Must Fly", *Air Progress*, July 1943, pp. 8-11, 61.

Reiss, George R., "Ahead of His Time", *Air Trails Pictorial*;
Part 1 - November 1943, pp. 18-19
Part 2 - December 1943, pp. 32-33

"What Has Become of Ford's Tri-motors?", *Southern Flight*, May 1944, p.68.

Leiding, Oscar, "One-Man Airline" (pp. 12-19), and "Two-Man Maintenance" (pp. 115-119), *Air Transport Operations and Maintenance Notebook*, McGraw-Hill Publishing Co., NYC, 1944.

Smith, Henry Ladd. *Airways (The History of Commercial Aviation in the United States)*, Alfred A. Knopf, NY, 1944.

"Ford and Aviation", 28-page press release, Ford News Bureau, undated; about June 1944.

Fahey, James C., *U.S. Army Aircraft 1908-1946, Ships and Aircraft*, NYC, 1946.

The Official CAA Directory of Certificated Aircraft - 1946, Haddaway-Reed Publishing Company, Dallas, 1946.

Aircraft Listing - July 1, 1949, Office of Aviation Safety, U.S. Department of Commerce, CAA. (Supersedes Chapter XVIII of the Inspection Handbook, i.e. aircraft of which not over 50 are in service), pp. 92-93.

Equipment of the Foreign Scheduled Common Carrier Airlines, March 1, 1950, Foreign Air Transport Division, Bureau of Economic Regulation, U.S. Civil Aeronautics Board.

Clark, R.J., "Tin Goose", *Aeronautica*, January-March 1952, pp. 6-8.

"Tin Goose", *Aeronautica*, July-December 1952, p.7.

Stocker, Joseph, "Those Fabulous Flying Fords", *Popular Mechanics*, June 1953, pp. 65-69.

"Stout Plans Tri-Motor Comeback", *Aviation Week*, December 28, 1953.

Mayer, Meyer, Austrian & Platt, *Corporate and Legal History of United Air Lines and its Predecessors and Subsidiaries 1925-1945*, The Twentieth Century Press, Chicago, 1953. pp. 65, 66, 299, 300.

"Backers Plan Tri-Motor Prototype", *Aviation Week*, May 17, 1954, p.18.

Weiss, David A., "Tin Goose of the Airways", *Coronet*, August 1955, pp. 105-108.

"The Return of the Tin Goose", *Bee-Hive*, United Aircraft Corporation, Fall 1955, p.24.

McKibben, Gordon, "Tin Goose Waddles To Jet Age Comeback After 25-Year Flight", *Wall Street Journal*, July 17, 1956, pp. 1, 9.

Technical Proposal 15-AT "Stout Bushmaster" STOL Type Aircraft for United States Army Aviation, Hayden Aircraft Corporation, Report No.312, September 1956.

Alder, Donald H., "The Tin Goose Waddles Back in Jet Age", *The Swath*, November 1956, pp. 5, 7, 13.

Northwest Airlines News, "30th Anniversary Issue", Vol.13, Nos.11-12, November-December 1956. (Devoted to the cross country flight of the Ford, 12 pages, over 44 photos).

"Ford Tri-Motor and Boeing Stratocruiser", "The Tin Goose", "Experience With A Ford Tri-Motor", "Airplane of Distinction", "No. 8419 Coast-to-Coast", *Antique Airplane News*, August 1957.

Harris, H.K., "Fighting Fires With Airplanes and Sodium Calcium Borate in Western Montana and Northern Idaho - 1957", Fire Control Notes, April 1958, pp. 66-67.

Bombard, Owen, "The Tin Goose", *Dearborn Historical Quarterly*, Dearborn Historical Society, May 1958.

Lafferty, George E., "The Air Tanker as an Initial Attack Tool", *Fire Control Notes*, Vol.19, No.3, July 1958, pp. 120-122.

Larkins, William T., *The Ford Story: A Pictorial History of the Ford Tri-Motor 1927-1957*, Robert R. Longo Co., Wichita, 1957.

Sweet, Bill, "King of the Tin Goose - Harold S. Johnson", *American Airman*, March 1959, pp. 20-21.

"Throughout the Midwest, folks turn out in droves when The Tin Goose Comes To Town", *The Power Plant* (Pratt & Whitney Aircraft Co.), Vol.XVII, No.18, October 21, 1960.

Olson, Gene, *The Tin Goose*, The Westminster Press, Philadelphia, 1961. (a novel)

Morrison, Duncan, "414H Rides Again", *American Airman*, January 1961, pp. 8-9.

Fisher, Herb, "Tin Goose Island-Hoppers", *Skyways*, January 1961, pp. 8-9.

Davis, W.E., "Mr. Ford's Tin Goose", *The American Legion Magazine*, May 1961, pp. 22-23, 49-50.

Christy, Joe, "Tin Goose: She led the Golden Age", *American Modeler*, February 1962, pp. 18-19, 52.

"Ford Flying Machines", *The Restorer* (Model A Ford Club of America), May-June 1962, pp. 9-24.

"TULE Overhaul Gets Unusual Job: Restore 30-Year-Old Tin Goose", *Flagship News* (AA), October 8, 1962, pp. 1, 6.

Larkins, William T., "American Airlines Ford Tri-Motor", *AAHS Journal*, Vol.7, No.4, Winter 1962, pp. 280-282.

Hufford, Robert G., "Yesterday's Airliner on Today's Airline", *AAHS Journal*, Vol.7, No.4, Winter 1962, pp. 280-282.

Juptner, Joseph P., *U.S. Civil Aircraft*, Aero Publishers, Fallbrook, Vol.1, 1962, pp. 215-218.

Winchester, James H., "Island Hopping in the Tin Goose", *Magic Circle* (Perfect Circle Corp.), June 1963, pp. 2-5.

"Jets, Phooey! Tin Goose Is Winging Again", *The Stars and Stripes*, June 12, 1963, p.6.

Friedlander, Paul J.C., "Coast To Coast", *New York Times*, June 30, 1963, Section 10, pg.1.

Chamberlin, Anne, "Last gasp of the Tin Goose; In a ramshackle museum piece, a dozen volunteers make a desperate journey down memory's airlane", *The Saturday Evening Post*, August 10-17, 1963. (LA to NY flight of N414H in 1963). A condensed version of this was published in *Reader's Digest*, December 1963, pp. 151-155.

Kidd, Stephen, "Jet-Age Journey in a Tin Goose", *Flying*, September 1963, pp. 46-47.

Mace, Kenneth D., "Flying the Old Tin Goose", *Clues*, Fall 1963, pp. 26-28.

United States Civil Aircraft Register, Federal Aviation Administration Control Systems/Flight Standards Divisions, U.S. Government Printing Office, Washington, D.C. Semi-Annual 1963-1978 averaging 1,500 pages per issue. (Continued in microfiche form 1980-1989 and available monthly from the government contractor, currently Anbacomp Inc., Oklahoma City, OK 73108).

Reiss, George R., "Island Airlines", *Esso Air World*, Jan-Feb 1964, pp. 102-104.

Downie, Don, "We fly the Ford", *Air Progress*, June-July 1964, pp. 59-66, 88-91.

Juptner, Joseph P., *U.S. Civil Aircraft*, Aero Publishers, Fallbrook, Vol.2, 1964, pp. 96-98, 160-161, 185-187, 209-211

Forero, Colonel Jose Ignacio, *Historia de la Aviation en Colombia*, Aedita, Bogota, Colombia, 1964.

Smith, Cal and Plecan, Paul, "Tin Goose Ford Tri-Motor Radio-Control Model" (Part 1), *American Modeler*, Jan-Feb 1965, pp. 40-44, 86. Page 43 has photos of the instrument panel in N8407 and N9683.

Wilson, A.H., "Reminiscences of a West Coast Pilot", *Canadian Aviation Historical Society Journal*, Fall 1965, pp. 67-70. (G-CATX in British Columbia).

O'Hara, Robert, "King of the Fords", *Air Classics*, August-September 1965, pp. 50-53.

Underwood, John, "The Tin Goose of Tayoltita", *Private Pilot*, April-May 1966, pp. 62-63.

Juptner, Joseph P., *U.S. Civil Aircraft*, Aero Publishers, Fallbrook, Vol.3, 1966, pp. 136-137, 273-275.

Roseberry, C.R., *The Challenging Skies*, Doubleday & Co., Garden City, 1966.

"Flying high in vintage Fords", *Business Week*, January 7, 1967, pp. 132-134.

"Island Lifeline", *Ohio*, January 1967, pp. 2-5.

Gardner, Harvey, "This airline still flies Tri-Motors!", *Mechanix Illustrated*, February 1967, pp. 83-86, 147.

"Modernized Tin Goose", *Air Progress*, March 1967, pp. 50-51.

"Another Ford in Our Future?", *Air Classics*, November 1967, pp. 54-61.

Larkins, William T., *The Ford Tri-Motor* (Profile No.156), Profile Publications Ltd., Leatherhead, England, 1967. (Includes 12 side view paintings in color).

Juptner, Joseph P., *U.S. Civil Aircraft*, Aero Publishers, Fallbrook, Vol.4, 1967, pp. 32-34.

Kirn, Thomas G., "Flights To Nostalgia", *Air Classics*, Vol.3, No.1, July 1968, pp. 16-20.

Ingells, Douglas J., "The Cry of the Tin Goose", *American Aircraft Modeler*, October 1968, pp. 18-20, 58-69.

Ingells, Douglas J., *Tin Goose - The Fabulous Ford Trimotor*, Aero Publishers, Fallbrook, 1968.

Maher, Theodore, "Pioneer Plane Is Reborn", *FAA Horizons*, December 23, 1968, p.6. (Regarding certification of the Bushmaster).

Linton, Jack, "The Venerable Tri-Motor", *Plane & Pilot*, July 1969, pp. 78-81.

Morrow, Ben H., "Henry Ford's Tin Goose", *Historic Aviation*, Vol.2, No.9, September 1969, pp. 11-26.

Birth Of An Industry, A Nostalgic Collection of Airline Schedules 1929-1939, Reuben H. Donnelley Corp., NYC, 1969. (Reproduction of one issue per year of The Official Airline Guide, with an Introduction by Robert J. Serling).

Ellis, F.H., "The Blitz of 'BEP", *Canadian Aviation Historical Society Journal*, Spring 1970.

"The Tin Goose Flies Again", *The Northwest Flyer*, June 22, 1970, pp. 1, 3. (Re N9645).

"By Any Other Name She's Still a Tin Goose", *Power Plant* (Pratt and Whitney Aircraft), June 26, 1970, p.7. (Re N9645).

Fulton, Fitzhugh L. Jr., "Flight Evaluation - Ford Trimotor - Model 4-AT-B", National Aeronautics and Space Administration, Flight Research Center, Edwards AFB, November 1970, p.9.

Peck, Edward, "Ancestor Aircraft of TWA", *American Aviation Historical Society Journal*, Vol.15, No.3, Fall 1970, pp. 178-180.

Towle, Tom, "Who Designed the Ford Trimotor? (#1)", *AAHS Journal*, Vol.15, No.3, Fall 1970, pp. 181-186.

Lee, John G., "Who Designed the Ford Trimotor? (#2)", *AAHS Journal*, Vol.15, No.3, Fall 1970, pp. 187-193.

Daniels, C.M., "Ford Had A Better Idea!", *Airpower*, September 1971, pp. 6-13, 54-57, 63.

Atkin, Jonathan B., "Passengers Flock to Tin Gooses", *The National Observer*, October 30, 1971.

Weiss, David Ansel, *The Saga of the Tin Goose*, Crown Publishers, NYC, 1971.

TWA Flight Operations Department, Legacy of Leadership, Walsworth Publishing Co., Marceline, MO, 1971.

Juptner, Joseph P., *U.S. Civil Aircraft*, Aero Publishers, Fallbrook, Vol.5, pp. 28-30, 92-94, 120-121.

McKay, William P., "Flying the Tin Goose", *Private Pilot*, January 1972, pp. 49-52.

Davies, R.E.G., *Airlines of the United States since 1914*, Putnam, London, 1972.

Kriz, Marjorie, "Flying School Bus", *FAA Aviation News*, January 1973.

Lewis, David L., "Ford's Boost to Aviation", *The Restorer* (Model A Ford Club of America), May-June 1973, pp. 11-21.

Poberezny, Paul H., "The Death of a Tri-Motor", *The Vintage Airplane*, August 1973, pp. 14-15.

Tallman, Frank, *Flying the Old Planes*, Doubleday & Co., New York, 1973, pp. 150-162.

Rice, Michael Stephen, Instruction Manual for Ford Trimotor, Aviation Publications, Milwaukee, 1973.

Forden, Lesley, *The Ford Air Tours 1925-1931*, The Nottingham Press, Alameda, 1973.

Turner, P. St. John, *Pictorial History of Pan American World Airways*, Ian Allen, London, 1973.

Smrz, Bohuslav and Smekal, Stanislav, "Ford Tri-Motor", Letecfin Kormonahfika No.75, Prague, 1973, pp. 584-587.

Considine, Bob, "The Tin Goose", *The American Way* (AA), February 1974, pp. 36-40.

Hardie, George Jr., *A Ford in EAA's Future*, EAA Museum Foundation, Franklin, WI, 1974. (Excellent survey of Ford Tri-Motor development including company advertisements, and the history of N8410).

Mc Carthy, Dan B., "The Kansas Clipper; Restored Ford Trimotor Flies On", *Air Classics*,

Bowers, Peter M., *Yesterday's Wings*, Aircraft Owners and Pilots Association, Washington, D.C., 1974, p.35.

Conrad, Max, "Max Conrad flys the Tin Goose", *Plane and Pilot*, January 1975, pp. 57-59.

Payne, Ralph L., "Ford's Tri-Motor Adventures", *Ford Illustrated*, Spring 1975, pp. 38-41, 50.

Gomez, Ing. Jose Villela, *Breve Historia de la Aviacion en Mexico*, Complejo Editorial Mexicano, Mexico City, 1975.

"Over Grand Canyon in an Elderly Ford", *Sunset*, May 1976, p.20D.

Hardie, George Jr., "Odyssey Of A Ford Trimotor", *Sport Aviation*, July 1976, pp. 16-19.

Downie, Don, "Grand Canyon Ford", *AOPA Pilot*, November 1976, pp. 67-70.

Leary, William M. Jr., *The Dragon's Wings* (CNAC and the Development of Commercial Aviation in China), The University of Georgia Press, Athens, Georgia, 1976.

Hendry, Maurice, "Henry Ford and His Stout-Hearted Flying Machines . . .",

Old Cars, January 25, 1977, pp. 24, 40-41.

"Those Fabulous Flying Fords", and "Island Airlines", *Captain's Log* (World Airline Hobby Club), Vol.2, No.4, January-March 1977.

Alsop, Ronald, "Crash of Tin Goose Means Hard Times for Ohio Airline", *The Wall Street Journal*, August 9, 1977, p.24.

Dean, Paul, "The Gallant Lady of the Grand Canyon", *Arizona Highways*, November 1977, pp. 38-41 and front cover.

Wojtas, Ed, "The Goose Lives!", *Airline Quarterly*, Vol.1, No.2, Fall 1977, pp. 52-63.

Book of Instruction, *Ford Tri-Motor All-Metal Monoplane* (Ford Motor Company 1929), Post-Era Books, Arcadia, CA, 1977.

Chee, Quan, Buerger, Giltz and Bieszczad, "It's A Stout Ford", *IPMS-USA Quarterly Journal*; Part 1 - Vol.12, No.3, 1977, pp. 117-125; Part 2 - Vol.12, No.4, 1977, pp. 208-214. (Many closeup photos of Island Air Lines 4-AT).

Litwak, Jerry, "Skinning A Tin Goose... the hard way", *Air International*, May 1978, pp. 251-252.

Mertens, Randy, "Barnstorming tri-motor returns to the midwest", *Pilot News*, May 1978, pp. 6-7.

Davies, R.E.G., "Development of the Transcontinental Air Service, Part 1", *AAHS Journal*, Vol.23, No.1, Spring 1978.

Fredericksen, Byron, "Fords Are Where You Find Them", *The Vintage Airplane,* April 1978, p.8.

Conrad, Max, "The Great Tin Goose", *Flying Classics*, September 1978, pp.

Norman, Marc, *Fool's Errand*, Holt, Rinehart and Winston, NYC, 1978. (Novel about flying dynamite in three Fords over the Andes to Bolivia).

Morgan, Len, "Flying the Ford", *Flying*, January 1979, pp. 50-54, 78-82. (Excellent color photos by Russell Munson).

Taylor, H.A., "Ford's Stout-Hearted Trimotor", *Air Enthusiast*, January 1979, pp. 38-50.

Reynolds, Lindell and Roos, Fred, "Union Electric's Airplanes", *Aeronautical History Society of St. Louis Newsletter*, February 1979, 4 pages.

Farrar, Fred, "The Resurrection of a Legend", *FAA World*, July 1979, pp. 6-8.

Smith, Gene, "Stout Bushmaster", *Air Progress*, August 1979.

Smith, Steve, *Fly the Biggest Piece Back*, Mountain Press, Missoula, 1979. (Re Johnson Flying Service).

"The Tin Goose", *The Illustrated Encyclopedia of Aviation*, Vol.9, 1979, pp. 1030-1033..

Nemecek, Vaclav and Tyc, Pavel, *Trimotorova Dopravni Letadla*, Prague, 1979, pp. 32-33, 58-63.

Ionne, Joe, "The Tin Goose Flies Again", *The Columbus Dispatch*, June 8, 1980, Sunday Magazine. (Photos of crash and rebuilding of N7584).

Air Enthusiast, April-July 1980, pp. 49-50. Three letters and editors comments on Fords in New Guinea and Spain.

Kidd, Stephen, "Ford Tri-Motor: The Golden Goose", *Aviation Quarterly*, Vol.6, No.2, Airtrails Inc., Plano, TX, 1980, pp. 100-129. (Includes beautiful two-page color painting of AA's restored N9683).

Norton, Clarence E., *Those Early Years*, M&W Printers, Dickinson, TX, 1980. (Photos and text by SAFE pilot who later flew Fords in Honduras).

Beckford, Mary, "Hershberger threw lifeline to islanders", *The Port Clinton News Herald*, December 5, 1981, pp. 1, 4.

Van Sciever, T.P., *Ford Air Transportation Department, A Chronology: 1901-1979*, V.I.P. Printing Company, St. Louis, 1981.

Juptner, Joseph P., *U.S. Civil Aircraft*, Aero Publishers, Fallbrook, Vol.9, 1981, pp. 82, 107, 108, 111, 123, 142, 149, 156, 186, 190, 192.

Hagelthorn, Richard L., "Dearborn's 'Spruce Goose'", *The Dearborn Historian*, Vol.22, No.3, Summer 1982. (Excellent illustrated history of the 14-A).

Hardie, George Jr., "Ford Trimotor update", *Sport Aviation* (EAA), August 1982, pp. 35-42. (Rebuilding of N8407).

McGoldrick, J.P., *The Spokane Aviation Story*, Part I, Ye Galleon Press, Fairfield, Washington, 1982.

Davies, R.E.G., *Airlines of Latin America since 1919*, Putnam, London, 1983.

Cohen, Stan, *A Pictorial History of Smokejumping*, Pictorial Histories Publishing Co., Missoula, 1983.

Murdoch, Simon, "The Tin Goose Story", *Aviation News* (England), 30 Dec 83/12 Jan 84, pp. 686-688, plus front cover.

Betts, Ed, "The Short, Salty Career of Old 620", *TWA Skyliner*, November 5, 1984, pp. 4-5.

Cooley, Earl, *Trimotor and Trail*, Mountain Press, Missoula, 1984.

"The World's Greatest Aircraft: Ford Tri-Motor", *The Illustrated Encyclopedia of Aircraft*, Vol.13, Issue 149, Aerospace Publishing Ltd., London, 1984, pp. 2965-2971. (Includes cutaway drawing and 3-view in color).

Farmer, James H., *Celluloid Wings*, Tab Books, Blue Ridge Summit, PA, 1984.

Creedy, Kathryn B., *Commuter Regional Airline News*; Part 1 - September 23, 1985 "Scenic Tri-Motor Provides Flight Into Past"; Part 2 - September 30, 1985 "Tri-Motor Brings Out Kid in ATC System"; Part 3 - October 7, 1985 "An American Panorama – The West"; Part 4 - October 14, 1985 "An American Panorama – The East."

Henderson, Dana K. and Davis, Lou, "Ford Tri-Motor Recreates Transcontinental Service", *Air Transport World*, October 1985, pp. 60-61. (LA to NYC flight of N414H in 1985).

Hunhoff, Bernie, "Clyde Ice", *South Dakota Magazine*, November 1985, pp. 6-12.

"A Piece of History Passes Through", *Pilot News*, October 1985, pp. 30-36.

Mirando, J. and Mercado, P., *Aviacion Mundial en Espana (Guerra Civil) 1936-1939*, Vol.1 "Aviones Americanos y Rusos", Silex, Madrid, 1985, pp. 74-77.

Yerex, David, *Yerex of TACA*, Ampersand Publishing Associates, Carterton, New Zealand, 1985.

Davisson, Budd, "Last of the Barnstormers", *Air Progress*, June 1986, pp. 70-79.

Kavelaars, H.C., "The Air Transport Department of the Shell Company of Ecuador 1937-1950", *AAHS Journal*, Summer 1986, pp. 92-105.

Petersen, Norm, "Ford Tri-Motor NC8407", *Sport Aviation*, EAA, Oshkosh, July 1986, pp. 48-56. (Rebuilding and flight of N8407, color photos including front cover).

Jerdone, Frank H., *Pilot of Fortune*, Vantage Press, NYC, 1986. Larkins, William T. "Ford 5-AT-11", Skyways, April 1987, pp. 2-7.

Larkins, William T. "Ford Details", *Skyways*, April 1987, pp. 8-12.

Larkins, William T., "Ford XB-906", *Skyways*, October 1987, pp. 32-35.

Rust, Kenn C., "Early Airlines, Accidents List 1926-1941", *AAHS Journal*, Fall 1987, pp. 213-223.

Davies, R.E.G., *Rebels and Reformers of the Airways*, Smithsonian Institution Press, Washington, D.C., 1987.

Davies, R.E.G., *Pan Am - An Airline and Its Aircraft*, Orion Books, New York, 1987.

Baker, John L., "Trimotor", *AOPA Pilot*, November 1987, pp. 48-57, 60-62. (Pilots report of N414H with 17 excellent color photos by Art Davis).

Classics of the Air, Exeter Books, NYC, 1988. (pp. 109-116 are a reprint of the article in the *Illustrated Encyclopedia of Aircraft*, No. 149).

Allen, Richard Sanders., "A Charter to Chicago", *Aviation Quarterly*, Vol.8, No.4, 1988, pp. 318-331.

Sedgwick, Rhonda Coy, *Sky Trails: The Life of Clyde W. Ice*, Quarter Circle A Enterprises, Newcastle, WY, 1988.

Rosholt, Malcolm (Editor), "Early Birds in China; Perry Hutton", *Annual Pictorial Magazine of the Flying Tigers of the 14th Air Force Association*, Rosholt, WI, 1989, pp. 54-59.

Leary, William M., *Aviation's Golden Age; Portraits From The 1920's and 1930's*, University of Iowa Press, Iowa City, 1989. pp. 1-17 "Henry Ford and Aeronautics During the 1920's", plus notes on pp. 149-152.

Bryan, Ford R., *Beyond The Model T - The Other Adventures of Henry Ford*, Wayne State University Press, Detroit, 1990, pp. 163-173.

"Great Aircraft of the World; Ford Tri-motor", *Airplane*, Vol.3, No.27, Aerospace Publishing Ltd., England, 1990, pp. 736-747. Slightly revised version of their 1984 text with some new color photos including one on the cover and a magnificent 11-1/2 x 34 inch fold-out airbrush drawing of a PAA 5-AT by Iain Nyllie complete with 24 captions.

Cook, Marc E., "Bushmaster 2000: Tri Again", *AOPA Pilot*, January 1991, pp. 42-48.

Gann, Ernest K., *Ernest K. Gann's Flying Circus*, Bantam Books, NYC, 1992. pp. 103-115 "The Tin Goose." Reprint of 1974 McMillan book. Text first published in *Flying*, August 1974, pp. 91-101 as part of the advance publicity for his book.

Holden, Henry M., *The Fabulous Ford Tri-Motors*, TAB Books, Blue Ridge Summit, PA 1992.

Vintage Airline Timetables

This folder effective September 20, 1928

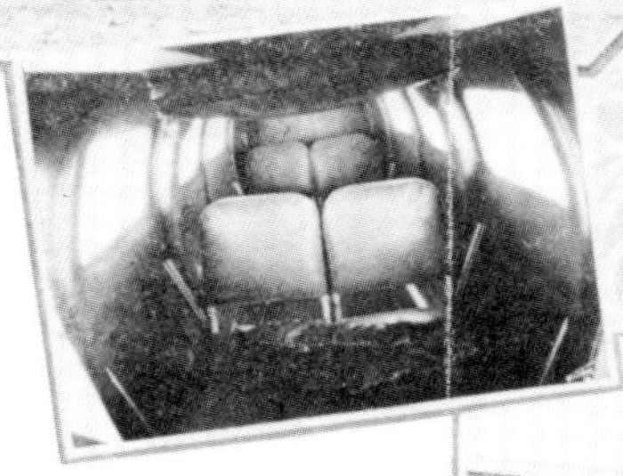

Upper: Lockheed Vega cabin monoplane for special trips. Right: Luxurious Lockheed passenger cabin.

THE experienced air traveler, knowing the safety today of air lines under government supervision, is more interested in ports of call and scenic beauties than other considerations. A growing network of lines throughout the United States offers him fast, direct contact between all progressive communities.

Comparisons between relative speeds of two air lines, or two types of equipment, mean little. Maddux Air Lines' equipment is built primarily to meet the basic requirement for safety, reliability, regularity. Speed is entirely secondary in its design. The air route at any pace allows so great a time-saving over other mediums that saving a few minutes more through superlative speed is unnecessary.

The regular traveler of the skyway will check, first of all, the economic and pleasure values of the route he takes.

Maddux Air Lines' California system offers travelers the widest range of possibilities. Daily service on the northern division covers Los Angeles, Bakersfield, Visalia, Fresno, Oakland and San Francisco. The southern division extends from Los Angeles through Long Beach, Santa Ana and San Diego to Agua Caliente, Mexico—the first daily international air line in American aviation history. The value to the traveling public of all these possible contacts cannot be overestimated. Tri-weekly service reaches Ensenada.

A "preview" of the scenic trip between Los Angeles and San Francisco may be encompassed in a brief description, "reading" northbound:

When the three motors blend in one solid tone, the huge air liner speeds down the runway into the wind. With a gentle, imperceptible movement it leaves the ground—no strain, no sense of lifting. The hangars and rows of toy-like airplanes take their place in the great pattern of Los Angeles, stretching to the hills and the sea, and the craft noses northwest, over the multi-colored roofs, gardens and shining boulevards of Hollywood and Beverly Hills. The foothills of Millionaires Row look up with uncounted mansions and canyons, laced with new roads that curve and climb in search of every virgin spot. Soon the impressive stretches of the San Fernando Valley are ahead, then under, then past—with a square block pattern of farms and encroaching subdivisions.

New hills appear, sharper, more rugged. To the right and left is the awe-inspiring yellow waste of the St. Francis Dam flood, a scar which man will not fully repair in years. Forks of dead yellow vengeance reach into many little valleys and canyons.

Upper: Daily Los Angeles-San Francisco air liner over the Santa Clara Valley. Lower: Daily arrival scene at terminal.

Ridge beyond ridge of the timbered Tehachapis appear on the right, and the famous Ridge Route, like a string thrown carelessly away by the gods, curls and snakes its way along under the plane. Hotel Lebec and Lebec airport are conspicuous landmarks. When peaks begin to grade down and the Ridge Route unravels itself into a smooth straightaway, look to the left, ahead, at Buena Vista Lake, the duck hunters' mecca. To the right of Bakersfield, looming up ahead, is Oil City, a forest of derricks on a round, smooth eminence.

Circling the field, the air liner glides down to a smooth landing.

With one powerful hydraulic wheel brake locked, it turns "on a dime" and taxis to the passenger receiving point, stopping as quickly and smoothly as any automobile.

Off again in a long sweeping run, the plane heads northwest, following the same straight line of its course from

Below: Ready to leave the hangar. Above, right: Typical airport scene. Left: Showing two pilots at dual controls.

Top: Three Maddux air liners over the timbered Tehachapis. Middle: Air view of the San Joaquin River. Below: The air liner's "Saturday Night."

Above, reading up: Oil City, near Bakersfield; three tri-motored all-metal Ford air liners of the Maddux fleet; a mountain view on the Los Angeles-San Francisco route.

Los Angeles. The next port is Fresno. Great squares and oblongs of verdant farming land pass in the wake of the ship. Prosperous, progressive cities, with many highways leading into them. A winding, tree-fringed stream. To the right the dim outlines of the High Sierras and sharper foothills; to the left, the coast range passing along like a smooth wall barring the invisible ocean beyond.

Fresno appears with a suggestion of spires and industrial buildings. Over a canal running through country rich with agricultural abundance, the plane glides into port, wheeling around to a perfect stop with military precision. The fuel crew take over the winged carrier as passengers step out for a walk around the hangars.

Three minutes after leaving Fresno, the San Joaquin River, running in endless half-turns, bordered by dense growth, winds across the route. In less than an hour the hills at the end of the valley appear, the air liner crosses the "hump" and the Livermore Valley is seen, brilliantly green. In a few finutes San Francisco Bay, Oakland, Berkeley, Alameda and other smaller cities are visible, with Mt. Diablo looming up against the sky. The landing at Oakland offers a wonderful view of a great airport retrieved from waste lands and shallow waters of the bay.

The short hop across the bay presents views unparalleled: land and cities, water and ships. On the right, downtown San Francisco looms at the water's edge—a fascinating skyline. Mt. Tamalpais and Twin Peaks, and the softly rolling hills of the peninsula, are the last remembered views. Touching ground smoothly, the big plane brings up short beside an iron gate. It is hard to realize that Los Angeles is 500 ground-miles away; 365 air-miles; four hours. In comfortable limousines the passengers are whisked to Market Street and the heart of San Francisco, carrying with them vivid memories of "the greatest show on earth."

ON the international line to Agua Caliente, Mexico, the daily air liner leaves Rogers Airport, Los Angeles, at 8:15 a.m., fifteen minutes after the daily plane for San Francisco. Over the Baldwin Hills and part of Los Angeles, Inglewood and several suburban communities the big ship wings its way south. Signal Hill, one of the most picturesque oil centers in the United States, Long Beach, San Pedro, Wilmington and the busy Los Angeles harbor are among the first views. Flying down the coast line, the air transport passes over the famous beaches of Southern California, from Long Beach south. Laguna, Del Mar and La Jolla are three of the most beautiful from the air. Fishing boats dot the waters below in occasional groups. The white line of a speedboat's trail makes a fleeting scar on the dark smoothness of the ocean. Breakers die gently on smooth sands and smash to death in white clouds on occasional great rocks.

There is no vantage point from which the blue of the ocean seems so vivid as from the skyway. Contrasting brilliantly with the water's deep tone are the white strands where bathers frolic in the sun, the peculiarly red-tinted cliffs rising from the water's edge at many points, the green hills and valleys and the riot of undersea plant colors so vivid they may be seen clearly from the sky. And perhaps no part of California shows more variety in color and architecture of buildings than the southern coast line.

Over the hills back of La Jolla the plane glides inland to Maddux Airport, opposite the Marine base at San Diego. In a minute's time the passengers for San Diego are on the ground and the plane is in the air again, bound for Mexico.

Over a variety of country the route leads straight for the border. Over Tia Juana and a range of low hills the air liner glides down into a beautiful valley, where Agua Caliente hotel, Casino, whippet track and three-score quaint Spanish bungalows present an interesting view. Taxiing up the landing field almost to the hotel, the airplane releases its passengers to enjoy the beauties and delights of Mexico. On Wednesday, Saturday and Sunday the plane continues on to old Ensenada.

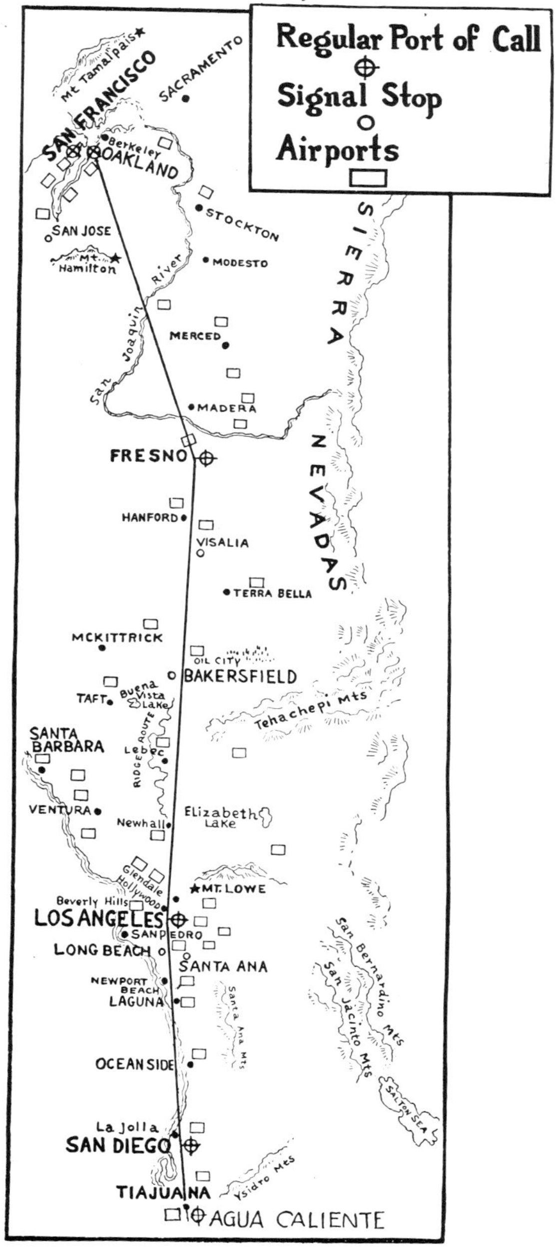

GENERAL INFORMATION

Regarding Daily Service in California and Mexico

THE MADDUX AIR LINER

STANDARD equipment for the daily passenger service of Maddux Air Lines is the Ford all-metal, 12-passenger, parlor monoplane, powered with three Wright Whirlwind motors, a single one of which carried Colonel Charles A. Lindbergh's "Spirit of St. Louis" across the Atlantic. Genuine comfort as well as the luxury of speed is the keynote of the huge craft, with its easy chairs, wide windows and ample foot-room suggesting complete relaxation and rest. No dust, dirt or smoke is associated with this transport, raising it above all other transportation mediums for cleanliness. A rest room is conveniently located. Rack space for hats, coats and other light encumbrances is provided, besides the regular luggage storage.

"FASHION HINTS" FOR THE NEWCOMER

In traveling from one city to another for luncheon, dinner, an interview or any other special purpose, dress exactly as that purpose demands. Do not add or detract anything for the air route.

LUGGAGE

Each passenger is allowed twenty-five pounds of hand luggage; excess will be charged for according to tariff of the various routes. Company's liability is limited to $100.

For excess rates, see first division of the parcel rates in this folder.

FARE REGULATIONS

Reservations will not be held later than twenty-four hours before departure, unless paid for. Refunds on reservations cancelled later than this will be subject to a 25 per cent cancellation fee subject to sale of seat. No refunds on reservations cancelled later than two hours before departure.

There are no half fares. Children charged full fares.

No dogs, cats, birds or other pets allowed.

The company reserves the right to refund fares in full and alter the published schedule without notice.

CITY CENTER-TO-AIRPORT SERVICE

Luxurious closed cars maintained by Maddux Air Lines leave 636 South Olive Street, Los Angeles, and 672 Market Street, San Francisco, at 7:15 a. m. This service is free of charge. Likewise, passengers arriving at either of these cities are carried to the same addresses. At Oakland, a car leaves the Hotel Oakland and the Crabtree Travel Office, 412 Thirteenth Street, at 7:35 A. M.

COMBINATION TRIPS

In providing transportation for the vacationer, Maddux Air Lines will arrange combination routes, gratifying to the one who seeks novelty and contrast.

OVER HIGHWAY AND SKYWAY

With the California Parlor Car Tours, Inc., a land-and-air trip over the heart of California has been arranged. Three days' time is required for the land trip, in palatial motor coaches, between Los Angeles and San Francisco, with overnight stops at two of the West's most famous hotels. The return by air is made in four hours, over the great San Joaquin Valley. The complete trip, one way land, one way air, is only $90.00.

THE PACIFIC SEA-AND-AIR ROUTE

With the Pacific Steamship Company, Canada, the United States and Mexico have been linked in one great coastwise air-and-water transportation combine. "Through" tickets may be purchased from any Puget sound port of the famous Admiral Lines to any airport of the Maddux system. From Seattle to San Francisco by steamship, and thence to Los Angeles by air, takes 42 hours of diversified travel—38 hours on the water, 4 hours in the air. As an example of rates, a round trip between Los Angeles and San Francisco, one way by water, the other way by air, costs only $52.50. Get details from any Maddux or Admiral Lines agent.

SIGHTSEEING TOURS

Regular scenic trips are conducted over San Francisco, Oakland, Los Angeles, San Diego and Agua Caliente, which present the ultimate degree of pleasure with an all-inclusive survey of the beauties of these California cities. Luxury is the dominating note of this new aerial sightseeing privilege, which is yet moderate in price—$5.00 per passenger.

CHARTER TRIPS

Maddux air liners may be chartered for business or pleasure, and offer advantages over any other transportation. Many California business firms have already learned their value, and film studios have enjoyed tremendous overhead savings in location work. Sportsmen may take week-end hunting and fishing trips which in the past have been prohibited by limitations of time. Maddux Air Lines have the large Ford three-motored, all-metal air yachts carrying two pilots and ten passengers, and for smaller parties swift, dependable Lockheed monoplanes carrying four besides the pilot.

EL PASO DIVISION

Plans are now being completed for an extension of daily passenger service with Ford three-motored, all metal air liners, from San Francisco, Oakland, Fresno, Bakersfield, Los Angeles and San Diego to Imperial, Phoenix, Tucson and El Paso. At the El Paso terminal other air lines will connect, providing service over Texas, through the South, East and North. Your nearest Maddux Air Lines agent will notify you of the definite inaugural date. Until that date, all service through the Southwest, east of Los Angeles and San Diego, is on a charter basis.

ENSENADA—IN OLD MEXICO

If all the attractions of Old Mexico were known to the average pleasure-seeker, the air, land and water routes to principal colonies of Baja California would be congested. As it is, only members of the wealthy class have ventured across the international border until recently. On July 4, 1928, Maddux Air Lines became the first international passenger air line of the North American continent by extending its southern terminal to Agua Caliente, the society resort three miles south of Tia Juana. Since then, capacity loads have been carried.

Now, service on Wednesday, Saturday and Sunday is available to Ensenada, sixty miles farther south. Ensenada has been famed for years for its unsurpassed hunting and fishing, its marvellous miles of perfect beach and beautiful harbor. It lays claim to the finest fresh sea food and wild game dinners on the Pacific Coast. And there is present, always, that indefinable but vital charm that is Mexico.

PARCEL EXPRESS

A very few business men do not yet realize the value of air express. Those who do have turned dissatisfied customers into boosters; retrieved deals apparently fallen through; beaten other organizations in delivering samples and first orders; and gained the reputation of being first in service. The difference in cost over slower shipping service is recovered immediately in increased business.

In Los Angeles and San Francisco, messenger service to the field is provided for all parcels delivered to the downtown offices before 7:00 a.m. Packages sent to these cities and Fresno are delivered from the airport to any address in the business district.

PARCEL EXPRESS RATES

PER POUND—SUBJECT TO MINIMUM CHARGE SHOWN

Between Points Named Below	San Francisco and Oakland	Fresno	Bakersfield	Los Angeles	San Diego
Fresno	$0.25	....	$0.25	$0.35	$0.50
Bakersfield	.35	$0.25	....	.25	.35
Los Angeles	.50	.35	.25	....	.20
San Diego	.65	.50	.35	.20	....

MINIMUM RATE CHARGE

Between Points Named Below	San Francisco and Oakland	Fresno	Bakersfield	Los Angeles	San Diego
Fresno	$1.00	....	$1.00	$1.50	$2.00
Bakersfield	1.50	$1.00	....	1.00	1.50
Los Angeles	2.00	1.50	1.00	....	1.00
San Diego	2.50	2.00	1.50	1.00	....

Coming into Port

The number of women air travelers is increasing rapidly.

RATES AND SCHEDULES AT A GLANCE

LOS ANGELES—SAN FRANCISCO DIVISION

*Stops on Reservation Only	North bound	South bound (Read Up)	Trip	Los Angeles	Bakers-field	Visalia	Fresno	San Francisco-Oakland
Los Angeles	Lv. 8:00 a.m.	12:30 p.m.	One Way R. T.	....	$15.00 27.50	$28.00 52.00	$30.00 55.00	$45.00 85.00
*Bakersfield	9:10 a.m.	11:20 a.m.	One Way R. T.	$15.00 27.50	....	15.00 27.50	15.00 27.50	32.00 60.00
*Visalia	10:00a.m.	10:25 a.m.	One Way R. T.	28.00 52.00	15.00 27.50	....	....	28.00 52.00
Fresno	Ar. 10:25 a.m. Lv. 10:40 a.m.	Lv. 10:05 a.m. Ar. 9:50 a.m.	One Way R. T.	30.00 55.00	15.00 27.50	....	....	25.00 46.00
San Francisco and Oakland	Ar. 12:30 p.m.	Lv. 8:00 a.m.	One Way R. T.	45.00 85.00	32.00 60.00	28.00 52.00	25.00 46.00	....

LOS ANGELES—SAN DIEGO—MEXICO DIVISION

*Stops on Reservation Only	South-bound	North bound (Read Up)	Trip	Los Angeles	Long Beach	Santa Ana	San Diego	Agua Caliente	Ense-nada
Los Angeles	Lv. 8:15 a.m.	Ar. 6:00 p.m.	One Way R. T.	....	$ 8.00 15.00	$ 8.00 15.00	$15.00 27.50	$20.00 37.50	$30.00 55.00
*Long Beach	8:35 a.m.	5:40 p.m.	One Way R. T.	$ 8.00 15.00	....	....	15.00 27.50	20.00 37.50	30.00 55.00
*Santa Ana	8:45 a.m.	5:30 p.m.	One Way R. T.	8.00 15.00	....	....	15.00 27.50	20.00 37.50	30.00 55.00
San Diego	Ar. 9:30 a.m. Lv. 9:35 a.m.	Lv. 4:45 p.m. Ar. 4:35 p.m.	One Way R. T.	15.00 27.50	15.00 27.50	15.00 27.50	....	5.00 10.00	15.00 27.50
Agua Caliente Mexico	Ar. 9:55 a.m. Lv. 10:10 a.m.	Lv. 4:15 p.m. Ar. 4:00 p.m.	One Way R. T.	20.00 37.50	20.00 37.50	20.00 37.50	5.00 10.00	....	10.00 17.50
‡Ensenada Mexico	Ar. 10:45 a.m.	Lv. 3:25 p.m.	One Way R. T.	30.00 55.00	30.00 55.00	30.00 55.00	15.00 27.50	10.00 17.50	....

‡Wednesday, Saturday and Sunday Only.

One may write in the air liner as easily as at home.

CITY	INFORMATION	
San Francisco	Maddux Air Lines, Inc., 672 Market—Sutter 5047	Mills Field
Oakland	Crabtree Travel Office, 412 Thirteenth St.—Oakland 1436	Alameda
Fresno	Maddux Air Lines, Inc., 1361 Fulton St.—Phone 27429	Municipal
Visalia	Hotel Johnson—Phone 17	Municipal
Bakersfield	El Tejon Hotel—Phone 3200	Municipal
Los Angeles	Maddux Air Lines, Inc., 2100 S. Figueroa and 636 S. Olive WEstmore 4111	Rogers' Airport
Long Beach	Globe Travel Service and Municipal Airport	Municipal
Santa Ana	Martin's Airport	Martin's
San Diego	Leading Hotels and Maddux Airport—Bayview 0808 3330 Barnett Avenue	Maddux
Agua Caliente	Agua Caliente Hotel	Agua Caliente
Ensenada	Casino Club	Municipal

Also—*"Ask Mr. Foster,"* Ames Bros. Co. Travel Bureaus, Peck-Judah, Thomas Cook & Sons, American Express or any principal travel agency.

From San Francisco: Marked airport car leaves Palace Hotel at 7:15 a.m. *From Oakland:* Car leaves Hotel Oakland and Crabtree Travel Office at 7:35 a.m. *From Los Angeles:* Car leaves 636 S. Olive at 7:15 a.m.

MADDUX AIR LINES

It is no longer necessary to "sell" air transportation to those who have learned its advantages. In a year the attitude of the traveling public has changed radically. What once was curiosity, now is a definite, enthusiastic, participating interest. Those who travel for business realize the value of time saved; pleasure seekers have learned the air route pays enjoyment dividends in a ratio of ten to one over all other mediums. The air liner carrying its burden above a complex pattern of twisting highways and grades, direct to its destination, serves both business and pleasure better than any earth-bound carrier. ¶ Maddux Air Lines pioneered in large-plane, inter-city passenger service in California and out of this has come a new conception of travel luxury, proving the superiority of the air route. The Los Angeles-San Diego daily run first popularized air travel in Southern California. Since the opening of the Los Angeles-San Francisco run April 14, 1928, thousands of passengers have been carried luxuriously in Ford all-metal air liners.

Spaciously accommodating ten, the passenger cabin of the Ford air liner is truly a revelation of air travel luxury.

TAT TRANSCONTINENTAL AIR TRANSPORT, INC.

TAT TRANSCONTINENTAL AIR TRANSPORT, INC.

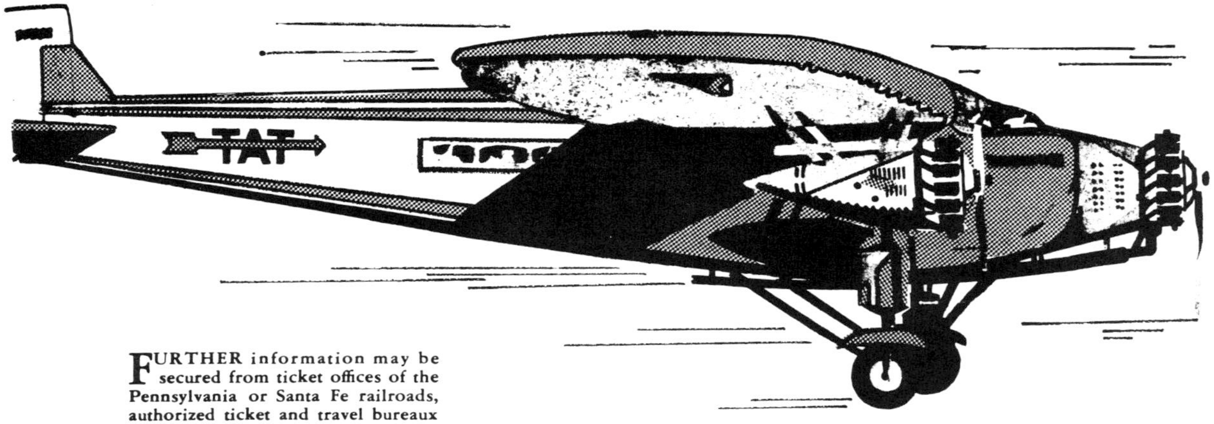

TRANSCONTINENTAL Air Transport, Inc.,* air-rail passenger service brings Atlantic and Pacific coast cities two days nearer to each other, and speeds up travel between local points in the TAT territory.

It is Modern Transportation's answer to the demands for faster travel without sacrifice of safety or comfort.

Two days of delightful sight-seeing in superbly appointed TAT multimotored planes, and two comfortable nights aboard deluxe Pullmans now bridge the gap of a heretofore tedious, four-day journey.

This is the simple story of TAT's air-rail transcontinental passenger service. It takes its place as an established method of travel, to save time for those whose time is too valuable to waste, and for those who desire to see America in the most interesting, comprehensive way.

Air Travel needs no introduction to the experienced tourist. In Europe and in many sections of America it is a commonplace method of transportation. TAT air-rail service is as safe, comfortable and convenient as world famed experts, headed by Colonel Lindbergh, can provide. Its equipment, airport system, airway lighting, communicating system and private weather bureau are the most modern in the world.

**A private carrier*

FURTHER information may be secured from ticket offices of the Pennsylvania or Santa Fe railroads, authorized ticket and travel bureaux or from Transcontinental Air Transport, Inc. offices at airports en route as well as from the TAT traffic offices listed below—

EASTERN TRAFFIC MANAGER
27 West 57th Street
New York City
Telephone: Wickersham 2630

WESTERN TRAFFIC MANAGER
520 Pacific Mutual Building
Los Angeles, California
Telephone: Vandike 3158

CENTRAL TRAFFIC MANAGER
1106 Syndicate Trust Building
St. Louis, Missouri
Telephone: Central 9100

Coast to Coast by Plane and Train

Transcontinental Air Transport, Inc.

9-11-28

Coast to Coast by Plane and Train

STEP aboard the perfectly equipped "Airway Limited" of the Pennsylvania railroad. It leaves New York at 6:05 P.M., and an excellent dinner is being served as you go aboard.

An hour in the club or observation car, a restful night in berth, compartment, or drawing room, and you arise from breakfast as the "Airway" approaches Port Columbus.

The great plane stands at the passenger station, its propellers whirring idly. Pilots and Courier are in attendance. Enter the cabin with nine fellow passengers, relax in the comfortable chairs with their reclining backs and prepare to enjoy your flight.

The earth floats lazily by below you—low level fields—wooded lands, ribbons of paved roads—bodies of water—small towns—America from a new viewpoint. You pause for fifteen minutes at Indianapolis, St. Louis, Kansas City and Wichita, the day's flight ending at Airport, Waynoka, at 6:24 o'clock.

In mid-morning a cup of bouillon is served aloft. A Fred Harvey luncheon is served aloft between St. Louis and Kansas City and in mid-afternoon hot or iced tea is served aboard the plane.

A set-out Pullman awaits at Waynoka, ready for immediate occupancy and is attached to the "Missionary" of the Santa Fe railroad later in the evening.

Another comfortable night in a Pullman, breakfast at the Harvey house in Clovis, New Mexico, a trip in the Aero car to Portair, Clovis, where the second day's plane trip begins.

West of Clovis the landscape rises toward the mountains, and wide desert spaces separate the ranges. Visibility increases and mountains as far away as 100 miles are easily seen.

America, seen from the air, is a country of magnificent expanses.

Luncheon and the mid-morning and mid-afternoon refreshments are again served aloft by Fred Harvey.

Brief stops are made, as on the previous day, at Albuquerque, New Mexico; Winslow, Arizona; Kingman, Arizona, and, late in the afternoon, Los Angeles, California. The Aero car takes you to downtown Los Angeles in ample time for dinner and the evening's business or social engagements.

You have crossed the continent in 48 hours.

You have traveled with the utmost comfort, luxury and speed—but above all you have gained a deeper understanding of the vast and beautiful country that lies between East and West coasts.

Passengers bound for San Francisco may leave by train the same evening or remain in Los Angeles over-night to leave by air early next morning.

TAT service, while transcontinental in its scope, is an extension of existing transportation facilities throughout the United States. The service will be found a convenience in connection with other transport schedules in the East, the Middle West and the great Southwest. It is, in a word, the highest achievement of American Transportation.

TRANSCONTINENTAL AIR TRANSPORT, INC.

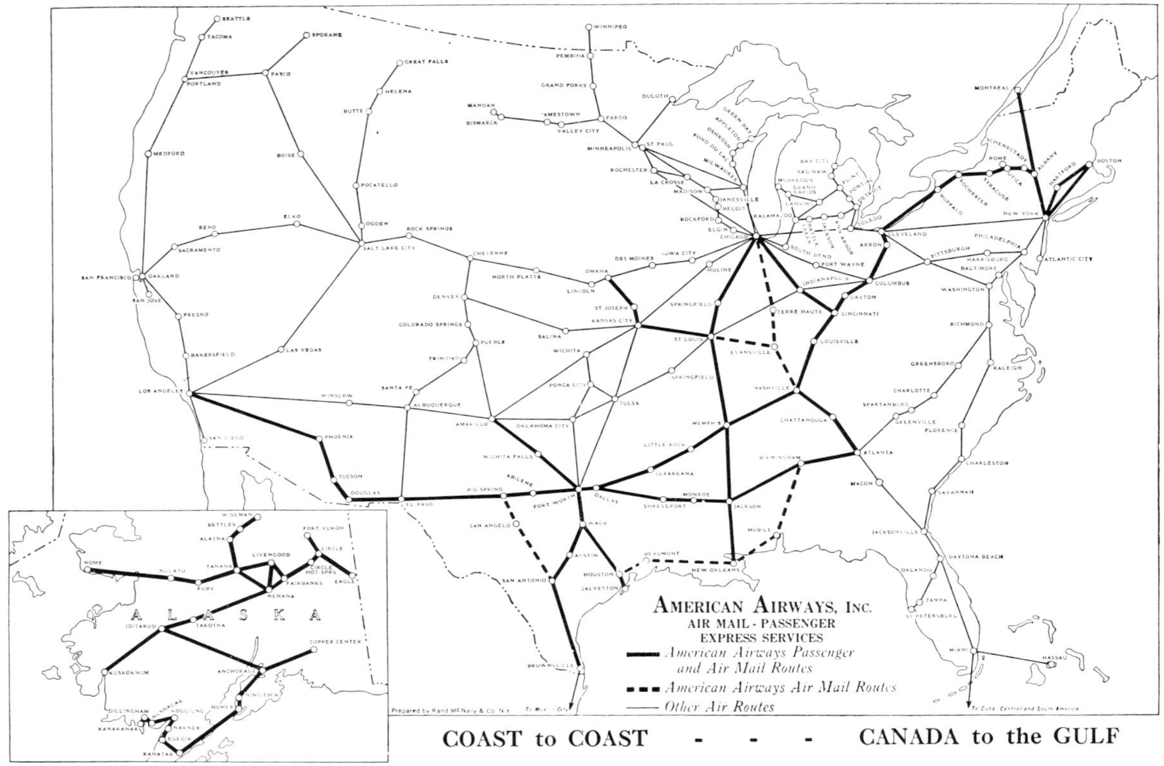

COAST to COAST - - - CANADA to the GULF

ALPHABETICAL INDEX

Cities served by American Airways or by Connecting Lines

Numerals Indicate Table Number

TWA

The Lindbergh Line

Complete

Air Service

NEW YORK PHILADELPHIA HARRISBURG PITTSBURGH COLUMBUS INDIANAPOLIS FORT WAYNE CHICAGO ST. LOUIS SPRINGFIELD KANSAS CITY WICHITA TULSA OKLAHOMA CITY AMARILLO ALBUQUERQUE WINSLOW KINGMAN LOS ANGELES SAN FRANCISCO

TRANSCONTINENTAL & WESTERN AIR, INC.
STANDARD AIR LINE OF THE WORLD

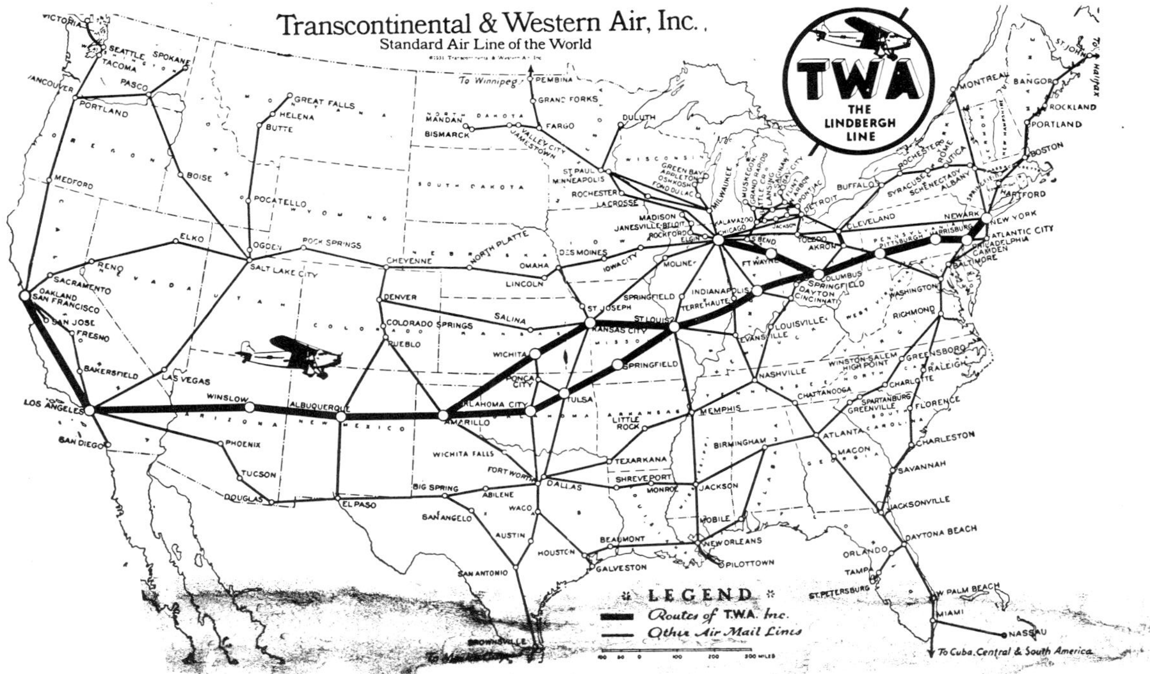

LUXURIOUS, SECURE, SWIFT—TRAVEL VIA T W A—"THE LINDBERGH LINE"

TRANSCONTINENTAL & WESTERN AIR, INC., is proud of its five year record. Passengers carried number more than 175,000. Miles flown with passengers, mail and express exceed 15,000,000. The company investment in buildings, land and flying equipment has grown each year until it has passed the $5,000,000 mark. Three gigantic hangars have been built at Columbus, Kansas City and Los Angeles to take care of the fleet of 50 big air liners.

MUNICIPAL AIRPORT, ST. LOUIS

TWA PASSENGER AIRLINER IN FLIGHT

Schedules show the same steady advance. Mail between New York and Los Angeles is now carried in 24 hours. The passenger schedule—even with a night's stopover at Kansas City—covers the same distance in 36 hours. Between New York and Chicago the time is 8 hours, St. Louis 10 hours, Kansas City 12 hours; between Philadelphia and Chicago 6½ hours.

Schedules have been synchronized with those of connecting air lines, and railroads, so that practically any point of destination can now be reached quickly by using the Transcontinental & Western Air, Inc. system—if not for the entire distance, to reach a connecting air line, or to make a distant railroad connection or steamship sailing date. Los Angeles is four days nearer Europe, via T W A.

The great economic advantage to American business—saving time—and conquering distance—can probably never be adequately measured. Transcontinental & Western Air, Inc., "The Lindbergh Line," now offers *the fastest possible method of shipping merchandise* and dispatching mail.

And this revolution in swift travel and shipping of goods is as near you as your telephone. Call any Postal Telegraph office. They will make reservations, deliver your tickets, put your baggage on board plane, if you wish, pick up packages you want to ship—and deliver

PLANE PILOT RECEIVING WEATHER REPORTS AND ORDERS FROM GROUND RADIO STATION

them at their point of destination. You may also call any Transcontinental & Western Air, Inc. office for information and tickets, any Pennsylvania Railroad ticket office, any associated railroad ticket office or other authorized travel agency.

Air travel is the *swiftest, cleanest, most delightful way to go.* Let us help you work out your schedule, whether you travel for business or pleasure.

General Information

BAGGAGE. Thirty (30) pounds of baggage will be carried free. Baggage weighing in excess of thirty pounds—up to a maximum of twenty additional pounds per passenger—will be charged for by the pound. Other baggage may be shipped to destination by air express or air freight.

CHILDREN'S FARES. Infants under two years of age, held in lap of parent or guardian will be carried free. All children under twelve years of age occupying seats, when accompanied by parent or guardian, will be charged half-fare and when unaccompanied will be charged full fare.

COMBINATION TRIPS. A number of combination trips by air, rail and water can be arranged upon application to any Transcontinental & Western Air, Inc., agent. A particularly delightful trip over and around America in sixteen days has been made possible in connection with the Panama Pacific Line.

SNOW CAPPED SAN FRANCISCO PEAKS FROM PLANE

ROUND TRIP FARES. Ten per cent reduction will be allowed on round trip air tickets. Return portions of tickets can not be used unless seat reservations have been made in advance.

STOP OVERS. Ten (10) day stop over will be permitted at any regularly scheduled landing field providing reservations are made in advance.

DINING SERVICE. The company provides meals served in flight. Other meals are at passenger's expense.

OVERNIGHT STOP. Arrangements have been made with principal hotels in Kansas City and Tulsa for overnight accommodation of through passengers at special rates.

RESERVATIONS. All seats are reserved. Reservations may be made at any company office, at leading hotels, travel agencies, steamship and railroad offices or through Postal Telegraph.

REFUNDS. All applications for refund should be addressed to the nearest office of Transcontinental & Western Air, Inc.

TAXICABS. Passengers desiring taxicabs at landing field should inform co-pilot, who will radio ahead and have cabs waiting on arrival of plane.

WASHROOM. Lavatory is located in the rear of each plane.

WEARING APPAREL. Cabins of all planes are heated or cooled as conditions require. Wear ordinary traveling apparel regardless of the season of the year.

INTOXICANTS. Under no circumstances will use or transportation aboard planes be permitted.

PETS. Animals and birds will not be carried.

DELICIOUS LUNCHEON SERVED ALOFT

TWA PLANES, PORT COLUMBUS

MUNICIPAL AIRPORT, KANSAS CITY

TWA PLANE AT LOS ANGELES

4 5 6

FAST MAIL AND EXPRESS PLANE USED ON TWA 24-HOUR COAST TO COAST SERVICE

Whenever Time Means Money

Use the Air Mail

5c first ounce or fraction thereof; 10c each additional ounce or fraction thereof; anywhere in the United States.

Use any postage stamp. Mark envelope plainly "Air Mail." Drop in any mail box.

Air mail can be sent Registered, Insured, Special Delivery and C. O. D.

Whenever Time Means Money

Ship by Air Express

Every airplane operated by T. & W. A. carries air express.

In addition to two 24-hour Coast to Coast services operated in each direction daily, except Sunday, air express is also carried on the 8-hour New York-Chicago service; between Columbus and Amarillo via St. Louis and Tulsa; on the 2 daily local services between San Francisco and Los Angeles, and on the 4 daily local services between New York and Pittsburgh.

Call Postal Telegraph for pick-up and delivery.

For detailed information as to rates and schedules, telephone any T. & W. A. agent or any Postal Telegraph office.

Whenever Time Means Money

Ship by Air Freight

T. & W. A. operates America's first overnight Air Freight Service daily, except Sunday, between New York and Kansas City.

Air shipping is no longer in the emergency class because of its cost. Now, at the lowest rates in air transport history, it is available for daily business use. Optional pick-up and delivery service offered TWA patrons at special rates by the Postal Telegraph Company.

For complete information on Air Freight Service, telephone any T. & W. A. agent, Pennsylvania Railroad freight or passenger agent, or call any Postal Telegraph office.

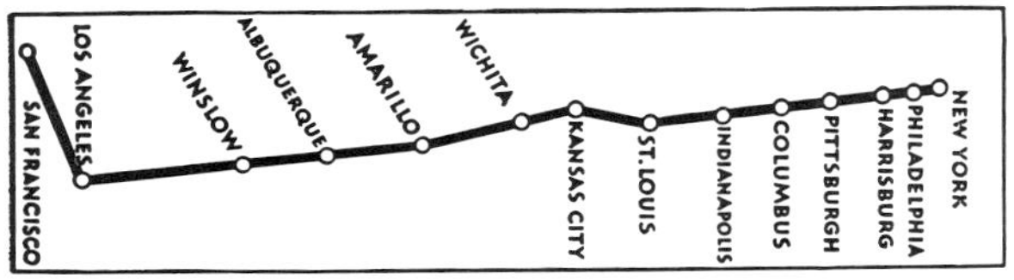

36-HOUR COAST TO COAST SCHEDULES

WESTBOUND READ DOWN	(Subject to Change Without Notice) (Standard Time)	EASTBOUND READ UP
FLIGHT 1		FLIGHT 4
L 10:45 AM ET A 11:28 AM	NEW YORK (Newark Airport) PHILADELPHIA (Camden Airport)	A 7:54 PM ET L 7:18 PM
L 11:38 AM A 12:37 PM	PHILADELPHIA (Camden Airport) HARRISBURG, PA. (Airport)	A 7:08 PM L 6:19 PM
L 12:47 PM A 2:30 PM	HARRISBURG, Pa. (Airport) PITTSBURGH (Curtiss-Bettis Field)	A 6:09 PM L 4:43 PM
L 2:40 PM A 4:15 PM	PITTSBURGH (Curtiss-Bettis Field) COLUMBUS, O. (Port Columbus)	A 4:33 PM L 3:13 PM
L 4:25 PM ET A 5:14 PM CT	COLUMBUS, O. (Port Columbus) INDIANAPOLIS (Municipal Airport)	A 3:03 PM ET L 12:32 PM CT
L 5:24 PM A 7:44 PM	INDIANAPOLIS (Municipal Airport) ST. LOUIS, MO. (Lambert Field)	A 12:22 PM L 10:25 AM
L 7:54 PM A 10:12 PM CT	ST. LOUIS, MO. (Lambert Field) KANSAS CITY (Municipal Airport)	A 10:15 AM L 8:20 AM CT
FLIGHT 3	Overnight Hotel Stop	FLIGHT 2
L 8:45 AM CT A 10:20 AM	KANSAS CITY (Municipal Airport) WICHITA, KANS. (Municipal Airport)	A 6:30 PM CT L 5:02 PM
L 10:30 AM A 1:17 PM	WICHITA, KANS. (Municipal Airport) AMARILLO, TEX. (English Field)	A 4:52 PM L 2:21 PM
L 1:27 PM CT A 3:09 PM MT	AMARILLO, TEX. (English Field) ALBUQUERQUE (T. W. A. Field)	A 2:11 PM CT L 10:42 AM MT
L 3:19 PM A 5:29 PM	ALBUQUERQUE (T. W. A. Field) WINSLOW, ARIZ. (T. W. A. Field)	A 10:32 AM L 8:33 AM
L 5:39 PM MT A 8:53 PM PT	WINSLOW, ARIZ. (T. W. A. Field) LOS ANGELES (Airport, Glendale)	A 8:23 AM MT L 3:30 AM PT

DIRECT CONNECTIONS BY AIR AND RAIL

To and from Boston, Hartford, Atlantic City, Washington, Baltimore, Wilmington, Akron, Cleveland, Detroit, New Orleans, Jackson, Memphis, Topeka, Salina, Goodland, Denver, Colorado Springs, Pueblo, Las Vegas and Santa Fe.

3½-HOUR NEW YORK-PITTSBURGH SCHEDULES

(Subject to Change Without Notice)—(Eastern Time)

FLIGHT 1	FLIGHT 9		FLIGHT 10	FLIGHT 4
L 10:45 AM A 11:28 AM	L 12:45 PM A 1:25 PM	NEW YORK PHILADELPHIA	A 12:40 PM L 12:04 PM	A 7:54 PM L 7:18 PM
L 11:38 AM A 12:37 PM	L 1:36 PM A 2:32 PM	PHILADELPHIA HARRISBURG	A 11:55 AM L 11:06 AM	A 7:08 PM L 6:19 PM
L 12:47 PM A 2:30 PM	L 2:42 PM A 4:20 PM	HARRISBURG PITTSBURGH	A 10:56 AM L 9:30 AM	A 6:09 PM L 4:43 PM
FLIGHT 7	FLIGHT 11		FLIGHT 12	FLIGHT 8
L 8:45 AM A 9:28 AM	L 2:45 PM A 3:26 PM	NEW YORK PHILADELPHIA	A 5:05 PM L 4:29 PM	A 6:23 PM L 5:45 PM
L 9:38 AM A 10:37 AM	L 3:36 PM A 4:32 PM	PHILADELPHIA HARRISBURG	A 4:20 PM L 3:31 PM	A 5:35 PM L 4:44 PM
L 10:47 AM A 12:30 PM	L 4:42 PM A 6:20 PM	HARRISBURG PITTSBURGH	A 3:21 PM L 1:55 PM	A 4:34 PM L 3:05 PM

DIRECT CONNECTIONS BY AIR AND RAIL

To and from Boston, Hartford, Atlantic City, Washington, Baltimore, Wilmington, Akron, Cleveland and Detroit

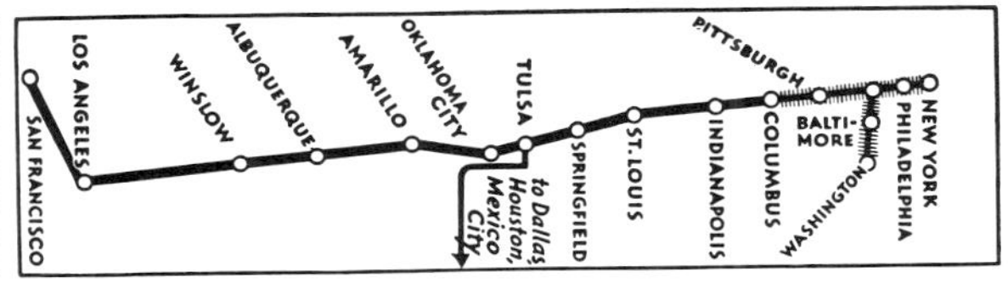

48-HOUR COAST TO COAST AIR-RAIL SCHEDULES

WESTBOUND READ DOWN	(Subject to Change Without Notice) (Standard Time)	EASTBOUND READ UP
Pa. R.R. Train 65 "Airway Limited"		Pa. R.R. Train 66 "The American"
L 7:05 PM ET	NEW YORK (Penna. Sta.)	A 9:02 AM ET
L 7:00 PM	HUDSON TERMINAL	A 9:11 AM
L 7:27 PM	NEWARK	A 8:50 AM
L 7:20 PM	WASHINGTON	A 8:45 AM
L 8:16 PM	BALTIMORE	A 7:48 AM
L 8:50 PM	NORTH PHILADELPHIA	A 7:16 AM
L 9:58 PM	YORK, PA	A 6:14 AM
L 11:05 PM	HARRISBURG	A 5:01 AM
	PITTSBURGH	A 11:10 PM
A 8:50 AM ET	PORT COLUMBUS	L 7:00 PM ET
FLIGHT 5		FLIGHT 6
L 9:05 AM ET	COLUMBUS, O. (Port Columbus)	A 6:34 PM ET
a Flag 9:31 AM	SPRINGFIELD, O. (Airport)	cFlag 6:10 PM
a Flag 9:45 AM ET	DAYTON (Vandalia Airport)	cFlag 5:57 PM ET
A 9:48 AM CT	INDIANAPOLIS (Municipal Airport)	L 4:00 PM CT
L 9:58 AM	INDIANAPOLIS (Municipal Airport)	A 3:52 PM
bFlag 10:35 AM	TERRE HAUTE (Dresser Field)	dFlag 3:18 PM
A 12:11 PM	ST. LOUIS (Lambert Field)	L 1:50 PM
L 12:25 PM	ST. LOUIS (Lambert Field)	A 1:35 PM
A 2:14 PM	SPRINGFIELD, MO. (Airport)	L 11:56 AM
L 2:24 PM	SPRINGFIELD, MO. (Airport)	A 11:50 AM
A 4:03 PM CT	TULSA, OKLA. (Municipal Airport)	L 10:20 AM CT
	(Overnight Hotel Stop)	
L 9:15 AM CT	TULSA, OKLA. (Municipal Airport)	A 5:53 PM CT
A 10:20 AM	OKLAHOMA CITY (Municipal Airport)	L 4:54 PM
L 10:30 AM	OKLAHOMA CITY (Municipal Airport)	A 4:44 PM
A 1:02 PM CT	AMARILLO, TEX. (English Field)	L 2:26 PM CT
FLIGHT 3		FLIGHT 2
L 1:27 PM CT	AMARILLO, TEX. (English Field)	A 2:11 PM CT
A 3:09 PM MT	ALBUQUERQUE (T. W. A. Field)	L 10:42 AM MT
L 3:19 PM	ALBUQUERQUE (T. W. A. Field)	A 10:32 AM
A 5:29 PM	WINSLOW, ARIZ. (T. W. A. Field)	L 8:33 AM
L 5:39 PM MT	WINSLOW, ARIZ. (T. W. A. Field)	A 8:23 AM MT
A 8:53 PM PT	LOS ANGELES (Airport, Glendale)	L 3:30 AM PT

a Will pick up passengers for St. Louis and points West thereof.
b Will pick up passengers for points West of St. Louis.
c Will discharge passengers from St. Louis and points West thereof.
d Will discharge passengers from points west of St. Louis.

DIRECT CONNECTIONS BY AIR AND RAIL

To and from Boston, Providence, Hartford, New Haven, Norfolk, Richmond, Roanoke, Albany, Schenectady, Utica, Syracuse, Rochester, Buffalo, Chicago, Springfield, Ill., Kansas City, Omaha, Dallas, and Fort Worth.

24-HOUR CHICAGO-LOS ANGELES SCHEDULES

WESTBOUND—Read Down				(Subject to Change Without Notice) (Central Time)	EASTBOUND—READ UP		
Santa Fe Railway Train No. 3	The Alton Railroad Train No. 9	Rock Island Railway Train No. 11	C. M. St. P. & P. R. R. Train No. 7-25		Rock Island Railway Train No. 4	The Alton Railroad Train No. 10	Santa Fe Railway Train No. 2
9:05 PM 8:10 AM	8:00 PM 8:00 AM	6:00 PM 8:00 AM	6:00 PM 8:00 AM	Chicago Kan. City	9:30 AM 9:00 PM	8:00 AM 8:00 PM	8:05 AM 7:55 PM

FLIGHT 3		FLIGHT 2
L 8:45 AM CT A 10:20 AM	KANSAS CITY (Municipal Airport) WICHITA, KANS. (Municipal Airport)	A 6:30 PM CT L 5:02 PM
L 10:30 AM A 1:17 PM	WICHITA, KANS. (Municipal Airport) AMARILLO, TEX. (English Field)	A 4:52 PM L 2:21 PM
L 1:27 PM CT A 3:09 PM MT	AMARILLO, TEX. (English Field) ALBUQUERQUE (T. W. A. Field)	A 2:11 PM CT L 10:42 AM MT
L 3:19 PM A 5:29 PM	ALBUQUERQUE (T. W. A. Field) WINSLOW, ARIZ. (T. W. A. Field)	A 10:32 AM L 8:33 AM
L 5:39 PM MT A 8:53 PM PT	WINSLOW, ARIZ. (T. W. A. Field) LOS ANGELES (Airport, Glendale)	A 8:23 AM MT L 3:30 AM PT

GREYHOUND BUS LINES NOW OFFER CONVENIENT CONNECTING SCHEDULES TO ALL CITIES AND TOWNS IN THE TERRITORY TRIBUTARY TO T. & W. A. COMBINATION AIR-BUS TICKETS MAY BE SECURED AT ANY T. & W. A. OR GREYHOUND TICKET OFFICE

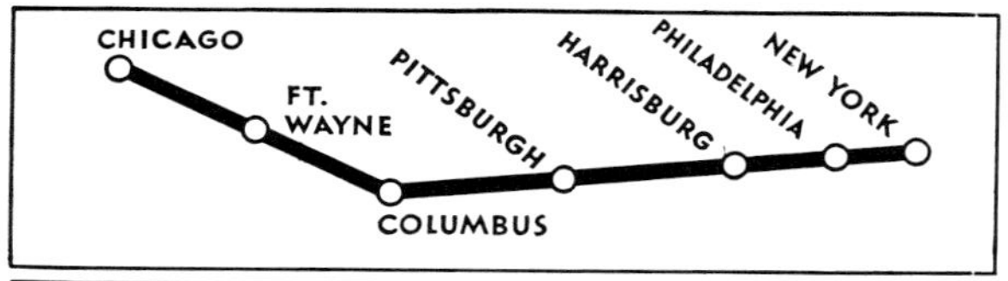

8-HOUR NEW YORK-CHICAGO SCHEDULES

WESTBOUND READ DOWN FLIGHT 7	(Subject to Change Without Notice) (Standard Time)	EASTBOUND READ UP FLIGHT 8
L 8:45 AM	NEW YORK (Newark Airport)	A 6:23 PM
A 9:28 AM	PHILADELPHIA (Camden Airport)	L 5:45 PM
L 9:38 AM	PHILADELPHIA (Camden Airport)	A 5:35 PM
A 10:37 AM	HARRISBURG, PA. (Airport)	L 4:44 PM
L 10:47 AM	HARRISBURG, PA. (Airport)	A 4:34 PM
A 12:30 PM	PITTSBURGH (Curtiss-Bettis Field)	L 3:05 PM
L 12:40 PM	PITTSBURGH (Curtiss-Bettis Field)	A 2:55 PM
A 2:15 PM	COLUMBUS, O. (Port Columbus)	L 1:32 PM
L 2:25 PM	COLUMBUS, O. (Port Columbus)	A 1:22 PM
Flag 2:55 PM	SPRINGFIELD, O. (Airport)	Flag 12:58 PM
Flag 3:10 PM ET	DAYTON, O. (Vandalia Airport)	Flag 12:45 PM ET
A 3:13 PM CT	FT. WAYNE (Municipal Airport)	L 10:50 AM CT
L 3:20 PM	FT. WAYNE (Municipal Airport)	A 10:44 AM
A 4:45 PM CT	CHICAGO (Municipal Airport)	L 9:30 AM CT

DIRECT CONNECTIONS BY AIR AND RAIL

To and from Boston, Hartford, Atlantic City, Washington, Baltimore, Wilmington, Akron, Cleveland, Detroit, Rochester, Minneapolis and St. Paul.

3-HOUR SAN FRANCISCO-LOS ANGELES SCHEDULES

SOUTHBOUND READ DOWN	(Subject to Change Without Notice) (Pacific Time)	NORTHBOUND READ UP
FLIGHT 15		FLIGHT 16
L 10:00 AM PT	SAN FRANCISCO (Bay Airdrome)	A 1:00 PM PT
A 12:45 PM PT	LOS ANGELES (Air Term., Glendale)	L 10:00 AM PT
FLIGHT 17		FLIGHT 18
L 5:30 PM PT	SAN FRANCISCO (Bay Airdrome)	A 8:30 PM PT
A 8:15 PM PT	LOS ANGELES (Air Term., Glendale)	L 5:30 PM PT

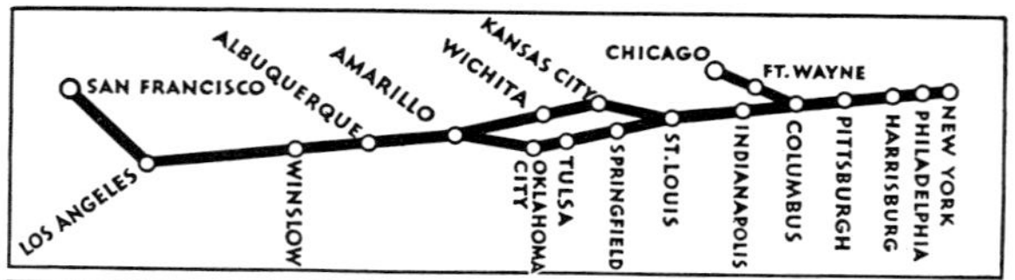

24-HOUR MAIL AND EXPRESS ONLY

Flight 5	Flight 3	Flight 1	(Subject to Change Without Notice) (Standard Time)	Flight 4	Flight 2	Flight 6
WESTBOUND READ DOWN				EASTBOUND READ UP		
No air mail handled between Columbus and St. Louis on Flight No. 5.	7:00PM (ct)	8:30AM (ct)	L NEW YORK ... A	9:30PM (a)	6:25AM (a)	No air mail handled between St. Louis and Columbus on Flight No. 6.
	9:45PM 10:21PM	10:45AM 11:28AM	L NEWARK ... A A PHILADELPHIA ... L	7:54PM 7:18PM	5:15AM 4:43AM	
	10:31PM 11:18PM	11:38AM 12:37PM	L PHILADELPHIA ... A A HARRISBURG ... L	7:08PM 6:19PM	4:38AM 3:54AM	
	11:28PM 12:50AM	12:47PM 2:30PM	L HARRISBURG ... A A PITTSBURGH ... L	6:09PM 4:43PM	3:44AM 2:28AM	
	1:00AM 2:16AM	2:40PM 4:15PM	L PITTSBURGH ... A A COLUMBUS ... L	4:33PM 3:13PM	2:18AM 1:07AM	
9:05AM 9:48AM	2:26AM 3:13AM	4:25PM 5:14PM	L COLUMBUS ... A A INDIANAPOLIS ... L	3:03PM 12:32PM	12:57AM 10:40PM	6:34PM 4:00PM
9:58AM 12:11PM	3:23AM 5:15AM	5:24PM 7:44PM	L INDIANAPOLIS ... A A ST. LOUIS ... L	12:22PM 10:25AM	10:30PM 8:50PM	3:52PM 1:50PM
12:25PM 2:14PM	5:25AM	7:54PM	L ST. LOUIS ... A A SPRINGFIELD ... L	10:15AM	8:40PM	1:35PM 11:56AM
2:24PM	7:15AM	10:12PM	L SPRINGFIELD ... A A KANSAS CITY ... L	8:20AM	7:00PM	11:50AM
4:03PM	8:45AM	10:30PM	L KANSAS CITY ... A A TULSA ... L	4:24AM	6:30PM	10:20AM
9:15AM	10:20AM	11:54PM	L TULSA ... A A WICHITA ... L	3:06AM	5:02PM	5:53PM
10:20AM	10:30AM	12:04AM	L WICHITA ... A A OKLAHOMA CITY ... L	2:56AM	4:52PM	4:54PM
10:30AM 1:02PM	1:17PM	2:31AM	L OKLAHOMA CITY ... A A AMARILLO ... L	12:45AM	2:21PM	4:44PM 2:26PM
1:27PM 3:09PM	1:27PM 3:09PM	2:41AM 4:04AM	L AMARILLO ... A A ALBUQUERQUE ... L	12:35AM 9:28PM	2:11PM 10:42AM	2:11PM 10:42AM
3:19PM 5:29PM	3:19PM 5:29PM	4:14AM 6:08AM	L ALBUQUERQUE ... A A WINSLOW ... L	9:18PM 7:39PM	10:32AM 8:33AM	10:32AM 8:33AM
5:39PM 8:53PM	5:39PM 8:53PM	6:18AM 9:02AM	L WINSLOW ... A A LOS ANGELES ... L	7:29PM 3:05PM	8:23AM 3:30AM	8:23AM 3:30AM

(a) Arrival time at General Post Office, New York.
(ct) Closing time at General Post Office, New York.

AIR FREIGHT IS HANDLED OVER NIGHT AT VERY LOW RATES BETWEEN NEW YORK, PHILADELPHIA, HARRISBURG, PITTSBURGH, COLUMBUS, INDIANAPOLIS, ST. LOUIS and KANSAS CITY

T. & W. A.—FARES IN DOLLARS—(10% REDUCTION GRANTED ON ROUND TRIP TICKETS)

SUBJECT TO CHANGE WITHOUT NOTICE	New York	Philadelphia	Harrisburg	Pittsburgh	Columbus	*Springfield, O.	*Dayton, O.	Fort Wayne	Indianapolis	*Terre Haute
New York	xx	$ 6.00	$ 13.00	$ 24.00	$ 36.00	$ 41.00	$ 41.00	$ 46.00	$ 49.00	xx
Philadelphia	$ 6.00	xx	7.00	18.00	30.00	35.00	35.00	40.00	43.00	xx
Harrisburg	13.00	7.00	xx	11.00	23.00	28.00	28.00	33.00	36.00	xx
Pittsburgh	24.00	18.00	11.00	xx	12.00	17.00	17.00	22.00	25.00	xx
Columbus	36.00	30.00	23.00	12.00	xx	xx	xx	13.00	13.00	xx
*Springfield, O.	41.00	35.00	28.00	17.00	xx	xx	xx	xx	xx	xx
*Dayton, O.	41.00	35.00	28.00	17.00	xx	xx	xx	xx	xx	xx
Fort Wayne	46.00	40.00	33.00	22.00	13.00	xx	xx	xx	xx	xx
Indianapolis	49.00	43.00	36.00	25 00	13.00	xx	xx	xx	xx	xx
*Terre Haute	xx	xx	xx	xx	xx	xx	xx	xx	xx	xx
Chicago	59.50	50.00	43.00	28.65	20.00	18.00	18.00	10.50	xx	xx
St. Louis	65.00	59.00	52.00	41.00	29.00	29.00	29.00	xx	16.00	xx
Springfield, Mo.	79.00	73.00	66.00	55.00	43.00	43.00	43.00	xx	30.00	30.00
Kansas City	82.00	76.00	69.00	58.00	46.00	46.00	46.00	xx	33.00	33.00
Tulsa	91.00	85.00	78.00	67.00	55.00	55.00	55.00	xx	42.00	42.00
Wichita	94.00	88.00	81.00	70.00	58.00	58.00	58.00	xx	45.00	45.00
Oklahoma City	98.00	92.00	85.00	74.00	62.00	62.00	62.00	xx	49.00	49.00
Amarillo	115.00	109.00	102.00	91.00	79.00	79.00	79.00	xx	66.00	66.00
Albuquerque	139.00	133.00	126.00	115.00	103.00	103.00	103.00	xx	90.00	90.00
Winslow	159.00	153.00	146.00	135.00	123.00	123.00	123.00	xx	110.00	110.00
Los Angeles	200.00	194.00	187.00	176.00	159.00	159.00	159.00	xx	151.00	151.00
San Francisco	200.00	194.00	187.00	179.00	169.00	169.00	169.00	xx	161.00	161.00

SUBJECT TO CHANGE WITHOUT NOTICE	Chicago	St. Louis	Springfield, Mo.	Kansas City	Tulsa	Wichita	Oklahoma City	Amarillo	Albuquerque	Winslow	Los Angeles	San Francisco
New York	$ 59.50	$ 65.00	$ 79.00	$ 82.00	$ 91.00	$ 94.00	$ 98.00	$115.00	$139.00	$159.00	$200.00	$200.00
Philadelphia	50.00	59.00	73.00	76.00	85.00	88.00	92.00	109.00	133.00	153.00	194.00	194.00
Harrisburg	43.00	52.00	66.00	69.00	78.00	81.00	85.00	102.00	126.00	146.00	187.00	187.00
Pittsburgh	28.65	41.00	55.00	58.00	67.00	70.00	74.00	91.00	115.00	135.00	176.00	179.00
Columbus	20.00	29.00	43.00	46.00	55.00	58.00	62.00	79.00	103.00	123.00	159.00	169.00
*Springfield, O.	18.00	29.00	43.00	46.00	55.00	58.00	62.00	79.00	103.00	123.00	159.00	169.00
*Dayton, O.	18.00	29.00	43.00	46.00	55.00	58.00	62.00	79.00	103.00	123.00	159.00	169.00
Fort Wayne	10.50	xx	xx	xx	xx	xx	xx	xx	xx	xx	xx	xx
Indianapolis	xx	16.00	30.00	33.00	42.00	45.00	49.00	66.00	90.00	110.00	151.00	161.00
*Terre Haute	xx	xx	30.00	33.00	42.00	45.00	49.00	66.00	90.00	110.00	151.00	161.00
Chicago	xx	xx	xx	xx	xx	xx	xx	xx	xx	xx	xx	xx
St. Louis	xx	xx	14.00	17.00	26.00	29.00	33.00	50.00	74.00	94.00	132.85	150.00
Springfield, Mo.	xx	14.00	xx	xx	12.00	xx	19.00	36.00	60.00	80.00	121.00	139.00
Kansas City	xx	17.00	xx	xx	xx	14.00	xx	35.00	60.00	80.00	120.00	138.00
Tulsa	xx	26.00	12.00	xx	xx	xx	7.00	24.00	48.00	68.00	109.00	127.00
Wichita	xx	29.00	xx	14.00	xx	xx	xx	21.00	45.00	65.00	106.00	124.00
Oklahoma City	xx	33.00	19.00	xx	7.00	xx	xx	17.00	41.00	61.00	102.00	120.00
Amarillo	xx	50.00	36.00	35.00	24.00	21.00	17.00	xx	24.00	44.00	85.00	103.00
Albuquerque	xx	74.00	60.00	60.00	48.00	45.00	41.00	24.00	xx	20.00	61.00	79.00
Winslow	xx	94.00	80.00	80.00	68.00	65.00	61.00	44.00	20.00	xx	41.00	59.00
Los Angeles	xx	132.85	121.00	120.00	109.00	106.00	102.00	85.00	61.00	41.00	xx	18.95
San Francisco	xx	150.00	139.00	138.00	127.00	124.00	120.00	103.00	79.00	59.00	18.95	xx

Fares do not include automobile transportation, but special low taxicab rates have been arranged for its passengers by T. & W. A. * Flag stops on certain flights.

GREYHOUND BUS LINES NOW OFFER CONVENIENT CONNECTING SCHEDULES TO ALL CITIES AND TOWNS IN THE TERRITORY TRIBUTARY TO T. & W. A. COMBINATION AIR-BUS TICKETS MAY BE SECURED AT ANY T. & W. A. OR GREYHOUND TICKET OFFICE

TWA

Passengers Mail
Express Freight

RESERVATIONS

Call any Postal Telegraph Office, any Pennsylvania R. R. or connecting rail or air line representative, authorized travel bureaus, porters of leading hotels or any T. & W. A. office listed below.

NEW YORK—Rm. 157, Penn. Station. Tel. Penn. 6-6000, Ext. 583-4.
NEWARK—Metropolitan Airport. Tel. Mulberry 4-1497.
PHILADELPHIA—Central Airport, Camden. Tel. Camden 8775, or 1613 Chestnut St. Tel. Rittenhouse 5800.
WASHINGTON, D. C.—Washington Airport. Tel. Metr'pn 0534.
HARRISBURG—Harrisburg Airport. Tel. 7880.
PITTSBURGH—Bettis Field (McKeesport). Tel. Homestead 4200.
COLUMBUS—Port Columbus. Tel. Evergreen 4514.
DAYTON—Vandalia Airport. Tel. Vandalia 75.
SPRINGFIELD, O.—Municipal Airport. Tel. Main 304.
AKRON—Municipal Airport. Tel. Jefferson 5152.
CLEVELAND—Municipal Airport. Tel. Clearwater 0158.
INDIANAPOLIS—Municipal Airport. Tel. Belmont 3023, or Riley 9331.
FORT WAYNE—Baer Airport. Tel. Anthny 6386 or Eastb. 1166.
CHICAGO—1027 Foreman Nat. Bank Bldg. Tel. Central 7200. The Travel Shop, P. R. R., 454 N. Michigan Ave. Tel. Central 7200. Air Passenger Bureau, Palmer House Lobby. Tel. State 7111. Union Station. Tel. Franklin 6700.
TERRE HAUTE—Penn. R. R. Tel. Crawford 1371.
ST. LOUIS—403 N. 12th Blvd. Tel. Central 9100.
SPRINGFIELD, MO.—Municipal Airport. Tel. 3622.
KANSAS CITY—1105 Baltimore Ave. Tel. Harrison 7755.
WICHITA—P. O. Box 544 or Municipal Airport. Tel. 4-8913.
TULSA—Municipal Airport. Tel. 6-3604.
OKLAHOMA CITY—Municipal Airport. Tel. 7-6222.
AMARILLO—English Field. Tel. 5600.
ALBUQUERQUE—T. & W. A. Airport. Tel. 3353.
WINSLOW—T. & W. A. Airport. Tel. 572.
KINGMAN—T. & W. A. Airport. Tel. Airport 20R1.
LOS ANGELES—636 South Olive St. Tel. Michigan 8881. Ambassador Hotel. Tel. Drexel 7000, or Biltmore Hotel, Tel. Faber 1011.
GLENDALE—Grand Central Air Terminal. Tel. Capitol 6111.
HOLLYWOOD—6407 Hollywood Blvd. Tel. Hollywood 7123.
SAN FRANCISCO—661 Market St. Tel. Sutter 1482.
OAKLAND—San Francisco Bay Airdrome. Tel. Alameda 6721.
BERKELEY—Travellers Union Ticket Office, 2482 Bancroft St. Tel. Thornwall 7499.
SACRAMENTO—Hotel Sacramento. Tel. Main 4558.

SCHEDULES EFFECTIVE NOVEMBER 1, 1931

10 11

Index

Also from the publisher

INNOVATIONS IN AIRCRAFT CONSTRUCTION

Thirty-Seven Influential Designs

Hans Redemann

Size: 8 1/2" x 11" 248 pp. hard cover Over 300 color and b/w photos

ISBN: 0-88740-338-7 $29.95

THE
FORD
TRI-MOTOR

this is to certify that

Bill Larkins

was co-pilot on a flight of
AMERICAN AIRLINES'
Ford Tri-Motor
N9683

5-17-65
DATE

Ed McNeil
CAPTAIN

MOX-AIR COLLECTION

ROUNDTRIP
$5.00

FLIGHT
SOUVENIR

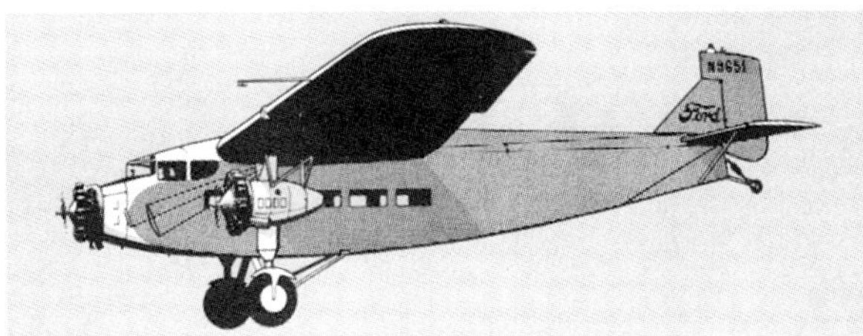

I FLEW IN THE ORIGINAL FORD TRI-MOTOR N-9651

"Graceful"